ADDITIONAL PRAISE FOR
Toward a More Perfect University:

"Eminently well-informed and pragmatic, Cole's work not only offers a clear-eyed analysis of the current state of higher education in the US, it also provides a detailed starting point for dialogues about the function and shape of the great American universities of the future. An ambitious and visionary examination of American universities and 'how to develop them still further so that they may maximize their full potential.'" —*Kirkus*

"Jonathan Cole's new work is a magnificent description of the history, evolution, and rise to global preeminence of America's research universities. With a mastery reflecting a deep understanding of the academic world, Jonathan unflinchingly confronts the challenges facing these institutions in an increasingly skeptical environment. He offers bold, sometimes provocative, innovative, and concrete proposals for insuring academic leadership for the United States. This is a must-read for those who care about our collective future." —MARY SUE COLEMAN, **president emerita, University of Michigan, and president elect, Association of American Universities**

"Jonathan Cole brings to bear on the problem of higher education's future viability his years of experience as an education theorist and university leader. He calls for communities and institutions to address the roadblocks we all see in higher education—access and rising costs among them—and to nurture the will to invest in and fortify the path of learning from pre-school to graduate school. Cole's prescription is bold and imaginative and will compel the best minds to undertake the challenge he poses." —HENRY LOUIS GATES, JR., **Alphonse Fletcher University Professor, Harvard University**

"In his new book, *Toward a More Perfect University*, Cole, a paragon of academic excellence and one of the preeminent writers and thinkers concerned with the strength and quality of American higher education, explores how today's universities can not only thrive but excel, while also expanding their ability to educate an increasingly diverse nation of men and women whose aspirations and abilities continue to be the engine of American progress. *Toward a More Perfect University* is an excellent addition to the study of the future of higher education in the United States." —VARTAN GREGORIAN, **president, Carnegie Corporation of New York**

"In *Toward a More Perfect University*, Jonathan Cole describes challenges to the eminence of American universities, both present and future. In a lively and engaging manner, building on his rich experience and deeply analytic perspective, he discusses the circumstances that created the country's great research universities and delineates proposals for change, presenting choices institutions of higher education must confront to continue to thrive as centers of learning, research, and innovation. His book should be of great interest not only to educators but to parents, civic leaders, and anyone with a stake in American higher education." —ROBERT J. ZIMMER, president, University of Chicago

Toward a More Perfect University

TOWARD
A MORE
PERFECT
UNIVERSITY

Jonathan R. Cole

PUBLICAFFAIRS
New York

Book Design by Milenda Nan Ok Lee

Library of Congress Control Number: 2015955566
ISBN 978-1-61039-265-5 (HC)
ISBN 978-1-61039-266-2 (EB)
First Edition
10 9 8 7 6 5 4 3 2 1

For Daniel and Nick, Nonnie and Gabe, Lydia
and Charlotte, Joan, and of course Joanna

Contents

Preface

I N LATE SEPTEMBER 1960, when I first walked through the 116th Street and Broadway gates as a freshman at Columbia College, I was in awe of McKim, Mead, and White's architecture. Could there really be such a beautiful and inspiring campus in the heart of New York City? I already knew something of Columbia and was apprehensive about how I, a "jock" with exceptionally good grades from a New York City public school, would fare in this intense intellectual environment. My older brother, Stephen, was entering his junior year there, and it was where my mother had studied for her Ph.D. in English Literature until my father, a stage, radio, and early television actor, had been blacklisted during the McCarthy era and the responsibility for supporting our family suddenly fell on her shoulders. Traversing the tree-lined College Walk, I thought of George Santayana's possibly apocryphal observation that when he walked the McKim campus he felt in the company of great minds. There was something inspiring about looking up at the facade of Butler Library and seeing carved in stone the names of Homer, Sophocles, Plato, Aristotle, Cicero, and Virgil, and those of Shakespeare, Milton, and Goethe, among many others whose work we would read in Columbia's required Humanities course. I was one of around six hundred others who were entering a journey at Columbia College.

Of course, the place was hardly as idyllic as I made it out to be. When I entered the college, there were no women (Barnard was the women's college at Columbia), only two African Americans—both talented academics and athletes—

and no Hispanics in my class. About 60 percent came from Jewish backgrounds. Many were first-generation Ivy League students, and perhaps 30 or 40 percent of them aspired to be either doctors or lawyers. So much for diversity. The first lecture I ever attended was for the entire freshman class and was given by Lionel Trilling, the literary scholar and public intellectual, on C. P. Snow's recently published essay *The Two Cultures and the Scientific Revolution.*[1]

The college was conspicuously "local" compared to its more famous sister "cosmopolitan" Ivy League institutions, Harvard, Yale, and Princeton. It was not even a fully residential college at the time—capable of housing only perhaps 50 percent of its undergraduate students. The rest found either off-campus apartments or commuted to school. Columbia College had its own proud faculty and undergraduates, and its students rarely took courses or seminars with professors with appointments in the graduate faculties. In fact, thick boundaries existed around each school. We all took roughly half of our total points required to graduate in the Core Curriculum—and we could concentrate, rather than major, in a particular discipline. Legend had it that we had the best curriculum in the country (we knew next to nothing about what existed at other schools), taught by dedicated professors and instructors. We believed in the legend. We were immersed in and committed to a liberal arts education despite an equal dedication to a career that would represent upward social mobility.

What I wanted, as Woodrow Wilson said when speaking of his own education at Princeton, was to have the experience of rubbing up against other interesting minds. I quickly became an "organized dilettante," taking courses with some of the extraordinary Columbia faculty regardless of their discipline, including Trilling, historian Richard Hofstadter, art historian Meyer Schapiro, sociologists Robert K. Merton and Daniel Bell, Nobel physicist Polykarp Kusch, and many others who were the stars of Columbia during those days—to say nothing of the younger, as yet relatively unknown, exceptional minds.

At the outset of my undergraduate years, I would not have predicted (nor would most others) that I would become an academic. Some might have thought that I would follow my father into the theater or aspire to something in baseball or an occupation outside the academy, but I secretly yearned for a life in academia, in part because of my family's values, my Columbia teachers, and my brother's influence, as well as the fact that I knew too much about the unpredictable world of the stage to think of it as a career.[2]

Perhaps a turning point came at the beginning of my sophomore year, when my father suddenly died of a heart attack and my financial aid was insufficient for me to continue at the college. Harry Coleman, assistant dean, saved me. When he heard my story, Coleman assured me that I could continue my studies and immediately increased my scholarship by $500 (a significant percentage of my total tuition bill at the time) without asking any questions or requiring me to fill out a sheaf of forms. I've never left Morningside Heights. But when I arrived, I had almost no idea about the contours of the house that I would live in for the next fifty years. I was a student at Columbia, and that was all that mattered at the time.

These autobiographical snippets are intended to provide a crude backdrop of what Columbia was like in the early 1960s, against which we can examine the evolution of this "older" research university. As an undergraduate history major, Ph.D. sociology student, junior and senior faculty member, teacher, researcher, and for fifteen years an academic administrator, of which thirteen were as the university's provost and dean of faculties, I witnessed profound changes at Columbia and the other great universities around the world. It seems popular these days to target all that is wrong with our universities rather than to focus on the improvements in the quality of study, students, faculty, and particularly the research conducted that has led to a plethora of discoveries and innovations as well as scholarly advances that have altered our world. There was, of course, great science and scholarship before the 1960s and 1970s, even if the headlines had more to do with student unrest or how universities had prostituted themselves to the federal government and intelligence agencies and thus had become just another part of the military-industrial complex that Eisenhower had warned the nation about in his farewell address.

In fact, the very character of these houses of higher learning was changing. They no longer fit neatly into the perceptive characterization of them by Clark Kerr, the first chancellor of the University of California, Berkeley, from 1958 to 1967, as "multiversities," which had no center and were a bunch of disconnected parts held together by a common interest in parking. But in design and practice, they were slowly becoming more perfect universities: more open, more meritocratic, more influential on our nation's social and economic growth and potential. Universities were increasingly open to women, minorities, and foreign scholars and students. They were being improved through technological innovation and the recruitment of more diverse and exceptional talent. They continued to struggle to adhere to the principles of academic freedom and free inquiry when they came under assault by the government and other powerful political interest groups. The way scholarship was conducted was moving from very Small Science to Big Science—and finally to very Big Science in some transdisciplinary projects. Multi-university collaborations were emerging; and the Internet, the World Wide Web, and the multitude of new computer technologies allowed for remarkable changes in how information could be found, stored, exchanged, and used. That technology changed how students could be taught as well. Scholarship without borders was slowly becoming a reality—and the hard boundaries that Kerr saw were disappearing. Some of the universities' great buildings were becoming symbols and architectural ruins—reminders of our past.

The size of the academy was growing exponentially; state universities were playing an increasingly important role in educating the majority of undergraduate, doctoral, and professional school students. Universities were taking on new functions. Consider just a few of the ways in which growth in size and complexity made a qualitative as well as a quantitative difference in the structure and governance of great research universities. We might begin just with the chief policy instrument of any university—its budget. When I entered Columbia, the university's budget was perhaps slightly more than $100 million, up from $50 million in the 1950s; today, it is rubbing up against $4 billion annually. The same can be said about all of the large research universities. There has been enormous growth in research and scholarly centers and institutes to accommodate new styles of research and learning; and new departments and schools have been formed. The curriculum has expanded to include many studies beyond those that were part of our Western tradition. Yes, there has been significant growth in the size of the faculties at the various schools, but that growth did not compare with the proliferation over time of the bureaucratic administrative offices of the university that were born in response to pressure from governments, students, faculty, and other constituencies of the institutions of higher learning.

The sheer number of government regulations (a new way to control academic institutions and limit their autonomy) related to students, experimental animals, conflicts of interest, and diversity, as well as other aspects of research led to a plethora of unfunded mandates and increases in staff to respond to these governmental requirements and other pressures. From 1989 to 2011–2012, universities and colleges in the United States added more than 500,000 administrators and professional employees. Andrew Gillen, a researcher at the American Institutes of Research, said: "There is a mind-boggling amount of money per student that's being spent on administration."[3] Mario Lalich, writing for the *Washington Monthly*, cites data from the Delta Project, which focused on university spending:

> Between 1998 and 2008, America's private colleges increased spending on instruction by 22 percent while increasing spending on administration and staff support by 36 percent. Parents who wonder why college tuition is so high and why it increases so much each year may be less than pleased to learn that their sons and daughters will have an opportunity to interact with more administrators and staffers—but no more professors. Well, you can't have everything.[4]

The growth of administration is also linked to the preferences, if not the demands, of students, parents, and faculty when they consider attending or working at Columbia or another institution of higher learning. Today, there are extensive psychological counseling services, health services, advising and job placement services, and large admissions and financial aid offices. Compared with the past, current students and their parents are demanding relatively plush residence halls and dining arrangements; they want Olympic-quality recreational facilities, an elaborate student activities center that houses a variety of extracurricular activities and is staffed by dozens of professionals, remedial learning centers, and information technology centers. There is a growing group of staff members who work on raising money for the university. The legal departments of the university have grown rapidly over time, and they handle an increasing number of cases or threats of lawsuits.[5]

Many of these requests are for services and facilities that are essential, required, or provide worthwhile support for the members of the academic community. But they come at a price. Expensive layers of bureaucracy have been added to meet a variety of legal requirements and constituency demands—and to become more competitive. The open question is: Have universities produced too much of a good thing, which has now become dysfunctional when they try to reduce costs?

The irony, perhaps, is that the resources spent on increasing the number of people actually teaching our students have not kept pace with the growth in administrative costs. Although less true at the most well-heeled universities, many colleges and universities have resorted to the unfortunate practice of reducing appointments of full-time faculty members while increasing the proportion of their faculty who are part-time adjunct professors with little or no job security and almost no fringe benefits.

The ways in which teaching and research are conducted at major research universities today are vastly different from the approaches used more than fifty years ago. The sheer size of the research enterprise—with much of the sponsored government- and foundation-financed research taking place on the institution's medical school campus—would be unrecognizable. Research has become bigger and far more collaborative—and far more international in scope. Teaching has used the fruits of new technology and is less likely to be found in the traditional format of professorial lectures. At most top universities in this country, students and faculty come from every corner of the globe.

Although Columbia had world-renowned scholars and scientists when I was an undergraduate (and I was fortunate to study with many of them), virtually every aspect of the university today represents progress for students and faculty members. But, like many of our finest institutions of higher education, Columbia faces a plethora of challenges and criticisms—often by observers who can't distinguish "fact" from "fiction." I'll consider many of these challenges in this book, but my central message is simple: As good as our system of higher learning has become over the past half-century, we still have a great deal to do if we are to approach the maximum potential of these institutions.

Over the decades that I've spent getting to know many of these top schools, I've come to see the ways in which these universities have served the nation well. I've also witnessed their limitations and what they don't do so well. I know the stresses and strains that they confront every day and the ways in which the outside world is increasingly uncertain of the role that these top schools serve in our nation. Social scientists are notoriously poor predictors of the future, and I'm sure I would be no better than others in pursuing that fool's errand. My objective is to analyze the threats to American preeminence in higher learning and research, but it is *not* to prognosticate what these universities will look like twenty or thirty years from now as they evolve in the ecosystem of American society.[6] Rather, my aim is to suggest what a great research university *ought* to look like within several decades. It is a normative rather than a predictive effort—one that argues that substantial changes in this high-achieving system should be made if these institutions are to approach their full potential. If there is going to be an informed conversation, or debate, over what the American research university ought to look like, then I am trying here to stimulate one.

Introduction

The University's role is not based upon a conception of neutrality or indifference to society's problems, but an approach to the problems through the only strength which a university is entitled to assert. It is a conservative role because it values cultures and ideas, and reaffirms the basic commitment to reason. It is revolutionary because of its compulsion to discover and to know. It is modest because it recognizes that the difficulties are great and the standards are demanding.

—EDWARD H. LEVI, PRESIDENT OF THE UNIVERSITY OF CHICAGO, 1968–1975

I BEGIN WITH A PARADOX. As of 2015, the United States has by far the greatest system of higher education in the world. By most reckonings, we have roughly 80 percent of the top twenty universities, 70 percent of the top 50, and 60 percent of the top 100. We win the majority of Nobel science and economics prizes and other internationally prestigious awards for scholarly and scientific achievements. Scholarship produced by our universities dominates most fields and has the greatest impact on discoveries in those disciplines. In fact, American universities have become the envy of the world. Because many of the brightest and most creative people in other nations want to attend them or work at them, they represent collectively perhaps the only American industry today with a favorable balance of trade.

There are, of course, many superb universities in other countries as well as highly distinguished institutes where research is carried out. One only need look to Oxford, Cambridge, or Imperial College London, to name just three in England, or to the Pasteur Institute in France, or to some of the Max Planck Institutes in Germany, or to a number of universities in Asia as evidence that exceptional institutions can be found elsewhere. Indeed, the advancement of knowledge would benefit if we had more great universities in other nations, as it would help to solve more rapidly the extremely complex social, economic, scientific, and health problems that confront us. But in the aggregate, there is no national system of higher learning that has come close to matching what the American universities have achieved.

Most of the educated American public think of our universities in terms of teaching and the transmission of knowledge, rather than the creation of new knowledge, and most critiques of higher education focus on undergraduate education. This point of view is understandable. Families are concerned primarily with the education of their children and grandchildren and its cost, and they relate to their own educational experience. Let me be emphatically clear: Excellent teaching of undergraduates and graduate students is critically important and an integral part of the mission of great universities. It is perhaps our first calling. But the fulfillment of this teaching mission is *not* what has made our research universities the best in the world. Rather, our ability to fulfill one of the other central missions of great universities—the production of new knowledge through discoveries that actually change the world—has produced virtual consensus about our preeminence.[1]

Most new industrial nations are striving to match the quality of our great universities. Unfortunately, they are trying to imitate what we were and what we are, not what we will be or should be.[2]

In fact, most educated Americans don't realize that lasers, FM radio, magnetic resonance imaging, global positioning systems, barcodes, the algorithm for Google, the fetal monitor, the nicotine patch, antibiotics, and the Richter scale were all born at our universities. Nor do they know that the development of buckyballs and nanotechnology, the discovery of the insulin gene, the birth of computers, the origin of bioengineering through the discovery of DNA, the improvement of transistors, and innovations in treating diseases through work on the mind and the brain also took place at these institutions. Few are aware that improved weather forecasting, cures for childhood leukemia, the Pap smear, and scientific agriculture were also spawned there. In addition, not many know that social and behavioral science discoveries such as the method for surveying public opinion or for projecting election results, or the concepts of congestion pricing, human capital, behavioral economics, and the self-fulfilling prophecy came from work at these institutions. Even the electric toothbrush, Gatorade, the Heimlich maneuver and, yes, Viagra, had their start there. And these are just a few illustrations of the thousands of life-altering discoveries and ideas that have emerged from these great universities.

So, if we are so good, why is there so much criticism of our system of higher learning and such concern about its supposed failures? Today, while we can easily find stories about higher education and university life in books, news media, magazines, blog postings, or on the Internet, few Americans understand what makes these universities extraordinary places, despite the challenges they face and the inadequacies of their current structures and methods of operation. Consider just a few of these challenges: The sources for building our universities with state, federal, and private foundations funding, especially in fields of science, mathematics, and engineering, have been drying up. We face enormous "pipeline" problems with our K–12 education programs, which feed students into our colleges and universities. High-anxiety testing is the fashion of the day and the metric used to compare our primary and secondary educational system against those of other nations. It remains unclear whether educational reforms such as "No Child Left Behind" or the "Common Core," which are built on assessing the nation's readiness by relying on the test result of students, will bear any fruit. Also unclear is whether these competency tests even approach measures of creativity or curiosity. The humanities are under attack yet again for their supposed lack of marketability and extrinsic value. Further, despite an increase in college attendance, graduation rates are well below what we ought to expect, especially at community colleges. Instead of increasing social mobility through our educational system, we are diminishing young people's ability to realize the American dream. Levels of upward social mobility in Europe now exceed what we find in the United States. The public and politicians view the cost of a university education as excessive and escalating—increasingly unaffordable for the middle class. The economic and intellectual value of a college or graduate degree is questioned, yet rarely fully discussed. The unacceptable level of student debt continues to make headlines. Yet, the cost of government mandates regulating the behavior of faculty and others at our universities are passed on to students in the form of tuition increases.

Within the colleges and universities, there is a belief that the traditional structures on which our best universities have been built are rapidly becoming ossified. People are calling for an end to academic tenure. Academic freedom and free inquiry continue to be under attack. Anti-intellectualism simmers at the surface of public attitudes. The public is questioning the universities' commitment to diversity, to transparency and accountability—terms used to trigger discontent. There is a belief that professors do not like to teach; that more of the actual teaching of undergraduates is done by an "underclass" of adjunct professors and lecturers. And students, we are told, don't study very much and place more value on the outcome—a job—than on the process of education, both in and out of the classroom. The organization and values surrounding intercollegiate athletics are in a sorry state.[3]

There is messianic hope that the system will be saved by new technology, represented most recently in the development of online educational courses. Preachers of "disruptive technologies" believe the cost and quality problems can be solved with more clicks and fewer bricks. People question the admissions system. They denounce the quality and exorbitant salaries of academic leaders.

Simultaneously, states are decreasing support for their flagship universities—including world-class institutions like the University of Wisconsin.[4] State legislators and governors across the country continue to starve their universities while asking them to teach more students and do a better job of preparing them for meaningful careers. At the same time, states are directing universities to hold down tuition increases. And finally, among other discontents, there is concern with sexual assault and sexual harassment on campuses.

Beneath all of these particulars is a fundamental erosion of trust between the government—at all levels—and our finest universities. There is a growing belief that our system of higher learning may be incapable in the future of fulfilling its compact with the nation: to provide avenues of upward social mobility, a better stock of human capital, a labor force capable of handling an increasing number of technologically sophisticated jobs, a better-informed citizenry, and to remain a key engine of innovation and discovery in our society. Little effort has been made to distinguish fact from fiction in these matters, but there is no shortage of assertions of facts in books and articles critical of the current state of affairs. What ought to be done?

This book focuses on the top American research universities—perhaps 120—rather than on all of the 4,500 or so colleges and universities in the United States. Despite representing only a small proportion of the total, these distinguished educational institutions have a disproportionate impact on the nation and the world. Changes that they make often set the stage for transformations at other colleges and universities. They also produce the majority of advanced-degree recipients and surely an overwhelming proportion of the most significant scientific, engineering, and social and behavioral science discoveries and innovations.

The Idea of a Research University

Our nation's Founding Fathers took a far more detailed interest in formulating a model for higher learning than do our current leaders. Thomas Jefferson described the "academical village" clustered around tree-lined lawns, where students and teachers lived adjacent to each other with the grand library at the focal point of the quadrangle,[5] and Benjamin Franklin envisioned a new type of college in Philadelphia.

The leaders of our first set of exceptional research universities,[6] beginning in 1876 with the opening of Johns Hopkins, participated in a debate about what the research university *ought* to look like and how it should differ from the best systems of higher learning in the world at the time, the German and British university systems. This debate filtered into a continuing discussion in the 1920s and early 1930s over the proper shape of a university. These leaders held remarkably disparate ideas[7] about the appropriate contours of universities, but the conversation led to structures and values that moved us closer to preeminence. What emerged was the system that took shape in the 1930s and began its ascent following World War II. That model provided the United States and our citizens with enormous social and economic returns, as well as better-informed and effective citizens, for more than seventy-five years.

The American university's rise to preeminence happened with remarkable speed.[8] Consider a few of the key factors responsible for this rapid rise.

Influences on Our Rise to Preeminence

The United States adopted a hybrid system of higher education that combined the emphasis on research found in both the German universities of the nineteenth and early twentieth centuries and the far older collegium system identified with Britain's Oxbridge colleges with its own independent adaptations to the needs of a growing and increasingly technologically advanced society. The fundamental idea that we still live with was more or less settled by 1950.

A robust value system was put in place on which great "steeples of excellence" could be built—organized around transmitting knowledge to both undergraduates and advanced and professional school students. That value system, much of which had its origins in the scientific revolution in seventeenth-century England, turned out to be both hearty and essential for building special spaces where knowledge could grow freely, relatively undisturbed from external and internal interference, and where there were mechanisms for combining the research and teaching enterprise.

American research universities, invoking the value of meritocracy (which was only partially realized), searched for talent from anywhere in the world; and the system allowed those identified individuals the freedom to pursue ideas wherever they might lead. Yet, the system demanded high levels of skepticism. An essential tension arose: These great universities tolerated the most radical ideas yet demanded strict, highly conservative standards of evidence and proof before accepting them.

In a remarkable move by the federal and most state governments, these institutions were offered relative autonomy from the state. Individuals could criticize the prince without fear for their jobs or safety, with a number of important historical exceptions when intolerance and fear for national security permeated the society. Even today, in many systems of higher education around the world, such security or meritocracy of ideas simply does not exist.[9]

It took more than a value system, however, to establish true distinction. Within the larger American society, there was a growing commitment to universal education, certainly through high school but also looking to increase significantly the proportion of the population with college degrees. The concomitant rise in the educated population was instrumental in creating the twentieth as the "American century." As educational achievement became more of a universal goal, there was also a growing belief, despite all of its contradictions, in the idea of meritocracy. Scientists, engineers, and other professionals were rapidly replacing ministers as society's most trusted experts.

Nationally, the federal government's involvement in expanding higher education, and facilitating entry for those not from privileged backgrounds, can be traced to the passage of the Morrill Act of 1862, signed by President Abraham Lincoln during the Civil War. The Morrill Act offered states free federal land that could be used or sold for the resources necessary to build land-grant colleges. Designed to foster higher learning throughout the country, the act also provided support for the creation of the historically black colleges and for the first agricultural research stations associated with these universities (which were part of the Morrill II Act of 1890, also known as the Agricultural Act). Eventually, these research stations would discover revolutionary methods of agriculture that would raise the productivity of the American farmer enormously.[10]

From its outset, this system of higher learning was very competitive. The University of Chicago, which opened in 1892, was bidding for the talent that existed at Harvard, and Harvard was bidding for talent wherever it existed. Competition among universities for the best talent, within both the faculty and student ranks, was extremely beneficial for the system as a whole. It forced universities to continually improve the quality of their research and educational infrastructures, it gave professors opportunities to launch new fields, and it increased the number of high-level academic jobs that were available for students with advanced training.

Although there was substantial foreshadowing in the mid-nineteenth century of later events, such as the growth of scientism and the changing definition of expertise, the great transformation was not visible until the final quarter of the nineteenth century.[11] By the turn of the twentieth century, scholarly disciplinary societies were taking hold and had begun to define what constituted "expertise" in a field. This actually helped places like Harvard, whose extraordinary president at the time, Charles Eliot, finally could feel that in order to hire faculty members he did not have to be a polymath. Other experts could judge the quality of work of proposed members of the faculty. The growth of these professional societies as well as the development of organizations like the American Association of University Professors, which were born out of conflict between the administrative leaders of universities and the faculty, began to define more clearly the division of labor at these great universities.

In fact, one of the remarkable features of the rise to preeminence of our research universities was how they managed to grow despite many social and economic obstacles. They withstood the paranoia about the subversive nature of the faculties and the heavy hands of university presidents and trustees who would not allow any dissent against American entry into World War I. They weathered the first Red Scare after World War I and the repression of free speech in the early 1940s and during the McCarthy period. They got stronger while surviving threats and punitive actions by the government and educational leaders. Despite being viewed by many legislators as bastions of sedition and radical thought that were indoctrinating students and subverting public policies, these universities prevailed.

In the process, these educational institutions incorporated into their faculties some of the most brilliant European minds who had emigrated because of the threat of National Socialism and the repression in Germany before World War II. In fact, until Adolf Hitler came to power, American educational leaders were jealous of these great German universities' discoveries and admired how they had placed research at the heart of their university enterprise. Under the Weimar Republic, between the two great wars, religious and political discrimination certainly existed in Germany before the Nazi regime, but it was a relatively good time for minority group members and dissidents. Quite a few of the most creative scholars in fields like physics, among others, were Jewish scientists.

Then everything changed. Hitler and the National Socialists took control of Germany in January 1933, and by April his regime had purged the universities of their intellectual leaders on ideological and religious grounds. German universities were devastated, and British and American universities became the beneficiaries of the intellectual migration that followed.[12]

The young Brooklyn, New York–born Columbia physicist I. I. Rabi—who would go on to win a Nobel Prize and spawn a generation of giants in physics—observed in the late 1920s and early 1930s that the United States had as much younger talent in physics as any country in the world, but it lacked intellectual leadership. That is what, at least in part, the émigré scientists provided. A new chemistry developed at the American research universities: one that mixed the horizontal mobility of the more sophisticated émigré scholars with the new possibilities for upward, or vertical, mobility for new American academics, many of whom were in fact Jewish—people like Rabi himself, but also others like J. Robert Oppenheimer and the still younger members of the scientific community, such as the brilliant Richard Feynman. By the 1940s, the United States was also producing an increasing number of talented young people who were interested in academic careers.

Until World War II, most distinguished universities were still relatively small and lacked significant resources. They were heavily tuition-dependent, which led to the large increase in tuition-producing professional schools during the early part of the twentieth century. Even the largest endowments of the older great American universities did not surpass $100 million until the 1940s, and Harvard's endowment was far larger than that of almost any of its competitors at the time. This would all change after the war.

The World War II years not only demonstrated the multiple capabilities of American scientists in their work on the Manhattan Project, anti-submarine warfare, the improvement of radar, the development of antibiotics, and many other discoveries that helped the Allies win the war; the war years also represented the beginning of Big Science in the United States, where large groups of scientists worked collaboratively to solve complex problems. But just as the government became heavily involved in funding defense-related scientific projects during the war, the scientists themselves became weary and began to have misgivings about sowing the seeds to create the atomic bomb. Many wanted to retreat into the world that they knew before the war, the world of Little Science in small laboratories at their own universities.

But there was no retreating from a changed world. The nation was obsessed with the fruits of wartime science, and there was a growing sense that great talent was out there to be cultivated and used for discovery. These talented scientists, who now appeared on the cover of *Time* and *Life* magazine, became household names. But what the system lacked, and was about to obtain, was a source of abundant revenue with which research could be conducted.

Vannevar Bush (no relation to the recent presidents), an engineer from MIT, was about to produce what would become the most enlightened science policy produced in our nation's history. A true master builder, Bush had become President Franklin Roosevelt's closest scientific advisor. When the outcome of World War II became clear in 1945, Roosevelt asked Bush what would happen to American science after the war—particularly in the area of American military superiority. Bush, who had led the effort to recruit the most able scientists to the war effort (including some of the intellectual migrants), told the president that a true national disaster could occur. Asked by Roosevelt to frame a new national science policy, Bush, aided by a distinguished set of scientists, educators, and business leaders, produced the groundbreaking policy document *Science, the Endless Frontier* (which was delivered to President Harry Truman after Roosevelt's death).[13]

For the first time in American history, the United States would use taxpayer dollars to support the growth of scientific knowledge. This had vast implications for the size of the scientific enterprise.[14]

The federal government reorganized the way it funded research, restructured the National Institutes of Health in 1948, and created the National Science Foundation in 1950 (which was not the model for funding fundamental scientific research that Bush preferred, because he wanted greater independence from government politics, but it was the eventual outcome of his proposed federally endowed National Research Foundation).[15] Bush never achieved the quasi autonomy from government that he desired,[16] but he had taken the first great leap forward: obtaining government agreement that scientific supremacy (which included military supremacy) was of such paramount importance that it warranted the use of public monies for its support.

Bush believed that the government should largely outsource research to the nation's universities, the selection of which would depend on a competitive peer review process. Proposals would be submitted and evaluated in terms of their intrinsic quality, potential impact, and the scientists' prior track record. The awards would be made to the universities, not directly to the researchers. The government would repay universities for the audited costs spent on facilities and on personnel required to carry out the research. This idea had a revolutionary effect on our universities and enabled them to link the advanced research and teaching missions in the laboratory—a phenomenon of which the public is still largely unaware. Virtually no other national university system is set up this way.[17]

One other step toward preeminence came with Clark Kerr's efforts to form (with others' help) the California Master Plan of 1960. Kerr was interested in building a state university system that was of the highest academic research quality and that opened the doors to Californians who otherwise might not have been able to afford college or to get into the major universities in the system. As one of the first educators whose goal was to include rather than exclude, Kerr created multiple avenues of opportunity for those who performed well. A student could, in theory, move from a community college to a state university or to one of the flagship universities in the system, such as Berkeley or UCLA. This was a brilliant and innovative plan for public universities whose missions were to serve large numbers of graduating secondary school students. Not without its setbacks, yet remarkably successful, Kerr's plan became the model used in other states.

For all of the excellent academic leaders that we have had at our great universities, until very recently we were fleshing out the model that was born in the 1930s and 1940s and settled by the 1960s. It has served us well since, leading to our unquestioned leadership in the world of higher education.[18]

Building Steeples of Excellence

With a revenue stream for research that far exceeded that of any of our competitors, American universities that were prescient enough to see how the wind was blowing, and that aspired to greatness, began to build what Fred Terman, Stanford's provost from 1955 to 1965, called "steeples of excellence." Perhaps more than any other institution, Stanford capitalized on the conditions at hand. Terman knew he could not build all of Stanford's departments into preeminent ones simultaneously, so he and President Wallace Sterling began with engineering and the sciences, including the medical sciences. Later, he and his successors became more concerned about Stanford's humanities and social science departments.

Terman also displayed an uncanny ability to recruit extraordinary talent. He brought in clusters of exceptionally able researchers, such as the polymath and Nobel Prize winner Joshua Lederberg, along with others that the academic leaders knew could work collaboratively. Terman also conceived of a strategy to recruit brilliant young faculty: Perusing the list of nominations to the National Academy of Sciences, he would bypass those who had been elected and instead focus on the talented younger scientists who just missed being chosen but were very likely to be elected in the short run. He went after them— realizing that they would command a cheaper price before, rather than after, election to the Academy. And, in this fashion, he began to build his steeples of excellence, which set Stanford on a course to becoming one of the premier research universities in the world, which it remains today.

But the irrepressible Terman was not finished. Since Stanford had a history of strength in engineering, Terman provided opportunities for young entrepreneurial students to develop innovative ideas on the Stanford campus that could morph into high-technology companies. This led him famously to allow Hewlett and Packard to start their enterprise in a small garage on the Stanford campus. And even more recently, the Google boys were working at Stanford when they developed their algorithm, which the university owned until it sold it back to the two students for hundreds of millions of dollars.[19]

An Enduring Value System and a Plethora of Unresolved Challenges

Universities' core value system, which consisted of a dozen fundamental merits, had been settled upon by the 1930s and would quickly become institutionalized among university faculties and most of their leaders—and remain with us today. These values include meritocracy (merit should dominate any personal characteristic of a student or scholar), organized skepticism (claims to truth or fact should be viewed with suspicion), free and open communication of ideas (keeping knowledge proprietary kills scientific and scholarly advances), academic freedom and free inquiry (scholarly investigation should not be restricted), disinterestedness (scientists should not profit directly from their discoveries), creation of new knowledge and excellence in research and teaching (these are the central missions of a preeminent university), a peer review system (review by peers is the best way to judge quality of research ideas), and governance by authority rather than by sheer power (leadership depends on support of the governed and on powers of persuasion rather than brute force), among others.[20]

These core university values continue, for the most part, to be precisely the set that we ought to maintain in the future. The problem is not with the values themselves but with the fact that some have eroded over time and important new values need to be incorporated into the fabric of the research university.

Yet, over time, an increasing number of challenges began to match the ever-growing discoveries that were coming out of these university structures. Restraints on the growth of knowledge and its transmission to students began to constrain the production of new and revolutionary innovations and discoveries. Government policies for funding research changed; federal regulations of research increased enormously; expectations for the universities, particularly state universities, also changed. Criticisms of our great universities were increasing and, along with so many other institutions, higher education was losing the trust of many in the American public. As Hunter Rawlings III, Cornell's former president and currently president of the Association of American Universities (comprising sixty of America's most distinguished research universities and two in Canada), said in 2012:

> Trust in universities, as in all other institutions, including government, private business, and churches, has diminished. In addition to the public outcry over tuition costs and student debt, the three pillars of institutional integrity, autonomy, neutrality, and authority, are under assault.... This is a conspicuous attack upon institutional autonomy, and it is nationwide. At the same time, ironically, states are asking more from their universities than ever before in the pragmatic realm of economic development. This pressure compromises the neutrality of universities.[21]

Perhaps what is most remarkable is the variance between the set of challenges and threats to the American research university that I discussed four years ago in my previous book, *The Great American University*, and those that are on the public and legislative minds today. I thought the essential threats our research universities faced were not outside the United States, but internal. I still believe this to be true. These threats may not influence our relative world standing among the great universities as much as they will continue to impede our ability to move toward still greater distinction.

Unfortunately, the threats I identified then, which I shall only enumerate here, remain. Generated more from the perspective of the university insider than from the point of view of the public or its leaders, they include familiar attacks on academic freedom and free inquiry; the obstruction of research and sometimes teaching by unnecessary rules related to national security (e.g., in the USA PATRIOT Act, which has been renewed several times); restrictive visa policies; the monitoring and prior restraint that is imposed on scientists and scholars before they can publish papers that the government feels could be harmful to national security; the limitation on foreign scientists publishing in American academic journals because their nations have been designated as supporters of terrorist activities (and the use of export control regulations to limit free communication of ideas); efforts to impose ideology on science, such as the overhauling of the Center for Disease Control's website to exclude family planning and to include abstinence as the method for reducing unwanted pregnancies; censoring papers by government and university scientists on global climate change when the point of view differs from the ideology of those in power; limitations on the production of new stem cell lines in an important area of scientific inquiry; the hammering of the arts and humanities on campuses; and the intrusions of political criteria into the peer review system.

Other identified threats include the increased tensions in a needed partnership among universities, government, and industry; attacks on the Bayh-Dole Act, which gave universities the intellectual property rights to discoveries sponsored by the federal government; the reluctance to change universities' budgets and other organizational structures to keep pace with the growth of knowledge; an absence of efforts to counter the natural tendency among students and faculty members toward intellectual orthodoxy, or what Yale's David Bromwich has called the herd of independent minds; and finally, the absence of sufficient faculty places for those with radical ideas in the sciences as well as in all other disciplines that challenge existing dogma.

When Barack Obama became president in 2008, there were great expectations that many of the problems mentioned above would be addressed by the new administration. And the rhetoric was clearly present when the president spoke before the National Academy of Sciences shortly after his inauguration, stating that our universities and research would be among our highest national priorities because they were so necessary for continued economic leadership. He promised to spend as much proportionally on these research missions as had been spent during the 1960s. His exceptional efforts to provide greater support and increased resources for bold new ideas in science and technology, such as the BRAIN initiative and the effort to create personalized medicine, have been consistently met with almost total resistance by Republicans in Congress. The promise for increased resources has not yet been met.[22]

Many expected that the days of the anti-science movement and efforts to introduce ideology into scientific matters, as well as the targeting of universities for potential terrorist activities, would shortly come to a close. The level of anti-intellectualism and the blatant attacks on those at universities who were critical of President George W. Bush's higher education–related policies have surely diminished significantly during the Obama presidency. It is hard to know, however, if President Obama has limited the surveillance of college students and faculty that was unleashed in the USA PATRIOT Act. In fact, during his two terms in office, he has expanded in many ways the level of generalized, invisible surveillance on all populations, including those who work at our universities. He has proposed a much-needed set of reforms in our immigration policy, which would include the immigration status of the talented groups that are educated and work at our most distinguished universities; but he has imposed new, dubious regulations on research and university activities.

Whether it is because of a dysfunctional Congress or a presidency that is unable to carry through with policies that would implement its values, much of what were challenges in 2008 remain so today. Many quarters of the academy have a sense of disappointment and unfulfilled expectations. When the older list of challenges is added to the most salient current concerns, the need for a new discussion on the structure of our great universities becomes imperative.

Academic leaders tend toward a conservative bias, often having a paucity of new ideas, the ability to implement them, or the stomach to engage with those within the academic community who resist change. At their best, most such leaders oversee limited changes within the existing paradigm. Yet, changes are needed in structure, in pedagogy, in ways that we conduct research, even in the way we organize our competition with others and model our own physical campuses. Of course, at our finest universities, the campus will not disappear; nor will laboratories or the need for student-teacher interactions or the desire for a vibrant campus culture outside the classroom. Only alarmists, without evidence, will suggest that we are about to tear down the walls of our great seats of higher learning.

This is neither a time for panic nor for yielding to the rhetoric of crisis. It is a time to explore new and bold ideas. The many proposals found here include ideas about how universities ought to be implicated in K–12 education, how to shape a class of students when we have discretion to do so, how to select undergraduate students and nurture them, how to reorganize and better integrate the preschool-to-college system, how to rethink the financing of higher learning, how to reorganize the growth of knowledge through structural changes that release intellectual energies, how to restructure research on extremely difficult problems, how to proceed with the internationalization of our universities, how to use rapidly developing new media technology to enhance the quality of our educational results, how to produce a more robust and interesting curriculum that will raise our students' critical learning skills and their levels of skepticism about what is presented to them as facts, how to rethink the governance of universities and the distribution of power and authority among its various protagonists, how to create a new cadre of leaders, how to feed the pipeline of students needed for the jobs of the future, how to begin to differentiate universities so that they don't all try to look alike, and how to create patterns of cooperation that differ significantly from the laissez-faire kinds of competition that served us well in the first fifty years of greatness.

I will also suggest ideas about how to carve out a revised compact between the federal government and research universities, how to grow closer to industry without selling our souls to the devil, how to prevent the erosion and subversion of our deepest values, and how to prevent becoming a commodity like so many of our other institutions. I will suggest how to bring the humanities back in, centering them once again at the heart rather than at the perimeter of the university. I will suggest ways to reconsider the roles that health science centers play in university life as well as ways to reassess the value of the other professional schools.

This book is also about people—those working at universities today who see what needs to be done. Although I focus less here on the fruits of our national system of innovation and the process of discovery than I did in *The Great American University*, I do suggest how knowledge is developing in such a way that we need to unleash the creativity and curiosity of our students and faculty engaged in research.[23] We do not, of course, have to start from scratch. There is so much in our system of higher learning that continues to be valuable and is worth maintaining and defending. These great universities remain the most dynamic force in the world in creating important new discoveries, and there is little reason to think that this spigot will be turned off quickly. Yet with the way in which discoveries are being made, the dependency on transdisciplinary research—which combines the deep knowledge of disciplines with the absolute need for collaborations among multiple fields—will continue to grow over time. Multiuniversity collaborations, which have begun to evolve, ought to be more rapidly developed—even if they lead to a limited loss of institutional autonomy. We must allow this growth of knowledge to advance unimpeded—indeed, facilitated.

At the opposite end of the educational continuum, we should recognize that there are exceptional K–12 schools that feed our best colleges and universities. In fact, tens of thousands of elementary and high school students are receiving first-rate teaching from dedicated and wonderfully imaginative and informed educators. But for all those students, mostly from the privileged strata of our society, there are even more, mostly from the less-privileged in the society, who are falling farther and farther behind. Not only are these students learning very little that they will remember, they also are not enjoying the learning experience itself.

The plight of our world-renowned public universities should be of great concern, too. If there is to be social mobility in this country, it will come mostly from our states' systems of higher education. For the past few years, until perhaps 2013 in some states, universities have been taking annual cuts of roughly 20 percent in state support. I'll address the bleeding of the state universities in far more detail in a subsequent chapter, but suffice to say here that these legislative decisions have huge ramifications for the health of the local, state, and national economy as well as the demographic composition of the state that cuts its support for its best universities. What most legislators fail to understand is that it is far more costly to rebuild lost excellence than to maintain it.

Hanna Holborn Gray, historian and former president of the University of Chicago, entitled her 2009 Clark Kerr lectures *Searching for Utopia*. While I may not be searching for a utopian set of universities in these pages, I am suggesting ideas that we ought to pursue over the next several decades that move us toward a more perfect American research university. That is what the founding fathers of our great research universities were searching for in the early part of the twentieth century; that is what we need to move toward now. If we have little reason to fear international competition, what is it that places our great universities at risk and that we should address as we try to make them still better? To paraphrase Pogo, the central character of Walt Kelly, the satirical political cartoonist of the 1940s and 1950s, "We have met the enemy and he is us."

CHAPTER ONE

Getting In

A child educated only at school is an uneducated child.

—GEORGE SANTAYANA

Everybody is a genius. But if you judge a fish by its ability to climb a tree, it will live its whole life believing it is stupid.

—ALBERT EINSTEIN (ORIGIN ACTUALLY UNCERTAIN)

Alison Foyer is a high school senior at a prestigious independent school in New York City. An African American from a middle-class background, she has a stellar academic record. Alison has been tutored at a considerable expense to her parents; and because of that, her SAT scores improved by more than 200 points. Still, at 2150 her scores are high but not off the charts for the Ivy League schools to which she has applied. Alison has played in the high school band and been involved in a few other activities to make her record look appealing to admissions officers. In fact, throughout her life she has been a model youngster. Getting into one of the Ivies would be a feather in her parents' cap as well as hers. Alison has taken the straight path to success.

Gabriel Jones is a computer whiz, and some of the software he developed has already garnered interest among investors. The product of an excellent New York City public school, he has a good grade point average, has done superbly well on the quantitative portion of the SAT, but has performed less well on the verbal section and about average on the writing portion of the entrance exams. He couldn't care less about community service or the high school band; and he hasn't shown a real interest in history and the humanities, consistently receiving no better than Bs in those subjects while earning A+ grades in some of the sciences. In part because his parents have pressured him, Gabriel too wants to attend a highly selective college. His guidance counselor has indicated that these top universities will be a stretch for Gabe because his class rank and SAT scores are simply below those of others who are applying to the Ivies and places like MIT. In fact, the C he received in European Literature in his sophomore year, he is told, is apt to stick out like a sore thumb to admissions officers.

Luke James grew up in a small farming town in Iowa and wants nothing more than to get away from it. His high school record is good, and his academic interests include the social and behavioral sciences, current events, and history. His SAT scores are high—in the range of 2200—but what Luke is most keen on is creating his political cartoon strip, which is satirical, original, and extremely clever. He has not played sports or engaged in a significant number of extracurricular activities during his high school days because they don't interest him. Yet he wants very much to go to one of the most selective schools in the country because he hopes to find others like himself who have unusual interests and passions.

James Puskin comes from a lower-class family in New Jersey and would be the first among them to attend college. A three-sport letterman, he has gained all-state honors as a football and baseball player. He does very well but not brilliantly in his academic subjects, receiving a majority of grades in the B+ to A− range. He is a highly sought-after athlete among coaches at Ivy League and similarly selective colleges; they like his ability and his character and believe he can make a difference on their team. James had no opportunity to be tutored for entrance examinations; and his SAT scores are roughly the same on each of the three parts of the test, for a total of around 1900, considerably lower than that of the average Ivy League–admitted student. He would like to play professional sports but wants to obtain a degree at a university with a rigorous curriculum that he can put to use should he not prove to be pro material.

Finally, there is Maggie Prince, who attends a good public school in California and who loves to read literature regardless of whether or not it is required for her courses. She is particularly taken with the works of eighteenth- and nineteenth-century novelists, especially Jane Austen. Maggie wants to be a writer and has been working on her writing, particularly poetry that she combines with music that she composes. She comes from a lower-middle-class background and never even thought about receiving coaching for her SAT exams. Although Maggie does extremely well in all subjects related to her interests, she is hopelessly lost when it comes to math or science. Consequently, her overall GPA is 3.5, and her SATs come in at 2000. Having shined in several national poetry contests, she has reason to believe that she has what it takes to be a published poet.

These five profiles could represent thousands of young people who are applying to selective colleges and universities. Suppose you had to choose only one student; which one would you select and why? Or would you reject them all—as might be necessary given the number of applicants relative to the number of places available?

Is it any wonder why high school seniors and their families suffer from extreme anxiety as they wait to hear from highly selective colleges that they have either hit the jackpot or, like more than 90 percent of those who apply, been rejected by the college of their choice?

Nonetheless, every November, hundreds of thousands of American high school juniors begin visiting colleges and thinking about the applications that will need to be filed within the next year. The annual school rankings published by the cottage industry of assessors have been released by then, and students and parents fret over which schools are in reach and which their college advisors insist are a stretch.

There is much to know about the admissions process, yet most of it remains mysterious to students and parents. Since undergraduate education is what most of the public think about when they consider our great universities, I hope to shed light on how the admissions process has taken on the character of an organized lottery and how it favors some students at the expense of others.[1]

Of course, most colleges and universities in this country need students. They are not highly selective. They accept students with varied levels of academic achievement and often with few outward signs of great academic potential. If a student from a state high school has a certain grade point average or class rank, he or she is entitled to attend college—whether at a community or state school or a top-tier research university in the state system.

Most students who are admitted to these community colleges and state schools are there primarily to obtain a degree. They are not motivated by a desire to study hard in order to receive a good education and to improve their critical thinking. In fact, in *Academically Adrift*,[2] Richard Arum and Josipa Roksa report that most college students in the United States don't improve their critical reasoning skills or their ability to think through complex problems in the first two years of college. Their writing doesn't improve significantly, either. This is not surprising given the authors' finding that those students surveyed study, on average, about twelve hours a week outside of the classroom; and 37 percent of them acknowledged that they studied less than five hours each week for their courses.[3] At its best, attending college provides an important avenue for upward mobility and acquisition of the skills needed in today's job market. This is not a bad thing, but it differs appreciably from what goes on at perhaps 120 or so private and public colleges and universities in the United States that are highly selective and that have their choice of students from a huge pool of applicants.

The numbers are staggering. For example, Harvard received more than 37,000 applicants for the Class of 2019, of which they admitted roughly 6 percent—not good odds even for the highly qualified and self-selected group who actually apply to that great university.[4] For the Class of 2018, or those admitted in 2015, Columbia College received roughly 36,000 applicants. Only 6.1 percent of those who applied were admitted. Yale, Princeton, and Stanford accept about the same proportion of their applicants.[5] Clearly, getting in is a crapshoot. The same kinds of numbers are seen at places like Williams, Amherst, and Swarthmore—admissions rates of about 15 percent, slightly higher than at the Ivy League schools, because these colleges more often lose out when both sets of schools accept the same person.

There is little doubt that more than 5,000 of the 36,000 students who apply to Columbia each year could do very well at the university and contribute greatly to it. But there are only about 1,450 positions available; so many extraordinary students are turned down. And the odds of being admitted are diminishing.[6] Despite sharply rising costs, the demand for slots at these top schools (and other private and public universities) is actually rising. Interestingly, Stacy Berg Dale and Alan B. Krueger found that using the College and Beyond data set and the National Survey of the High School Class of 1972, "we find that students who attended more selective colleges earned about the same as students of seemingly comparable ability who attended less selective schools."[7]

At these highly selective colleges, the goal is to "shape a class," which involves trying to admit qualified and diverse students who will learn from each other as well as from their experiences in the classroom. These are the students who have the greatest potential to use their education in productive ways and to contribute to their own well-being and to the needs of the larger society. Diversity is not defined here as solely race, ethnic, or gender, although that weighs on decisions, but on a range of interests and talents that students can develop and share with others during their college years. These are high-minded goals.

Undergraduate admissions decisions rest in the hands of a staff of well-trained and highly motivated young people: the dreaded admissions officers.[8] They travel around the country touting the virtues of their school, train students to give campus tours, and provide professional videos of what life is like at their institution. A director of admissions, usually significantly older and more experienced, oversees their work. Faculty members, however, rarely have any input in these undergraduate admissions decisions. In fact, at most elite colleges and universities, the faculty have almost nothing to say about admissions policies or what criteria should be emphasized in admitting students. Even at the Ivy League schools, there is almost never a discussion with the faculty about how the admissions office defines a "success" or a "failure" in a past admissions decision. Despite their considerable abilities, most admissions officers are arguably not as talented or as interesting as the thousands of students who are applying to these schools—many of whom will be rejected. The smartest, most imaginative, and most creative administrators ought to be located in the office of admissions. They rarely are, despite the admissions office's dedication and determination to admit the most qualified students. That's unfortunate, because shaping an undergraduate student body is one of the most critical tasks of a university.

There is a superabundance of applicants who are extraordinary by almost any of the standard numerical indicators: GPA, SAT, and ACT. But as much as applicants would like to think that there is some inherent rank of quality applicants from, say, 1 to 36,000 at Columbia, there is not. Instead, diversity guidelines are set, including race, ethnicity, gender, and geographic distribution. It is not simply by chance that the proportion of students in each of these categories rarely varies much from year to year. These may not be quotas, but they certainly represent goals or targets. Beyond demographic and geographic criteria, there are also athletic teams that have to be filled, bands that need a trombone player, alumni children that need a break, and talented students in a variety of disciplines that need to be recruited. For colleges and universities that don't have deep financial aid pockets, the ability to afford the education may also be a factor that is considered along with the student's record. Contrary to the opinion of some secondary school guidance counselors, these colleges are looking for a well-rounded class as much as for well-rounded individuals. And yet the nation's elite colleges betray their ability to make difficult decisions and rarely take the kind of chances some of us would like to see them take. They are too often guided by what the final result will look like in numerical terms compared with their competition—and how that might play out in *U.S. News & World Report* rankings.

An empirical study by Patricia Conley, a political scientist at Northwestern University, of 300 admissions applications at a highly selective college demonstrated that although admissions officers talk about having a good deal of discretion in making decisions that circumvent customary attributes, College Board scores, GPA, race, gender, ethnicity, legacies—the standard factors that can be easily examined in an application—are by far the most significant determinants of the admissions decision.[9]

An informal pact has developed between college counselors at secondary schools and the admissions officers at select colleges. The college counselors want a good track record of getting their kids into the schools they apply to, and the colleges want to get the counselors to send them their "best" students, who are generally defined as those with stellar academic records and College Board scores. If you are not a kid who has gone down the straight and narrow path for your entire high school career, doing exceptionally well in everything and racking up impressive scores, you are rarely advised to apply to one of these highly selective colleges—unless you fall into some category (e.g., a star athlete) where it is well-known that lower standards are applied in terms of College Board scores and other academic credentials. Within the group of outrageously high achievers, whose SATs and GPAs are already off the charts, youngsters are pushed by their parents and secondary school teachers to differentiate themselves from the thousands of others by doing something special in extracurricular activities. So they volunteer for something, not necessarily because of true passion but for the record. But the brilliant poet, distinguished novelist, or political cartoonist of the future who just did not care about that physics course in his or her sophomore year (and received a grade that showed it) is told that he or she doesn't have a prayer of getting into one of the selective schools. So is the kid who starts out entertaining tourists on the street but who will eventually do extraordinary work as a performance artist. There is an appreciation for diverse talents, but only if they go hand-in-hand with great College Board scores and uniformly high GPAs.

But that should not be the way the world works. If Columbia can produce a poet of Allen Ginsberg's quality, who cares if he was lousy in mathematics? And if the university can produce a physicist as brilliant as the eventual Nobel Laureate Julian Schwinger, does it matter if he had no interest in high school European history?

By gauging the achievement of secondary school students according to current admissions standards, many of the top schools have taken the quirkiness out of the student body—and the rebelliousness of intellect, style, and thought that is often critical to doing something important in fields other than law or medicine. And it shows. Rarely are students today willing to challenge their teachers in class. Occasionally, I have asked my students to indicate with a show of hands whether they have ever withheld their intellectual punches in a seminar because they feared that their comments might hurt their final grade. Virtually every hand went up. For too many of these students, who occupy cherished seats at great universities and colleges, a terrific undergraduate education amounts to a higher probability of being admitted to a great professional school. College becomes an instrumental bridge between high school and graduate school—or to a good job. Our current admissions process leaves behind some of the most talented kids. Of course, many of these youngsters go to other places and thrive—and have wonderfully productive careers pursuing their interests. It is unfortunate, however, that the admissions criteria used by the most selective schools classify the exceptionally talented but "one-sided" youngster as "not eligible" for admission.

The highly selective colleges reap what they sow. They advise students and their families that following the beaten path rather than the road not taken is the way to get into their schools, and they select students using current standardized metrics. But the resulting proclivity to "do everything right" limits students' impulses toward the rebellion and inquisitiveness that could lead to greater skepticism and creativity.

Overlooking the exceptionally talented but quirky student is related to what I call "the law of the 5 percent." That is, in virtually every field, 5 percent of the population will be responsible for 60 to 70 percent of the creative and truly original work. Derek J. de Solla Price and others have shown this to be empirically true in fields of science. But my observations would extend this to virtually every occupation and profession. That does not mean that other students don't count; it simply means that in shaping a class, these highly selective institutions try hard to identify those who will eventually be in the 5 percent—as difficult as that is to predict when the students are relatively young. The problem is that current admissions policies are not designed to identify those 5 percent: SAT scores don't necessarily correlate well with creativity; and, although recognizing qualities that will later make individuals truly creative is difficult under the best of circumstances, the admissions officers who are shaping the class would not be able to identify those characteristics if they saw them on an application. So they muddle through by using standard and widely accepted metrics to determine tautologically those who are "the best and the brightest."

Straying from Meritocracy

As noted, Ivy League universities and other similarly high-quality institutions, both public and private, receive far more applicants than they can possibly accept; and those who apply are highly "self-selected," meaning that academically weaker students don't even consider submitting an application.[10]

This presents a dilemma. Who should be admitted and on what basis? I've outlined some of the factors that go into the decisions under the current system. However, is this the fairest way to admit students to these schools? The status quo perpetuates the myth that there are real, meaningful differences among hundreds, if not thousands, of applicants. It also assumes that whether or not an individual is admitted is not a result of the luck of the draw—that is, which two admissions officers happen to read his or her application and what they particularly value, to say nothing about whether they had an upset stomach at the time.

Let's consider the university I know best, Columbia, and its main undergraduate college, Columbia College. In order for admissions officers to fill the class of roughly 1,400 from the 36,000 applicants, they have to accept about 2,300 students, because some who are admitted will choose to go elsewhere.[11] Now assume that we had no early decisions at Columbia, and all students typically found out their fate in early April. Further suppose that Columbia concludes that there are roughly 5,000 of these 36,000 students who are truly extraordinary in almost every way. They are surely smart enough to benefit from a Columbia education; they could contribute mightily to the broader educational environment of the university by displaying their multiple talents; and they would make the university proud of them as graduates. The pool of 5,000-plus extraordinary students includes every racial, ethnic, and religious group; they have already begun interesting "careers" with their work in the sciences, arts, public service, and humanities; and they have toiled for the public good even while having to deal with the awful constraints of high school. It is, in short, a spectacular group. Suppose, then, that in January of their senior year, Columbia wrote a letter to each of these 5,000 students that was worded something like this:

Dear Lydia,

Congratulations! You have demonstrated in your years prior to college and in your application and achievements a remarkable set of abilities and talents. You are fully qualified for admission to Columbia College. We write to tell you so and to tell you that we believe that you are a truly remarkable person with a great future ahead of you. There is no doubt in our mind that you are fully capable of handling the rigorous Columbia College curriculum.

Unfortunately, you are one of 5,000 out of 36,000 applicants who are roughly equally qualified, and we have accommodations for only 1,400 students as freshmen at Columbia next year. Therefore, we have decided that the fairest way to admit students into the class this coming fall is to do so through a lottery system. Your name, along with the other roughly 5,000 qualified applicants, will be part of that lottery. The class will be selected through a highly developed scheme of random selection.

We are sorry that we must choose the class this way; but because there are so many more extraordinary students than we have room for, we can see no fairer way of selection. In fact, it would be essentially impossible and misleading to rank order each of you among this highly qualified group.

In early April you will hear from us about the results of the random selection process. We wish you good luck, and we know that if you are not selected through this method, you will continue your education at another exceptionally fine school.

Sincerely,
Dean of Admissions
Columbia College

Which of the two systems of admissions do you find fairer for the applicants? Would any proposed lottery system be better than the one currently in use, which creates the illusion that the applicants can be ranked from 1 to 36,000 plus? The reaction of my students, aside from the fact that they are beneficiaries of the current system, is an example of the "just world fallacy."[12] This is the widespread assumption or cognitive bias that holds that a person's actions always result in morally fair and fitting consequences for that person. People get what they deserve. So the secondary students who are rejected, despite being every bit as talented as, and perhaps more so than, many who have been admitted to the selective college, create a narrative that accounts for their rejection: They find something that they have done that "justifies" the decision. This bias can be (and has been) applied to many situations, including those of economic outcomes for individuals. People want to see the world as rational, so they construct at their own expense a narrative that confirms this belief.

Consider another way in which current admissions practices stray from meritocratic principles: Between 15 and 20 percent of the entering class at the top private colleges and universities are recruited athletes.[13] They are not walk-ons; they are actively recruited, and there is a great deal of competition within and beyond the Ivy League for the best of these athletes in order to produce winning sports teams. In contrast, about 5 percent of the students at athletic powerhouses like the University of Michigan, Notre Dame, and the Pac-12 schools are recruited scholarship athletes. What is going on here? The Ivy League and their smaller liberal arts companions are not really contending for national athletic titles in the major sports, and yet they claim to admit "student-athletes"? All of what follows, I confess, comes from a former jock; many years ago I competed in both baseball and basketball for Columbia, and I remain an avid sports fan.

This plethora of recruited athletes at Ivy League schools is not a secret. In fact, James L. Shulman and William G. Bowen (the former president of Princeton and later the president of the Andrew G. Mellon Foundation) revealed this fact and many more in *The Game of Life: College Sports and Educational Values*, published almost a decade ago.[14]

How did the number of recruited athletes reach today's proportions at these elite schools? First, in 2015, the Ivy League supports more athletic teams than does any other conference in the nation. Harvard has 42 varsity teams; Cornell, Yale, and Columbia have around 30 or more each. Correlatively, the University of Michigan has 27, Notre Dame has 21, and UCLA has 23. Also, Title IX, which has made a world of positive difference for women athletes, requires that schools attempt to reach gender parity in their athletic programs. Consequently, the number of women's teams has expanded over time, which has had, of course, a large effect on the number of recruited athletes. Further, since the Ivy League adheres to a "need blind admissions" and "full need financial aid" policy, no students are given athletic scholarships to attend these schools, and no athletes at these schools lose financial aid if they decide to quit their team after being admitted. In fact, this happens frequently. In big-time athletic programs, students are offered athletic scholarships based on their ability and the expectation that they will participate in the sport for which they were recruited. If they fail to go out for the sport, or decide to quit, they lose their athletic scholarship.

In the Ivy League programs, athletes recruited for the high-profile sports of football, basketball, and hockey (not all Ivy League schools have a formal hockey team) have a substantial advantage in the admissions process. Some are what are known as "coaches' picks" and, at least for the big-time sports, their SAT scores are generally more than 100 points lower than the class average, yet they have about a 30 percent advantage in getting admitted compared to non-athletes in the applicant pool.[15] Recruited athletes tend to finish their college careers in the lower third of their graduating class, and many of them drop off their teams long before their graduation. Allowing for significant attrition, Ivy League schools recruit more football players each year than do the national champions. On the bright side, though, Ivy League athletes graduate at almost the same rate as other students in their class (more than 90 percent), and they do very well afterwards, both economically and in terms of their involvement in and service to their communities.

The policy issue is not, of course, whether there should be athletic teams at these schools. If nothing else, winning teams tend to increase social cohesion on campuses (e.g., Berkeley) that are often divided and in conflict on a wide set of political and social issues. Rather, the question is why—given the extraordinary number of superior candidates with diverse interests and talents who apply to the Ivy League schools—these institutions are using almost a fifth of their slots on recruited athletes. In concrete terms, if Columbia has a freshman class of 1,400, that means around 250 slots are allocated to recruited athletes. The Ivy League was, in fact, formed as a football conference, but it was also intended to exemplify the values of the student-athlete, that is, the student who participated in athletic competition rather than, say, reporting for the campus newspaper but was essentially indistinguishable from the rest of the class in terms of academic ability and career goals. The objective never was to win national championships; it was to provide opportunities for bright youngsters to participate in athletic competition and to live up to that old cliché of having a sound mind and a sound body. If national championships were won—which happened occasionally in lower-profile sports such as fencing, tennis, and lacrosse—that was unexpected icing on the cake. But the gradual growth in the number of recruited athletes and the illusion that these schools are truly competing at the national championship level in all but the low-profile sports has begun to undermine the central mission and values of these elite schools. The mission is not to produce athletic powerhouses (something that is impossible without athletic scholarships and lower standards than the Ivy League will permit) but to advance the work of youngsters with extraordinary talent who are apt to make very important contributions to society in a variety of institutional spheres, the least likely of which will be professional athletics.

The idea of the scholar-athlete has been largely lost at the Ivy League. Too many students who would otherwise be admitted, who are headed for exceptional careers as artists, dancers, physicists, philosophers, neuroscientists, and sociologists, are being passed over—losing their spots to recruited athletes, many of whom will never go out for teams once accepted. Athletics has become a backdoor ticket into some of the nation's leading universities and colleges, and this practice ought to be stopped.

There is a widespread belief that "big-time" intercollegiate athletics is a source of significant revenue for large Division I sports programs. Shulman and Bowen refute that argument, noting that few programs actually earn money for the university and that alumni of athletic teams do not donate more to the university than do other alumni.[16] A 2012 report from the American Institutes for Research, called the Delta Cost Project,[17] leaves little doubt that the prior estimates by Shulman and Bowen were not only accurate but probably underestimated the cost of intercollegiate athletics to universities that are struggling today to contain expenses. As Donna Desrochers, the author of the report, notes, "Participation in intercollegiate athletics in the United States comes with a hefty price tag, one that is usually paid in part by students and institutions." Terry Hartle, a senior vice president at the American Council of Education, argues that in pouring money into these athletic programs, universities have created a "financial arms race."[18] He notes that between 2005 and 2010, "athletic costs increased at least twice as much as academic spending at institutions with top-tier athletic programs."[19] At these institutions, the median athletic spending per athlete was $92,000 in 2010, compared with median academic spending per full-time student of less than $14,000. The cost per athlete was even higher in the "power conferences," such as the Big 12 and the Big East.[20] With football coaches' salaries often in the multimillion-dollar range, is it any wonder that these costs (plus facilities costs) leave average academic costs in the dust? Given concern about rising tuition and other college costs, these figures should be sobering.[21]

What, then, should be done? The Ivy League presidents and provosts, along with their counterparts at the elite private liberal arts colleges, should commit themselves to rolling back the percentage of recruited athletes over the next decade or so. They could identify perhaps one high-profile sport—perhaps men's and women's basketball—for recruited athletes. Because it takes only one or two truly outstanding players each year to form an excellent team, these individuals should be given athletic scholarships—an exception to the need-blind, full-need policies that these schools tend to have.[22] All other sports would gradually stop recruiting, and those teams would play against other nonrecruiting teams at other schools to retain competitive parity, even if at a lower level than one sees at the powerhouse athletic schools.

If the selective private colleges wish to maintain some national presence in athletics, they ought to consider being honest about what they are trying to do and adopt a model similar to Stanford's. As of 2015, Stanford has won the Sears Cup, which is given to the university with the most successful overall athletic program, for twenty-one straight years. Stanford offers athletic scholarships to its recruited athletes for its thirty-six teams. Offering athletic scholarships has certainly not hurt Stanford's international or national reputation as a great university. But what does Stanford do when a scholarship athlete decides that she or he is no longer interested in playing the sport that they were recruited for? Like the Ivy League, Stanford maintains a need-blind, full-need financial aid program for all of its non-athletes. When a recruited athlete leaves a team for one reason or another, she or he is placed back in the regular financial aid pool. They are not thrown out of school or given no financial aid. They receive financial aid in accord with their family's ability to afford the cost of attending Stanford, just as they would in the Ivy League. Some of the athletes leave Stanford; others stay on within the new financial aid parameters. The highly selective Ivy League and other selective colleges could adopt the Stanford model, still maintaining the principles of fairness, while lowering the proportion of recruited athletes in the class.[23]

Almost all sports, then, including football, would move to the Division III level. The select colleges would meet the full need of each student, depending only on his or her economic circumstances. These schools would withdraw from the NCAA and form their own association. As is, they get little from the NCAA while having to comply with many regulations that really don't apply to the Ivy League–type schools. A number of sports would necessarily have to be eliminated. Athletics cost the universities money; they are not a source of positive revenue. The idea is to recreate the real world of student-athletes and to reduce the numbers of recruited athletes so that other applicants with

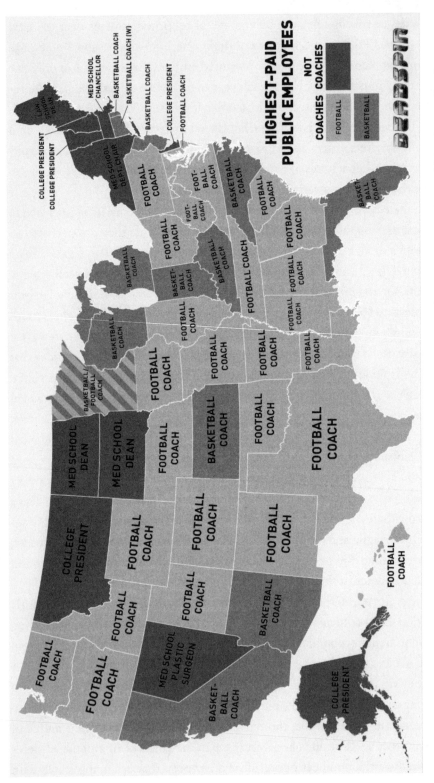

FIGURE I. Highest-paid public employees, by state. *Source:* Reuben Fisher-Baum, "Infographic: Is Your State's Highest-Paid Employee a Coach? (Probably)," http://deadspin.com/infographic-is-your-states-highest-paid-employee-a-co-489635228.

exceptional talents could be admitted to these top schools. What has happened over the past several decades is nothing less than a perversion of academic values. Take a look at Figure 1, which identifies the highest-paid public employee of each state in the United States. Coaches of college athletic programs dominate the map.

Colleges and universities have become training grounds for professional sports.[24] This is good for the professional leagues, especially the National Basketball Association, the National Hockey League, and Major League Baseball, which can reduce their costs by eliminating minor league teams that were once used to develop players; but it is bad for the colleges and universities whose mission is not to produce professional athletes. In Europe, there are no intercollegiate teams (although Cambridge and Oxford field some teams). If there are colleges and universities outside of the most selective ones that wish to retain the status quo, let them do so and let them form athletic colleges and universities that are devoted to developing world-class athletes.

This will be a very difficult change to effect at the top schools. For one, former athletes represent a powerful and highly vocal interest group among alumni. There also would be resistance from those in intercollegiate athletics departments and even from faculty and students who would argue against a different style of athletic competition. There is also apt to be leadership inertia. Presidents of these universities may be unwilling to spend the time and personal capital fighting to slowly redress this problem. I've known university presidents who quit their jobs (or were forced out) because they simply advocated changing the mascot for the university's teams from an offensive to a benign symbol. Think of how much harder it would be to come to grips with these kinds of gradual pullbacks. Finally, individual schools will have a difficult time making these changes unilaterally. It will take agreement among the league presidents to produce such modifications. It won't be easy, but I think it is necessary if we are to strive for still greater fairness in admissions and a more interesting student body at these elite educational institutions.

A New Way of Doing Undergraduate Admissions

Is the transformation of the admissions system doable? For many colleges and universities, it may prove too costly in terms of both faculty time and dollars spent. But at the top schools in the nation—with their relatively large endowments—resources can be transferred and properly used in the admissions process. The quality of the institution depends almost as much on the inter-esting nature of its student body as it does on its faculty members. Of course, the two elements are highly correlated. Consequently, as discussed, student admissions ought to be one of the main functions of the university and its fac-ulty. The job is too important to leave to well-meaning young administrators. It requires intervention and guidance—indeed, decision making—by faculty dedicated to admitting students with what Harvard developmental psycholo-gist Howard Gardner calls multiple intelligences, and providing them with an exciting and creative learning environment. In *Multiple Intelligences*, Gardner originally described and provides examples of seven types of intelligence, in-cluding musical, bodily-kinesthetic, logical-mathematical, linguistic, spatial, interpersonal, and intrapersonal intelligence.[25] Of course, some individuals possess several forms of intelligence, and there is some overlap among types in Gardner's classification. Since the original publication of *Multiple Intelligences*, Gardner has added several more and rejected other proposed types of intel-ligence. All too often, college admissions officers favor individuals with only one or two types of ability—those that show up on standardized tests.

There ought to be a standing committee of experienced and judicious fac-ulty members who work on shaping the class. They will be the "truffle dogs," with the ability to sniff out talented individuals who may have gone against the grain but who have exceptional potential. Being part of such a committee ought to be as prestigious as being part of a tenure review committee.[26] Admissions committee faculty members should serve three- to five-year terms, should ro-tate on and off, and should be given a reduced teaching schedule (or substan-tial additional compensation) for agreeing to be part of the process. Their first order of business would be to define the types of students they seek and how those students will fit into the education offered at their institution. Obvi-ously, the criteria for admissions are apt to be quite different at a place like MIT than they would be at Amherst. The admissions staff, which would be composed of people with experience identifying talent and potential in the various domains of intelligence,[27] could make the first big cut.[28] When the number of students has been winnowed from, say, 35,000 to 3,500, the faculty committee should discuss these applicants. Of the 3,500, perhaps 2,000 would be interviewed by two of the faculty on the admissions committee—as is done in the final phase of admissions to medical schools.

Academic leaders and faculty members should be trying to create an envi-ronment where those interested in writing, computer science, physics, cognitive psychology, anthropology, earth sciences, and economics can join together and use their abilities in an optimally creative way. This is what David Kelley, founder and head of IDEO, a world leader in user-centered design, products, services, and environments, has achieved in his "d.school" program at Stanford. Students there have very different forms of intelligence and build on each other's creative ideas. Along similar lines, Scott E. Page, the University of Michigan's professor of complex systems, political science, and economics, has found that diversity in forms of skills and intelligence leads to better group decisions, more productive firms and schools, and ultimately to a more creative society.[29]

The great state universities, which embrace a different mission from the private schools, face more difficult problems in recasting their admissions systems. Although private universities ought to be dedicated to access as well as excellence, access is a key part of the goals of great state universities. For universities in states where there is not a multitiered system, as there is in California or at the City University of New York, the admissions process ought to be highly differentiated. These institutions should admit students to honors colleges that would rely on the same criteria as the private universities, but they should also be guided by the need to provide opportunity to those who come from low-income and minority backgrounds. Here, the admissions process ought to embrace a form of affirmative action that is not based solely on race or ethnicity but also considers the income of parents. For those students who need it, there ought to be online remedial efforts available before they enter college (as have been successfully implemented at the City University of New York), and the students ought to be admitted into specific programs that will offer them the opportunity to major in areas where they can find better-paying jobs upon graduation. The schools should have well-defined mechanisms by which those students from more socially and economically deprived backgrounds can move within the university to programs that are restricted to high-achieving students. The state and federal government should set up incentive plans that induce these students to make an effort to move within the system to the most advanced courses of study. Greatness will be achieved, as President Michael Crow of Arizona State has said, not by who is excluded in the admissions process, but by who is included.

These public universities ought to make use of online technology as a teaching tool for those who are hard-pressed to afford life on campus, with the understanding that all students will spend some time on campus prior to graduation.

Even at the great state universities, the faculty should be brought back into the undergraduate admissions process at the final point of selection—and they should assess a random sample of those students who are slated to be rejected to see if the criteria that they have set are being followed during the first and possibly second cut.

For students who have exceptional artistic talent, the great universities ought to adopt a system of final selection similar to that used at the Juilliard School or Cooper Union. Many arts schools and conservatories gauge potential and actual skills through the use of tests that attempt to measure specific abilities that they covet. At Juilliard, the faculty "seeks students whose talent and commitment to excellence promise future achievement in their chosen areas of major study. The Committee on Admissions selects students on the basis of their performance at competitive auditions held at the Juilliard School and in selected cities around the country. All auditions are evaluated by members of the faculty."[30]

The conservatory model is not easily transferrable to an undergraduate college at a great university that has 30,000 applicants. However, there are ways to produce new forms of examinations and new tests of potential and ability that ought to be tried as substitutes for the current examinations that almost intrinsically favor those who come from privileged backgrounds. And it is the faculty who make these decisions, not well-intentioned but nonfaculty staff. A similar process is followed by Cooper Union, where a student's portfolio trumps all other test scores.

A New Way to Meet National Needs

There is one other important aspect of admissions at our great universities that ought to be changed. It has always seemed to me that high school tends to be a nightmare for most youngsters and that the rigidity in the grade-level system and its curriculum constrains the creativity of many students. I start with the premise that it is in the national interest to generate exceptionally talented students in all fields to compete in the high-technology world of the twenty-first century. Certainly, a major theme in conversations about American education has been our failure to generate home-grown STEM students—that is, students who will focus on science, technology, engineering, and mathematics. In fact, our needs go far beyond STEM subjects to all areas of knowledge. If we don't improve the quality of the curriculum and demonstrate through assessments that students are learning the content of their courses, we face a time when our citizens will be in no position to make considered judgments on complex issues. There will always remain some need for examinations or tests that measure competency in subject areas (rather than pretentiously claiming that they measure innate aptitude) without yielding to structures of teaching that focus only on the test.

Therefore, the federal government should increase its influence on the field of higher education as it did 150 years ago through the Morrill Act of 1862, which, as mentioned earlier, set up the land-grant colleges in the United States, and later the Morrill II Act of 1890. Now we ought to create a Morrill III Act, some of whose elements I describe here and others in later chapters.

A fitting effort as broad in scope as that found in the passage of the original act would be for the federal government, as part of the Morrill III Act, to stimulate achievement among the most promising students by establishing secondary schools located on the campuses of the top 100 research universities in the country. If a state does not have a research university among the top 100, the federal government would place the school at the best university in the state so that every state would have at least one such school. Admission to these schools, such as the North Carolina School of Science and Mathematics,[31] the Illinois Mathematics and Science Academy, or Hunter College High School in New York, would be based upon admissions criteria similar to those discussed above. These would be elite, but not elitist, schools.[32]

Because the schools would be located on the campuses of the universities, students would be offered housing during the school sessions. As an incentive, the federal government would match state contributions to enhance the quality of the facilities and teachers at these secondary schools. Most teachers would have Ph.D. degrees in their subject and would be highly informed about current research in their field. They would be paid the same as the university professors of comparable rank and experience, would receive the same benefits as faculty members at the associated university, and would have full access to the university's facilities. Further, the university would try to lend its prestige to the teachers at these secondary schools. Students' achievements would be linked to their secondary school teachers as well as to the professors at the university with whom they have taken courses. These educators would serve as facilitators and advisors as well as teachers—directing qualified students to explore possibilities at the larger university and creating opportunities for them to participate in university courses, workshops, and research programs.

Perhaps most importantly, students would move between grade levels according to their ability rather than their age. The boundary between the secondary school and the university would be permeable, depending on the ability and maturity of the students. It would be conceivable, for example, for an extremely able fifteen-year-old student to take advanced courses at the university if she or he were qualified to do so. Some faculty members at the university would teach occasional courses at the secondary school or offer lectures or seminars there. Students would use Internet technologies to gain access to some of the university's courses and would have discussions based upon the lectures given. Graduation would depend on achievement and assessment of that achievement rather than on passing the requisite number of courses that often are thoroughly boring for highly creative minds. Most of the students in the secondary schools would be offered admission to the university if they excel in the school; although they would, of course, not be compelled to attend the university to which the school is attached. We ought to create schools without borders.

The laboratory schools would be research as well as learning sites. An annual budget for research ought to support efforts by university faculty members to understand better the idea of multiple intelligences, different learning styles, and cognitive functioning. Research would provide a better understanding of what forms of pedagogy work to foster and extend curiosity and critical reasoning skills. Other benefits would flow from the network patterns established at these precollegiate schools. For example, such schools would inevitably foster great social cohesion and increased friendship across departments and schools at the university—at least for those faculty members whose children attend these schools. Because children do not sort themselves in school by discipline, parents of these children would interact with each other on the basis of their children's activities.

None of this can be done, of course, if we continue to worship at the feet of the gods of standardized intelligence testing. And the great universities ought to come together (through associations like the Association of American Universities) and openly refuse to participate in surveys and assessments by profit-making organizations like *U.S. News and World Report* that overly rely on the derivatives of the standardized test.

The Examination

> The examination combines the techniques of an observing hierarchy and those of a normalizing judgement. It is a normalizing gaze, a surveillance that makes it possible to qualify, to classify and to punish. It establishes over individuals a visibility through which one differentiates them and judges them. That is why, in all the mechanisms of discipline, the examination is highly ritualized.... The examination as the fixing, at once ritual and "scientific," of individual differences, as the pinning down of each individual in his own particularity (in contrast with the ceremony in which status, birth, privilege, function are manifested with all the spectacle of their marks) clearly indicates the appearance of a new modality of power in which each individual receives as his status his own individuality, and in which he is linked by his status to the features, the measurements, the gaps, the "marks" that characterize him and make him a "case."[33]

—MICHEL FOUCAULT, *DISCIPLINE AND PUNISH*

This book is *not* about primary and secondary education. However, surely the future of our great colleges and universities depends on the people who will enter higher education and then become distinguished faculty members and researchers or our leaders of industry, business, and parts of the labor force in the twenty-first century. Therefore, I need to address what is going on in the public school system at present and how that ought to change if we are going to produce the quality of human capital that we will need to maintain the most distinguished—and nationally beneficial—universities in twenty-five or thirty years.

Let's start with the current high-stakes testing mania. From its inception, the testing movement has been a brilliant way of classifying people as either "gifted," "average," or "challenged" ("challenged" is the current jargon that replaces such terms as "dumb," "stupid," or "not bright"). These labels, often applied to students at an early age, stick with people for the rest of their lives, affecting their own definition of self as well as how they are viewed by others. Those who are currently in positions of power and wealth control the content of the IQ, ERB, SAT, ACT, and other tests administered to youngsters before they enter college; and these tests can be skewed in any number of ways.

These examinations not only classify people into various groups, but they also offer vastly different opportunities depending on how one is classified. Thus, the American reward system is built by those who control the examination and creates the illusion that those who do poorly on these exams are not as worthy of recognition as those who do well.

Perhaps the most extraordinary outcome of the testing movement is that over time it has gained widespread legitimacy. It is as if these tests are real measures of a person's innate intelligence or aptitude and should not be seriously questioned. This utter nonsense continues to prevail, and it is all too useful for those who are currently in dominant positions in the society. Since those who are wealthy and highly educated have substantial human and cultural capital to pass on to their children, they have a leg up in seeing that their children are the next generation's beneficiaries of the testing regime.[34] They can afford to hire tutors and have their children enroll in special testing programs; and they can, or hope to, improve the testing capacity of their children in a variety of other ways, some of which are increasingly being contested. Despite whatever protests against these tests have arisen over the years, beginning with preeminent journalist Walter Lippmann's scathing 1922 critique of the early forms of the tests, those who believe in the accuracy and appropriateness of the sorting power of the tests in K–12 education continue to hold most of the power to formulate policy. As Lippmann opined long ago, if the tests took hold, those creating them, who controlled the content and classification scheme, would "occupy a position which no intellectual has held since the collapse of theocracy."[35]

In our society, the youngster who does relatively poorly in four years of high school (holding *only* a B+ cumulative average) but scores a 790 on the verbal portion of the SAT and 800 on the math section is labeled an "underachiever." But the same person, with the exact same profile, could easily be described, but rarely is, as an "overtester." In short, the test is viewed as right and the child's performance over four years as wrong. The correlative situation is equally damning: The student who achieves an A cumulative grade point average in secondary school but scores a mere 600 on the math and verbal portions of the SAT is almost invariably seen by family, friends, and college counselors as a "grub" or an "overachiever" rather than as an "undertester."[36] Howard Gardner has spent most of his career combating this point of view, insisting that there are multiple intelligences and that the standardized tests measure only one small aspect of a range—and even that in an uncertain way.[37] The result: The high-scoring youngsters get the coveted places in the most selective colleges, then at the most selective law schools or business schools, and so they are defined as the most able.

The situation in the K–12 years is even more pathetic. The quality of schools and teachers in the public schools is being measured disproportionately by how students do on standardized tests. This leads, of course, to perverse incentives, since the teachers are also being evaluated on the results of their students. Teachers teach to the tests, for their own careers depend on how their students do on them. In the most extreme cases, teachers modified answers on children's exams to improve the students' scores so that the teachers could keep their jobs. As one prominent educator said of the Common Core: "I have only one problem with the Common Core. It forgot about the children." What a system.

Furthermore, only two subjects are being assessed—math and reading skills—at several ages; and we hold the results up, inappropriately, to some vague international comparison that is essentially meaningless given the difference in the societies and the absence of any real thought about what these tests are measuring. If the United States finishes sixteenth out of thirty nations' kids taking the exams, a catastrophe for the society is envisioned, and one ill-conceived policy follows another on how we can close the "testing gap." In addition, concentrating on the two subjects on which children will be classified not only tends to force out of the curriculum subjects that may be of great interest to students and conform to their talents, such as art and music, but also pushes aside areas of the curriculum that might well have far more meaning for these young people once they become adults. There is an increasing amount of empirical evidence that success in school and later upward social mobility depends far more on what families do for their children in the early years, and how students respond to the possibility of failure, than on how they perform on standardized tests. James J. Heckman, University of Chicago economist and Nobel Prize winner, put it this way:

> Life success depends on more than cognitive skills. Non-cognitive characteristics—including physical and mental health, as well as perseverance, attentiveness, motivation, self-confidence, and other socio-emotional qualities—are also essential. While public attention tends to focus on cognitive skills—as measured by IQ tests, achievement tests, and tests administered by the Programme for International Student Assessment (PISA)—non-cognitive characteristics also contribute to social success and in fact help to determine scores on the tests that we use to evaluate cognitive achievement…both cognitive and socio-emotional skills develop in early childhood, and their development depends on the family environment.[38]

Stanford psychologist Carol S. Dweck suggests that individuals tend to have one of two mind-sets: They believe either that intelligence is immutable—a fixed characteristic that does not change over time—or that it can develop over time. Those who believe in IQ as a fixed trait tend not to learn from experience because they believe that they will demonstrate the fixed trait—that they are very intelligent or not. Dweck cites herself as a person who grew up believing that intelligence was a fixed characteristic, only to learn that, in fact, ability can change over the course of a lifetime. Those individuals who adopt the second mindset and who are willing to push themselves to overcome obstacles are often more successful in their lives than those who believe in intelligence as a fixed trait.[39]

There are multiple reasons why our love affair with high-stakes testing ought to be curtailed. The exams, whether IQ or achievement tests for precollege children, are deeply problematic as predictors of talent. The College Board admitted as much in their 2014 announcement that they were going to make significant changes in the SAT exams over the next few years. For decades, experts have pointed out the problems with taking the results of these exams too seriously—and how misleading those results can be. Although these tests try to measure one form of intelligence, even in that role they turn out not to be very good predictors except in a tautological sense. They measure the speed at which a person can get what the examiner defines as the "correct" answer; they are slightly correlated with first-year college grades[40] and with how well the test taker does on subsequent examinations of the same kind—such as the GREs, LSATs, or MCAT examinations for entrance to professional schools. Basically, if you're good on these kinds of tests, you'll be good on these particular tests—but how good are the tests themselves in measuring quality of mind and potential?

In *The House of Intellect,* initially published more than a half century ago, the Columbia historian and university provost Jacques Barzun offers a superb critique of the SAT examination, demonstrating that the preferred answer by the examiner is anything but clear, and that each of the alternatives in fill-in questions is arguably correct—if one has a subtle mind.[41]

To some extent, this kind of testing and the anxiety that accompanies success or failure on it is almost like a form of psychological torture for young people, who don't often recover easily from how well they do on "the examination." The anxiety begins long before the students are contemplating the SAT or the PSAT—sometimes even before they arrive in high school. The haunting presence of the test hovers over them throughout their primary and secondary school career. As provost at Columbia, I created a K–8 laboratory school in order to attract younger academics who insisted on superior schooling for

their children. The first principle was that there would be no standardized testing for children who were five or six years old. We could learn more from interviews with parents and through interaction with the children than we could
through subjecting these children to ERBs.[42] The Columbia School for Children rapidly became one of the best and most diverse private schools in New
York City.

Perhaps periodic tests of content and some fundamental principles are necessary to determine a student's strengths and weaknesses.[43] Such tests can be
useful educational tools for teachers, students, and their families. But employing them to classify children is not necessary and ought to stop. It has also become increasingly clear that the use of high-stakes testing methods is not apt
to improve our schools.[44]

It is time to return, even if most people who espouse it don't realize it, to
some of the fundamentals that John Dewey discussed in his philosophy of education more than 100 years ago. Dewey espoused the pragmatist's idea of
"learning by doing."[45] He believed in the value of learning from engagement
with life—from experiences that are actually interesting and that lead students
to formulate new questions for which there may not be answers at the back of
some textbook. Primary and secondary schools should stimulate the creativity
of children to work as individuals and as part of groups to have fun solving problems. Also, we need to make students understand that they learn from failure. It
is not evidence of their lack of ability; it is testimony to their need to practice
more and work harder at gaining skills. Great teachers give students confidence
to fail because they know they can succeed. Finally, we need to instill in students a thirst to pursue their own interests, even if it is at the expense of creating
the "well-rounded" student. We want to produce young people with enormous
curiosity who have developed talents and skills in a finite set of areas that conform to their type of intelligence—youngsters who are at least as much interested in generating provocative, unanswered questions as in producing answers
to existing questions. This is what all institutions of higher learning ought to be
looking for as they consider applicants for admission to their schools.[46]

Transforming the System

There is a widespread myth that "progressive," "constructivist," or "experiential"
learning through doing is not rigorous. In fact, those who enjoy learning
through experience are likely to retain knowledge longer than those students

who are forced into rote memorization. We need to resist reinforcing the cottage industry of counselors whose sole job is to help improve scores on high-anxiety tests. The great universities can take the lead here by making the results of these tests less important in admitting young people to their institutions.

We should not abandon testing altogether. But the nature and purposes of these tests ought to be changed. We need an innovative new testing movement in the United States, one that replaces the aged IQ-type tests, such as ERBs, PSATs, SATs, and professional school entrance examinations that have dominated the educational landscape for more than 100 years. We need a group of extremely smart cognitive psychologists, neuroscientists, statisticians, and evidence-based educators who believe in the multiple dimensions of intelligence to create a new set of examinations. These exams will not be used primarily for classifying but as reliable diagnostic tools that will measure critical reasoning skills, creativity in the arts, aptitude in the sciences, basic skills, and various other domains of knowledge and abilities—including athletic and other physical forms of intelligence. These new test innovators would develop companies that would compete with the College Board and the ACT examiners for legitimacy and the preferences of teachers and people interested in making sure that all forms of aptitude and potential in our children are recognized and reinforced.

Rather than ridding ourselves of testing, we simply ought to change how and what we test to make sure that we don't leave large portions of the population feeling like failures. Instead, they should be shown where they have outstanding abilities that can be fostered within our systems of lower and higher education. Only then will we begin to release ourselves from the hammerlock that these test machines hold over our population.

CHAPTER TWO

Thoughts on Undergraduate Education and Its Future

I believe the faculty is at the heart of this place, and I believe that at the heart of the faculty in a place like Yale is the teaching function. All the research we want to do, all the obligations we must carry out as faculty, are in some sense nurtured by and versions of that first calling, which is to teach our students.

—A. BARTLETT GIAMATTI, PRESIDENT OF YALE UNIVERSITY, 1978–1986

A PREVAILING MYTH AMONG THE AMERICAN educated public is that prominent scholars and scientists attend only to their research and are not interested in teaching undergraduate students—and that because research is the road to international recognition and rewards, this is the road that they take. This is a grossly distorted notion, certainly for faculty members employed at top-tier universities and liberal arts colleges. In fact, there is a slight positive association between the faculty's assessed classroom performance and the impact and quality of their research.

Teaching performance is a critical part of most professors' personal measure of their professional success, even if it is less visible than their research discoveries or publications. Of course, some faculty members are just not good teachers, and others don't particularly care about undergraduates; these professors leave their students highly disappointed with their classes. But what is surely wrong is the notion that the great researchers at the world's top universities uniformly don't care about undergraduate teaching and the welfare of their students—and care only about their research and graduate students. Consider the responses of seniors from a number of prestigious liberal arts colleges and larger, private universities who were asked in 2010 about their educational experiences.[1] In evaluating the quality of instruction they received, 94 percent said that they were either "generally satisfied" or "very satisfied." Ninety-three percent were generally or very satisfied with the discussions they had in their classes, and fully 92 percent felt similarly about the "intellectual excitement" they experienced in their courses. They also found that the faculty was very helpful (roughly 92 percent fell into the categories of generally and very satisfied), and more than 95 percent felt similarly when asked about the faculty's "availability."[2] The strongest disapproval was in the areas of advising, where roughly 10 percent of the students said they were "very dissatisfied" with "premajor advising" and another 7 percent felt the same way about "advising in the major."

It is true that those teaching at the smaller liberal arts colleges and the undergraduate colleges within larger universities have a somewhat easier time being successful teachers because their classes tend to be smaller than those at the great state universities.[3] To be sure, there is a wide variation in the quality of teaching in these massive courses, where it's hard to make personal contact and to communicate with individual students; and too often, these courses are offered by bright but inexperienced teachers. But the best of the professors at these schools, which may well be a majority, do care about whether they are effective and even entertaining teachers. As the humanist J. Hillis Miller, professor of comparative literature at the University of California, Irvine, recently put it: "Helping students share in my joy of the text is what I do as a humanist and feel I ought to do."[4]

But regardless of the size of the institution, high-quality teaching is a function of not only the ability of the professors teaching courses; it is also the result, at least in part, of the *interaction* of the students with the faculty members. For instance, if students fail to do the reading assignments and act bored, it becomes difficult for a professor to hold a meaningful and perhaps even formative discussion with them. If students don't care much about the lecture courses that they are taking, except to the extent that they can pass them or receive a good grade, and if they do not do the necessary preliminary work or cut classes, the professor is unlikely to continue to be motivated to offer a quality learning experience. For this reason, I believe that seminar participants ought to evaluate their fellow students as well as the professor. Nonetheless, this is not a particularly significant problem at the highly selective undergraduate institutions, since most of the students are determined to achieve high grades because of either true interest in the class or their desire to obtain a high overall grade point average (GPA) so that they will have a good chance of getting into their desired graduate or professional school program. But the tone of a class can be set by the students as much as by the motivation and ability of the professor.

The Goals of College

The goals of going to college and graduating are apt to be quite different depending on points of view: those of the faculty, those of students, and those of the parents. If we examine the motives that lead young people to college today, those motives do not always fit neatly into the idea of the college or university that is held by those who work at them. Even at the great state and private universities, the proportion of students who enter college with lofty ideals of making the world a more perfect place, of learning for its intrinsic value, or of exploring some variation on the idea of "the good life" has yielded excessively to those students who think about college as a means to a larger end—generally, a prestigious graduate school and/or a high-paying job. Parents, who often foot the bill for the cost of this education, may be those whose point of view is most instrumental; and that is truly unfortunate. I certainly don't want to dismiss the idea that college degrees are needed to obtain more highly skilled workers and better-paying jobs, but parents of children who are already privileged are more often looking for a college that they wish they had been able to attend (mostly because of the prestige it carries) than for one that represents the proper fit between their child's needs and what the college has to offer. They live vicariously through their children, and this happens perhaps more often at the most selective colleges and universities than elsewhere.

Of course, we must not underestimate the importance of undergraduate education as a means of social mobility. Families still have a greater effect on the social outcomes of their children than do schools. But after accounting for the ways in which families "educate" their children almost from birth and for the parents' occupational and educational achievements, the students' educational level makes the greatest difference (with the possible exception of sheer luck) on their socioeconomic attainment.

The students, taking the lead from their parents, often feel tremendous pressure to accept a place at the most prestigious school that admits them, rather than attend a college where they might really have a better learning experience. Add to this the supposed cash nexus between one's college and future earnings, and you have perfect conditions for psychological coercion.

There is also a reverse phenomenon: Students from poorer socioeconomic backgrounds who come out of high school after demonstrating enormous ability but who feel, as do their parents, that they are not "Ivy material" (a mistaken idea that is often supported by secondary school college counselors). These are students who are "undermatched." Their secondary school achievements and their potential would actually enable them to handle without difficulty the curriculum at the most selective colleges, but they fail to apply there.[5]

These youngsters, who are often from minority backgrounds, ought to be systematically identified early on and counseled by both college counselors and parents to apply to schools of the first rank. Empirical data brought together by economist Caroline Hoxby and Christopher Avery did exactly this by examining IRS income data by zip code, real estate evaluations, and some other sources. They identified approximately 35,000 twelfth-grade students whose grades placed them in the top 10 percent nationally and whose family income was in the bottom quartile. Hoxby and Avery found that almost 60 percent of them didn't apply to a single highly selective college or university.[6] It is equally important that the larger state universities set up honors colleges that can accommodate students with this kind of talent, but who, for one reason or another (financial or social), decide not to attend the most selective private colleges and universities. Although there is a downside to this form of stratification within university colleges, the upside effects seem to outweigh the potential feelings of the "haves" and the "have-nots." Many of our best state universities already have honors colleges, but their expansion represents an important role for the state universities—a role that ought to be supported financially by alumni donors as well as by the state and the federal governments.

What, then, are some of the experiences that ought to be part of the undergraduate curriculum and of each undergraduate's experience? Andrew Delbanco, a professor of English and Comparative Literature at Columbia University and a keen observer of American colleges and universities, recently identified five qualities of mind and heart required for reflective citizenship:

1. A skeptical discontent with the present, informed by a sense of the past.
2. The ability to make connections among seemingly disparate phenomena.
3. Appreciation of the natural world, enhanced by knowledge of science and the arts.
4. A willingness to imagine experience from perspectives other than one's own.
5. A sense of ethical responsibility.[7]

These principles help shape a young person's quality of mind. Delbanco correctly sees the college student as navigating a tricky path between adolescence and adulthood. We should not lose sight of this transformation of personal identity, but should also realize that the task of coming to an understanding of that identity and the qualities of mind that are associated with it doesn't end in college. In my experience, few college students, even after four years of intense study, have "found themselves" or can demonstrate a sophisticated ability to think in the ways that we would set as goals for them.

Among educators, there is apt to be a certain degree of overlap among their "lists" of ideals for a truly exceptional college experience. There are also likely to be differences in substance and emphasis. Howard Gardner, professor of developmental psychology at Harvard and the father of the idea of multiple intelligences, acknowledges the quality of Delbanco's list of principles while enumerating his own, which he suggests remain ideals not achieved even at our very best institutions of higher learning. They include (and I'm truncating the exposition a bit here):

1. The opportunity to spend extended periods of time with scholars from different disciplines and perspectives: learning what they do and how they do it; having a chance to become part of the process of mastering established lore and of creating new knowledge.
2. The opportunity not only to master one subject area, one discipline, but also to sample areas of knowledge that broaden one's perspective, to synthesize that knowledge, and to participate in a culminating or capstone course of the sort that was common a century ago.
3. The opportunity to live in proximity to peers who come from very different backgrounds and have different life experiences and aspirations: not just living, but sitting next to these peers in class and having the chance to exchange views—and, at times, to disagree in a respectful fashion.
4. The chance to receive intelligent, personalized feedback on work and on projects, with the opportunity for face-to-face, eyeball-to-eyeball discussions with teachers and peers.
5. The chance to participate in, and perhaps even initiate, activities that are fun, activities from which one can learn, and activities that serve the wider community.

6. Last, but perhaps most valuable: the creation and maintenance of a community that embodies the best of human values—intellectual, social, and ethical. Recognizing that the outside world falls short, but that a better community is possible, is a crucial lesson that can be conveyed through high-quality residential education. This is a reason why alumni so often return to campus; they think of their college experiences as the best years of their lives.[8]

In her 2009 Clark Kerr Lectures, Hanna Holborn Gray, historian and former president of the University of Chicago, summarizes some of the planks in the platform for outlining excellence in a liberal arts course of study:

The modern view sees the liberal arts as, literally, liberating, as freeing the mind from unexamined opinions and assumptions to think independently and exercise critical judgment, to question conventional doctrines and inherited claims to truth, to gain some skill in analysis and some capacity to deal with complexity, to embrace a certain skepticism in the face of dogma, and to be open to many points of view. These ideas came increasingly to shape the directions of liberal education in the universities and colleges.[9]

I think that each of these three representations of what we seek in a great undergraduate education is spot on and complements the others. Perhaps what is missing from these humanistic points of view, which I largely share, is the role of technology (which I discuss in more detail below) in changing the shape of some of the forms of education hidden in these principles and how technology can improve in some ways the quality of the undergraduate experience and, in fact, increase opportunities for some who do not otherwise have access to some of the great minds in a field.

I want to include a few additional axioms for an exceptional undergraduate education that are not explicitly covered in the above reflections and on which I will elaborate momentarily:

• All students must learn to think for themselves in a highly skeptical and critical way. They should graduate with a clear sense of what they believe the concepts of justice and meritocracy mean and what would make for a just society.

- There should be far greater integration of the curriculum across fields—this includes schools that have a strict core curriculum, a set of distributional requirements, or no formal content requirements at all. There are some essential ideas or concepts that all students should be familiar with in order to be actively engaged citizens; and our students should have mastered the concepts, if not the mathematics, of these core concepts. The absence of integration reflects the current structure of the university, which is divided into "knowledge units" that are defined by individual disciplines rather than by the knowledge needed to address complex problems.
- Students should read and analyze texts not only in their own tradition, but should become familiar with works produced by other societies. They should have the ability to project themselves into the position of "the other"—those who have different values and priorities from those that dominate our society.
- More of the undergraduate curriculum should be active rather than passive. Students should be engaged in active research projects, internships, and externships, and should be collaborating with each other and the faculty on these projects. There should be more learning by doing.
- There should be a capstone examination for graduating students to ascertain whether they have mastered the fundamental principles that the university feels is essential for one of its graduates.
- Every student should be familiar with the core values of their institution and how the "house" is built. These students live in this house for four years, yet the vast majority have no idea about how a university is organized, what is going on in the various rooms of the house, and how they relate to the fundamental organization of this special place called a "college" or "university." (It would not be a bad idea if the faculty were asked to obtain the same knowledge since few of them know about the place they often live in for decades.)

The admissions office should be looking for students who can thrive in an environment that emphasizes most of these academic priorities. Of course, it is difficult for students to internalize and master these core principles. If we think about telling a story about the events that attended or caused World War I, for example, consider how difficult it is to do so, as told by one of Britain's leading historians, Christopher Clark of Cambridge University:

The historian who seeks to understand the genesis of the First World War confronts several problems. The first and most obvious is an oversupply of sources.... In short, the great European documentary editions were, for all their undeniable value to scholars, munitions in a "world war of documents." ... The memoirs of statesmen, commanders and other key decision-makers, though indispensable to anyone trying to understand what happened on the road to war, are no less problematic. Some are frustratingly reticent on questions of burning interest.... There are, moreover, still significant gaps in our knowledge. Many important exchanges between key actors were verbal and are not recorded—they can be reconstructed only from indirect evidence or later testimony. The Serbian organizations linked with the assassination at Sarajevo were extremely secretive and left virtually no paper trail.[10]

Think of the undergraduate student trying to get a fix on the needed evidence to make a reasonable case in writing a paper on a subject that has spawned more than 20,000 books with no consensus about what caused the war. Think of how difficult it is (and the time required) to evaluate the quality and veracity of this evidence. And then think of putting together a causal argument that you can defend. This is a formidable task for a professional academic, let alone a bright undergraduate. This is no less true, of course, in learning how to do science or the social and behavioral sciences well. To learn to think independently and critically is a very difficult job for a twenty-year-old—and is something that more often than not eludes adults who have not had further formal training in this kind of thinking. Nonetheless, this is our ambition for these young, bright students at our finest universities and colleges. We should recognize, however, that the task of mastering the essential principles articulated here only begins during the undergraduate years.

Although a university curriculum must create an excitement about discovery and the dissemination of knowledge, a good curriculum should be unsettling for its students while respecting the values of academic freedom, free inquiry, and diverse viewpoints. It must never shy away from discussing public issues in the most candid way. Recently, students have been demanding that universities provide a "safe environment." Of course, study and learning cannot progress without such an environment. But when students assert that inviting a speaker to campus whose opinions they find opprobrious is creating an unsafe environment, it suggests that they have not learned what the essence of a university is about. Moreover, the university must demonstrate to its students that no one speaks for the institution, for fear of having a chilling effect on dissenting views that need to have a home at any great university and in any great undergraduate curriculum.[11] In short, obtaining a good, solid education should be fun; receiving a truly rigorous and advanced education should not only be fun but also hard work. And we should not forget what Harvard's former president said: that reforming the curriculum was like moving a cemetery.[12]

A superior undergraduate education should challenge students' biases, presuppositions, and beliefs. The college curriculum should be unsettling. Yet, in 2015, at our most selective colleges we witnessed an outbreak of what sociologist Todd Gitlin has called "a plague of hypersensitivity." At Columbia, which is but one among many institutions experiencing this disease, students are asking that books in the curriculum be reviewed for content that *might* make student readers "uncomfortable." Columbia's students have focused on its famous core curriculum, where they would have the college discard Ovid's *Metamorphoses* from the reading list because it has what they see as "sexually violent content." And, if the readings that have sensitive content are not nixed from the list—those that some "grand inquisitor" decides might offend the sensibilities of some unidentified students—then the college ought to attach "trigger warnings" (verbal or written trailers) to these readings or, minimally, have professors warn students that they might find some of a book's content disturbing. There are appropriate ways for students to voice their views about books or articles on reading lists. For example, students might point to an imbalance in the curriculum, one that has no course on the Quran but many courses on the Old and New Testament of the Bible (which was in fact the case at Ivy League schools until quite recently) or the absence of courses that teach basic concepts that provide scientific and technological literacy. In those core curricula, such as the one at Columbia, there is room for student criticism of the point of view of those who created a reading list decades ago that has hardly been altered. Students can certainly suggest that books representing a changing or different point of view might be substituted for some of the older readings *because* understanding changing points of view is an important part of the educational experience.

But criticism based on a book producing an "uncomfortable" feeling should not be one of them. We could be harking back to a time when books like *Huckleberry Finn* were banned from our libraries, and now our university curricula, because Mark Twain frequently used the "n" word in his dialogue.[13] Universities and colleges must not bend to this kind of student pressure. There is a world of difference between keeping a college a physically safe place and censoring works of literature of fiction or nonfiction, or works of art, because they might have some words or content that disturbs some of the students.[14] As Gitlin puts it: "No one ever promised that the truth would be comforting. History, Western and otherwise, is (among other things) a slaughterhouse." Here is where faculty members and academic leaders can show some courage while providing students with an education about why unsettling works are included in any first-rate curriculum. In any future undergraduate curriculum, the quality of the work and the moral, ethical, historical, and social problems it poses should be the sole criterion on which it might be included on reading lists.

Let me move from these general principles to specific changes—some small, some large—that ought to be implemented in undergraduate colleges where they do not yet exist.

The Structure of the Curriculum

In American higher learning, there has been a seventy-five-year debate on how structured an undergraduate curriculum ought to be: how much to stress liberal arts requirements rather than have an open curriculum that can be largely constructed by students with the support of advisors and faculty members. Should undergraduate education be job-oriented or skill-oriented—a place where young people begin the difficult process of thinking for themselves and attending to the complex issues described above. In fact, there has evolved many different responses to this debate. At one extreme is the totally structured four-year curriculum at St. John's College in Annapolis/Santa Fe, a small college of roughly 450 students per campus, where every student is required to take the same liberal arts and core courses featuring the great books of Western Civilization in each of the four years. In addition, students are required to take four years of literature, philosophy, and political science in seminars; four years of mathematics; three years of laboratory science; four years of language; and a freshman-year chorus and a sophomore year of music.

The best-known structured core curricula can be found at Columbia College and at the University of Chicago. At Columbia, roughly half of all points needed for graduation are in required courses. The humanities course, known as Lit. Hum., surveys great books in the Western canon and has not changed too much in its content over the years. In its inception, students read Homer's *The Iliad,* Virgil, Aeschylus, Sophocles, Euripides, Herodotus, Thucydides, Aristophanes, Plato, and Cervantes as well as Goethe and Shakespeare. The Bible was added after World War II, as were Dostoevsky, Austen, and still later Virginia Woolf and Toni Morrison. A few works were discontinued; and several were added.[15] For years, students were given short quizzes every week on details of the readings, in part to ensure that they actually read them. In recent years, a bit of choice has entered the course, given the preference of the individual instructor.

The course is taught in sections that cannot exceed twenty-two students, necessitating the use of many top-quality graduate students to oversee some of the sections. The value of the course is viewed variably. On the plus side, because virtually all first-year students are reading the same texts at the same time, they can discuss them both inside and outside the classroom. Faculty, most of whom love the core, will tell you that it is, in fact, reinvented every generation and is "a course about problems people have never been able to solve" and problems that are related to the books but vary depending on changes in the larger society. Critics of the course see it as too static and overly focused on the Western canon. Yet, even a literary scholar like Edward Said, who created a field through his writings about "orientalism," was not one to criticize what was in Lit. Hum. Students should read everything, Said believed, books in the Western canon as well as the literatures from other parts of the world. Columbia created an Asian humanities course in 1947, although it was not required, and over the years, there has been a dramatic increase in non-Western literature entering the curriculum.

Equally historic is the core course Contemporary Civilization (CC), also required of all Columbia students, which was founded in 1919–1920 by Professor of Literature John Erskine as a course focused on war and peace issues—particularly salient at the time of World War I. It has evolved over the years but retains its format—small, seminar-size discussion groups—and focuses on the kinds of political, social, moral, and religious communities we form and the values that inform and define such communities. In addition, Columbia requires all students to take Frontiers in Science as well as a semester of Art and Music Humanities. Most students also take a freshman expository essay-writing course. Although the faculty is somewhat divided over the merits of the core, there is enormous pressure from alums to keep this approach intact—it is the sacred cow of Columbia's undergraduate education, and if the alums had their way, hardly a reading in Lit. Hum. or CC would be altered—ever. (Of course, many alumni come to love the core only many years after taking it.)

The most discouraging aspect to the core curriculum at Columbia is the belief on the part of alumni and faculty that all of the works are irreplaceable and adjustments should never be made to the reading lists. Yet times change. So, too, should the selections that are part of the core. Some will say that the readings have changed: Female writers are now read; slightly more contemporary works are examined. But, in fact, almost all of the books found in the Lit. Hum. course at Columbia in the 1930s and 1940s are still there today; and Contemporary Civilization, although its structure has changed more than Humanities over time, still ends basically with the reading of selections from Freud. I haven't seen the formative work of Daniel Kahneman and Amos Tversky on decision-making under conditions of uncertainty on any of the core curriculum lists. Yet reading these works on fundamental cognitive aspects of decision-making may be as important today as reading Freud's *The Interpretation of Dreams* or one or two of his case studies in hysteria.

The University of Chicago followed Columbia in establishing a core that focused on the "great books." President Robert Hutchins, fighting against substantial faculty resistance to this innovative course of study, imported two scholars from Columbia's philosophy department to make his case: the Thomist philosopher Richard McKeon and Mortimer Adler. The latter was so disparaged by his colleagues at Chicago that Hutchins had to strong-arm the Law School into granting him an appointment. Had Hutchins had his way, the entire undergraduate curriculum might have been made up of a core set of studies in philosophy, science, and other Great Books subjects. But the tussles between Hutchins and the faculty, who wanted more of an opportunity to offer majors in their disciplines, led to the core as it has evolved today. The tightness of the Chicago core has loosened somewhat over the years; today, Chicago students are required to take a set number of quarters in humanities, civilization studies, and the arts. Nonetheless, perhaps the hallmark of undergraduate education at both Columbia and Chicago can be found in their staunch defense of the idea of a set of great books, as well as great works of art, poetry, music, and science, which all students should confront as undergraduates. In fact, these courses, which involve large numbers of students in different classes closely reading the same books at approximately the same time, lead, in theory, to greater critical reasoning skills—not long-term knowledge of each text.

Equally important to the structure and content of these core curriculum courses is how they help shape the culture of these universities—particularly undergraduate education—and the abiding commitment of leading scholars to excellence in teaching. John W. Boyer, the distinguished historian and long-time Dean of the College at Chicago, puts it this way:

> Like the Chicago Symphony Orchestra [which Boyer much admires], the University of Chicago is one of the city's most venerable institutions and like the CSO it is an ensemble filled with scholars and teachers of the highest intellectual caliber. We can be a very good university and college on most days of the week, even walking in a trance, and I suspect that we can even be a great university and college without giving the matter a great deal of thought. But our goal, as Stuart Tave reminded us 40 years ago, should be something quite different: to be a teaching college and a teaching university of consistently superior proportions, day in, day out, which in this context means that we must provide both a level of educational clarity and rigor and a level of personal encouragement and moral support for all of our students, undergraduates and graduate, that is (almost) unparalleled in American higher education today. The struggles of our predecessors to create and to define this great University's teaching programs were often tense and conflicted, because they were not only struggles about structural formalities. They were infused with a strong sense of pride and a profound sense that our work as educators would have a dramatic impact on the resilience of the fundamental values and the style of intellectual life that must define the University.[16]

Perhaps the best-known attempt of a faculty member to think through what an undergraduate ought to obtain from general education can be found in the Harvard 1945 Red Book (officially known as *General Education in a Free Society*), which outlines what its great late-nineteenth-century president, Charles W. Eliot, began to introduce decades earlier in the form of distribution requirements—moving Harvard away from the more rigid course of study that had existed until his presidency, beginning in 1869. Eliot was opposed to the idea of a pre-professional education, but he did not offer up a coherent structure to his curriculum. The Red Book focused on the concepts and specific authors that Harvard students ought to encounter during their first several years. It suggested courses and authors in each of the liberal arts areas.

As Hanna Holborn Gray has pointed out, President Hutchins of the University of Chicago did not favor Eliot's approach: "Hutchins maintained that the modern university lacked unity of intellectual purpose and failed to offer an education in fundamental ideas and questions that should shape human thought and investigation. He deplored excessive specialization and saw it as overwhelming the world of learning and as reinforced by the departmental system."[17]

Demonstrating its usual tenacity, Harvard faculty has periodically returned to the original question of what should be included in a general education. The latest iteration, co-chaired by literary critic Louis Menand, completed its work in 2011. Now consisting of more than 400 courses, the general education distribution requirement at Harvard is, according to Menand, "about showing people that the way things seem is not the way they completely are, and giving students the knowledge and skills to see that on their own. This is true of pretty much every discipline."[18]

The majority of our great universities subscribe to some form of general education but most follow the Harvard model of distribution requirements and include their own combination of designated courses in the humanities, social sciences, physical and biological sciences, and mathematics. A few outliers have gone down a different path. One wonderfully successful example was Brown University under its president Vartan Gregorian, an historian and humanist who led the university from 1989 to 1997. During his tenure, Brown eliminated all requirements for graduation and built an exceptional reputation as a university that only selected students who adhered to the principle of "freedom with responsibility," a mantra often heard from Brown students and supportive faculty. Here there was an enormous self-selection of students who were exceptionally creative in a particular field (but not necessary accomplished in others)—from applied mathematics and computer science to English literature and cultural studies—who wanted to be at Brown at almost any cost. They created their own programs of study from the existing course (with the close guidance of the faculty), and they worked hard at what they chose to do. The experience that most had was, and still is, exceptional.

I have taken and taught the Columbia core curriculum. Although I believe there is value in guiding students toward new ways of thinking—and the core does this, if nothing else—the approach is hardly for everyone. Here is just one criticism: In this type of curriculum (and in almost every undergraduate curriculum with which I am familiar), students study great works of literature and philosophy in one course, social science in another, and, in a third course, some of the great scientific discoveries dating back to at least the seventeenth century in England. But if, after they have finished this sequence of courses, students are asked to discuss the general historical or social context of a particular year or decade or generation, more often than not they respond with blank stares. It is not their fault that they cannot make these kinds of connections, since there is little curricular integration that consciously goes on. No one has helped them place the works of the core, including the development of science, into a larger framework, or, at the very least, a timeline.

Over the next decades, the curriculum at our colleges and universities should be integrated across subjects in the same way that multidisciplinary research is becoming the norm. Some great universities, like Stanford, are already moving in this direction.

The larger point is: Contrary to the myth that great universities and colleges don't give a damn about their undergraduates, the best institutions of higher learning are continually trying to improve the quality of curriculum—and invariably the faculty of these institutions take the lead in efforts, often not successful, at reform. The latest that is noteworthy is Stanford's 2012 effort to revise its undergraduate curriculum—the work of a seventeen-member committee, most of whom were faculty members. It was the first major rethinking of the curriculum since 1993–1994. The results focus on developing core skills in addition to disciplinary content, thus making Stanford much like Harvard and other great universities with a set of options within the core curriculum. The committee identified seven skill areas that it believed were important for all of its undergraduates to have upon graduation. They included: "aesthetic and interpretative inquiry; social inquiry; scientific analysis, formal and quantitative reasoning (two courses in each); as well as one course in engaging difference, one in moral and ethical reasoning, and another in creative expression."[19] The committee also added a collection of courses called "Thinking Matters" to the first-year-student curriculum. These courses had considerable range, from the "Art of Living," which bridges philosophical concepts developed in Greece to modern-day France[20]; one entitled "Freedom, Equality, Security"; another called "The Science of MythBusters," which focuses on the biological and physical sciences; one on "Brain, Behavior, and Evolution"; and another on "Everyday Life: How History Happens."

Although there are different approaches to the core offerings at these great universities, each one has a well-thought-out purpose and is designed to have major professors involved in the teaching of undergraduates. The movement is clearly away from substantive content per se and toward "thinking about thinking." One might respond to this set of illustrations: "But you are talking about a few universities with enormous prestige and resources." True enough, but the way these great universities think about the teaching of undergraduates has substantial influence on the formation of the undergraduate curriculums at hundreds of less-renowned universities and liberal arts colleges—and may, in the end, through their graduates, influence the way the educated public views undergraduate education.

Perhaps the most ambitious effort to alter the undergraduate curriculum comes from an unlikely source: Arizona State University (ASU). Since 2003, when Michael Crow became president, this one-time rather sleepy and relatively young university has been a cauldron of change, which is perhaps easier done in the Tempe setting than in Cambridge, Massachusetts. Limiting our glance to undergraduate education, the school has eliminated 69 academic units while creating 30 new ones; many of the older disciplinary units have become part of interdisciplinary units. Students are asked to focus on innovation and work that could be categorized as part of Pasteur's quadrant—that intellectual place that fosters discovery in which both basic and applied knowledge are relevant. New schools have been initiated, such as one of historical, philosophical, and religious studies; and ASU has tried to recruit faculty members who are interested in teaching largely interdisciplinary courses. The idea is to create a new type of university that differentiates itself rather than competes with the older, private, and predominantly Eastern institutions. As President Crow, who spent a decade at Columbia as its executive vice provost, likes to say: ASU wants to be known more for who is included rather than who is excluded, and to meet the national needs of students and the nation's needs in the twenty-first century.

Whatever the form of the curriculum, there is an essential need for undergraduates to partake of a variety of basic courses in the arts and sciences that introduce them to the various disciplines and the history of thought in those fields. In the process, these young men and women ought to be introduced to some key concepts that are necessary for being an informed citizen. My favorite example is the need for some fundamental knowledge, albeit conceptual rather than formally mathematical, in statistics and probability. It is almost impossible to read, understand, or criticize assertions of fact that appear in newspapers and other media (or, for that matter, to navigate daily life) without possessing an understanding of the basic concepts of statistics and probability.

Perhaps the greatest deficiency in today's undergraduate curriculum at smaller liberal arts colleges and selective research university colleges is the extremely weak curricula that focus on scientific and technological literacy and conceptual competence. This is particularly important because a majority of students never take a science course after they have completed the final requirement in high school. What they know about science and technology must, then, come from the various news media, social media, and from whatever teaching they may receive in American history during high school, college, or graduate school. We ought to embed in the undergraduate curriculum various ways in which students learn about scientific concepts—not necessarily the content of science, which is always changing. And limited progress has been made to make this happen.

Given the extraordinary contributions of science and technology to contemporary culture and the economic well-being of Americans, one might expect some significant representation of the development of science and technology, and the processes of scientific discovery, in the works of recent American history. In order to examine whether our most widely used history textbooks offer any introduction to these scientific concepts, I did a content analysis of the leading history textbooks sold in the United States. I found almost no references to science. There was the occasional mention of the development of the atomic bomb and of Albert Einstein, but when I compared references to science against those to contemporary culture, I found more references to the singer Madonna than to Watson and Crick, the discoverers of the structure of the DNA molecule.[21]

While there is no single, best way to structure a curriculum, they should all be rigorous and aim to achieve the goals mentioned above. In fact, differentiation among universities, more than there is today, would be a good thing and would offer students greater choice. Whatever the structure, students must be taught that it is hard work to attend to the goals of thinking that we have outlined here, and their development is not apt to stop upon graduation. One size does not fit all. A tightly organized core curriculum simply is not for everyone, but may be just what some students need and want. If we are to encourage organized dilettantes—those students who roam the curriculum in search of the best minds at the university rather than focus on a particular subject matter— then we need greater flexibility in requirements as well as a faculty who can steer students toward extraordinary minds.

And we ought to be moving all of the undergraduate curriculum toward more active, rather than passive, participation by our students. The hallmark of American higher education, which even our German counterparts of great stature admired when they came here to escape the Nazi regime, was the openness and ability of graduate students to participate on equal footing with their professors in the science labs. Now we ought to extend that to undergraduate education. The century-old style of the almighty professor lecturing to the passive students should increasingly be rare. Instead, we should encourage interactive experiences between undergraduates and professors as well as among students—a really good use of technology that is interactive—and that will allow undergraduates to learn by doing. This is not only apt to be of greater interest to them, but it is likely to have a great impact on their futures.

Finally, I believe that we ought increasingly to allow undergraduates to move at their own pace. There should be no real borders between undergraduate and graduate or professional courses if the undergraduate has demonstrated the ability to work at an advanced level. Of course, many universities allow students to take graduate courses while they are undergraduates, but my sense is that we ought to let them move as rapidly as they are able to the highest levels of content and research. We need to have a curriculum without borders and methods of accounting for students enrolled in various parts of the university so we can set up balance-of-trade agreements. Whatever sense of identification with a specific graduating class a student loses in this process will be replaced by a broader identification with the core values and opportunities at the university as a whole.

Another feature of the curriculum might well be changed. Today, students are encouraged to major or double major in one or two disciplines. They believe that this will make them more attractive to professional schools or in the job market. There is no evidence that this is so. In fact, universities and colleges ought to experiment with having no majors at all or concentration in a particular subject (which would require fewer courses). Of course, an undergraduate student who already has well-defined interests, who has known since she was five years old that she wanted to be a geologist, can take as many courses as she likes in the subject for which she holds a passion. But more often than not, students have no intellectual passions coming into college. They tend to be guided by practical concerns; but if they were encouraged to canvass the breadth of the curriculum to see what they might discover serendipitously, youngsters who come to college without any knowledge of music or of science, for example, might wind up wanting to pursue careers in the areas in which they discover an intellectual passion.

A great college education requires inspired teachers and curious students. Even those organizations that are noted for their support of research recognize

this critical fact. One illustration of this is the 2014 announcement by the Howard Hughes Medical Institute (HHMI) that it would support fifteen scientists
as HHMI Professors. These individuals would each receive $1 million over five
years "to introduce innovative approaches in teaching science to undergraduates." This will undoubtedly become a highly prestigious award. It signals that
one of the leading supporters of biological research in the nation also feels, as
Bart Giamatti said: "All the research we want to do, all the obligations we must
carry out as faculty, are in some sense nurtured by and versions of that first
calling, which is to teach our students."

University Identity

Every great university, every great liberal arts college, either has a cultural
identity or is searching for one. It is often unclear whether that culture is captured by the university's motto or mission statement. More often than not, such
pithy statements fail to capture the actual ethos of the institution. In part, that
identity is a result of the internalization of fundamental values and norms that
are never lost from view at the place of learning. This is the case at the University of Chicago with its deep-seated commitment, if not always realized, to
academic freedom, free inquiry, interdisciplinary discourse, and its form of general education. Columbia's identity is shaped to a great degree by its location—it
is, after all, Columbia University *in the City of New York*. But it is also shaped by
the creative impulse that guides research and, I would submit, the nature of its
manifest commitment to great books and great works of the mind.

To my knowledge, there has been no comprehensive comparison of the diversity of cultures represented by the many great research universities and
liberal arts colleges in the United States. What is it that distinguishes the
University of North Carolina at Chapel Hill from Chicago or Harvard; what
distinguishes Stanford from nearby Berkeley or UCLA, or the University of
Wisconsin, or the University of Michigan—other than the obvious differences
in the quality of their athletic teams? Are there significant and necessary cultural differences between public and private institutions; between research universities and liberal arts colleges; and if so, what are they?

The great public research universities, which have a somewhat different mission than the great privates, have a much harder time of it. For one, there is the
obvious fact that these schools have much larger and more diverse student bodies. It is extremely costly and difficult to staff small seminars for all first- or

second-year students, and there is more of a push among students and parents for a "preprofessional" education. It is more difficult for these universities to carve out a clear identity through their curriculum. So, these public universities, which educate the majority of our students, must create multiple curricula for their student bodies. What they ought to do is resist the push of legislators and parents for premature preprofessional education. All of the students ought to be well-versed in the liberal arts before taking on more concentrated work, faculty and advisors of every kind ought to make an effort to promote the value of a foundational education in the liberal arts that may actually benefit the students more than an undergraduate major in business or journalism or social work. In fact, perhaps the place for online learning should be predominantly focused on practical aspects of preprofessional education, since it may be more adaptable to that form of instruction. Furthermore, universities ought to do a better job at enlisting leaders of the business community to publicly support the value of a liberal arts education. They can also dispel the widespread belief that a prevocational undergraduate education prepares a person better for the "real world" and succeeding in a job.

Whatever the differences between the private and public great universities, the identity of a place, and of its students and faculty, is shaped in some measure by the structure of the undergraduate experience and contributes greatly to that cultural identity and its derived values and norms. What strikes one in reading so many diatribes against a culture of learning and a commitment by faculty to undergraduate education is how much it diverges from what one actually sees in the classrooms and outside of it at the best of our nation's universities.[22] In the future, we ought to make this commitment to young minds—who are not always ready for the work asked of them, or who have already been worn out by the culture of examinations and achievement—far more apparent to the educated public and its leaders. Thus far, too few know of that commitment and the passion that so many of the faculty at great institutions of higher learning have for their subjects and their undergraduate and graduate students.

The Informal Curriculum

At its best, undergraduate education (not to mention graduate education) is far more than what one studies in courses. The brilliant philosopher George Santayana, in speaking on schooling, once said: "A child educated only at school is an uneducated child."[23] Students benefit from being with people who come from very different backgrounds from their own; they form social bonds and networks that often represent the beginnings of lifelong friendships; they join clubs and athletic teams, campus newspapers and radio stations, and local service organizations—all of which enhance their education.

If we are going to improve on what currently exists for undergraduates, what ought we to do to augment these many forms of engagement? Through the creation of various forms of society within the larger community, we can enhance what students obtain from their teachers. Let me provide an example from Columbia, the Rabi Scholars Program. Named after Columbia's Nobel Laureate physicist, I. I. Rabi, whose students won many Nobel Prizes, this program brings together students who are interested in science and provides a space and programming where they can hear talks by scientists and their fellow students. Faculty members in the program have more direct contact with these focused students than they would otherwise. Rabi scholars are selected at Columbia at the point of admission, but there is no reason why selection cannot come after students have been able to navigate their way around the curriculum and even change their focus of study.

There could be similar types of smaller intellectual communities created around interests in the humanities, the social and behavioral sciences, and the arts. Each university could create such subcultures and name them after some of their illustrious former faculty members. Weekly or monthly meetings with substantive programs mixed with social interaction could enhance still further the education of these undergraduates. As new multidisciplinary courses of study develop, such as programs in cognitive neuroscience, universities should expand the number of subcommunities, which incidentally have proven extremely attractive to donors. There is probably no better way to lead students toward lives of the mind than through this kind of experiential learning.

Our great universities ought to introduce another form of learning that is combined with community building that few, if any, have at the moment. College students often work in study groups, but there is a form of learning that complements such modes of learning, which is beyond the formal curriculum but that enhances one's enjoyment of literature and that furthers the college's ultimate goals. I'm thinking about small informal reading groups that take pieces of literature and read them out loud to each other, without advance preparation, and then stop to have a discussion after each participant has completed his set number of pages. They might, for example, read novels like Charles Dickens's *Bleak House* in "numbers," the way in which it was published. Or they could read William Faulkner's *Light in August*, Zora Neale Hurston's *Their Eyes Were Watching God*, F. Scott Fitzgerald's *The Great Gatsby*, Herman Melville's *Moby Dick*, or perhaps the even more modern Patrick Melrose novels by Edward St. Aubyn. Individuals who are interested in nonfiction could also form groups that would read aloud sections of great works of history, anthropology, economics, or sociology. It might take several months or more to complete the reading of a single book, but it would serve both an intellectual and social function within the college. If it is difficult for the students to form these groups, an academic dean could help jump-start the process.

In order for our undergraduate students to gain a better sense of our nation's history—history that will ultimately be relevant to their coursework—the great universities ought to construct a set of perhaps twenty films that they ask their incoming students to watch at their leisure during their first year in college. At the end of the year, they will be given a short quiz to be reasonably sure that the students have carried out the assignment. Each of these films would be selected on the basis of a moment in history that the school would like their undergraduates to be aware of. Given their date of birth, there is no reason to expect the students to be familiar with important themes in our nation's history—much less the history of other nations or civilizations.

There are other local resources in university communities that we ought to try to preserve or create in the future. As convenient as it is to order books almost instantly from Amazon, or to go on the Internet and obtain copies of manuscripts, documents, and books in digital form (technologies that have revolutionized both study and research), the existence of scholarly bookstores remains an important ingredient in the cultural mix of colleges and universities. It has been sad to see the virtual disappearance of these stores. Almost always, they are replaced by a local Barnes & Noble, which emphasizes the selling of paraphernalia more than interesting scholarly books—the kind you might find reviewed in the *Times Literary Supplement* or the *London Review* or the *New York Review of Books* but are very unlikely to find mentioned in the *New York Times* Sunday Book Review. One may go into a store like that for textbooks, but not to browse through an array of titles selected by people who know good books. These scholarly bookstores are gathering places as well: small communities that sponsor talks by authors about their books, lectures by prominent authors on topics of current interest, and an introduction into a world of books that even the well-educated may not have known about prior to their engagement with these kinds of bookstores.

If these are a small number of the goals of undergraduate education, we should be certain that these goals are attainable. To do so, we must make sure that those who are capable of learning at this level can afford to attend college and that they have an opportunity to rise to the level of their demonstrated ability. It becomes imperative for our universities and for the nation, therefore, to find ways to create curricula that are treasured by those who are immersed in them and affordable for those who can benefit from it.

CHAPTER THREE

A House Built on a Firm Foundation

I know of no safe depository of the ultimate powers of the society but the people themselves; and if we think them not enlightened enough to exercise their control with a wholesome discretion, the remedy is not to take it from them, but to inform their discretion by education. This is the true corrective of abuses of constitutional power.

—THOMAS JEFFERSON, LETTER TO WILLIAM C. JARVIS,
SEPTEMBER 28, 1820

A HISTORIAN OF MEDIEVAL FRANCE and one of America's premier students of the theory and practice of historiography, Gabrielle Spiegel is also an accomplished teacher of many years at a number of universities, but principally at Johns Hopkins. A recipient of many honors for her work, Spiegel is a member of the American Academy of Arts and Sciences, one of the nation's oldest and most prestigious scholarly organizations and, perhaps even more striking, was elected by her peers as President of the American Historical Association in 2007.

Gabrielle Spiegel is, quite simply, one of the nation's distinguished humanists. When she moved to UCLA as Dean of the Humanities, though, she was confronted by a student reporter who asked her to respond to the following statement: "In the modern world, studying the humanities is a waste of time." As Spiegel has noted, the reporter might have asked for her reaction to the following: "No one ever died of English," or "Why study all those dead languages and civilizations?"[1] A group of Chinese leaders of higher learning that I visited several years ago in Nanjing asked me about the essential components of a truly great university: "Why do we need to include the humanities and most of the social sciences? Can't we create great universities without the humanities?"

Within the American Academy of Arts and Sciences there has been continual discussion of the causes for the decline in the percentage of undergraduates who major in the humanities; beyond those walls, a congressionally requested report released in 2013 by the academy has triggered a good deal of public debate over the state of the humanities. *The Heart of the Matter: The Humanities and Social Sciences for a Vibrant, Competitive, and Secure Nation,*[2] a report produced by a distinguished group of humanists, artists, and business executives who were members of the academy, argued for the advancement of three large goals: (1) To "educate Americans in the knowledge, skills, and understanding they will need to thrive in a twenty-first-century democracy [and that can be found only in the study of the humanities]"; (2) to "foster a society that is innovative, competitive, and strong"; and (3) to "equip the nation for leadership in an interconnected world."[3]

The academy report does not try to offer yet another defense for the intrinsic worth of the humanities (although it certainly acknowledges that value) but argues instead for the utilitarian benefit of having students well trained in humanistic disciplines. That alone would be sufficient to elicit a heated response from some humanists who despair when they hear arguments for the humanities on pragmatic grounds.[4]

In my view, the objectives of the sciences, humanities, and the behavioral and social sciences are not as different as they are often made out to be. The most serious deficiency in the academy report is that it treated the humanities as set apart from the other components of a liberal arts education rather than as an integral part of them. All of these liberal arts disciplines are committed to a search for facts and truth. They try to improve students' critical reasoning skills; they seek to discover, to innovate, and to enhance the quality of knowledge that citizens have to make informed decisions about their own lives and about their nation. The liberal arts are also committed to change: The sciences to changing our fundamental knowledge and to promoting downstream a set of discoveries that will improve the public's health and cure disease as well as answer the difficult questions about our origins and our evolution. So, too, with the humanistic and social sciences. Through their critical posture—to be sure, in a murky area between hard facts and values—they try to criticize existing patterns of behavior after understanding them and to promote changes in the institutions in which our citizens are embedded. In a fundamental way, the well-known antagonism between the sciences and the humanities, which has existed at least since C. P. Snow's *The Two Cultures and the Scientific Revolution,* is a false dichotomy that ought to be abandoned.[5] The commonality of interests has over time become clearer than perhaps it was in Snow's day; but although the disciplines that make up these large liberal arts enterprises have distinctly different methodologies and orientations, they have very common goals. Despite those similitudes, there is, as Berkeley historian David A. Hollinger says in a 2013 essay in the *Chronicle of Higher Education*, a "wedge driving Academe's two families apart" despite, he argues, "the deep kinship between humanistic studies and natural science."[6]

The Depth of the Problem

If the humanities and social and behavioral sciences, as well as the sciences and engineering, are the foundations for building reasonably independent-thinking individuals, then it's clear that the nation is failing in producing citizens with an acceptable level of knowledge for making informed decisions.[7] Consider a few findings from a recent survey of basic knowledge that American citizens have about their own history. It is not as if Americans don't think it is important to know something about their own history: 90 percent of those who took the survey entitled *The American Revolution. Who Cares?* did consider it important. Yet on the twenty-seven-question test, 83 percent received a failing grade.

For example, only about 10 percent of those surveyed identified John Jay as the first Chief Justice of the U.S. Supreme Court; "many more Americans knew that Michael Jackson authored *Beat It* and *Billie Jean* than knew that James Madison was the Father of the Constitution, or that Alexander Hamilton was the first treasury secretary; one-third did not know that the right to a jury trial is covered in the Bill of Rights, while 40 percent mistakenly thought that the right to vote is."[8] As discouraging as these finding may be, it may be equally disconcerting that when asked to grade themselves on their knowledge of the American Revolution [before taking the test], "89 percent gave themselves a passing grade, while only 3 percent gave themselves an F, and 8 percent gave themselves a D."[9]

The Annenberg Public Policy Center's Judicial Survey of 2007 also produced some startling results. For example, although about three-quarters of the population surveyed knew there were three branches of government, only 36 percent correctly named them.[10] Fewer than 20 percent of Americans could correctly name John Roberts as Chief Justice of the Supreme Court; two-thirds of Americans could not name a single member of the Court (whereas 66 percent knew at least one of the judges on the television show *American Idol*); fully one-third of the sampled population believed that Supreme Court decisions could be appealed; and less than half realized that a 5-to-4 Supreme Court decision carries as much weight as a 9-to-0 decision. Finally, to cite only one more finding, fully 60 percent of Americans believed that the president should follow a Supreme Court ruling he disagrees with, and a third thought that the president should instead do what he thinks is in the best interest of the country.[11] Clearly, we have a severe problem of ignorance—and that ignorance is not being diminished by our educational system, although level of education is positively correlated with greater knowledge of American history, various aspects of our government's structure, and the occupants of key positions.

Perhaps a bit more exposure to classics, history, English and comparative literature, philosophy, the arts, languages, musicology, religion, and the social sciences, whether they result in majoring in the subject or not, would serve these students well in their jobs and in later life.

Of course, the angst about the condition of the humanities can be found both inside and outside the nation's major universities. The so-called "crisis of the humanities" has been with us for generations. And for every perceived crisis, remedies are tried. In 2012, Harvard announced that it would mount a program to bolster the undergraduate humanities with changes in its curriculum and improved advising of its students—yet another attempt by Harvard to grapple with the problem that it perceives is faced by students interested in the liberal arts but who are fearful that they will not find jobs if they follow their interests. At the more advanced level of study, Stanford is experimenting with a five-year-maximum Ph.D. program, and some universities are considering doing away with the required doctoral dissertation in favor of completion of several publishable papers.

Some critics with a practical orientation argue that graduate Ph.D. education in the humanities is a sham: a way of obtaining surplus labor to staff large college courses through the hiring of adjunct professors without providing any hope for full-time employment. Others argue that the time it takes to obtain a Ph.D. is far too long, given that half of the doctorates in these fields will find employment outside institutions of higher learning. Any effort to create links between the humanities and the social and behavioral sciences or the natural sciences is viewed as a prostitution of the real purposes of the humanities by means of trying to find practical applications for the expertise developed by Ph.D.'s in the humanities. Still others bemoan the movement of the fields away from a strict analysis of literature, poetry, art, music, and languages to identity-based politics—with the introduction of race and gender studies into these disciplines. They attribute the demise of the humanities to the culture wars of the 1990s. All this departs from the good old days—the golden past that never existed.

The actual causes of the fall from grace of the humanities—from those supposed golden years of the 1960s—are not well-understood and perhaps somewhat exaggerated. There are grains of truth in a good deal of what able humanists moan about. We have created an inordinate number of underpaid and poorly served "adjunct professors"; we have not monitored the job market well or convinced students that there are fabulous jobs outside of the academy for which they are uniquely qualified. We have been through a period of "group think" and the conflict between "insiders" and "outsiders," about which the Yale intellectual David Bromwich has written insightfully. It does take too long for humanists to earn degrees, not because the job market that looms ahead of them is so bleak after ten years of study, but because it takes far too much time to complete their dissertations—most of which never see the light of day. For those privileged few whose thesis is published by a prestigious university press, no more than a few hundred people will read it.[12] The central ideas in the thesis are generally contained in one or two chapters that could have been converted into scholarly papers and published in more broadly circulated journals. In fact, it is questionable whether young humanist scholars are publishing their manuscripts in order to make an impact on their fields or to impress the tenure promotion committees with the fact that Harvard, Stanford, Yale, or some other top university press has decided to publish their book.

Perhaps the most insidious and destructive damage done to the humanities and to the sciences as they try to make the case for universities to the outside world is the continual internal follies of those ideological and sometimes romantic humanists who represent the anti-science movement and of those scientists who try to assimilate the humanities into the scientific enterprise, as Steven Pinker did in a 2013 essay entitled "Science Is Not Your Enemy." Finally, there is the endless whining and back and forth between the two cultures that the sciences have taken over the center of the university and are to blame for the current state of the humanities.

We know that there has been a significant erosion of students who major in the humanities, but the percentage of the total was never very high: only 7 percent today, compared with 14 percent a half-century ago. And although there have been a plethora of possible explanations for this decline—from the withdrawal of humanists from a more expansive view of teaching students critical reading of literature and poetry into the mode of encapsulated conversations among themselves, to the claim that focus on the humanities has no payoff after college—it remains unclear what the true causes of the decline are. And there are some data being reported that there are actually more humanities majors today than a decade ago.[13] The humanities indicators project of the Academy claims that there are 115,000 more students who earned a baccalaureate degree in the humanities in 2011, a 20 percent increase in absolute terms over the number a decade ago.

If there has been, in fact, a long-term decline in interest in the humanities, there may be reasons for this other than the absence of charm or good teaching within the disciplines. Consider only one: Nate Silver, the statistical analyst of voting behavior and predictor of elections, had enough spare time after the 2012 elections to reflect on the sources of decline. His explanation, based as usual on a wealth of data, was quite at variance with the ones typically reported in the newspapers. He argues that there has been essentially no decline in the proportion of male undergraduates who major in the humanities, but a drop by roughly 50 percent in the number of female undergraduates who major in subjects like English and classical and romance languages over the past 50 years, because women now have opportunities for jobs in businesses and industries as well as in the professions that were simply closed to them a half-century ago. According to Silver, it is the American opportunity structure, not the bad behavior of humanists, that accounts for these declining proportions.

Whatever the real causes of the decline over the longer term, the unit of study may be the wrong one. The proportion of those undergrads that major in the humanities does not adequately reflect the impact that taking humanities courses can have on college students. I daresay some of the students who loved Professor Spiegel's course on the Middle Ages at Hopkins are probably public health majors. Some who aim to go to medical or law school may take her course as an elective—and it may change their lives and perhaps even how they treat patients or clients. So, in part, the debate over the humanities has taken a wrong turn. We should not be as concerned about the number of undergraduates who major in these fields as we should be about whether or not during the course of their college experience they come to grips with the fundamental questions that inspired teachers in these fields raise in their classes.

The absence of any real public understanding of the importance of the humanities is demonstrated further by proposals from political figures as prominent as Governor of Florida Rick Scott. In 2013, Scott made the shocking (and now widely cited) proposal that students who major in the humanities should be charged higher tuition than those who chose more "practical" fields such as business and STEM subjects—those that supposedly lead directly to jobs. At roughly the same time, Pat McCrory, North Carolina's Republican governor, said: "If you want to take gender studies, that's fine, go to a private school and take it. But I don't want to subsidize that if that's not going to get someone a job."[14] In short, the humanities are of little practical value in obtaining jobs, so let's create disincentives for young people interested in music, languages, literature, philosophy, history and art history, as well as the creative arts, to taking such a course of study. Further, concrete evidence can be seen in the federal government's paltry funding of the humanities compared with the sciences and social sciences.

It is unfortunate that elected officials lack a sophisticated idea of what the humanities has to offer students, but perhaps more disheartening is that they don't even have their facts right. A 2014 study by the Association of American Colleges and Universities of the incomes of college graduates over a career, suggests that although humanities majors start off with lower incomes, over the longer haul they do quite well in comparative terms. The study showed that immediately following college, graduates who majored in the humanities and social sciences earned, on average, $26,271 in 2010 through 2011—slightly more than those majoring in science and mathematics, but less than those in engineering and in professional and preprofessional fields. But during years of peak earnings—between the ages of fifty-six and sixty—social science and humanities majors earned, on average, $66,185—some $2,000 ahead of professional and preprofessional majors. Engineers do better than all of these groups, but they represent roughly 10 percent of the entire population of college graduates. One reason that the pattern of peak earning looks better for humanists and social scientists is that a relatively high proportion of them, 40 percent, earn advanced degrees and benefit from their added value.[15]

If we want to explain the importance of the humanities to the educated public and to public officials and employers of college graduates, it would be best if humanists addressed the problems in our society that call for greater study of history, languages, arts, and philosophy. We may recognize the intrinsic value of reading great novels and poems, and of studying great works of art, but that will not persuade those who are in positions of power to support humanistic studies with increased funding and verbal confirmation of their value in life after college—including doing well in the job market.

There is, of course, great intrinsic value to studying the humanities. Socrates, in his famous dictum, said "the unexamined life is not worth living for a human being." As philosopher Martha C. Nussbaum, among others, has pointed out, this became the basis of much of the Western liberal arts educational tradition. "One of the reasons for giving all undergraduates a set of courses in philosophy and other subjects in the humanities is that they [educators] believe such courses, through both content and pedagogy, will stimulate students to think and argue for themselves, rather than defer to tradition and authority—and they believe that the ability to argue in this Socratic way is, as Socrates proclaimed, valuable for democracy."[16]

When properly taught, the humanities enable us to develop more acute critical learning and analytic skills; they force us to confront our own biases and presuppositions, as well as our orientation to the world. They allow us to shape and better understand the values that govern our actions and the decisions we make. They enjoin us to consider questions about the nature of the good life that have been debated since the time of the Greek philosophers. Beyond all of this, the humanities can provide us with enormous personal pleasure when we read memorable works of fiction and poetry, and they can help us interpret works of art in a social and cultural context.

But these arguments for support for the humanities have not achieved much traction in the world beyond the academy. Nussbaum, referring to Marcus Aurelius—although I suspect she need not have gone back quite so far in history—suggests that for us to become world citizens we need to "cultivate in ourselves a capacity for sympathetic imagination that will enable us to comprehend the motives and choices of people different from ourselves, seeing them not as forbiddingly alien and other, but as sharing many problems and possibilities with us. Differences of religion, gender, race, class, and national origin make the task of understanding harder, since these differences shape not only the practical choices people face but also their 'insides,' their desires, thoughts, and ways of looking at the world."[17] And this, of course, is the task of the humanities and of social and behavioral science disciplines.

Moreover, although there are undoubtedly varying opinions among humanists as to the principal function of the humanities in the curriculum—and why they are worth studying—a large sector of leading humanists think that the core of the humanities lies in their critical posture toward society. Lionel Trilling, the influential Columbia University literary critic, once said that the humanities and the public intellectuals most often housed at our great universities represented "an adversary culture." Part of the mission of the humanities is to assess and criticize the values, public policies, and the lack of moral authority found in the larger society. They most often take on this critical role within the sanctuary of the university. Rarely, however, do humanists carry their argument to the larger set of powerful individuals outside the academy. They have failed to make the case for the needs of students and citizens to wrestle with competing values, morality, and ethics and to think critically about these subjects. Indeed, one of the frequent criticisms of humanists over the past fifty years has been their narrow and clubbish orientation and their timidity in taking on powerful voices external to the academy.

Not all have lacked that courage. Another Columbian, Edward Said, had a different angle of vision on what humanistic studies are about:

> To understand humanism at all, for us as citizens of this particular republic to understand it as democratic, open to all classes and background, and as a process of unending disclosure, discovery, self-criticism and liberation. I would go so far as to say that humanism is critique, critique that is directed at the state of affairs in, as well as out of, the university (which is certainly not the position adopted by the carping and narrow humanism that sees itself as an elite formation) and that gathers its force and relevance by its democratic, secular, and open character.[18]

Berkeley's David A. Hollinger has placed this role in historical perspective:

> The academic humanities in the United States after World War II were a major institutional apparatus for bringing evidence and reasoning to domains where the rules of evidence are strongly contested and the power of reason often doubted. These domains, on the periphery of an increasingly science-centered academic enterprise, embraced the messy, risk-intensive issues left aside by the more methodologically confident, rigor-displaying social sciences. These domains constituted the borderlands between *Wissenschaft* and opinion, between scholarship and ideology... many of the least clearly mapped cognitive and demographic frontiers of the larger, shared academic program of bringing evidence and reasoning to inquiry were confronted by humanists.[19]

The absence today of a "case for the humanities" conceals the many recent efforts to argue for their increased importance within the liberal arts curriculum and, by extension, greater national funding for them.[20] In fact, in *The Great American University* I argue that the humanities are a part of the web of knowledge of a university and that you can't build a truly great university without paying attention to the perspective and criticism brought to the enterprise by the humanities. Drew Faust, Harvard University's president and a historian, said: "When we define higher education's role principally as driving economic development and solving society's most urgent problems, we risk losing sight of broader questions, of the kinds of inquiry that enable the critical stance, that build the humane perspective, that foster the restless skepticism and unbounded curiosity from which our profoundest understandings so often emerge."[21]

Recall Professor Andrew Delbanco's five qualities required for reflective citizenship discussed in Chapter 2. Beyond a "skeptical discontent with the present, informed by a sense of the past," Delbanco calls for an ability to join apparently disjointed phenomena, to develop an appreciation of both the arts and the sciences, to see the world as seen by the "other," and to develop a "sense of ethical responsibility."[22] He is speaking normatively about what a good undergraduate education should produce—and as much as he is a distinguished humanist, he is more than willing to acknowledge the need for some scientific and technological literacy and a sense that a college curriculum should prepare young people to become more active citizens.

Alexander Meiklejohn, philosopher and former president of Amherst College, expressed similar thoughts in his writings on the First Amendment. He noted: "[There] are many forms of thought and expression within the range of human communications from which the voter derives the knowledge, intelligence, sensitivity to human values: the capacity for sane and objective judgement which, so far as possible, a ballot should express. [The] people do need novels and dramas and painting and poems, because they will be called on to vote."[23]

Here are just a few of the questions that familiarity with the humanities allows students to confront as they mature into adulthood:

1. What are the elements of a just society? How do we define justice, and how might we arrive at a system of justice? Harvard philosopher John Rawls, who spent many years developing his *Theory of Justice*, grapples with these issues in ways that cannot be dealt with by scientists but which are just as important as scientific discoveries.

2. How do we deal with the statement that because we have the right to do something, is it the right thing to do? How do we use our moral

center to confront unjust laws and regulations—and what should we be willing to give up to adhere to our moral core? When is it appropriate to break laws?

3. What are the personal elements of the examined life—and what, for the individual, represents a full and good life?

4. What is the appropriate level of inequality of wealth in a society?

5. Should the United States conduct moral wars? Although we may have the power to intervene, under what conditions is this form of intervention warranted—and how is this predicated on our respective beliefs about universal truths?

6. What, if anything, can we learn from prior history, and why is our track record of learning from our past experiences so poor?

7. How can our sense of self-identity be expanded and intensified by knowledge of the customs in other cultures?

8. How do we make decisions, and why do we make so many that turn out to be wrong by our own assessment?

9. How are our own experiences enhanced through a deeper understanding of the languages, music, and art of different historical periods drawn from different societies and cultures?

Of course, there are other questions that can be raised, all of which require discussion, confrontation, and contemplation—where there is no right answer per se.

We must also face the difficult question of whether in a highly commoditized world, which increasingly includes even the best American universities, students are actually interested in asking these types of questions.[24] There may not be anything in our so-called winner-take-all society that makes it evident that students should be trained to ask such questions. And in universities that are increasingly driven by marketplace competition, students may not be inclined to think such questions are a fundamental part of their education. Perhaps having a high-paying job after college negates that need to ponder how a student defines a "good life"—or even to ask "How did I get here?"

When arguing for the practical value of studying the humanities, one can find a point of departure, perhaps fittingly, in the observations of one of America's great twentieth-century mathematicians, MIT's Norbert Wiener, who wrote with substantial prescience in 1949 on the potential dehumanization of the machine age (with the development of robots and computers):

These new machines have a great capacity for upsetting the present basis of industry, and of reducing the economic value of the routine factory employee to a point at which he is not worth hiring at any price. If we combine our machine-potentials of a factory with the valuation of human beings on which our present factory system is based, we are in for an industrial revolution of unmitigated cruelty . . . the machines will do what we ask them to do and not what we ought to ask them to do . . . if we move in the direction of making machines which learn and whose behavior is modified by experience, we must face the fact that every degree of independence we give the machine is a degree of possible defiance of our wishes. The genie in the bottle will not willingly go back in the bottle, nor have we reason to expect them [sic] to be well disposed to us. In short, it is only humanity which is capable of awe, which will also be capable of controlling the new potentials which we are opening for ourselves. We can be humble and live a good life with the aid of machines, or we can be arrogant and die.[25]

With the growth of scientific and technological knowledge that we have witnessed since Wiener made his observations more than a half-century ago, we have the ability not only to potentially create machines that learn from their actions in order to self-modify their behavior but perhaps also to clone human beings, to create nanostructures that may well be able to "think" for themselves, and to produce forms of biological materials that can cause mass destruction—or serve highly useful purposes. How we approach these advances in scientific knowledge is going to be largely dependent on our values, our moral sensibilities, our understanding of the potential for good and evil in these advances, and our ability to build in legal and other precautions to help us avoid choosing options that may well harm us. Trying to understand these ethical and moral dilemmas and to make good choices requires the work of humanists as much as scientists—perhaps more so. This then may be the point at which we can shift to a discussion of how the humanities ought to move beyond the idea of their intrinsic value and without abandoning that perspective, add to it a practical side that is essential for our society and that ought to be taught at our great universities.

In November 1944, when it became clear that the end of World War II was near, President Roosevelt put four questions to Vannevar Bush, the architect of much of America's scientific efforts during the War that helped bring us victory: "How to foster the diffusion of the scientific knowledge gained during the war? How to deploy science against disease? How to stimulate scientific research in the public and private sectors? And how to encourage the development of trained scientific talent?"[26] Roosevelt and Bush feared that after the war, scientists, particularly those who had worked on the Manhattan Project and at places like the MIT Radiation Laboratory, would want to retire to their home universities and retreat from national projects deemed important for the security of the nation but with questionable moral outcomes. As I suggested in the Introduction, Bush answered Roosevelt's four questions in *Science, the Endless Frontier*, and those answers changed the nature of scientific work in the United States and produced the greatest stimulus for exceptional university-based research in our nation's history.

Suppose President Obama or members of Congress asked similar questions related to the future of humanistic studies and their practical consequences for our nation. Among the queries might be: How can the study of the humanities reinforce core American values of fairness, opportunity, and justice? How can such study influence scientific and technological choices in ways that are consistent with the best features of a democratic society? How can we use the humanities to help our national security? How can the humanities further heighten our citizens' critical reasoning skills to improve the civic engagement of the population? How does the study of the humanities prepare one to live an examined life? And, perhaps, how does the study of the classics, literature and foreign languages, anthropology, sociology, art, music, and history prepare Americans for a better understanding of, and wiser choices in, a more global society? Of course, formulating a response to these queries is what *The Heart of the Matter*, the Academy report, was attempting to do. We need these answers in order to ensure a critical role for the humanities in the great research universities that will exist twenty-five or thirty years from now.

We can begin to answer Obama's hypothetical questions, at least in part, by returning to the responses Professor Gabrielle Spiegel gave to that young student reporter at UCLA. Here Spiegel tries to "recast the importance of grasping the notion of 'humanity' on a new basis" and places her argument in a compelling historical context:

We are heirs to a world—that of World War II and its aftermath—when states like Nazi Germany claimed that there was such a thing as "a life unworthy of life," the basis on which Germans claimed the right to terminate the lives of the mentally ill, those with birth defects, and those they simply scorned and hated, like gypsies, Jews and communists. Anyone who says "no one ever died of the humanities" has not thought much about what happens when states claim the right to define what humanity is, or who is good and who is evil, and therefore justify movements like ethnic cleansing.... The great and abiding task of the humanities is to cultivate appreciation for the immense variety of the ways that peoples and societies live and think.[27]

Professor Spiegel goes on to describe how crucial it is that our college graduates understand "the Other":

Given the current situation in the world [post-9/11], I can't think of anything more important than reaffirming the intrinsic humanity of all peoples, however different ethnically, religiously, politically or even medically. The great and abiding task of the humanities is to cultivate appreciation for the immense variety of the ways that peoples and societies live and think.... The notion that there is something that can be called "a life unworthy of life" should become, quite simply, unthinkable. The humanities teach this most importantly of all the disciplines in that they require an imaginative, not merely objective or logical, investment in their investigations.[28]

In the National Defense

As English has become the lingua franca throughout the world, American students have neglected the study of foreign languages and cultures. To many, the word globalization, if there is any meaning left in it, translates into American cultural and political, as well as economic, hegemony. Many students see little need to learn the languages of other societies and about the historical and cultural forces that have shaped those countries or cultural groups. This has gotten us into a great deal of trouble as a nation over the past half-century. A strong argument can be made that since World War II the military endeavors of the United States would not have taken place had we had a better understanding of the cultures and the historical roots of the societies that we have waged undeclared wars against. Perhaps the Iraqi and Afghanistan wars are two quintessential examples. By the Pentagon and the CIA's own admission, we had almost no one working in those two national defense agencies who knew the languages spoken in these societies, making it extremely difficult to gather useful intelligence. Soldiers and officers did not speak the language of the people they interacted with and were expected to act as much as cultural liaisons to the average citizen of Iraq or Afghanistan as they were military personnel. The same may be said for our distorted perceptions of the Palestinian people and culture when they became "the enemy" and certain Palestinian groups were labeled as terrorist organizations. In the 1970s, for example, two things seemed clear: The Palestinians were viewed harshly by other Arab nations, who saw them as intellectual snobs; and Israelis and Palestinians had far more in common than one might think in terms of values and interests. Thus, a great opportunity was lost during the 1960s through the 1980s in bringing the two cultures together.[29]

Unless one simply believes that we carry out military expeditions in order to sustain our own military-industrial complex, it is our ignorance of the "other" and our demonization of them that has led us into misguided and extremely costly military interventions. But whatever one's opinion about the necessity of these wars, it is unarguable that we entered into them without in-depth knowledge of the character of the countries, the ethnic and historical divisions within them, the latent conflict that would make nation-building near impossible, and the varieties of religious experiences and political philosophies that the people of these nations held. Again Spiegel is correct when she points out that "American society and government has never needed the kind of historical, linguistic, ethical, and cultural instruction offered by the humanities more crucially than at the present time. The exercise of power without a sense of ethical responsibility is dangerous; the exercise of power without historical and cultural knowledge is a prescription for disaster."[30]

As we look to the future, have we sorted out the ethics involved in drone attacks in nations that have not permitted us to cross their borders? When, if ever, are assassinations legitimate, and are they any more lawful for us to carry out than for our enemies? When, if ever, should we permit what the Geneva Conventions define as torture? When we are data mining massive amounts of information using algorithms that yield a significant number of false positives, how suppressed are our core civil liberties—and when will they be restored? These are questions of the moment that should be the basis of vigorous discussion in humanities and social science classes at institutions of higher learning—not because they do or do not lead to higher-paying jobs, but because they become the basis for our lifelong beliefs, attitudes, and values, as well as our level of skepticism about what the government tells us.

As University of Chicago legal scholar Geoffrey Stone has articulated in his book *Perilous Times*, the United States has a long history of curtailing fundamental civil liberties in times of national emergencies, or perceived crises, only to recognize subsequently that the deprivation of those liberties went too far. Our students need to be able to independently assess what is the proper balance, for example, between the need for national security and the preservation of those civil liberties that have been the hallmark of our society. They must be trusted with information that they are now not given. That balancing act is not an easy one, but it is precisely the type of issue students will face in their lifetime and on which they should not remain mute. They should, at the very least—based on their knowledge of history and of some aspects of constitutional law, as well as their views on our core civil liberties—be able to make a cogent argument for their thoughts on these matters. Few students today are able to do so.

In the twenty-first-century great university that we are building, we must retreat to a moment in time, not long ago, when we had greater respect for other cultures, languages, and literatures. Since the 1960s, the ethnocentrism that marked much of what was taught to undergraduates has evolved into a far more global perspective. Departments of comparative literature have been created, often in conjunction with English departments, that offer courses in different literatures and cultures. The expansion of the humanities curriculum, even the core curricula where it exists, to include works by great writers from other nations has developed in ways that surely expand the cognitive frame of students studying literature and the important questions raised in the books, stories, plays, and art that is the focus of classroom conversation. We can't continue to believe that our way is the best and only way; that our values are the best and only defensible values; that our cultural mores and practices are the only acceptable ones—especially in a global world where greater diversity and understanding of that diversity is essential. The myth of "American exceptionalism," which to this day is reinforced without evidence by our president, needs rethinking.

As Professor Spiegel implores us:

More powerfully than other disciplinary domains, knowledge of the historical past and the humanities help to frame for our students what it means to belong to a nation, committed by design to freedom and to the rule of law, and what it can mean to commit ourselves to the maintenance of humane and tolerant civil societies throughout the world.... I believe that this new mission for the Humanities in the contemporary world is in no way incompatible with the traditional goals of a humanistic education. For, in the end, what we wish for our students, and for ourselves, is that we all live our lives so that, as T. S. Eliot once put it, "you shall not cease from exploration. And the end of your exploring will be to arrive where you started and know the place for the first time."[31]

The humanities (and the social and behavioral sciences) are essential to furthering this increased awareness and understanding. It is difficult to convince many humanists that they should have anything to do with national defense. In *Who Paid the Piper?*, Frances Stonor Saunders, the British journalist and historian, documents how many prominent intellectuals and academics contributed to a secret campaign during the Cold War, some knowingly and some without knowledge of their role, to discredit communists and left-wing organizations in Europe. Some were paid for their efforts by funds secretly funneled through nonprofit organizations like the Ford Foundation. The lack of transparency in those operations, chronicled now in many books,[32] angered prominent liberal academics, especially humanists, and reinforced their idea that participating in any way with the military or the government to improve our understanding of other cultures was tantamount to conspiring with the enemy, represented by the American intelligence agencies.

In the aftermath of the 9/11 attacks and the assessment of our lack of knowledge of foreign languages and cultures within the Department of Defense, a conference of leaders in government, industry, language associations, and other academics issued a white paper, a "Call to Action," which argued that cultural and language competency was as important to the national defense as were investments in science and technology after the Russians launched the first space satellite, Sputnik, in 1957. The government referred to these competencies as "the Sputnik moment" in humanistic studies.[33]

To date, these arguments have gained little traction in most of our great universities. The white paper argues that "Americans became complacent with the end of the Cold War. Although we now know that al Qaeda was formed in 1988, at the end of the Soviet occupation of Afghanistan, its existence as a powerful, potentially threatening, organization was not described to government officials until 1999." Americans saw Afghanistan, according to the commission, as a remote place that had little bearing on the United States, while al Qaeda members saw the United States as being very close by. Afghanistan was more globalized than America was at the turn of the twenty-first century. Professor Spiegel concludes that there "is the need to globalize the curriculum, to extend our coverage of history, literature, languages, anthropology, political science and the like to all corners of the world."[34]

Building a More Skeptical and Critical Public

Our great universities of the future will need to promote far better analytic skills and skepticism among their students than we have managed to achieve thus far. Our universities, even the great ones, are not "unsettling" enough. Students are not forced to confront as much as they should their own presuppositions, biases, values, and beliefs. The great university a generation from now must focus on how critical reasoning skills can be enhanced and knowledge of the "other" expanded. This involves both content and methods for getting students to think independently and critically about social and economic policies, as well as scientific and technological innovations, about which they, as citizens, will need to hear.

This belief informs the structure of the two advanced undergraduate courses I teach at Columbia College, "Fact and Fiction" and "Law, Science, and Society." Here we discuss such issues as how knowledge grows, why we should be highly skeptical of claims about facts (such as the harmful effects of *dietary* cholesterol on mortality rates), why eyewitness testimony is so often believed yet faulty, and how we ought to think about privacy issues. We discuss who "owns" history and how much of "history" is fact and how much is "fiction." We talk about decision-making under conditions of uncertainty and the kinds of errors in decisions that are commonly made and why they are made. We discuss the adequacy of evidence that performance-enhancing drugs actually enhance performance among baseball players, along with a host of other issues. In short, we create a space for testing one's beliefs and weighing them against existing evidence, much of which is, of course, unfamiliar to the students. None of these issues are strictly scientific matters. The students are faced with continual challenges to their own views of "facts." In the process, one hopes that they not only sharpen their ability to think independently but also to become more skeptical and critical about materials that are passed off to them as truths.

In the great universities of the mid-twenty-first century, we should teach the humanities, in part, as a way of creating a better-informed public as well as of educating our political leaders in the nature of societies that are often labeled incorrectly as less advanced, more aggressive, and even more primitive, than we are. A 2015 letter to Iran's leader, signed by forty-seven Republican senators, was designed to teach the people of Iran about the American Constitution. Putting aside the questionable wisdom of sending such a letter (which was full of errors), there is the implied assumption that the missive was being sent to a bunch of barbarians. These senators probably didn't even realize that many of the Iranians had been educated in the United States.

It is also time for humanists to recognize that resources for the study of languages, arts, culture, history, and literature are more apt to come if the government sees some practical value in what the humanities are producing.[35] What we need are two essential paths for those who study the humanities: one that takes the traditional route and is based on the intrinsic interest that these subjects hold for our students; the other that leads to jobs with highly practical value.[36]

One of the ways to teach young people how to think critically for themselves is to expose them to others—in this case their teachers and a wide range of students—who have sharply analytic minds and put their powers to work on literary texts, pieces of art, social and economic problems, or scientific puzzles and questions without answers at the back of the book. The movement at many universities, spurred on by those who think of the outputs of universities in terms of jobs rather than analytic skills, takes us in precisely the wrong direction. Today, students talk of majors and even proudly about their double majors. Many of their guidance counselors reinforce this inclination. This high level of concentration is perceived as helping them either obtain jobs in a certain business sector or as producing a better ticket into a superior professional school. In fact, what students ought to be offered in addition to such high levels of specialization is the ability to become "organized dilettantes" at college— individuals who seek out the most intriguing minds at the university and take their courses—not on the basis of what is written in course bulletins, but on the basis of what these individuals are known to believe in and to have written about. At the undergraduate level, students ought to be given the option of concentrating without majoring in a subject, which would entail taking fewer courses in that discipline while roaming the campus and "experiencing" the minds of scientists, humanists, and social and behavioral scientists.

Mixed Signals and Human Capital

For several decades now, major employers and industry leaders have sent mixed signals to college graduates and their families. Most recently, we have heard as much from politicians as from employers that they would like students to study subjects that offer them practical possibilities for reasonably good jobs after graduation. Members of the business community have sent ambiguous signals at best about the importance of what a liberal arts education can "buy" a student after college.

Rosemary G. Feal, executive director of the Modern Language Association, said: "If you interview anyone in the business community, they'll say, 'Give me someone who knows how to write and is deeply literate, and I can teach them the particulars of the industry. Without those skills I can't teach them very much."[37] If Ms. Feal is accurate, then the business community has certainly failed to get its message through to the Governor of North Carolina, and I daresay to many other governors—to say nothing of college students or their parents. On the one hand, employers emphasize preprofessional training in business, journalism, engineering, and applied computer science, among other subjects. On the other, they often argue that what they want to see in college graduates are young people who are highly literate and widely read, can compose an argument, and who have those basic writing and analytic skills that we often associate with a liberal arts training—particularly in the humanities. These are the qualities, they say, that are most adaptable to training in the workplace.

So what are the poor college students and their parents to make of these contradictions? They tend to believe that the real value of a college education is the practical training it can impart. I believe that the contrary is true, and there is solid evidence to support this position. The authors of *The Heart of the Matter* refer to a survey of employer attitudes toward a "liberal education," which is defined as "a college education [that] provides both broad knowledge in a variety of areas of study and knowledge in a specific major or field of interest. It also helps students develop a sense of social responsibility, as well as intellectual and practical skills that span all areas of study, such as communication, analytical, and problem-solving skills, and a demonstrated ability to apply knowledge and skills in real-world settings."[38] The results showed that 94 percent of the employers said that a liberal education was either very or somewhat important; and when asked whether they would recommend such a course of study for their own child or a young person they know, fully three-quarters said "Yes."

To suggest that good jobs and successful careers are less possible for students of the humanities than for those who take preprofessional courses of study is simply absurd. Yet the myth that this is so persists.

Note that when it comes to medical school, studies suggest that an outstanding student of the humanities, who has taken none of the current premedical courses, can be admitted to a top medical school and (after one summer of an introduction to medical concepts and practice) wind up doing just as well as those students who came close to nervous breakdowns studying organic chemistry and physics.[39] The simple fact is that doctors don't learn to be doctors by taking premedical courses, nor do lawyers learn how to practice law from their undergraduate or even professional school training. They learn sets of highly valuable skills that can be applied to the practice of law or medicine. They learn how to think like lawyers or doctors, but they don't learn to practice law or medicine until they hold jobs. The same applies to business. The exceptionally able, wide-ranging literature, language, or philosophy major is going to be as well prepared as a business major to perform the highly skilled work that will be needed in the twenty-first century.[40] It would be a great mistake if we allowed politicians and a few outspoken businessmen to dictate educational policy and restructure our curricula so that it conforms to their ill-advised premature professionalism.

Creating Great Language and Culture Centers at Distinguished Universities

As noted, Americans' ability to speak and read foreign languages can only be described as abysmal. We assume that in the globalized world, English will become the common language and that there is little need to train students in foreign languages and culture. Although the use of English has spread enormously around the world since the 1960s, the assumption that we no longer need to learn foreign languages and about foreign cultures is false. There ought to be a renewed effort, spearheaded by government financing through the National Endowment for the Humanities, to create perhaps twenty world-class language centers (as postbaccalaureate degrees and certificates) that are outsourced to universities.[41] There are examples, here and abroad, of such centers having enormous success. The Defense Language Institute Foreign Language Center, which started as a secret enterprise in 1941 to prepare a set of qualified GIs to speak and read Japanese, still exists—including a branch in Washington, DC, where "low-density" (relatively rarely used) languages are taught—and teaches more than forty languages today. Some of our leading scholars of East Asia after World War II began their careers at these centers.

But we need to move beyond the Defense Department for mastery of these foreign languages and cultures. Universities have great humanities departments that produce language training and research on foreign cultures. This ought to be expanded through a significant government effort to train young people in the many languages that are needed to maximize participation in global commerce, industry, and scientific and technical collaborations.

Financing the Humanities

I've never seen a report, whether from an internal university review committee, the National Academy of Sciences, or the American Academy of Arts and Sciences, that doesn't call for greater investments in whatever they have studied. So it is true with reports on the humanities. But unlike many other areas within a great university, the humanities have been starved over the past forty years. Earlier, I referred to the recent report card on the humanities by the American Academy of Arts and Sciences, which notes: "federal support for research in those [humanities] disciplines accounted for less than one-half of 1 percent of the money given to colleges for science and engineering." Some of this difference can be attributed to the cost of doing scientific, as opposed to humanistic, research; but part of the exceptionally low funding of humanities research is a result of ideological politics and a sense among many legislators that the outcomes of this research have little practical value.

The lack of financing of the humanities is also due to the simple fact that, despite the rhetoric to the contrary, the state and federal legislators of the United States don't seem to value higher education of superb quality. Or, at least they are unwilling to pay for that quality. To be fair, the major players in higher education have done an abysmal job of explaining the cost factors and returns to higher education. State budgets have been tight since the recession of 2007–2008, and budget cuts and lack of funding result in larger classes, longer times to graduation, higher dropout rates, increased use of adjunct professors rather than full-time faculty, demoralization of the faculty because they receive no financial rewards for their work, increased numbers of out-of-state students and higher tuition rates to offset the state cuts, and a loss of public confidence in these institutions. Meanwhile, politicians play a foolish blame game—it is the university's fault because they can't control costs, when expectations are that these same institutions of higher learning are to educate increasing numbers of students with less money from the state.

In fact, the situation is even more perverse than one might think. If universities are successful at finding resources to make up for state cuts in their finances, the state simply cuts more, claiming that the universities have the ability to find the resources that they need by themselves. Consequently, the kind of small group interaction, which is certainly not cost-efficient, withers and makes the experience of college far less rewarding than it ought to be. Of course, any tax increase for education that is even hinted at by a state legislator is generally a ticket to defeat at the next election, since these same political figures are failing to educate the public on why increased financial allocations for education are needed—even if higher taxes, especially on the very wealthy, are required to sustain or enhance quality. Consequently, the price for a university education (tuition alone), which can now exceed $200,000 for four years at private universities, creates sticker shock in parents, despite generous financial aid packages that often allow youngsters from economically disadvantaged families to attend these private colleges almost for free—or at least without paying tuition costs. But as the former president of Cornell, Hunter Rawlings III, among others, has observed, this environment leads parents to pressure their children to choose practical majors (ones that will lead to a job—almost any job) rather than to the study of the liberal arts. The fear of large student debt and consequences of deep cuts in educational costs contribute to the drift away from the humanities—just when a humanities education can prove of great value.

The states have produced the conditions needed for a self-fulfilling prophecy. They withdraw support from the university; they demand greater productivity and transparency; they want more demonstrated quality; and yet they allocate insufficient funds, which ensures that their predictions of a lack of financial responsibility by academic leaders will almost always come true. And through their withdrawal of financial support, they create the potentially disruptive situation that leads them to predict that the cost model of higher education cannot be sustained. Of course that will be true if the state allocated only 10 percent or less of the budgets supporting their top universities.

So what ought to be done? In Chapter 5 of this book, I consider the cost of higher education. Here let me simply reiterate that our federal, state, and local governments must begin to create incentives for the education of our youth, linking, for example, the federal allocation of financial aid (which should be in-creased) to state increases in allocations to higher learning. At the same time, universities that increase their tuition at rates significantly higher than cost factors associated with higher education (the higher education cost index is different from the more widely cited Consumer Price Index)—and thus are asking the states and federal government to pay for inefficiencies in their institutions—ought to be penalized for raising costs extravagantly. Moreover, since the institutions with the largest endowments generally graduate students with the lowest levels of student debt (because they can reduce the sticker prices for those in real need), the government ought to support the accrual of larger endowments. Rather than Congress threatening universities because they have large unspent endowments, the government ought to be offering further incentives to private individuals of wealth to invest in our universities through their contributions to endowment funds.

These are the values that humanists and scientists and their colleagues in the social and behavioral sciences must be committed to and articulate to the broader public if we are to become still greater universities. These are the principles that are on display in the short Kalven Committee Report and that are articulated in Gabrielle Spiegel's response to her young UCLA reporter. This represents the soul of the humanities that must be strengthened in the great universities in the future.

Perhaps the best expression of support for the arts and the humanistic en-terprises can be found in the words of President John F. Kennedy in his remarks on October 26, 1963, at Amherst College in marking the death of the poet Robert Frost, who had read a poem at Kennedy's inauguration:

> Our national strength matters, but the spirit which informs and controls our strength matters just as much.... When power leads man towards arrogance, poetry reminds him of his limitations. When power narrows the areas of man's concern, poetry reminds him of the richness and diversity of his exis-tence. When power corrupts, poetry cleanses. For art establishes the basic human truth which must serve as the touchstone of our judgment.... The art-ist, however faithful to his personal vision of reality, becomes the last cham-pion of the individual mind and sensibility against an intrusive society and officious state.... If sometimes our great artists have been the most critical of our society, it is because their sensitivity and their concern for justice, which must motivate any true artist, makes him aware that our Nation falls

short of its highest potential. . . . I look forward to a great future for America, a future in which our country will match its military strength with our moral restraint, its wealth with our wisdom, its power with our purpose. I look forward to an America which will not be afraid of grace and beauty, which will protect the beauty of our natural environment.[42]

And What About the Social and Behavioral Sciences?

It is a natural question why I'm writing here about the social and behavioral sciences in a chapter devoted principally to the humanities. The answer is that over the past fifty years, there has been a great deal of connection and fluidity between the disciplines that have historically been classified as in one domain or another. For example, history used to be classified squarely as a social science in many, if not most, of our large universities. Today, many of our elite universities have reclassified history as a humanities department. The same may be true in terms of intellectual boundaries of anthropology and certain types of qualitative sociology, although these two fields remain classified as social and behavioral sciences. And psychology, which was largely social psychology for decades, has become much more like the sciences and has moved into that classification at many institutions. One conclusion is that these broader classifications now make little sense; another is that the substantive and methodological development of the disciplines have changed significantly over time. Anthropologists, sociologists, and even economists and political scientists often hold joint appointments in the history department. A good deal of joint appointments have taken place, which further complicates the traditional classification schemes. Economics has both more mathematics and more linkages with features of social psychology then it had in the past. Because fields like anthropology, history, and sociology have such a large place in the humanities these days—and will have an even larger place, I suspect, in the future—some discussion of the place of the social and behavioral sciences is in order.

Like the humanities, the social and behavioral sciences find themselves under continual assault by legislators or the public. Because a good deal of social science research has political implications, and is often critical of government policy, it is targeted for its attention to subject matter that disturbs the sensibilities and ideological perspectives of legislators. When American anti-intellectualism raises its ugly head, it is often directed toward work in these fields. For example, it is extremely difficult for social scientists who are studying the transmission of disease, such as HIV/AIDS, to study sex workers as a mechanism for finding out whether or not this is one of the causes of such transmission. Almost every year, some member of Congress proposes to dramatically cut funding to the social and behavioral sciences—except for work that is ideologically compatible with his or her own beliefs—such as work on national security and terrorism. In Chapter 9, which focuses on a great university's core values, I'll point to specific recent attacks on the social and behavioral sciences. Here I want to highlight how the work that flows from our research universities in fields like economics, sociology, anthropology, and political science has made major contributions to our understanding of everyday behavior. I will also suggest that, like the humanities, these fields often become their own worst enemies. I also will propose (in blueprint form) how these fields ought to evolve in order for them to make even greater contributions to the growth of knowledge.

The disciplinary structure of the social and behavioral sciences is only about 100 years old. When I was a graduate student at Columbia from 1964 to 1969, I wasn't fully aware of how young my discipline was in America. Nonetheless, in the subsequent fifty years, important original research has come from sociology and its sister social and behavioral science disciplines, from behavioral economics to human capital research, theories of cognitive dissonance and game theory. I could extend this list many times over, but it should suffice to suggest that these disciplines continue to have a major role to play at our great universities and in our larger society.

Almost all of the pathfinding work was conducted within formal disciplinary structures, more often than not by individual scholars and only relatively recently as products of collaborations and of transdisciplinary work. Here are several ways in which I think social and behavioral science research ought to change over the next twenty years. In fact, much of what I advocate has already begun, but there is too little transdisciplinary collaboration and too little collaboration with other academic disciplines, both of which we need to see more of.

Although the work of what Sir Isaiah Berlin called "hedgehogs" ought to continue—there is a need for deep, focused research within disciplines—the social and behavioral sciences ought to begin to contribute significantly to the work of scientists. With new conceptions of the relationship between nature and nurture, the role of behavior on health and disease is so significant, along with genetics and neuroscience, for example, that there ought to be organized collaborations between these two groups. Each should train itself, at least at a broad conceptual level, with the basic ideas and concepts of the other's discipline, allowing for more effective collaborations. But the social sciences should no longer be only stand-alone disciplines. There has, of course, been some integration of the social and behavioral science—economists like Gary Becker have used economics concepts to study certain types of sociological behavior—but there has been relatively little collaboration, except among epidemiologists and biologists, between the social scientists and colleagues in biology, chemistry, or physics.

If the behavioral sciences ought to move toward greater internal and external collaborations with other disciplines and other universities, they also ought to clean up their act as well. Consider the field of economics, which is full of many brilliant scholars. Although much important research has come from them, there has emerged in recent decades a worshiping of mathematical modeling and unwillingness, more often than there ought to be, to consider alternative explanations for the phenomena that they study. Although mathematics can often clarify vague concepts, it also can be used to distort what is being studied. Jon Elster, the political scientist, has referred to this as "hard obscurantism."[43] Although economists have used elaborate mathematical models in their world of finance, and sophisticated econometric models for almost all types of empirical work on economic and social patterns of behavior, they too often draw ludicrous inferences from their models, which are built on highly questionable, if not outright wrong, assumptions. And these models have real consequences. Take, for example, the research done by economists on the marginal deterrent effect of capital punishment on murder rates. Making assumptions that have little to do with reality (e.g., they never even examine whether the patterns of murders among people who know each other differ significantly in causes and consequences from those that involve strangers), they will construct regression models that will provide at least two things: estimates of the marginal deterrent effect of executions, and causal interpretations that rest on a matrix of questionable correlations. Courts will use these results without truly understanding the models; other social scientists, accepting the veracity of the models, will make moral arguments in favor of capital punishment based on the idea that each execution "prevents" twelve to eighteen murders. It becomes morally appropriate, they argue, to take the one person's life to save the dozen or more. This is poor social science hiding behind obscure models that most readers do not understand. Ignorance of mathematics or econometric models does not, in itself, mean that the work is not correct, but too often published work that becomes highly visible is based on incorrect assumptions and techniques. The same problems exist with theories of trickle-down economics. No matter how often this theory has been falsified, there is a blind adherence to its value by extremely bright economists. These individuals too often cannot imagine alternative explanations that would show their theory to be wrong.[44]

These problems are not limited to economics. A good deal of work in political science on comparative politics or in sociology, involving data mining and curve fitting, are fraught with the same distortions. Over the next several decades, we ought to alter the reward system of the academy so that it takes a very hard look at what is useful, well-done social science and what is merely an illusion of scientific analysis.

Doing so requires us to confront the guild aspect of disciplines and their prevailing dogmas. Economics again is a good example. In my experience, and that of other former provosts, presidents, and deans of major universities, the discipline of economics has set up its own highly efficient market. This leads to only certain types of research gaining widespread publication and recognition and a reward system that is built to benefit those who control the marketplace. The dogmatism that I allude to leads, as Columbia philosopher Akeel Bilgrami suggests, to the suppression of counterevidence and counterarguments by "outsiders" who are not part of the inner circle of powerful disciplinary leaders—such as professors at leading departments of economics or editors of high-impact journals. Bilgrami proposes that academic exclusion exists when those who "control" a discipline systematically "circle the wagons around our own frameworks for discussion so that *alternative frameworks* for pursuing the truth simply will not even become visible on the horizon of our research agenda."[45] He believes that this is a pernicious form of "academic unfreedom" that is more widespread within the academy than we like to admit.[46] Although Bilgrami focuses principally on economics, "academic unfreedom" also can be found in sociology when it privileges insiders versus outsiders, and the reward system requires that quotas be met of scholars with particular racial or ethnic characteristics. This also leads to forms of exclusion of points of view that are outside the central dogma of the moment.

The most distinguished economists, or their equivalent in other fields, are well aware of this type of dogmatism. When Bilgrami raised this issue with Nobel Prize–winning economist Joseph Stiglitz, his response suggested that Bilgrami was being naïve. Stiglitz opined: "Akeel, I agree with you about economists, but I don't understand why you are so puzzled. One would only be puzzled if one were making the wrong assumption about economics. What you should be assuming is that—as it is done by most economists—economics is really a religion. And so why should you be puzzled by the fact that they cling to and never give up their views despite frequent falsification?"[47]

When social and behavioral scientists are working on problems that have real-life consequences, they must not only be willing to have their results replicated but they ought to highlight their assumptions so that they may be closely scrutinized during the peer review process prior to publication. And, finally, we ought to devise mechanisms, and this will not be easily done, that break down the dogmatism in social and behavioral science fields (and the sciences and humanities are, of course, not immune from this phenomenon) and open these disciplines to contrary points of view that rarely see the light of day and are almost never rewarded. These mechanisms ought to be institutionalized within the academy.

If the behavioral and social scientists need to place their house in order, then outsiders also must recognize the value of the knowledge generated by those working in these disciplines. Not only are they making discoveries that change our lives, but they also are necessary components of a university that conducts far more interdisciplinary research. If we do not support these disciplines and the scholars who work in these vineyards, we will lose a great deal of new and important knowledge. If we constrain their growth because of ideological differences with the products of the disciplines' work, we will narrow what great universities can achieve.

CHAPTER FOUR

The Contours of the University

The life of the law has not been logic; it has been experience.... The law embodies the story of a nation's development through many centuries, and it cannot be dealt with as if it contained only the axioms and corollaries of a book of mathematics.

—OLIVER WENDELL HOLMES, *THE COMMON LAW* (1881)

Our government... teaches the whole people by its example. If the government becomes the lawbreaker, it breeds contempt for law; it invites every man to become a law unto himself; it invites anarchy.

—LOUIS D. BRANDEIS

Medicine is my lawful wife and literature my mistress; when I get tired of one, I spend the night with the other.

—ANTON CHEKHOV

WRITING HIS CRITIQUE of the most distinguished American research universities of the time, Thorstein Veblen, the economist and sociologist, labeled the leaders of higher learning "captains of erudition" who were part of the "bootless conventional race for funds and increased enrollments." With equal scorn, he characterized America's leading universities as "merely administrative aggregations, so varied, so manifold, so complex that administration itself is reduced to budgeting, student accounting, advertising, etc."[1] Veblen was part of the debate, involving social critics and the first and second generation of leaders of our most distinguished American universities, on the ideal American university. Part of this contentious discussion focused on what a great university should include. How should it expand beyond the arts and sciences disciplines as well as law and medicine? Opinions varied enormously, as did the outcomes. That is why among our finest universities today, you will see the presence of very different schools.

Although the debate might appear to have been about high-minded principles and theory (and the Founding Fathers were capable of a principled argument), it contained a lot more pragmatic reasoning. Academic leaders such as William Rainey Harper and Nicholas Murray Butler were willing to develop educational programs in a wide variety of fields—principally as a mechanism for enlarging the size of the university (which was used as a key indicator of quality in those days) while increasing its resources through new sources of tuition revenue. In those early days, none of the great universities could count on the yield from large endowments to offset the cost of their educational operations; so they searched for veins of gold in programs representing multiple fields, from journalism to social work. Later, when Big Science became an essential component of the great research universities, it took only a couple of decades for the federal government to pull back from its earlier commitment to fully fund research on college and university campuses. Federally sponsored research is not a source of "profit" that can be used to enhance the quality of other activities at the universities. In fact, in 2015, research grants don't cover nearly their full cost, and that fact has become a major bone of contention between the universities and government.

The search for increased revenue through the addition of academic programs beyond the liberal arts and sciences drew the ire of the staunch critics of the new American university. For example, Abraham Flexner, an educator best known for his 1910 devastating report on the quality of American medical schools (which led to the closing of many and the revamping of the curricula of those that remained), envisioned a university where the various parts were inextricably bound together. But as Clark Kerr, the architect of the innovative University of California Plan of 1960, would write, Flexner's conception of what ought to be was essentially dead on arrival in 1930.

Other critics put forward their views of the essential character of these new universities if they were to thrive. According to Veblen:

> The conservation and advancement of the higher learning involves two lines of work, distinct but closely bound together: (a) scientific and scholarly inquiry, and (b) the instruction of students. The former of these is primary and indispensable. It is this work of intellectual enterprise that gives its character to the university and marks it off from the lower schools. The work of teaching properly belongs in the university only because and in so far as it incites and facilitates the university man's [sic] work of inquiry.[2]

Even more vituperative critics questioned not only the accretion of academic units but also the ethics of the connections between university presidents and large, powerful corporations, as well as universities' ties to national political leaders. Upton Sinclair focused on presidents of universities, like Butler, whom he described as "a man with a first-class brain, a driving executive worker, capable of anything he puts his mind to, but utterly overpowered by the presence of great wealth."[3] He was disturbed by these linkages and the consequent influence of what the sociologist C. Wright Mills would later call the "power elite" in the governance of these universities. The "interlocking directorates" (another term coined by Mills) consisted of leaders of academia, politics, and industry, and it was not a rarity that university presidents could move from their seat of leadership in a place of advanced education into a seat of power in Washington, as Woodrow Wilson demonstrated in a short period of time between 1910 and 1912, in which he moved from presidency of Princeton to that of the United States. The Carnegies, Rockefellers, Roosevelts, and other power brokers of the Gilded Age were deeply implicated in the governance of these newly minted research universities. In fact, some of the richest men of that era created universities or great centers of learning. John D. Rockefeller provided the resources to begin and to expand the University of Chicago in the early 1890s while also developing from scratch the Rockefeller Institute for Medical Research—the senior oilman's two proudest charitable efforts.

When Wilson wanted to develop a professional graduate law school at Princeton, his trustees thwarted his effort. Princeton, with some of the greatest graduate programs in the world today, actually has few graduate schools compared with some of its peer institutions. The University of Chicago, which became one of the nation's leading institutions of higher learning in just over a decade, always had the idea that its professional schools would be small and limited in number compared with the school of arts and sciences. Robert Hutchins, who became its president in 1930, argued forcefully for a limited and structured curriculum and favored separating the research faculty from the teaching faculty, with the professorships being limited to those who taught. Many Chicago faculty members reacted hostilely to these proposals.

In fact, none of the most active participants in the first great debate over the idea of the American university succeeded in determining the course of university development over the following several decades. Hutchins didn't get his separation of research from teaching faculty; Flexner didn't get the level of integration that he sought; and the critics of higher education who opined against the close relationship between these institutions and the very wealthy and political movers and shakers were also disappointed with the outcome. What emerged during the first three decades of the twentieth century was, as I have indicated, a hybrid of the English and German university systems, but with an entirely new set of activities grafted on, multiplying the foci of higher learning—to say nothing of the number of constituent groups that tried to influence university policy.[4] The most distinguished American universities were on a course to becoming "full-service" organizations that would educate professionals, artists, writers, filmmakers, public policy makers, nurses, and dentists, among others, as well as provide a home for the research and teaching of those in the core arts and sciences disciplines.[5] This educational and organizational "creep" began in the early decades of the twentieth century and did not abate until close to century's end, when it became popular at our great universities to speak of "selective excellence," even if they rarely followed through by implementing the idea.

Although there are significant exceptions to this full-service model, such as Princeton, MIT, Cal Tech, and the Rockefeller University, it is not uncommon for major universities to have a total of fifteen or so distinct schools. Perhaps more importantly, over the past half-century, the professional schools, including most notably the health sciences schools, have represented an increasing proportion of a university's total operating budget. So, for example, more than 50 percent of Columbia University's 2014 budget of almost $4 billion was spent *outside* of the arts and sciences. This is typical for universities with medical centers. The open question is: Has the proliferation and growth of the professional schools and the revenues that they generate undermined the centrality of the core arts and sciences disciplines?

A New Set of Flexner Reports

How ought the full-service university with its multiple appendages be altered—in terms of both the individual colleges' or divisions' relationships among themselves and with the principle missions of the university?[6]

The Flexner Report precipitated a transformation in the American medical school. Given the current state of professional education at our great universities and the absence of substantial change in them since their inception, there is probably a current need for perhaps five or six new Flexner reports focusing on various professional schools. These investigations could explore such issues as how much value added is there by pursuing a degree at one of the professional schools rather than gaining experience by working full-time in the associated occupation? Given the power that professional guilds wield when it comes to designing the schools' curriculum and establishing graduation requirements, are the faculties really preparing students for their profession? With the ossification that has set in on ancient curricular requirements in many professional schools, is it not time to take a hard look at what today is required to be an extraordinary lawyer, physician, social worker, or journalist? Finally, in what ways is the scholarship of the faculty at these schools contributing to the growth of knowledge, to new forms of teaching, and to the professions? The "Flexner II" reports would be produced by carefully chosen, prominent individuals in the field and by those in allied disciplines that are selected by an organization like the Institute of Medicine to carry out the analysis and make recommendations for major changes, even closures, where required.[7]

There is, of course, precedent for downsizing universities—although given the growth of a host of advocates and constituencies, it has become increasingly time-consuming and difficult to eliminate programs, much less schools, at universities. Few leaders have had the strength or will to eliminate schools that contribute little, if anything, to the evolving missions of the university. Even altering the curriculum in a significant way rarely occurs. Nonetheless, old schools of mining, which once made up much of what engineering schools did, have been eliminated, and there have been a significant number of closings of library schools where those faculty members and leaders were wedded to old-fashioned, if not rigid, views of the role of information in the twenty-first century.[8]

Let me suggest what ought to be explored in each of the new reports, beginning with the schools that have been part of many of the great universities for well over one hundred years: the schools of medicine and of law.

Premedical Education and Medical Schools

Consider the entrance requirements of medical schools. Undoubtedly, members of the profession who control the licensing of physicians constructed these prerequisites. This is not intrinsically a poor place to rest authority, but what seemed academically necessary one hundred years ago may be quite unnecessary in light of subsequent history and our increases in knowledge.

There have been consistent and even strident calls for reforming premedical education ever since the time of Flexner's report. These calls began in 1904 by the American Medical Association's Council on Medical Education. It was, in fact, the Flexner Report that recommended essentially the requirements that exist today, including physics, chemistry, organic chemistry, and biology. By

1930, these requirements became standardized in the premedical curriculum. Over the past twenty or twenty-five years, various groups, to their credit, have weighed in strongly on why that basic curriculum ought to change. Among the critiques noted by Dr. David Muller, the dean of medical education at Mount Sinai Hospital, are that

> the pace of scientific discovery and its clinical application have outstripped the requirements; that information technology has made memorizing vast amounts of content unnecessary; that the requirements lack clinical, scientific, and social relevance; that they're used to cull the herd of talented aspiring physicians; that they disadvantage minority and female students; that they crowd out studies of bioethics, social justice, and health policy; and that rigidly structured premedical and medical school curricula hinder students from becoming self-directed lifelong learners.[9]

Then, there are those who believe that the requirements foster excessive competition for grades that conflicts with the basic precepts of medical professionalism.

Perhaps as troubling is that, despite all of the calls for change, little has occurred over the past half-century. Muller claims that universities "are neither equipped nor motivated to create new courses for medical school preparation. They have limited resources, siloed departments, educational inertia, and faculty with ingrained teaching habits."[10] Excluding those young people who train as physicians but are fundamentally interested in medical research, how many of these doctors will need to use organic chemistry, for example, in their practices? How much does the subject sharpen their skills as a practicing clinician; how much do they even remember a year after taking the course?[11] Yet, organic chemistry is used perversely today as a filter to reduce the number of young people who apply to medical school, regardless of whether or not they will be good physicians.[12] This prerequisite is generally supported by chemistry departments that can justify the size of their faculty on the basis of large undergraduate enrollments in such premedical courses. This is the "guild" talking, not necessarily the people who have a good idea about what it takes to be a caring and able practicing physician. In order for physicians to read medical journals with appropriate skepticism about what is claimed as fact, they would be far better off taking courses in statistics, probability, and research methodology than organic chemistry.[13] They might well be better off even taking a humanities course on medical ethics or a course on concepts surrounding directed therapies. Yet these latter subjects are not yet part of the prerequisites for applying to medical schools.[14] Indeed, in recent years there have been experiments that suggest that heavily trained premedical students do little better, if at all, in medical school than those who majored in the humanities and who were rapidly prepared for medical school and who have certain personality traits, like empathy.[15]

After a century of tinkering with the best way to train medical school students, we ought to be rethinking how these premedical courses might be overhauled or replaced—especially as new scientific techniques will become increasingly important in diagnosing and treating disease. If it takes a second Flexner-type report to legitimize these changes, so be it. In fact, as Muller notes: "Flexner's proposals for more structured curricula were right for his era and revolutionized the teaching, investigation, and practice of medicine. But we have failed him by allowing premedical curricula to ossify despite advances in science, clinical practice, and technology. Our times, too, require the objectivity, commitment, and courage to pursue better ways of preparing students for careers in medicine and biomedical science."[16]

Similarly, over the past two decades, there has been substantial trumpeting within the biomedical community of the value of the "translational researcher." Typically, these are doctors who have been part of M.D./Ph.D. programs. The "translation" refers to trained physicians who are able to move seamlessly from the scientific bench to the bedside. Plainly, a physician should be extremely well schooled in how research is done, how to assess the work of others, and how to apply that knowledge to patient care. But with a few exceptions, it is a myth that we could create a cadre of physicians who are *both* original discoverers of fundamental knowledge and gifted clinicians. Generally, such people wind up choosing either research or practice. Why not accept reality and work to foster better collaborations between the two groups? Correlatively, if there is substantial evidence that translational research in medicine has made a significant difference in patient outcomes or in research discoveries, then the new Flexner report should uncover it and describe where this combination really works.

In addition, there ought to be greater emphasis on finding cures and treating patients and less emphasis on the vast array of other clinical activities that go on at most medical schools. Many decades ago, physicians were the gods of the medical complexes; researchers were "backbenchers." That has been reversed. The gods of the medical centers are the basic biological scientists who make pathbreaking discoveries—ones that often lead to election to elite acad-emies, run Howard Hughes labs, and occasionally win Nobel Prizes or other prestigious awards. There ought to be more focus on the scientific work of top researchers and of those who are working directly on inventions and discover-ies that need to be tested. Some, not all, great universities should eschew large patient care operations—ceding this role to affiliated or independent hospitals. Most medical schools should maintain patient facilities that accommodate a relatively small number of patients, perhaps a maximum of one hundred, which would be used for testing the efficacy of the new treatments or devices that re-sult from the scientific discoveries. For example, specific work on a vaccine for a disease such as HIV or on targeted genetic therapies might involve a small, selected group of patients who are treated at the small hospital-type facility associated with the university's medical school. This is the model that was used at the Rockefeller University for many years.

For the foreseeable future, high priority must be placed on basic science and technology related to the cure and treatment of disease. The fundamental dis-covery feature of this work ought to be carried out at great universities; the ap-plication to patient care ought to be carried out at teaching hospitals. For this reason, it is important that in the future we make sure that we link more closely the work in the basic biological sciences that is conducted at university medi-cal centers with the basic sciences carried out where the arts and sciences and engineering research are located. There is apt to be more affinity between the basic biomedical sciences and the other sciences, computing, and engineering on campus than there is between these efforts at fundamental discoveries and patient care.

There are many universities where doctors join practice plans and see their patients at the university's or hospital's facilities. The revenues generated are "passed through" to the physicians who are "taxed" by the medical school for the use of space, equipment, and other facilities. These practice plan pass-throughs distort the size of the university's budget, making it seem larger than it really is, because most of the revenue that comes in goes to the physicians who practice there. At Columbia, the patient care revenue in 2012 totaled roughly $870 million of the entire $3.4 billion budget; patient care expenses, roughly $740 million. In turn, many of the physicians teach medical students (and most say they enjoy teaching) without pay—although that commitment is generally limited to a few lectures, occasional grand rounds, and instructing interns and residents in patient care. Research physicians also teach Ph.D. students and postdoctoral fellows, the resources coming principally from their grants and contracts.

But where should these activities be located? Medical school faculty tend to like the association with the university and are technically often the employees of the university, but what most of them do could easily and perhaps more effectively be performed at affiliated hospitals. Teaching hospitals are critical to the future of good health care in our country. But there is no reason why physicians at hospitals cannot participate in the teaching of medical students and be paid for their time as instructors.[17] Nursing and dental research should be the dominant feature of the training associated with the university; practice should be part of the hospital's enterprise. Moreover, there is no intrinsic reason why schools of public health need to be located at medical centers. The research and training conducted in public health is linked often to the social and behavioral sciences as much as to medicine. More of our great universities ought to move toward a model that downsizes medical centers and emphasizes basic research, including medically related research, and uses teaching hospitals to test approved new treatments. Although some of our preeminent universities may wish to continue to incorporate large-scale clinical care within the university, many ought to consider placing that care in the hands of their affiliated hospitals. The finances of the university and the hospitals ought to be kept separate.

Law Schools

More than any other professional schools, law schools have been highly insulated from the rest of the university campus. They have resisted interaction with other schools; have restricted their students from taking more than a handful of courses elsewhere at the university; and almost all of them, until recently, have refused to participate in university-wide reviews for academic tenure. They insist that they should be allowed to manage their own affairs. The processes that lead to faculty appointments tend to be limited to graduates of a very limited number of other top law schools. The schools also often assert that they are being used as "cash cows" for the less well-heeled schools in the university community. The consequence of this posture is that law schools invite in a small number of non-legal experts from outside their school; they do not embrace the abundance of extraordinary faculty in different schools and departments who could offer important substantive courses to their students.[18]

Top law schools assert that they place a very high premium on excellence in teaching; surely, many faculty members display this talent.[19] In many cases, they have clerked for leading federal judges, and many have done so for Supreme Court Justices. Unlike any other discipline, law schools' top scholarly journals, law reviews, are run by current law students rather than by the faculty or professional peers. The faculty members do not have to publish much to gain tenure—although the scholarly requirements for tenure have increased over the past several decades—and they do not have to support themselves with external research grants or contracts, unlike many at medical schools and those who run laboratories in the arts and sciences. Although they don't live the lives of partners at the large law firms, they do represent how "the other half lives" within the university. They rarely are forced to test their ideas with empirical evidence of any kind—and any suggestion that they might do so is viewed skeptically by most of these extremely able faculty members. If a paper with empirical data is published in a law school review, nine times out of ten, it is apt to be authored or coauthored by a law school faculty member who has a Ph.D. in economics, sociology, or psychology (or some other social science field). It is not unusual for internal struggles to break out between those at the law school who would like to hire more "scholars" trained in philosophy, economics, sociology, psychology, and even English literature and those who prefer faculty members with basic legal training and experience.

Law schools do a remarkable job of making students think analytically and critically in a certain way. It is not at all like scientific thinking; but at the best places, it is rigorous and changes the way first- and second-year law students approach problems and make arguments.

Nonetheless, there are significant issues that ought to be addressed as we move to improve legal education in this country. First, is there in fact a need for a third year of law school? Does it provide any demonstrable value added for the student? It surely provides value added by way of tuition for the school. In 2015, the total cost for a year of law school—without financial aid—was about $85,000 at Columbia. This third year certainly adds to the indebtedness of the students and, as a consequence, often dictates why they choose a job at a white-shoe firm over much less lucrative public service type jobs.[20]

The bulk of "legal" education takes place in the first and part of the second year of law school. By the end of the second year, students are well-versed in legal methods, torts, contracts, civil procedure, constitutional law, and evidence, and generally in how lawyers "think." They are rarely taught, however, about the core competencies of being a lawyer. Law schools could place a greater emphasis within their curriculum on how lawyers can become wise counselors and astute leaders "who are capable of acknowledging and grappling with their obligations to clients, to the legal system, to the institutions in which they work, and to the broader goals of society."[21] Moreover, young lawyers, well trained in law schools, will find in their practices of law a world that is far more complex than they might have imagined. Linking legal knowledge and methods to those found in a variety of other university disciplines could improve greatly the preparation of lawyers for their jobs at law firms or at other types of businesses.

The question of what to do with the third year takes on even greater meaning when the market for lawyers is such, as was the case at least until the recession of 2008, that most of the students at the superior law schools already have been offered high-paying jobs by the time they enter their final year of school.[22] When this occurs, many of the students choose courses that they think will be interesting but that do not require real effort. It remains unclear whether third-year students would learn more about being a lawyer by practicing for a year than they do by taking a potpourri of courses that often have little to do with the practice of law or legal philosophy. These students have effectively "checked out." Curtailing the third year of law school would reduce student debt while providing them the opportunity to earn another year of income.[23]

Law school faculties have grappled with this problem, and they continue to do so. They tinker with the old model, much as medical schools do. But they have not done much, other than producing interesting clinical programs, to reform the third year in a way that has any lasting meaning or impact for law students. Perhaps we need to rethink the merits of reintroducing the three-two programs that existed at research universities for decades. In these programs, a certain number of students complete three years of undergraduate education and then are admitted to law school, where they take two years of courses. They then receive both an undergraduate and a law degree. Or students could take the full four years as an undergraduate, but also complete law school in two years.

When Benjamin Cardozo graduated from Columbia College Phi Beta Kappa in 1889, he entered Columbia Law School. At the time, the school had a two-year program, but while Cardozo was in law school the program was extended to include a third year. He declined to take the third year, did not receive the law school degree, but was allowed to take the bar exam, which he passed and went on to an extraordinary legal career. Of course, much has changed in the legal profession since then, and not every student is a Cardozo. But even today it remains unclear what the continuing rationale is for the third year of law school other than to support a larger number of faculty members, staff, and programs.

If a great university wishes to maintain a third year as an option, let's make it worthwhile for the students. Let them loose on the university to pursue courses that will not only interest them but will also help them in practicing law.[24] Consider just two examples: The students might take a course in scientific and behavioral science methods or statistics so that they can more competently litigate complex cases that with increasing frequency involve analyzing quantitative information. Doing so would put them in a better position to choose experts for cases and to understand what the experts claim that the data show. They also might take courses in the sciences and learn how the thinking of scientists differs from that of lawyers. And, as I suggested above for medical students, they might even take courses in philosophy or other humanities subjects that will add to the tools they bring to their work as lawyers.

But is the additional year of education, regardless of the courses taken, more useful, intellectually or vocationally, than the experience gained by practicing law for a year?[25] Some law schools will argue that the third year is an essential part of legal training, yet they are unable to demonstrate this empirically—other than through anecdotal responses of faculty members and a selective group of students. Perhaps the law schools could allow third-year students to take a master's degree (at one of the other schools at the university) that would offer training in a subject that is related to the area in which these students want to practice law.

Some universities might decide to allow students the choice of taking two *or* three years of law school. There would be two degrees offered, providing a distinction depending on the option selected by the student. All of the core law courses would have to be taken to receive either degree. Experiments ought to be done for these larger courses as to whether what is known as a "flipped classroom" would offer more effective and longer-lasting knowledge than the current lecture and quasi-Socratic method used today at top law schools. The flipped classroom would include an online course offered by one of the school's great teachers—and those lectures (no longer offered to groups of one hundred students or more) could be viewed by students at any time, with the possibility of repeating parts of the lecture that are captured in the online format. Then, there would be a set of smaller seminars devoted to responding to questions that the students had about the online lecture, as well as trying to solve problems posed by the leader of the seminar. Having the option of two or three years of schooling would allow students to decide what they want to do, would accommodate changes in the job market, and would allow these future lawyers to either take the bar after the second year or to wait one year after their first job before taking the bar exam.[26]

Like almost every aspect of higher learning, there is no single model that works or that ought to exist. At many of the most prestigious law schools, there are in fact multiple tracks that students follow. Some want to graduate and start practicing as soon as possible. Perhaps a third year is not essential for them, since many of them already have offers that they have accepted from law firms or public service organizations. There is another set of students who want to obtain a deeper knowledge of subjects that they have been introduced to in the first two years, such as tax or antitrust law, before entering practice. For these students a third year may also be very useful. Then there are those who are not sure what they want to do with their law degree and during the third year hope to explore a variety of clinical possibilities, such as working as an intern at the ACLU or for the Legal Aid Society. Still others may want careers as legal scholars and professors and would benefit from taking a wide range of courses—from statistics and probability to deeper studies in economics, psychology, or sociology—that they believe will help them in preparing scholarly works in the future. They also may benefit from working on a law review. In short, students, de facto, sort themselves into several tracks, and a different number of years of schooling may be appropriate for those on different tracks. That flexibility ought to be allowed and should not be held hostage to formal guild requirements for a set number of course hours necessary to hold the JD degree.

Turning to the creation of knowledge by law school faculty, we have very little data, to my knowledge, about the influence of their publications on judges, legislators, partners, and others at law firms. Citation analysis could be done of legal opinions by judges and Supreme Court justices to see who nominally has influenced their views, and surveys could be conducted of members of prestigious law firms about how, if at all, they use the literature produced by legal scholars. Undoubtedly, there are good examples of legal scholarship having an impact on the thinking of members of these various groups. For example, the entire law and economics movement has influenced law in a variety of areas, such as antitrust law. But how extensive has the influence been, and what form does it take? How has legal scholarship influenced efforts in other academic disciplines? And how often are the high-impact published papers the work of faculty members employed by law schools but trained in an arts and sciences discipline? To go to the extreme, how often have papers by legal scholars impeded clear thinking by lawyers and judges about complex social problems, especially when the legal scholars depend on, but do not fully understand, the empirical social and behavioral sciences or more applied fields like criminology?

Changes also have to be made in the guild and legal accrediting organizations. For example, how are law libraries used, and how will they need to be structured in the future? When we think about what a law school should look like in twenty-five or thirty years, we should not rely solely on insiders to supply us with the answers. One change is certainly necessary: Law schools should be mandated to adhere to the general university review process for tenure and to the larger standards of excellence of these great universities. Using their own jargon, the burden of proof has to shift to the law schools and their faculties to demonstrate conclusively the value of the third year and of the scholarship that they produce. They must also rethink how articles are accepted or rejected for publication at law journals. In the twenty-first century, it is inappropriate not to rely heavily on faculty peer review. Although running the journals may be a good experience for students, it is not helping the growth of knowledge. And it is on these publications that tenure is often denied or granted. No one would advocate the elimination of our nation's law schools (although a few might not need to exist if the training they offer students is very poor). But how those law schools organize their activities ought to be changed, just as the nature of their curriculum changed to the case method in the late nineteenth century. For this we probably need a Flexner-type review of the schools.

Business Schools and Schools of Public Health

The ability of other professional schools to blend arts and sciences disciplinary knowledge with professional practice knowledge has been remarkably varied at America's best universities. Some, such as business schools and schools of public health, have proceeded far faster than others at this essential linkage—and have established a better argument that their curriculum imparts more than what a person might learn from working in the field. Both of these schools recruit Ph.D.'s from key disciplines related to their field of practice.

Business schools are perhaps the best example. We often find world-class economists on business school faculties today, as well as psychologists, decision theorists, and sociologists, among representatives of other disciplines. In fact, a significant proportion of appointments at the best business schools are shared with arts and sciences departments. This enables business schools to expose students to knowledge that they could not possibly access while in the workforce and that might be critical to their future success. Many of the leading business school economists consult for the largest corporations and banks in the United States, and others serve as advisors to international and national organizations. Aside from teaching sophisticated financial modeling, business schools are now educating students in advanced methods of network theory as applied to business (see, for example, University of Chicago professor of business and sociology Ronald Burt's work on social networks within business organizations[27]) and decision theory developed by the school of scholars that are direct or indirect "descendants" of Amos Tversky and Daniel Kahneman, and methods of marketing research drawing upon advanced techniques in survey and data analysis developed in the fields of sociology and statistics. Although business schools tend to recruit social and behavioral scientists to their faculties, they can hardly be classified as schools without borders. As good as many of the business school faculty trained in social science disciplines are (in part, the recruitment is made easier because the business schools are able to pay far higher salaries and provide more research benefits than are arts and sciences departments), we would hardly say that business school students rarely are able to explore fully their interests beyond the boundaries of their school. That ought to change, and it would be far more easily accomplished if budgets of many of these great universities were not so decentralized.

Similar scholarly cross-fertilization is found in schools of public health, where students studying biostatistics are taught by professors of statistics, while epidemiology students use the research of demographers and sociologists and study with faculty members trained in these fields. Experts on aging, who have backgrounds in the arts and sciences, contribute to the research conducted on disease expression and the general health problems of the aged. Moreover, expert social scientists at these schools are beginning to work closely with geneticists and other biomedical scientists to understand the complex interactions between heredity and environment. In fact, the relationship between genetics and social factors in determining disease is being recast because of this research.

No longer are we stuck on the nature versus nurture controversies of the past, which most often examined the relationship between innate intelligence and social factors. Instead, social variables are considered as independent determinants of whether or not people who may be genetically predisposed to a disease actually get it, and when they may notice the first set of symptoms. In the future, there ought to be far more rigorous studies of causation rather than simple correlates of disease. Unfortunately, schools of public health as well as schools of medicine produce papers that show sets of correlations and models of those correlations without coming close to generating conclusive causal analysis. When these papers are published and picked up by the media, they lead to the diffusion of fictions rather than facts—fictions in the public's mind that are often very difficult to extinguish.

In the great universities of the future, we will need closer collaboration among the social, behavioral, and biological sciences and the core disciplines of public health to make more rapid progress in discovering the causes, correlates, and onset of disease. This interaction may also provide us with clues on how to intervene more intelligently and effectively to prevent or cure diseases. Such work has begun in trying to understand better the causes or correlates of various forms of Alzheimer's disease and autism. The future great university ought to make these collaborations easy to initiate—both within universities and across university borders. (Since I consider engineering disciplines, including computer science, as among a university's core disciplines, I won't include them in this discussion of professional schools.)

Other Professional Schools

Law, medicine, business, and public health schools—as well as schools of public policy, international affairs, and architecture—have demonstrated their value as educational and research arms of our distinguished universities, and they have proven their value beyond what might be gained from practicing a profession for a comparable period. Now let's consider a few professional schools where the value added is less clear, such as those focused on social work, journalism, and the arts. Social work schools recruit relatively few non–social work doctorates as faculty members. These tend to be among the strongest in the school; produce the most important research; and train most of the Ph.D.'s, or doctors of social work. But these schools are principally in the business of offering master's degrees in social work practice and in psychiatric social work.

By standards set by the guild and critical for accreditation, professors who received their Ph.D.'s in arts and sciences disciplines are not permitted to teach core courses. A good deal of the course work is structured, with core courses and supervised fieldwork. Efforts by the leading schools of social work—such as Washington University in St. Louis, the University of Michigan, the University of Chicago, and Columbia—to change in significant ways the curriculum and the requirements for who may teach basic courses have met with repeated resistance. The parts of the program that deal with public policy, such as family and work policy or health care policy, could be folded into the curriculum of schools of public policy and international affairs. I've not seen studies, and I doubt whether any exist, that demonstrate that the *current* curriculum, which has a minimal infusion of arts and sciences knowledge, provides students with more tools and expert knowledge than they would obtain with two or three years of work in the field. So a Flexner-type report is long overdue for the field of social work—again carried out by people not tied to the professional guild.

Journalism schools pose a different set of dilemmas. Columbia and Berkeley may be the two universities in the United States that offer only graduate-level degrees in journalism. Elsewhere, almost all of the journalism programs are offered, often as part of programs in communications, at the undergraduate level—with some universities also offering master's degrees in these fields. The importance of the subject is not in question. The press and various forms of new media are critical intermediaries between the government and every other institution and the educated (and often not well-educated) public. Without a free and distinguished press corps, it is hard to see how democracy can work. Yet the quality of journalism is often deeply problematic. Even at the gold-standard places such as the *New York Times* there has been a move from extensive, detailed, and highly accurate journalism toward opinion pieces.[28] Journalism used to think of itself in guild terms: Any decent reporter given forty-eight hours could write a good story on almost any subject. That is no longer true—if it ever was. Good science reporting, for example, requires specialized knowledge and skills. So does first-rate reporting on politics or business. And education reporting seems to occupy the low place on the totem pole in the hierarchy of media reporters—a fact that has damaged universities substantially over the past few decades. With fundamental transformations taking place in the business model of news reporting and its distribution, students have to learn far more than in the past because they not only have to gather the information for their stories, but they often have to produce and/or write the story for broadcast from faraway places.

So, what should be the curriculum for young journalists at a great university? I'm deeply skeptical about an undergraduate journalism education that is not steeped in the liberal arts and sciences. Good reporters should not only write well, but also have an extremely good liberal arts education. Undergraduate journalism tends to be too professionally oriented, which is a fine objective for some of our universities but limits the opportunity for undergraduates at our best universities and colleges to travel across the liberal arts curriculum before settling on a vocational destination. A rigorous course of study in almost any arts and science field will provide these students with far better critical reasoning skills and depth of knowledge than they are apt to receive from undergraduate journalism programs. The curriculum in journalism schools ought to change from instruction on how to become a beat reporter working on tight deadlines to one that emphasizes extensive knowledge in a student's field of interest as well as in the modern technologies of new media. A few graduate journalism schools are trying to take such steps, but a thorough analysis of their curricula and the quality of their faculties for teaching and research in journalism would go some distance to determining the added value of the degree programs in journalism.

Let me mention briefly the role of education schools in the United States today. Some are relatively small and concentrate on educational research; others prepare young people to teach or become educational administrators; and still others are directly involved in the nation's public schools. But the nature of these schools has changed over the last half-century—and not necessarily for the better. Fifty years ago, schools that prepared teachers for K–12 education tended to have extremely bright female students who could not find jobs in law, medicine, or in other professions, including academia. Now, women have more opportunities. Consequently, education schools—at least at the undergraduate or master's degree level—do not attract exceptional talent.[29] That is unfortunate and is not only the result of past gender discrimination. The public does not hold elementary and secondary school teachers in particularly high regard, and they don't pay them well. They also don't recognize how difficult it is to teach five classes a day to students who are variously prepared to take an academic course of study. We should not forget that next to family influences, the influence of a great teacher on a young person's future is very often a profound one.[30]

We have not produced the proper incentives for talented young people to enter education—except for those few who enter it through programs like Teach for America. Even those with idealistic views often leave the system within a few years, either to take positions in affluent private schools or in some other occupation altogether. Consequently, in fields like physics or chemistry, fewer than 20 percent of those who teach these subjects actually hold certificates in these fields. Until we can alter this pattern, the teaching guild should allow college graduates who have majored in other subjects to teach in K–12 schools without the requisite pedagogy. It is not that pedagogy is unimportant—it is, and many university professors would do well to take a course or two in it. But in order to get brighter and more highly trained people into K–12 education, we should relax this guild requirement. In the laboratory schools that I would set up on the top university campuses, I would enable those schools to hire outside of the guild and allow professors to teach in the high schools. And students would be encouraged to take courses at the college or graduate level if their competence allowed them to do so. Changing the requirements of the teaching degrees and certificates could enhance rather than detract from the quality of people entering the profession and encourage graduate students who cannot find jobs in universities of their choice to teach at the secondary school level with the same compensation as assistant professors.

Finally, consider the value in arts education—given the tuition that is charged. I'm referring particularly to education in film, creative writing, and fine arts. Much of the value added in these schools probably depends on the quality of fellow students as much as on the quality of instruction. Those who attend these schools and praise their time there often note that the schools give them opportunities to use exceptionally good facilities to conduct their filmmaking or studio art. The student networks that are formed are viewed as invaluable as is the critical feedback received from faculty members and fellow students. Many long-term associations are begun at these schools and carry over to the students' professional careers. What we need are better measures of these effects in order to demonstrate the value of pursuing a degree in the arts. A great university should want to spawn the careers of exceptional artists, writers, poets, and those who will be curators. But how do these schools add to the overall value of the university? Where in the web of institutional affiliations can they be located; and how do these schools, beyond their intrinsic value (which may be enough) add to the luster of their universities?

The professional schools can play an important role in creating great universities, but only if they are willing to become collaborative players with the arts and sciences divisions at their own and other universities. To update and upgrade what they do—and to be sure that they add value to the university—we ought to generate those new Flexner-type reports to help legitimize our ability to reorganize and, in some cases, rebuild some of our professional schools.

CHAPTER FIVE

The Affordability and Value of Higher Education

Fact and Fiction

There's a tsunami coming.... [But] I can't tell you exactly how it's going to break.

—JOHN HENNESSY, PRESIDENT, STANFORD UNIVERSITY

THERE IS NO SENSE in sugarcoating it. The leaders of American higher education have done an abysmal job of explaining the affordability of a college education to the public as well as to our national and state legislators. Instead of a well-framed message, we almost invariably read about how the cost of tuition exceeds $50,000 per year and that student debt now reaches new highs, making college increasingly unaffordable. Consider just two examples. In *Higher Education*, economist Andrew Hacker and former *New York Times* staff writer Claudia Dreifus hammer the reader at the outset with alarming statistics: "$192,520: that's the bare-bones cost for four years at Kenyon College, a well-regarded liberal arts school in rural Ohio. We cite it because its tab is fairly typical for colleges having known names.... Altogether, 62 percent of its students have to take out loans to pursue a Kenyon degree."[1]

Along similar lines, Columbia religion professor Mark Taylor, who has had a long-standing love affair with online education as a way of handling the escalating expense, paints a bleak (and quite misleading) picture of the costs of higher learning in his 2010 book *Crisis on Campus*. He offers statistics showing the projected costs of attending college, beginning with a figure for 2012–2013 of roughly $219,000. Using a tuition inflator of 6 percent, he projects a four-year cost in 2020–2021 of almost $350,000. To dramatize the situation even further, Taylor extends his projections out until 2034–2035, when four years will cost a family a staggering $788,000.[2] This widely referenced book and his estimated numbers would surely scare anyone who bothered to examine them.

Most informed Americans believe these assertions are true and attribute them to the irresponsibility of colleges and universities in controlling costs. One consequence is that families that are not well off simply don't believe that college is affordable for their children. Yet many of these asserted "facts" are either misleading or downright fiction. Furthermore, few educators (and there are notable exceptions) have tried to explain the cost-value proposition resulting from achieving college graduation in a timely way.[3] With so-called authorities making claims like Taylor's, and with the public being bombarded with such numbers by the media, it is all the more difficult to extinguish these "facts" from the public mind.[4] When the rhetoric is so extreme, it becomes harder to create a correct narrative about a subject with many subtleties.

Perhaps the more significant questions associated with the cost of college are: In the future, can our society provide access to institutions of higher learning for youngsters from disadvantaged backgrounds? Can we contain the costs for families that earn a very good living—say, between $100,000 and $150,000 a year—but that have two or three college-age children whose total tuition (after taxes and financial aid) comes to more than half of their total income? (This is the great dilemma of the cost of private higher education for the middle-class family.) Can we make it possible for able youngsters from these backgrounds to attend college, graduate on time, and limit the debt that they are burdened with upon graduation? Finally, how can families that have managed to pay for undergraduate education afford the cost of advanced education in schools with limited, if any, financial aid?

Over the past several decades, the number of young people attending college has gone up. In fact, until recently, the United States had a far higher percentage of its young people graduate from college than did any other nation. Yet, millions of qualified young Americans today never get a chance to go to college; or, as William Bowen and his colleagues have pointed out, they often attend colleges that are inferior to those that they are qualified to attend—they are "undermatched." Moreover, of those entering college today, fewer than 60 percent actually graduate.[5] The probability of graduating on time or at all goes down, not surprisingly, the lower the socioeconomic background of the student. The odds of going to college for a youngster who is born into a family in the bottom quartile of the income distribution in the United States are about one in five. For a member of an African American, Hispanic, or Latino family, the chances are lower than for whites in this same quartile.

The affordability of a college education is not a single problem. The top twenty-five private research universities in the nation, many of which hold hefty endowments, face a very different situation from public universities—even the flagship public institutions. Poorly endowed private colleges face different challenges from those that are highly endowed; public colleges, in general, have different situations from private colleges; and community colleges and for-profit colleges face still other issues.[6] As of 2014, American higher education had roughly 4,600 colleges and universities, public and private—some that were relatively poor, others that were extremely wealthy (i.e., some that were tuition dependent, and others that were not); some that were large and diverse, others that were small; some that were highly selective, granting admission to as few as 6 to 8 percent of the students who applied, while others admitted almost anyone who submitted an application.[7]

These institutions of learning also have sharply different missions, and that too affects their cost structures and their goals for their students. Some universities do almost no research; others are research intensive. Some are governed by independent boards of trustees while others ultimately must report to a Board of Regents that is often composed of political appointees. Some states offer universities substantial sums to construct new buildings; others offer nothing. Each of these categories of schools faces different problems regarding affordability. But whether we consider public or private universities, one fact is certain: Tuition does not cover the full cost of educating a college student.

The problem of cost and value is also linked to broader social and political issues that the nation as a whole must face. The sources of the problem are multiple and include the features of educational institutions; the larger economy in which universities and colleges are embedded; and perhaps most importantly, the values, interests, and constraints of legislators and the people they represent. Determining the cost versus value of a college education involves making decisions that are not always easy to make—especially if individuals lack the information needed to make informed choices. Affordability rests as much on the public's "revealed preferences" as on their stated preferences.[8] The elements in this drama, which I'm reluctant to characterize as either a tragedy or a comedy, include, among other things, the actions taken by colleges and universities, the demands families and students as consumers make on universities and colleges, and state and local government policies toward institutions of higher learning and the relative priority given higher education in their annual budgets.

In short, understanding the forces that drive increases in tuition and fees at colleges and universities and what forces mitigate those increases is about as complex as interpreting the American tax code. To comprehend college costs requires that we grasp the complexity of the society that produced them; to simplify the process is a challenge because change involves dealing with so many often-incompatible interests, values, preferences, and economic and social pressures at work in society. That is why the story is difficult to tell.

The Cost of Higher Education over Time

How much has tuition, which is the focus of much of the public criticism, climbed over time? On the surface, there appears to be a real problem. The distinguished historian of education Roger L. Geiger uses data from thirty-three private and sixty-six public universities to show that "the costs of higher education borne by students nearly doubled in real terms from 1978 to 1996. In the same years, gross domestic product (GDP) and disposable personal income each grew slightly more than 50 percent. The cost of going to college, then, grew nearly twice as fast as the economy."[9]

William G. Bowen, who has probably done more influential empirical work on various aspects of American higher education than any other contemporary scholar or academic leader, also concludes that the cost of higher education has historically risen at a more rapid rate than inflation.[10] Looking backwards from 1964 to 1904–1905 at the direct costs per student (of which tuition is only one component) compared with an index of overall economic trends, Bowen notes: "Excepting war periods and the Great Depression ... cost per student rose appreciably faster than an economy-wide index of costs in general. The consistency of this pattern suggested to me then [this study was done originally in the 1960s and was labeled by Clark Kerr as Bowen's Law], as it does today, that we are observing the effects of relationships that are deeply embedded in the economic order."[11]

And, in 2012, Sandy Baum, Charles Kurose, and Michael S. McPherson used data from the American Institutes for Research's Delta Cost Project to conclude that "education and related expenditures per FTE (full-time equivalent) student increased at an average annual rate of about 1 percent beyond inflation at *all* types of public universities from 2002 to 2008."[12] For many years, the cost of private university education was rising more rapidly than was the cost of education at its public counterparts. The reverse has been true over the past decade, and change in relative costs has accelerated after the Great Recession of 2007–2008. Prior to this reversal, Charles T. Clotfelter, professor of public policy and economics at Duke University, studied cost escalation at several elite universities up until 1998 and found confirming evidence of rising costs: "Beginning around 1980, these costs [in higher education], measured in real, inflation-adjusted dollars, began to rise rapidly. Growth was especially rapid at private institutions.... Throughout most of the past three decades, the average tuition and fees charged by colleges and universities in the United States tended to increase faster than the overall rate of inflation."[13]

In *Why Does College Cost So Much?*, published in 2011, Robert B. Archibald and David H. Feldman concluded that: "Tuition and fees at colleges and universities consistently go up faster than the inflation rate. We don't like this, so it is a problem. The first cause one might consider is that colleges and universities are doing something wrong. Colleges and universities have indeed served up some pretty fat targets in recent years, so this approach might appear to be quite fruitful."[14] But as these two economists suggest, the story is a complex one.

Over the past thirty years, the average in-state tuition and fees rose 257 percent for students taking four years to complete their studies, an increase from roughly $2,400 to $8,700.[15] If there is any hopeful news on the cost of a college education, it has come from recent reports that the rate of tuition increases has slowed since 2012. In-state tuition and fees rose by 2.9 percent for students at four-year public colleges, the lowest rise since 1975–1976. At private colleges and universities, the rate of increase was 3.8 percent, somewhat lower than in recent years, according to Sandy Baum, who tracks these data for the College Board. The average tuition sticker price at four-year public institutions was up about $250 over the previous year to $8,893 in 2013–2014; at private nonprofit four-year colleges, it grew from $28,989 to $30,094 in 2012–2013.[16] After adjusting for financial aid, the cost of college (including tuition, room, and board) for those attending all four-year institutions reached an average of $12,620 in 2013, up $220 over the previous year. It rose to a total of $23,290, an increase of $700, at private four-year colleges and universities. Finally, at two-year public colleges, the average tuition and fees grew about $100 over the prior year to $3,264.[17]

The aggregate data on student debt, however, are more troublesome. Student debt has now topped $1 trillion, and the rate of default on these loans has continued to increase to the point where one in ten students now defaults within two years of starting to repay them, according to the Department of Education. To help pay for their college costs, in 2012, 36 percent of undergraduate students received an average of $3,650 in federal Pell Grants, which are the primary source of support for needy students.[18] The students may also have taken out low-interest loans from the federal government, such as Stafford and Perkins loans, and may have received support from individual state programs. The federal government also provides help through education tax credits and tuition deductions, which amount to about 60 percent of the total Pell Grant allocations.[19]

This is the view from 30,000 feet. A closer inspection of pricing and actual cost is more instructive. Let's first examine two of the nation's largest public university systems—the City University of New York (CUNY) and the University of California system. Over many decades, the colleges in CUNY have assimilated hundreds of thousands of children of immigrants and have permitted access to deserving students from lower socioeconomic backgrounds. It has been one of the exemplar institutions that has fostered upward social mobility in the United States. With a current enrollment of roughly 270,000 students among its community colleges and four-year colleges, it continues to do that today.[20]

The cost of going to college is not limited, of course, to tuition and fees. Students also have to pay for their books and supplies, for room and board, and often for travel to and from school, among other things. So, tuition and fees give us only a partial picture of the overall cost of a college education. In the case of CUNY, the tuition for full-time students at four-year colleges was $5,730 in 2013; if a student came from outside of New York State, the tuition was either $15,330 per year or $510 per credit. CUNY also has a technology fee, a student activities fee, and a Consolidated Service Fee. These fees, for full-time students, total around $200 a year, on average. But CUNY also recommends that students living at home or with relatives budget an additional $7,110 to cover the costs of the items mentioned above plus personal expenses. For students who do not live at home, CUNY recommends a budget of $19,858 for expenses in addition to tuition and fees, most of which (more than $10,000) goes toward the cost of housing. Thus, New York State residents living away from home and attending a CUNY college full-time would be wise to budget their total expenses at around $25,000 per year. The estimated costs for the substantial percentage of CUNY undergraduates who commute to college would be around $14,000 a year.

As mentioned, eligible students can reduce the sticker price of tuition and fees[21] through federal Pell Grants and tax credits, as well as through New York

State's Tuition Assistance Program (TAP), which offers grants based on a complex set of calculations of a family's financial circumstances.[22] Consider the full-time CUNY student from a low-income family: He or she might receive the maximum Pell Grant for a year of study, which in 2012–2013 totaled roughly $5,645.[23] If he or she also applied for TAP, he or she might receive another grant up to about $5,000 per year. Since Pell and TAP programs are not loans, the money does not have to be repaid. The total amount received from these two financial aid programs, which were specifically designed to increase access to college education for youngsters from poorer socioeconomic backgrounds, could cover the total cost of tuition and fees at CUNY. In fact, in 2013 about 60 percent of full-time students attending CUNY colleges paid *no* tuition and fees at all.[24] Yet many of these students graduate with some level of debt because they've needed to take out loans to meet the additional expenses of school, such as those mentioned above. A look at the actual indebtedness of CUNY students is revealing: Fewer than 20 percent of students graduated with debt in 2013; the default rate on their loans is roughly 6 percent on an average total debt of about $13,000.

Now consider the situation in California, which has had the greatest system of public higher learning in the United States. Unlike CUNY, in which all components of the system report to a single chancellor, California has a tripartite system of community colleges, a California State University system (CSU), and the research universities that are part of the University of California (UC). As of 2011, roughly 235,000 students attended one of UC's ten campuses, including Berkeley and UCLA. These institutions had almost 20,000 faculty members and close to 200,000 staff members. The California State University system had another 437,000 students at twenty-three campuses and more than 44,000 faculty members and staff. Finally, the community college system enrolled about 2.4 million students at 112 colleges. In the aggregate, these three components of California state higher education comprise the largest and most complex system in the nation, although New York might contest that by bringing together both the State University of New York (SUNY) and CUNY systems.[25]

A California student from an impoverished or low-income background also has access to Pell Grants and to state student aid. The amount of tuition, fees, and other expenses associated with attending each of the three tiers differs, of course. The estimated cost for community college students in the 2013–2014 academic year came to about $14,000, of which roughly $1,100 was the cost of tuition and fees for a twelve-credit program. Tuition and fees at the CSU system were about $6,600, but with additional costs, the total came to about $25,000. Finally, for UC students, tuition and fees were $13,200, with estimated total costs coming to $32,400. These are not small sums for parents with little savings and low-wage jobs, but even the full sticker price for a Californian who attends one of the world's top universities is not wildly expensive. As with CUNY, if a student comes from an economically disadvantaged background yet has the credentials to be admitted to one of the UC institutions, the discounted price for a year of college could come to around $3,000 if he or she received full amounts from both Pell Grants and the California entitlement award, which is similar to the New York TAP program. If the student also qualified for need-based aid because of "high potential," he or she might receive another $1,500, bringing the total charges for tuition and fees to about $1,500 per year. Again, this student might be forced to take out loans to cover the cost of books and living expenses. And depending upon the need for housing or to commute to school, he or she might incur debt of perhaps $10,000 to $15,000 a year. That is no small chunk of change for a youngster who has never had much money to begin with. Over a four-year period (assuming the student graduates within four years, which is not true for many), the amount of debt grows to a significant sum.[26] The student who commutes to community college, which is where many enter the education system before moving up to either the CSU or UC system schools, can attend school without paying any tuition and fees.[27]

One further obstacle for prospective college students and their families who come from poorer economic backgrounds is the highly skewed levels of knowledge about how a student might receive financial aid in order to reduce the sticker price of a college education. In 2015, the College Decision Survey of these prospective students showed that "students were least likely to be familiar with Pell Grants (44 percent), tax credits/deductions (35 percent) and the Supplemental Educational Opportunity Grant program (27 percent)." Some "88 percent of prospective students and recently-enrolled students said the cost of college and availability of financial aid were important or very important factors in deciding to attend a specific college," yet a minority of those in this study were familiar with basic ways of lowering the cost of education. Rachel Fishman, who directed the study, notes: "Only 44 percent of students with a household income of less than $50,000 expected to or had received a Pell Grant, even though U.S. Department of Education data show that 92 percent of students who applied for federal student aid from that income level received Pell."[28] We must find mechanisms to change this and also to simplify access to information about federal financial aid programs and how families can use the tax credits available to them to lower the cost of higher education.[29]

The loan repayment and default problem hits students at community colleges hardest because they have the highest probability of dropping out of school. Nationally, only about 25 percent of community college students graduate, and a high proportion need student loans to be able to attend college in the first place. When they don't graduate, they don't reap the economic rewards of a college education; and, saddled with debt, they all too often default on their loans. This is not nearly as large a problem at either four-year universities or the prestigious private universities, where the graduation rates exceed 90 percent and the default rate on government loans is very low. Far more focus on the debt situation of community college students is needed, and policymakers ought to devise ways to keep these students in school and to reduce their debt burden.[30]

If a high-achieving high school student of modest means wins the lottery of getting into one of the most selective universities, then he or she is in for more good luck. Despite what the media would have us believe, these are the very small number of institutions where the difference between the nominal cost of attending the university—$50,000 tuition and fees—and the actual cost for students from low-income backgrounds is the greatest.

Let's look at Princeton University, which had a $21 billion endowment as of June 2014. On a per-student basis, Princeton is probably the wealthiest major research university in the nation, although Harvard's endowment is significantly larger ($36.4 billion in the same year).[31] Princeton's tuition and fees total slightly more than $50,000 a year, and 75 percent of their students graduate debt-free. The average debt at graduation for those who do take out loans is between $5,000 and $6,000. As mentioned, all of the Ivy League undergraduate colleges have a need-blind admissions policy that is coupled with a full-need financial aid policy. What this means is that applicants are reviewed regardless of their need and are admitted, ostensibly, only on their merit. We know, of course, that legacy children and athletes have significant advantages in the admissions process, as do youngsters of color and to a lesser extent those who come from economically disadvantaged families.[32] But like a number of the Ivy League universities and a few others, about a decade ago Princeton adopted a no-loan financial aid policy. Consequently, the amount of borrowing by even economically disadvantaged students is very low. Princeton's average student debt upon graduation is the lowest in the country, but it is not alone in the category of those truly distinguished colleges at research universities whose students graduate with little or no debt. All of this is possible because these schools have substantial endowments that cover part of the cost of attending them, and they have a deep commitment to supporting students who do not come from privileged economic backgrounds.[33]

At Yale, which has a sticker price of about $54,000 a year, graduates have an average debt of $9,254 after four years, and only 28 percent have to borrow for their education. Again, this is because the school commits a large part of its endowment to financial aid (in fact, much of the endowment for financial aid is restricted by the terms of the gift for financial aid use); its annual financial aid budget for undergraduates is close to $120 million per year.

Finally, Harvard's undergraduate tuition, room, board, and fees for 2014–2015 were nearly the same as Yale's—almost $59,000—but only 34 percent of its undergraduates have to borrow to get through school. The average debt is a bit more than $10,000 for four years at Harvard. For 2014–2015, the school awarded $166 million in financial aid—a 77 percent increase over the amount designated for aid in 2007. Harvard initiated the major move to have students graduate without any debt. Its website tells the story clearly:

> Your financial circumstances have never kept you from great achievement, and they will not keep you from Harvard.... 20 percent of our parents have total incomes less than $65,000 and are not expected to contribute. Families with incomes between $65,000 and $150,000 will be asked to pay proportionately more than 10 percent, based on their individual circumstances.... Home equity and retirement assets are not considered in our assessment of financial aid.... Foreign students have the same access to financial aid funding as U.S. citizens [which is not true at most other highly selective colleges].[34] Harvard lets prospective students know that approximately 70 percent of our students receive some form of aid, and about 60 percent receive need-based scholarship and pay an average of $12,000 per year. Twenty percent of parents pay nothing. No loans required.

Beyond the most selective colleges and universities, the actual cost of higher education is apt to be greater; and the loans that result from lower or nonexistent endowments create a larger debt burden for less-well-off students. Excellent universities, such as Brown University, or colleges, like Bowdoin, do not have the endowments to allow for this low level of indebtedness. But as should be plain, the real costs of going to college in the United States differ enormously for varying types of schools.

A report from the Institute for College Access & Success,[35] an independent nonprofit organization that works to make higher education both more affordable and more attainable for individuals from varying backgrounds, underscores the extreme variability in the debt of undergraduate students who received their diplomas in 2012.[36] Although the average debt climbed to $29,400 in 2011–2012, details varied by state and type of college. The report presents aggregate data on so-called high-debt states and low-debt states, but these numbers can be misleading until one looks at specific institutions and the actual proportion of graduating students who leave college with a debt burden, as we have done. Among the 71 percent of recent graduates from four-year colleges who held loans, the amount varied by state from $18,000 to $33,650, and the number of students holding debt ranged from 41 to 78 percent. But more importantly, the report shows even greater variability in debt among colleges—even in the same state—ranging from an average of $4,450 to $49,450 in the aggregate for four years.[37]

Among the highly educated and wealthiest 1 percent or even .1 percent of those in the United States and abroad, price is not a determining factor in their decisions to have their children apply to the top schools or attend if admitted. Perceived advantages in such areas as admission to professional schools, future income, prestige, networking, and "assortative mating" (i.e., marrying others who come from a similar background), whether rational or not, drive the decisions of this limited group. Consequently, under their need-blind admissions and full-need financial aid programs, these schools charge substantially more to students of the very wealthy than to those who come from needy backgrounds. This is a social policy adopted by these universities—one that involves the belief that those with wealth should contribute to the welfare of the less economically fortunate. If greater financial support doesn't come from either the state or federal government, then the schools have taken it upon themselves to create a progressive policy that will enable the less affluent but remarkably able youngsters to attend these elite schools. This is a form of social engineering. But not all private colleges and universities, as wealthy as they may seem to outsiders, are in a position to compete financially with Harvard, Yale, and Princeton (HYP).

The affordability crunch falls on neither the 1 percent nor the .1 percent, nor on those at the bottom of the income hierarchy, but on those in the middle class whose annual family income ranges from, say, $50,000 to $150,000 and who may have more than one child attending college simultaneously. How should one handle this group in the middle? The wealthiest of the top universities adopted a no-loan policy for either everyone (in the case of Harvard) or for students whose families earn less than around $200,000 a year. This is an admirable practice, but many institutions that are competing with HYP cannot afford such generosity. Yet they have, in the name of competition, adopted such policies ostensibly to compete with those better-endowed universities. Take Columbia, as an example. The University's prestige and place in the public mind has been significantly elevated over the past generation, but its endowment is simply not in the same league as HYP and Stanford. Yet its "discount" rate has risen from around 25 percent to well over 40 percent of tuition in a generation. That is a great deal of money that might otherwise be spent on faculty salaries, greater financial aid for graduate students, better laboratory facilities, and upgraded classrooms and library facilities. The money might be better spent on, for example, attractive undergraduate programs that might lure students to the university than on a no-loan policy. In short, there are large "opportunity costs," as economists would say, to adopting a no-loan financial aid policy. Whether it is even appropriate that a student attend a great university at no cost is another issue.

Public institutions of higher learning have historically adopted a regressive form of taxation on those families whose children attend them—and most people see this as fair or just.[38] If Steve Jobs's third daughter, Eve, who was born in 1998, decided to attend Berkeley rather than Stanford or some other highly selective private university, is there any reason why her family should not pay more for her education than should the immigrant parents of an equally talented first-generation child who struggle to make ends meet? The only form of progressive "tax" comes in the form of financial aid eligibility that would distinguish the child of the poorer first-generation family from Jobs's child. But to go to one of the greatest universities in the world for about $14,000 in tuition a year is a bargain for a child of such wealthy parents. Total costs for students living away from home are almost double the cost of tuition.[39]

Although the media tend to focus on the sticker prices of a handful of top universities, these institutions represent a tiny percentage of the schools that educate most of the nation's college students. The state universities and colleges, as well as the community colleges, teach most of our college students, and their escalating tuition and fees should be the primary focus of our concern and of media attention.[40] At the end of the day, however, the United States in 2013 had the highest proportion of its appropriate-age cohort graduating from college than it ever has had in the past.

Finally, most Americans who consider the cost of our higher educational system think that the level of student debt in other countries is far less than that in the United States. This is not true. In Sweden, where college is free, students still typically graduate with $19,000 in loan debt. In the United Kingdom, where students do pay fees and tuition for college, the average debt at graduation is roughly the equivalent of $40,000—more than in the United States. In Chile, which has both public and private universities, roughly 50 percent of the population between the ages of eighteen and twenty-four go to college. This figure can be misleading if we ignore the fact that more than 90 percent of youngsters from the wealthiest 10 percent of the population go on to higher education, compared with fewer than 20 percent among those who come from the poorest 10 percent of the nation. Of course, the wealthiest Chileans tend to send their children to the top universities; those from disadvantaged backgrounds tend to wind up in lesser institutions. The dropout rate also reflects the great economic disparity in the country: About 50 percent of Chilean students drop out, and the overwhelming majority of them come from the most economically disadvantaged groups. They take on debt and often struggle to repay it, just like Americans. Clearly, the phenomenon of debt incurred to cover the cost of higher learning is not a peculiarly American problem.[41]

The Economic Value of Higher Education

Unfortunately, Americans tend not to see allocation of national and state resources in education as a form of investment in the nation's future. In a 2010 telephone survey of 1,000 Americans, "six out of ten Americans [said] that colleges today operate more like a business, focused more on the bottom line than on the educational experience of students."[42] And 60 percent agreed either strongly or somewhat with the statement that colleges should admit a lot more students without lowering quality or raising prices.[43] How the colleges were supposed to do this was not a question asked in the survey. Although most Americans viewed a college degree as being more important than it was in the past, somewhat fewer thought that they would be able to afford to send their children to college. Finally, more than 80 percent of those that responded said that students had "to borrow too much money to pay for their college education."

There are many different estimates of the monetary value of a college degree.[44] In the 2006 report *A Test of Leadership: Charting the Future of U.S. Higher Education*, Margaret Spellings, then secretary of education and of the nineteen-member commission she appointed to conduct the study, concluded that the transformation in the American economy, which increasingly depended on a highly skilled and educated workforce, made a college education that much more valuable.[45] The report estimated that as of 2003, now more than a decade ago, "the median average salary of an American worker with only a high school diploma was $30,800, compared with ... $49,000 median for those with a bachelor's degree.... Over a lifetime, an individual with a bachelor's degree will earn an average of $2.1 million—nearly twice as much as a worker with only a high school diploma."[46]

A 2012 study using census data also demonstrated the significant added returns to higher education. Individuals with a bachelor's degree earned a median income of $50,360 compared with a little more than a $29,000 median income for those who earned only a high school diploma. And those with graduate degrees earned a median of $68,064, or approximately 35 percent more than those with bachelor's degrees. The study also demonstrated, not surprisingly, that those individuals without a bachelor's or higher degree were more vulnerable to job loss during the economic downturn of 2008.[47] A 2013 report by the Organization for Economic Cooperation and Development compared the returns to higher education in different countries. The authors found that "the average person who has graduated from college (either two-year or four-year) and has any earnings makes about 57 percent more than a counterpart with no more than a high school education. In the United States, the comparable earnings premium is 77 percent." The study also showed that taxpayers benefit greatly from having a more skilled, educated population. The return to taxpayers of a college, rather than a high school, graduate is estimated at about $231,000.[48] Finally, a 2013 study from College Summit, a nonprofit organization dedicated to increasing access to college, showed that college graduates earned 80 percent more than did high school graduates.[49]

But the importance of investments in higher education is surely not only a matter of individual and collective economic well-being. The 2012 special report *U.S. Education Reform and National Security*, published by the Council on Foreign Relations, chaired by Joel Klein, former head of New York City public schools, and Condoleezza Rice, former provost at Stanford University and secretary of state, concluded that "educational failure puts the United States' future economic prosperity, global position, and physical safety at risk." A lack of educational preparedness "poses threats," the report concludes, "on five national security fronts: economic growth and competitiveness, physical safety, intellectual property, U.S. global awareness, and U.S. unity and cohesion."[50]

Perhaps the most comprehensive and sophisticated studies of the value of education can be found in *The Race Between Education and Technology*, published in 2008 by Harvard economists Claudia Goldin and Lawrence F. Katz. Theirs is an historical work whose central message is that the twentieth century was the American century largely because of our commitment to mass education that could meet an increasingly technological society's need for increasingly skilled labor. Goldin and Katz use econometric models and other data to suggest that the substantial returns on education in the United States during the twentieth century were instrumental in our world economic leadership; but during the century's last thirty or so years, other nations, which held a much more elitist view of higher learning, were rapidly catching up, and even surpassing us in some cases, in both the numbers of their citizens earning higher degrees and the quality of the education. This, they argue, poses a threat to American prosperity in the future. It is the basis for their argument that the United States must improve both access to higher education and its quality if we are to remain an economic leader.[51] And although we may have more students between the ages of eighteen and twenty-five graduating from college than ever before, that does not mean that these young adults are being trained in a way that fits the needs of the twenty-first century economy.

However, plainly there is a substantial economic return to education, which makes the debt incurred relatively low—although it seems large initially—over the working life of an individual. Although most economic and sociological studies present aggregate estimates of the value of a higher degree, most also fail to show the variations in the value when a variety of other factors are considered. For example, Caroline Hoxby, professor of economics at Stanford University and one of the nation's leaders in understanding education in the United States, demonstrated that the degree of selectivity (difficulty of gaining admission) was related to longer-term incomes. Comparing eight different levels of selectivity of colleges, Hoxby showed that a student who graduated in 1982 from one of the most selective colleges was apt to earn $2.9 million over his or her career compared with a student from one of the less selective colleges, whose lifetime earnings were estimated to be about $1.76 million—a rather substantial difference. Indeed, economists have shown, ironically, that the best predictor of future earnings is the sticker price of the college the student attended.[52] The higher the sticker price, the more the graduate was likely to earn in the future—a finding that is consistent with those reported by Hoxby.

Economists have also demonstrated that performance in college has an effect on future earnings, as does the field in which a student majors—but this has always been true. Those students who major in STEM fields and/or plan careers in business, law, or medicine have always had a better chance of earning more than those who major in the arts or humanities. But money isn't everything and clearly should not be the sole criterion when choosing a major or line of work. Unfortunately, but not unexpectedly, there are data that suggest that students who come from families with incomes of less than $50,000 a year tend to underestimate the returns to education, which can lead to lower enrollments among this group of prospective students.[53]

Just to place these tuition numbers into some perspective, consider that a single B-2 bomber has a price tag of $3 billion. It is rarely used, and many in the military don't see the value in continuing its production. If we assume that the cost of tuition at a first-tier state university is $12,000 a year without any discount, then for the price of one B-2 bomber we could cover the college tuition cost of almost 250,000 students for one year or about 62,500 students for four years. One military drone cost approximately $17 million in 2013. That money would have paid full cost for almost 350 students to attend four years of college. In short, these are questions of values as much as finances.

There are, of course, many reasons why a university education is valuable well beyond the increased economic returns. In theory, students improve their reasoning skills so that they can become better citizens and enjoy richer lives. Students exposed to exceptional teachers learn to think about thinking—and how great minds do this. They have opportunities to explore different worlds, ones that may have been unimaginable prior to entering college. These are not easily measurable outcomes. For example, an undergraduate classmate of mine at Columbia College had never heard a piece of classical music. After taking a core curriculum course on the history of music, his life was transformed. He fell in love with music, abandoned his aspirations to become a doctor—the profession his parents coveted for him—and became a composer and professor of music. Higher learning at its best has had this effect on thousands of students for generations, and we must not lose sight of the value of these transformations, even if we can't put a price tag on them.

If affordability is a real problem, but one that is exaggerated by the media, a more significant problem is the rate at which college students complete their degrees within a reasonable period. The good news is that more Americans are attending college than ever before. The bad news is that a very high proportion of students in lower socioeconomic groups or who attend certain types of colleges don't usually graduate in six years, and most of those students never finish. Prestigious private universities have completion rates above 90 percent, but this is because getting into these schools is much more difficult than flunking out. In short, completion of college is highly stratified by class and race. Although almost 80 percent of students who attend the more traditional private or public colleges and universities graduate within six years, when we look more closely at demographics and types of colleges, we see far more alarming figures. For example, part-time students, who often have to work in order to pay for college or to help their families financially, have a graduation rate of less than 20 percent. These are often community college students. Public universities as a whole have a graduation rate of less than 60 percent; the rate is only about 10 percent higher for those at private, nonprofit institutions of higher learning. What is more disquieting is that the completion rate for Latinos is 8 percent lower than the average and fully 18 percent lower for African Americans. There are many reasons for this dropout crisis. Although economics obviously plays a role in some cases, other causes remain speculative and often fail to enter the media narratives about colleges and universities completion rates. And this is a crisis not only because it undermines efforts to establish racial and socioeconomic equality in the country but also because it is a fundamental and tragic loss of human capital.[54]

The Hidden Cost Problem

When legislators discuss higher learning in America, the focus is almost entirely on undergraduate study. Yet, the debt problem for students considering graduate or professional school is actually more formidable in some fields than for undergraduates. In part, this is a result of many professional schools having less endowment for financial aid.

The public often dismisses the size of the debt because fewer students go on to graduate school and because of the assumed higher earnings potential of those graduating with advanced degrees. If, for example, a student attends Harvard Business School or the Berkeley School of Law, he or she is apt to leave with a debt burden that may be well over $100,000, but the public will not cry for that person because they believe that his or her earnings will be high enough to easily cover the loans. This is not necessarily true; and a very heavy debt burden creates a disincentive to practice medicine or law, for example, for the public interest. If we turn to the lower-paying professions, such as social work, architecture, the arts, or journalism, the debt burden of going to graduate school can become crushing. These students rarely receive significant financial aid, and they enter a job market that has few high-paying jobs. Many of these professionals are burdened with debt for years, leading them to question the added value of the higher degree. They may not be wrong.

There is also a reliance on debt to complete Ph.D. programs. Although there are fellowship programs for arts and sciences disciplines that are supported by federal agencies such as the National Science Foundation (NSF), the National Institutes of Health, and the Department of Defense, as well as private foundations, few resources exist to support work in many of the other disciplines. In the highly competitive world of the most prestigious and wealthiest institutions, graduate students are fully supported for five years, including tuition and a stipend that ranges, depending on the discipline, from $25,000 to $35,000 a year. But most Ph.D. programs in the United States cannot afford such financial support. According to a study released by the NSF in 2013, in 2002 about "16 percent of doctoral recipients graduated with $30,000 or more in debt";[55] in 2012, more than 18 percent did. A total of 37 percent of Ph.D. students graduated with some debt, ranging from $10,000 or less to more than $30,000, depending on the Ph.D. program from which the student graduated. An anthropologist reported having $96,000 of debt from graduate educational costs, and a sociologist reported owing $209,000. Many of these students, who are committed to paying off their debt, will be doing so for decades, which will seriously affect their lifestyle. And many of them will not obtain tenure-track positions. Beyond all of this, Ph.D. education is basically open-ended. The expected duration of a Ph.D. program may be five or six years, but in fact, in many disciplines the number is closer to eight years. This is not true in the other professional schools where the program of study is of a fixed duration. Few media outlets discuss this problem and its significance for the training of exceptionally skilled young people who are working toward the most advanced degree that Americans can pursue.[56] As Mark K. Fiegener, a social science analyst at the NSF, said: "Everybody thinks they're going to be the best, be an NBA player, and they don't realize how few people get tenure-track jobs at the best schools."[57]

Even if the cost of an undergraduate or a professional education is often reported as greater than it may actually be, universities are not experts at re-allocating resources in ways that might hold down the cost borne by its students. Let's consider a number of reasons for the increasing costs of higher education.

The American Way of Death at Our Universities

Universities are places where new ideas thrive. Over the past century they have grown dramatically, not only in the size of their student bodies and the number of degrees that they offer but in the amount of research that is carried out and the number of institutes and centers that they support. At Columbia during the 1990s, there were more than three hundred independent centers—a staggering number of entities that had come into being over decades but that reported to almost no one. Many received support from a school or the central administration—even when for years no one had evaluated the center's productivity and value to the larger enterprise or even questioned whether the university should be in that "business" any longer. Universities are geniuses when it comes to the creation and gestation of ideas that always seem to require formal structure and funding outside of the normal department or school boundaries. But universities are terrible at death.

Consider this story, borrowed from a former president at Teachers College (TC), which is corporately independent but affiliated with and offering degrees from Columbia. As a new president, he spent several months of his first year trying to get a fix on the organization of the College. There were an inordinate number of independent centers; many seemed to be functioning well, but others were at best on life support. Understanding that faculty members at any university tend to be conservative when it came to change in their own institution, he was careful in his assessment of how to save costs through the elimination of moribund centers. After a year, he called a faculty meeting to announce the results of his review. He spoke positively about the work of many of the centers but also noted that the positive value of some was less obvious. He identified one center, which had been in existence for roughly forty years and was taking money from the College but, as far as anyone could tell, was not producing anything. He announced that he intended to close that center. Suddenly, a well-meaning faculty member stood up in the back of the assembled faculty crowd and said in a booming voice, "Ah, give it a chance!" After the nervous laughter subsided, the net result was that the center was not closed. Why does this happen? For one, closing academic units of a university is seen as a faculty prerogative. But there's a psychological component; many members of the faculty think, "There but for the grace of God go I," and they resist change. Also, closing down any unit of the university, no matter how small, has enormous transaction costs. Closing a department of four tenured faculty members or eliminating a single sport from the portfolio of athletic teams may mean that the president, provost, dean, and trustees will have to spend a year fending off incessant attacks from one constituency or another.

Academic Budgets as Cost Centers

The great university academic leaders never let control of the budget—because it deals with dollars—fall primarily into the hands of financial people. These are academic choices expressed through numbers. But budgeting is often done in a way that leads to waste, beyond the inert centers and institutes just discussed. Because of two budgeting practices commonly used by most institutions of higher learning, universities often do not investigate how they can save resources or redirect them. One of these practices might be called incremental budgeting; the other, "solving for tuition." Both have cost implications.

Universities use a variety of budgeting systems, but they all tend to use incremental budgeting techniques. Essentially, this means that the point of departure tends to be last year's budget. The university then figures out what incremental costs it will incur through increases in faculty salaries and benefits, incremental debt service for new buildings and facilities, new facilities that do not use debt, new faculty and staff hires that it feels are essential to maintaining its quality and prestige, labor contracts, improved technology and libraries, expenses of the general counsel's office, and auxiliaries such as dining or residence halls, among many other lines in the expense budget (e.g., predicting the cost of heating, which might include buying oil or gas futures). Having computed expenses above and beyond last year's bottom line, the university calculates its revenues, which will include items such as tuition and fees, current gifts, yields from endowment, revenues from research contracts and grants, income from auxiliaries, as well as revenue from physician practice plans, again among many other items. If all of these thousands of calculations— from central administrative costs to costs in the schools (which if the university lives in a decentralized environment must also be balanced with revenues)—equals the projected income from basic sources, then the administration will call the budget in balance. Everyone is happy, and the institution's leaders hail their ability to balance their budget for the "nth" time in a row. And then the trustees (who follow very little of what actually goes on at the university) are also happy.

Universities almost always use what is known as "historical budgeting" techniques, in which people question only increments to the historical budget. But these universities, to my knowledge, never go through a "zero-based budgeting" exercise, where every line item within the university must be approved and that starts essentially from zero and builds up a budget based on demonstrated or argued needs and costs. They therefore rarely question the cost of carried-forward, or historical, budget items.

There are good reasons for using the historical budgeting method. Zero-based budgeting is extremely time-consuming, and it is often difficult for managers, such as department chairs or deans, to justify every line item in their budget. (How do they justify having a Shakespeare scholar as well as a Milton scholar on the English faculty, but not a scholar of twentieth-century African American literature—or the need for a medievalist despite low enrollment in those courses?[58]) At universities, the governance structure does not easily lend itself to such budgeting practices because leaders are in a precarious position if they try to question the faculty about the value of certain activities. Nonetheless, a decanal effort at such budgeting might lead members of the university community to think harder about its real and changing needs, and about the value of programs with long histories that may no longer be relevant or a high priority to the university. Whether by discovering certain administrative activities that could be outsourced at a cheaper price while maintaining equal or improved quality or by eliminating cost-ineffective operations that can be streamlined, zero-based budgeting could lead to reductions in overall expenses. In some sense, this effort would be akin to creating a strategic plan with dollar signs next to the activities that make up a university.

Since universities use historical budgeting practices and tend to look for justifications only for additional expenses, there is a tendency for them to "solve for tuition." This practice, which has taken hold at universities more often than it should, involves producing the expense side of the budget, creating the income side without filling in the line for tuition and fees, and then looking at the difference in the two ledgers. If the projected expenses exceed the projected income, then the difference is made up by raising tuition and fees in the amount necessary to close the gap. Thus, the problem of cost is solved by determining tuition rates that will balance the expense and income equation. Obviously, this is an easy way to balance a budget; but it also tends to drive up tuition and fees more rapidly than would otherwise be the case, since the cost of additional programs or increases in academic or administrative budgets is simply being pushed onto the students and their families. To be fair, universities will try to hold down costs, especially through lower increases in salaries, so that tuition rate increases don't move beyond the point where they stick out like a sore thumb compared with their competition. However, if the market continues to accept these increases and the quality of the enterprise is not affected—in fact, it keeps faculty and staff happy by giving them the incremental dollars or positions that they are asking for—then there are few incentives or pressures to lower the rate of increase in tuition and fees. And, finally, it obviates potential conflict and the need for faculty members and administrators to make hard choices.

The Role of Government

Over the past several decades, most state governments have disinvested in higher education. Although these states want to hold down tuition, fees, and other costs of college, and ask their universities to educate more students—and do a better job at educating them for the workforce of the future—they simultaneously are starving these universities to death. Year after year, states such as California, Michigan, Wisconsin, Arizona, and Florida have allocated fewer dollars to higher education. Many of the cuts have been dramatic. James Duderstadt, former president of the University of Michigan, sardonically speaks of these universities as moving from state-supported to state-assisted to state-located seats of higher learning. In fact, the University of Michigan, which had received as much as 78 percent of its general funds budget from the state in 1960, received roughly 17 percent of its budget from the state in 2012.[59] Today, this world-class institution receives less than 10 percent of its total operating budget from the state. It is in effect no longer really a state university, although a state Board of Regents has the ultimate control over much of the university's financial future.

A report on state spending on higher education published in the *Chronicle of Higher Education* in January 2013 noted: "During the past five years...all but 12 states have reduced higher-education spending overall, including cuts of nearly 37 percent in Arizona and 36 percent in New Hampshire. More than a dozen states have slashed tax dollars for colleges by more than 20 percent since the 2008 fiscal year."[60] The result is that Americans work longer hours, incur more debt than in the past, and devote a higher proportion of their total income to paying for the college education of their children.[61] Today, tuition and fees make up about half of public universities' budgets compared with about 25 percent a quarter of a century earlier.

How are universities to make up the shortfall in state allocations, improve access and quality, and hold costs to prior levels? When we read that places like California spend more on incarceration and prisons than on higher education, we begin to wonder what are the values of the people of the state—especially when the cost of maintaining a single prisoner is about five times the annual cost of tuition and fees at the University of California system. Put another way, we could pay for the cost of tuition and fees for about five students for every person left in a California prison for being arrested for holding (for the third time) a few ounces of marijuana.

In short, states are bleeding a stone.[62] They can't seriously believe that state allocations can move below 10 percent and that universities can cut faculty, programs, staff, library resources, and technology allocations to make ends meet without raising tuition and fees, and without affecting the quality of education. If these universities do not have the option of increasing tuition and fees to fill the gap produced by reduced state allocation, they will sacrifice quality or begin to increase the student population of out-of-state students who pay far higher tuition than those from inside the state. To make ends meet, the University of California, Berkeley has been forced to do this in recent years.

The problem is really not universities' alleged hunger for more funding; rather, it's the core values of our citizens. People assume that without cuts in *unnecessary* expenditures, there is no way to maintain the quality of their best universities. Let me be emphatic: There are ways for universities to cut costs and enhance quality, but doing so is not easy and may not be the preferred solution if we are intent upon remaining the greatest system of higher learning in the world. Other major factors contribute to the relative increase in college tuition and fees compared with the consumer price index. But as long as the nation tolerates an increasing inequality of wealth and a stagnation of middle-class family income and refuses to increase its marginal tax rates or to legislate special measures to support education, the problem will be harder to solve.

The federal government also has much to answer for in creating the cost problem at colleges and universities. Three examples should suffice to illustrate its hand in creating part of the problem, each of which I will cover in greater detail later in the book.

First, the government offers student loans at more favorable rates than those available at neighborhood banks (whose loans are often guaranteed by the federal government). But the interest rate is not 1 percent or zero; and the government actually earns substantial sums from student loans. One estimate was that in 2013 the government profited by $66 billion from student loans on which they charged an interest rate of 4 to 6 percent.[63] The federal government charges banks about 1 percent interest for borrowing money. Massachusetts senator Elizabeth Warren has raised the question of why the government should be charging students far more interest than it charges the banks. If students and banks were charged the same, which Warren proposes, the cost of student loans and students' future indebtedness would go down proportionately and steeply, since most student loans today are federal loans.

Second, the original compact between the federal government and the universities, as envisioned by Vannevar Bush, was that the government would cover the full cost of federally funded research at universities. That agreement persisted for some time after World War II but, like many other government programs, was modified severely over time. Now, due to changes in federal policy and existing foundation policies, research actually loses money for universities. Most people don't realize this. To some extent, fundraising and endowment payouts are used to cover the shortfall, but often there is a cross-subsidy of research from student tuition and fees. This puts pressure on universities to increase their tuition beyond what it might be otherwise.

Third, the federal and state governments have imposed a staggering number of compliance regulations on the universities that add significantly to staff and overall costs. This has become a major area of conflict between universities and the government, which I will discuss and suggest solutions for in Chapter 10. If trust were reestablished between the government and the universities, and if the universities could demonstrate that they can police themselves, universities could save resources and adhere better to their core values.

The Cost Disease

In the 1960s, William J. Baumol and William G. Bowen, two Princeton economists, tried to explain why the costs of the performing arts—from string quartets to dance companies—did not respond to technological advances in the larger society. The costs tended to rise over time more rapidly than did the general cost-of-living index. As a partial explanation for the phenomena, Baumol and Bowen developed the concept of the "cost disease,"[64] and they found that the concept could be generalized to various sectors of the economy beyond the performing arts that are dependent on personal services, such as health care or higher education. The concept has been widely used in economics, but is little known to the general educated public or to many state and federal leaders who are attempting to understand why the cost of education continues to rise more rapidly than inflation and the general cost of living indexes. One reason for this concept's force is that it elaborates on the general idea produced by Nobel Laureate in Economics Robert Solow, suggesting that the major determinant of incremental economic growth in a country like the United States results from advances in technology.

What are the salient features of the cost disease? Baumol explains the idea by dividing the economy into two sectors—a "stagnant sector" and a "progressive sector."[65] Over time, the products "produced" by the stagnant sector (e.g., the arts, health care, and higher learning) will be relatively unaffordable compared with the products of the progressive sector (e.g., computers and automobiles). Some industries, typically those that provide personal services, are likely to be above average in their cost growth because their cost is not easily influenced by labor-saving technologies. These personal services industries may improve their quality using technological innovations without lowering their costs. Other industries will be below the average growth in costs because they can benefit from productivity-enhancing technologies. Nonetheless, Baumol strongly asserts that no matter how rapidly stagnant costs grow relative to inflation, they will never become unaffordable to the larger society. "This," he says, "is because the economy's constantly growing productivity simultaneously increases the community's overall purchasing power and makes for ever-improving overall living standards." He makes two other important points: "The other side of the coin is the increasing affordability and the declining relative costs of the products of the progressive sector" and that "the declining affordability of stagnant-sector products makes them politically contentious and a source of disquiet for average citizens. But paradoxically, it is the development of the progressive sector that poses the greater threat to the general welfare by stimulating such threatening problems as terrorism and climate change." Baumol is suggesting that if we put constraints, for political or other reasons, on the growth of the progressive sector, the balance between it and the more stagnant sector can be adversely affected. Finally, Baumol notes that as productivity grows "so too will our ability to pay for all of these ever more expensive services," and "If governments cannot be led to understand [the cost disease], then their citizens may be denied vital health, education, and other benefits because they *appear* to be unaffordable, when in fact they are not."[66]

A concrete example may help us better understand why the cost disease does not have to cripple our ability to send our children to college—even if the growth rates of tuition and fees exceed average price indexes. Suppose a person has $100 to spend, and $50 goes to rent and basic food and living costs. That would leave, hypothetically, $50 to spend on other things. Suppose further that the price of an item in the progressive sector is lowered—for example, the cost of a thirty-five-inch television, by 30 percent—but the cost of tuition rises by 4 percent a year. The money the person saves on the less-expensive television set, which was made possible through advancements in technology, could go toward paying for his or her child's education. Such savings might even exceed the additional education costs. Although education costs may rise annually, while the life of a television extends for a number of years, a choice remains between buying a new television with a sixty-inch screen at the same price as the old set or living with the smaller unit and putting the money not spent into savings for a college education. In fact, the lowered cost in the progressive sector may result in greater discretionary income. In subsequent years, the person may also benefit from lower prices on other manufactured items, such as computers.

Baumol places the problem of relative costs and affordability of higher learning in just such a larger context. Investment in these different sectors of our lives, he suggests, is as much a matter of values as of economics. The cost disease is also related to the assumption that there will be overall rising wage levels in the economy, which enable us to shift our allocation of personal resources from one type of investment, such as lower-cost computers, to higher-cost personal services, such as education. But what happens when wages in most of the society remain stagnant or decline while growing massively for a small percentage of the population?[67] For roughly thirty years before the financial crisis of 2007–2008, the incomes of America's middle class had hardly changed. But now, as Nobel Prize–winning economist Joseph Stiglitz starkly puts it, "the six heirs to the Walmart empire command wealth of $69.7 billion, which is equivalent to the wealth of the entire bottom 30 percent of U.S. society."[68] The stag-nation of family income requires that families sending their kids to college resort to debt financing. Again, the growing inequality of wealth in America poses a real problem, and it is the one that the U.S. middle class faces today when it contemplates investments in education.

Some scholars, such as Robert B. Archibald and David H. Feldman, do not believe that the cost disease is the major determinant of the affordability prob-lems facing higher education. It is not that they reject the concept of the cost disease, but they argue that the primary reason that tuition and fees have in-creased more rapidly than inflation over the past several decades is that they "are driven more by changes in state subsidies and in the American distribu-tion of income than by rising costs."[69] They note that if we wanted to increase productivity at these universities, we could simply change the structure of education by doubling class size—increasing the "productivity" of the faculty. But the goal at great universities is to hold down costs *without* diminishing quality. As Archibald and Feldman point out, if any family is asked "if they want their son or daughter to learn in small group seminars taught by tenured professors, or if they prefer giant impersonal lectures or online chat rooms monitored by adjuncts who answer lots of email questions," the answer is obvious—they prefer the former to the latter option.[70]

Also, about 70 percent of those employed by major universities hold at least a college education and could be said to work in the personal services industry—the stagnant sector. If the gap in wages between those who hold college de-grees and those who don't increases over time, then the expenses of universities will rise relative to average inflation and to overall mean incomes. Perhaps iron-ically, what we are trying to achieve—a higher percentage of the population with at least a college degree to enable them to hold jobs in a knowledge-based economy and to increase their earning power—is one of the reasons for the higher-than-inflation costs of universities and colleges. In addition, the tech-nological innovations at universities, and there have been many, tend not to be of the cost-saving type. In order for colleges and universities to compete with each other and to improve their quality, they often must adopt non-labor-saving technologies. If technological progress is the driving force behind the cost dis-ease, then when technological innovation slows down, so will the rising costs in higher education. When technological progress picks up, so will the relative cost of higher learning.[71]

Archibald and Feldman explore other factors leading to higher costs, and they place a greater emphasis on these influences than on the cost disease. One, which is especially true among top universities or those seeking similar standing, is competition. Recruiting superstar faculty members involves competition to provide higher salaries, state-of-the-art laboratories, and a host of other enticements, including luxury housing and financial support for the schooling of faculty children. There is also increasing competition for top students—at the undergraduate as well as the graduate student and post-doctoral fellow levels—and junior faculty members. The competition for undergraduate students takes such forms as nicer dormitories, housing suites, and apartments—some that would make the Four Seasons proud—student activities spaces, athletic facilities, quality food services, counseling services, and employment placement offices. There is an argument that colleges and universities are being managed inefficiently, which drives up costs. But there is little evidence that they are more inefficient today than they were in the past. Administrative bloat is also viewed by some as a reason for the increased cost of tuition, but Archibald and Feldman argue that these increased costs, which have risen in recent decades, are not significantly different from those in other industries, where the overall costs of products have not risen as rapidly as university tuitions and fees. Competition, I argue elsewhere,[72] has been a highly positive force in driving the system of higher education toward its current preeminent position. But there is no doubt that we are in a form of arms race that can be expensive.

Finally, many tuition-dependent universities use a portion of their tuition to fund capital projects that could not otherwise receive funding without the university going further into debt—and jeopardizing its bond rating by floating additional bonds for capital projects. (These bond ratings are often more of an indicator of prestige than a substantial cost savings at most universities.) Part of the tuition is transferred into an account that finances projects that often benefit students, but these transfers represent moving increased tuition to other lines in the university budgets. Since students and their parents are not familiar with the budgets, they don't realize that these tuition dollars are being spent to improve the quality of student life.

Archibald and Feldman argue that we ought to be asking ourselves: "Over any given span of years, once you account for all price changes and all changes in family income, can a family purchase the exact same set of goods and services as before, and have more money left over to buy other things?"[73] This is the correct way to frame the question about college costs. The cost problem results, to a significant degree, from the growing inequality of wealth in our country, due to stagnation of income growth in the middle and lower classes over the past three decades. Nonetheless, there are things that colleges and universities can do, and ought to do, that would reduce the burden of increases in tuition and student debt. I turn now to a number of potential ways of handling the affordability problem.

CHAPTER SIX

An Accessible, High-Quality Education for All

Social and economic inequalities... are just only if they result in compensating benefits for everyone, and in particular for the least advantaged members of society.

—JOHN RAWLS, *A THEORY OF JUSTICE*

I T IS A LOSS TO OUR NATION, and to our American ideals, when individuals with talent and curiosity are unable to pursue their interests for a lack of financial means. Not everyone needs or wants to attend a college or university. Being a large nation, we can educate many individuals in important, and needed, trades and occupational pursuits without requiring of them a formal college education. But the tragedy surfaces when individuals who want to pursue advanced education believe that the doors are closed to them because they simply cannot afford it. This is as true for families who fall in the middle of our income distribution as for those who are in the lowest quintile.[1]

An attentive reader can find scores of prognosticators who warn us that higher education's business model is about to be rethought and remade by the disruptive effects of new technology. As evidence, they point to the transformation of the music industry as well as the book and magazine publishing businesses. And there have been fundamental changes in those sectors. But will reasoning by analogy hold true for those who see the future of higher education in the use of online learning and new forms of educational software that will replace the older models of instruction? And will these new technologies be able to reduce the costs of education while improving its quality—particularly at our most selective colleges and universities?

Will Clicks Eliminate Bricks?

In 2015, the rage among the saviors of higher education was often new technology, such as massive open online courses (MOOCs) and the role they could play in harnessing the cost of higher education. Much has been written about various online platforms, such as Udacity and Coursera (a profit-making company founded by Stanford's Andrew Ng and Daphne Koller that began offering free online courses in 2008 and quickly enlisted distinguished academic partners, including many elite universities). Similarly, edX, which as of this writing is a nonprofit online course enterprise begun at Harvard and MIT, has quickly been adopted by a set of prestigious universities. Each of the partners creates a limited number of MOOCs that are available for online learning. Will online learning centers become the future of higher education, negating the campus and the need to build new residence halls, laboratories, and classrooms?

I do not believe that technology will solve the seemingly perennial cost problem at the most selective and research-intensive universities. But it *ought* to be one of the new ways in which we improve how we reach students by increasing knowledge of cognitive learning styles (through the collection of massive amounts of data on learning), and it will replace some of our universities' ancient structures. Let me briefly discuss what I see as the limits of MOOCs for these schools and then describe some examples of technologies that may have more of an impact on higher learning for undergraduates at our finest schools.

As journalist and author Fareed Zakaria writes:

> MOOCs are courses that can be taken online by watching videos of lectures and completing assignments and tests that are graded by computer programs or humans. In some cases, students engage in virtual classroom discussion through structured chat rooms or bulletin boards.... The larger idea behind them is simple. A course that could be taken by a few hundred people at a university is now available to tens of thousands, even hundreds of thousands, across the globe.[2]

MOOCs represent only the latest messianic technological movement in which its adherents produce extravagant claims about how the technology will disrupt and then save higher education. Although most of the focus is on containing or reducing costs without lowering quality—and doing this without a traditional learning environment—MOOCs are also an attempt to use "star" teachers to reach audiences through a technology that is free of the lecture method of instruction.[3] As noted, students can view these lectures online at their leisure, more than once if necessary, and, in principle, can discuss the problems presented in the lecture in small sections taught by regular, or more often adjunct, faculty or students—the so-called flipped classroom. Because they have the potential to reach large audiences worldwide, perhaps the greatest claim for MOOCs is that they will have a democratizing effect on higher learning. It seems to me that this is the way they could ultimately have their greatest impact. Thus far, there has been almost no discussion about whether the American dominance of this technology and the production of content leads to a view of the world that is consistent with our values, rather than with the values of people in the foreign nations that the MOOCs reach. This might not matter in a course in elementary statistics, but it could make a huge difference in a course on, for example, the politics of the Middle East.

Efforts to use new technology to improve content or lower costs are hardly new. Over the past seventy-five years, we have seen attempts to employ correspondence courses for educational credit and to use television as a medium to deliver knowledge. For example, in the famous series *Sunrise Semester*, which appeared on CBS and was developed in conjunction with NYU, faculty members who were outstanding teachers delivered lectures early in the morning. The series, which ran for almost twenty-five years, presented courses with titles such as "From Stendhal to Hemingway." To receive credit toward their degrees, students paid $25 per point. More than 175 students took the first course for credit, but it was watched on CBS for free by some 120,000 others. This revolutionary form of distance learning demonstrated that the new technology, television, had the potential to educate an attentive and early-rising public; but it did not alter the structure of the traditional college or university.

During the dot.com boom (and bust) of the late 1990s, many universities thought that they had discovered a potentially transformative use of new Internet technology to deliver high-end content to an engaged public, including lifelong learners. Columbia was among the entrants in that field—in several forms, the most famous of which was Fathom, an online-learning platform designed to appeal to those looking for high-level, certified knowledge and comprising a distinguished consortium of institutions, including great universities in the United States and Britain as well as major museums in each country.[4] Fathom (and many lesser products) was a success in concept, but not in implementation. The technology of the day was not good enough to deliver the product (most viewers were still using telephone connections to the Internet that were so slow it took several minutes to download a single image), and the cost of producing high-level, multimedia content proved more expensive than we had anticipated. Now, only a decade or so later, the technology has improved so greatly that the technological barrier that we faced with Fathom could be overcome. This ought to be a lesson for us. Good ideas for the use of educational media should not be discarded prematurely. In the longer term, they can have dramatic impacts on certain types of learning among various audiences.

Nevertheless, online education will not (and should not) replace residential campuses at the great colleges and universities in the United States. At selective colleges, MOOCs will be one of many forms of new technology that will be useful: mostly for courses for which there is a "right answer at the back of the book." This has already been demonstrated, especially at places like Georgia Tech, Carnegie Mellon, and Arizona State University, among others. For all other courses, where there are subtleties in interpretation, where there is a need for argument and critical thinking and for a close-knit community of participants, MOOCs will be less useful. As Columbia biologist Stuart Firestein puts it: "Questions are more relevant than answers. Questions are bigger than answers."[5]

Richard Levin, the former president of Yale University, echoed this belief in 2014 when he signed on as CEO of Coursera and explicitly noted that MOOCs "couldn't replicate the traditional four-year residential education model." Certainly MOOCs have the potential to produce a democratizing effect, and this is what Levin emphasized, quite correctly, when he joined Coursera: "We're going to address the needs of millions who don't have access to that [residential model]," said Levin. "Technology now gives us the means to extend the reach of high-quality education around the world and to provide millions of people with access to learning and opportunities for advancement."[6]

Jumping prematurely on the MOOC bandwagon suggests a form of institutional mania where each university almost mindlessly decides that it is better to get on board early for the possible first-mover advantage than to seriously consider what the university really wants to obtain from these online platforms—other than an alternative income stream (that is hardly guaranteed). A few smart educators, however, have begun to think of special audiences for whom online courses make a great deal of sense and offer a way for them to earn credits toward a degree or certificate. Although the new technology holds out a great deal of hope for the expansion of quality education, we do not yet have sufficient empirical evidence to support claims that it will become a game changer. Consider:

1. Thus far, there is no clear business model in place for the larger platforms such as edX or Coursera, at least none that suggest that they will generate significant income (beyond costs) for the participating institutions of higher learning. As of March 2015, the developers of Coursera could say with some pride that it had more than 12 million users (not necessarily unique online students) from 190 countries enrolled in one of roughly 1,000 courses generated by 117 colleges and universities. In 2013, it claimed to have generated $1 million through fees for tuition and verified certificates, introducing students to potential employers and recruiters, tutoring, and sponsorships.

2. Although the technology of online education has improved dramatically over the past decade, the cost of creating high-quality content that involves more than the equivalent of an old-style lecture hall is high. Estimates that I have received from members of edX suggest that the cost per course varies but often is between $100,000 and $300,000. Thus, although the marginal cost of providing the course a second or third time is low (yet often underestimated because there is a continual need to update these courses), there is no evidence that MOOCs will lower costs of tuition—at least at the most selective colleges and universities.

3. There is no uniform method or policy for dealing with the substantial problems of who owns the content or how the intellectual property is to be divided among the creators of the platform, the university, and the faculty members who have created the MOOC. edX is leaving this critical matter up to the schools, but one can easily envision the most successful MOOC teachers beginning to sell their talents to the highest bidder in the academic job market. They also might form their own companies in order to own a substantially greater share of the "business" than they might be able to obtain by staying within the university.

4. Unfortunately, as of 2015, there is no good evidence that MOOCs have a democratizing effect, meaning that they allow those without a college education—and who cannot afford to attend a residential

college located in another part of the world—to obtain one online. In fact, thus far, those who take these courses in foreign countries are those who already have an undergraduate or more advanced degree.[7]

5. There is no good evidence on how people with different learning styles respond to the flipped classroom and a MOOC culture on campus.

6. No good methods have been identified to examine the thousands of people taking online courses without monitoring who exactly has taken the course and who is taking the test to earn a certificate or degree. We know that there is massive cheating in foreign countries when students are required to pass language requirements or to do well on standardized examinations in order to be admitted to institutions of higher learning. Nothing short of monitoring these exams guarantees that cheating on them won't be rampant. Again, this is a known problem that online producers are trying to address.

7. There is some, but no good, evidence profiling those users who drop out of these courses; nor are there good data on why they sign up for them or on whether or not they take another MOOC course after having experienced their first one. The ability to collect massive amounts of data on those who sign up for these courses should enable their creators ultimately to provide such information in detail.

8. In a recent poll of faculty members who teach MOOC courses online, 72 percent said they did not think their students deserve credit, even if they did well in the class. This poll was of a sample of professors who teach these courses, which means that in a random sample of faculty the percentage could be even higher.

9. Researchers at Glasgow Caledonian University examined the results of 400 students who took the Harvard Medical School's "Fundamentals of Clinical Trials," a MOOC offered to health professionals through edX.[8] They found that these students took a passive approach to learning; avoided collaborations with other students; studied to obtain passing grades; and did not have good retention of the materials. There was little peer interaction.

10. Sebastian Thrun, one of the creators of the MOOC platform Udacity, worked at Stanford for some time and mostly at Google. Most of his MOOC courses, which were not offered for credit, were short, focused on artificial intelligence, and had hundreds of thousands of students who signed up. Thrun's name was all over the media as he

trumpeted the value of these online courses. Reality struck sometime in 2014. He voiced his own skepticism about his work on Udacity when he summed up his feelings this way: "We were on the front pages of newspapers and magazines, and at the same time, I was realizing, we don't educate people as others wished, or as I wished. We have a lousy product.... It was a painful moment."[9]

Although there may be increasing skepticism about MOOCs, let's not be too hasty in assuming that some of the new technologies (that we don't even know about at the moment) will not be extremely helpful in a variety of ways. We might not be seeing the democratizing effects of MOOCs yet, but we are in an early phase of their development; and we may be using ineffective mechanisms for reaching those able youngsters in African, South Asian, and Latin American societies who could benefit significantly from these types of courses. Small-scale studies that support our presuppositions should be examined skeptically, and we should think hard about alternative ways that we can enrich the lives of students around the world through the use of these new technologies.[10] At least, there is in existence proof of the democratizing effect of MOOCs. Jima Ngei, who lives in Nigeria, reports that he has completed and passed 250 MOOCs through Coursera since 2012. He took a wide variety of courses, and he asserts that "taking MOOCs through Coursera was the only way I could get a high-quality education, and I had this unrelenting fear that this miracle of free access might evaporate soon."[11] And there are glowing reports from Georgia Tech, Arizona State, Carnegie Mellon, and other large universities on the number of students who have taken MOOCs and who do as well as those who take regular classes. For highly specific courses designed to meet the needs of a specific type of student, some MOOCs might indeed prove effective. But the empirical evidence of their value remains thin.

Nonetheless, those who believe that clicks will replace bricks don't really understand how college works—at least at the best schools, whether public or private. Undergraduates who are finding themselves have a deep need for community, for conversation, and for forming and building lasting social networks. As A. Scott Berg, one of Woodrow Wilson's more recent biographers, noted: "Wilson found that the most rewarding elements of college came not through the formal academics ('No undergraduate can be made a scholar in four years') but in friendship, that immeasurable influence twenty-year-olds have upon one another before their personalities have hardened." Wilson himself said: "the very best effects of university life are wrought between six and nine o'clock in the evenings, when the professor has gone home, and minds meet minds, and a generating process takes place."[12] That is still true today. One of the most influential mathematicians of the twentieth century, Yakov G. Sinai, professor of mathematics at Princeton, credited the intellectual environment there for helping inspire the work that earned him the 2014 Norwegian Academy of Sciences $1 million Abel Prize and many other honors. He said that at Princeton, "I always can find a person to ask the right questions."[13]

What are some of the noncurricular activities that make campus life essential for a full, undergraduate experience? Sherry Turkle, MIT's Abby Rockefeller Mauzé Professor of the Social Studies of Science and Technology, has spent years studying the social effects of new technologies and artificial intelligence programs on young people. In *Alone Together*, she discusses some of the unintended consequences of the obsession of some youngsters with computer simulation games and the amount of time they spend on their computers and digital devices: "Technology is seductive when what it offers meets our human vulnerabilities," says Turkle. "And as it turns out, we are very vulnerable indeed. We are lonely but fearful of intimacy. Digital connections and the sociable robot may offer the illusion of companionship without the demands of friendship. Our networked life allows us to hide from each other, even as we are tethered to each other."[14]

What Turkle and others are speaking to is a form of contemporary alienation. Of course, we all benefit from the advances in technology and, in particular, computer technology. But there is a darker side to the consequences of these advances—and one dark cloud may come in the form of alienation that we ought to be working to reduce. The exclusive use of online learning to contain educational costs and to offer degrees to large numbers of individuals who are connected only via their computers may result in individuals who are largely divorced from community and the interpersonal communications that take place in a physical setting. It is, perhaps, an open question as to whether subsequent generations can experience fulfilling lives without much human contact, without direct conversation and argumentation, and without the interaction with peers that makes up so much of the educational experience. We ought to be looking to create MOOCs and other learning technologies that are embedded in the regular curricular and extracurricular programs of great universities—ones that are designed to enhance the quality of an education rather than reducing cost. Some things of great value carry costs with them—and a great education may be one of those that is well worth the cost.

At the most selective schools, students learn from each other when they eat together, read together, form study groups together, converse together, and sleep together. If nothing else will save the residential college, sex will. Of course, websites like the one for the Kahn Academy, where short, highly focused courses are offered, will be appealing to some fraction of the student body—and those who are seeking admission to the most selective colleges and perhaps even their parents. So will blended education—the mixture of online and in-person learning experiences. Those who simply want certification in order to obtain slightly better jobs will find value in websites such as the one for the University of Phoenix, even if they know that their "attendance" in these digital universities involves a substantial personal loss of social interaction. If certificate granting is the business of Coursera or edX, then there may be some hope for them as businesses, but not as replacements for the structure of existing campuses and curricula at the best institutions of higher learning. Even if they involve some interaction, these online courses are not the way our students ought to learn at our greatest universities, professional schools, and liberal arts colleges. They may be part of the experience, but not all of it.

What we ought to do is allow innovative faculty members to develop digital platforms that are far more interactive and that are focused specifically on the courses that are offered both at a single university and to those members of the new academic leagues that ought to be formed (which I'll discuss in Chapter 7). A creative academic like Professor Brian Greene—who formally teaches physics and mathematics at Columbia University but wears many hats, including as a public intellectual and author of *The Elegant Universe*, which has been translated into scores of languages and has sold hundreds of thousands of copies around the world—is such a person. The brilliance of Greene's work is that his platform allows young students as well as Nobel Prize winners to consider concepts, puzzles, and ideas that are more closely related to how science really operates. Greene launched two free online courses in 2014 as part of the World Science University, a place on the World Wide Web where students can ask science questions, explore topics guided by world-renowned scientists, and take university courses. This "university" is an extension of Greene's annual World Science Festival, which is held in New York City and involves discussions and talks by renowned math and physics faculty members and holds demonstrations for youngsters. One offering is a three-week course on space and time that examines how reality behaves at very high speeds, and the other is a ten-week course. "I don't want to use the Internet," says Greene, "as a new delivery vehicle for old-style teaching." Instead, he aims "to create a new kind of learning experience that makes science more visual, interactive, and compelling ... I launched this project with the aim of using digital innovation to make it easier, more exciting, and more gratifying for students to learn science."[15] Interestingly, Greene filmed his talks not in a standard classroom but in a Manhattan loft for, as he puts it, a more compelling experience for those who sign up for the course. "When students can visualize abstract ideas through carefully crafted animations, play with new concepts through interactive demonstrations, be led by the hand through exercises and problems, and have many confusing issues addressed through guided question session, they learn the material more deeply."[16]

In fact, we need not only more customized platforms that are tailored to specific audiences but also far more experimental and empirical work on learning styles and cognition. Although this work is taking place at great universities, few outside of the Academy know about it. Consider just three examples.

John Robert Anderson is an award-winning professor of psychology and computer science at Carnegie Mellon University, which has historically been one of the world's leaders in discoveries related to digital technology and the Internet. Anderson has used functional magnetic resonance imaging to study how students learn with intelligent tutoring systems. The cognitive architecture that emerged from these studies showed that patterns of errors that students made in solving problems could be discerned and that specific digital tutoring programs could be constructed to help them. Most of Anderson's work has been in mathematical problem solving; the result has been a cognitive architecture called ACT-R, which mimics the behavior of students and in a personalized way predicts, or perhaps "guesses," what the students' difficulties will be. Although not a MOOC, it makes use of new technology in a way that instructs us about various learning styles and develops special interactive programs to help those students overcome their difficulties in solving problems. Today, Cognitive Tutors for Mathematics is being used in thousands of schools across the United States.

Eric Mazur is a Harvard physicist who offered polished lectures and demonstrations to extremely bright undergraduates—mostly premedical students and engineers. The students gave his courses excellent evaluations at the end of each term. After seven years of teaching these types of courses, seemingly very successfully, Mazur, in his own words, discovered that his success as a teacher "was a complete illusion."[17] He acknowledged that these smart students could improve their ability to handle equations and formulas; but when it came to really understanding what they were being taught, "they basically reverted to Aristotelian logic." According to Mazur, "After a semester of physics, they still held the same misconceptions as they had at the beginning of the term.... They floundered on the simple word problems, which demanded a real understanding of the concepts behind the formulas."[18]

Mazur read about a simple test developed by Arizona State University professor David Hestenes that checked whether his students really understood one of the most fundamental concepts in physics—force. The test showed that most students had learned almost nothing from the introductory course. Mazur had found the same results at Harvard that Hestenes had found as ASU. What Mazur did was purely serendipitous. After some frustration in trying to teach the students the concepts addressed in the test, Mazur said to his class: "Why don't you discuss it with each other?" "It was complete chaos," said Mazur. "But within three minutes, they had figured it out. That was very surprising to me—I had just spent *10 minutes* trying to explain this." Mazur began to experiment with what is now referred to as "active learning" through interactive pedagogy, which was intended to turn passive learners into active ones. For Mazur, "the person who learns the most in any classroom is the teacher." The active-learning professor tries to reevaluate what can be accomplished during a lecture class and uses a different approach if necessary. Mazur observed "lectures are a way of transferring the instructor's lecture notes to students' notebooks without passing through the brains of either."[19] Finally, he concludes:

> I think the answer to this challenge [of getting students' attention] is to re-think the nature of the college course, to consider it as a different kind of animal these days.... A course can be a communication across time about a discrete topic, with a different temporal existence than the old doing-the-homework-for-the-lecture routine. Students now tap into a course through different media; they may download materials via its website, and even access a faculty member's research and bio. It's a different kind of communication between faculty and student.[20]

Accordingly, Mazur dropped the lecture model and instead works closely with students in what is a learning/teaching endeavor. It is part of a two-step process of information transfer and making sense of and assimilating the information.[21] Mazur is teaching physics, and yet he begins his classes with a question. He asks his students to think the problem through and commit to an answer, which each student records using a handheld device, such as a smartphone. A central computer statistically compiles and tabulates the initial results and, unless there is a clear consensus, the students proceed to peer instruction. A student finds another person with a different answer and makes a case for his or her own response. Pandemonium ensues. Mazur circulates around the room and listens, especially to incorrect reasoning, so he can "resensitize myself to the difficulties beginning learners face." After a few minutes, the students vote again, and typically the proportion of correct answers improves dramatically. Then Mazur repeats the cycle in an effort to "turn our students into *real* problem solvers."[22] Mazur is not using MOOCs or other sophisticated technology, but he has reoriented his teaching by employing a fundamentally different strategy, one that is more consistent with Dewey's idea of learning by doing—and collaborating.[23] Many faculty members at Harvard and other top universities are experimenting with better methods for teaching their undergraduates, using either an intuitive sense or a more formal cognitive idea of how young people with different learning styles can benefit most from their undergraduate courses.

Consider now the extremely popular classes at Stanford's d.school (an institute for design innovation). The students come from every field: sciences, engineering, social sciences, arts, and humanities. David Kelley, one of the school's founders, says the students are taught to develop "empathy muscles." They are also taught to forgo computer screens and spreadsheets and focus on people. At the d.school, says Kelley, "We learn by doing." The school has been a huge success, with students churning out dozens of innovative products and start-ups (one assignment led to a news-reading app that was bought by LinkedIn for $90 million). Students work in a cavernous space, which seems like a nod to the Silicon Valley garages of lore. The classes often get four times as many applicants as there are seats available. Their creativity comes from interactions, from open discussions, from the formation of a sense of community. Ideas occur as the students eat together or as they put Post-it notes on chalkboards. This kind of experience won't happen with MOOCs.

We ought to have many more such experiments in ways of teaching that are geared toward how students learn best, rather than adhering to 600-year-old methods of formal lecturing. But there is no one way of doing this—with or without new digital technology. These great educators are working hard to understand how people learn best, not because they are trying to economize, but because they want to become better teachers for smart, young people. Our future as great universities ought to depend more and more on these various forms of innovative thinking and empirically based methods of teaching and learning—where the student becomes a more central component in the process.

Caroline M. Hoxby, the Stanford economist, suggests that we cannot view online learning, whether in the form of MOOCs or other types of platforms, as having similar effect at the most highly selective colleges and universities as at those of lesser standing.[24] The educational needs and forms of teaching differ among these institutions. Consequently, the role played by these new technologies in the curriculum must also be viewed differently. Hoxby argues that the top schools operate on business models akin to those at venture capital firms—where the university invests heavily in today's student body in order to instill in them the types of loyalty and commitment that accompany generous gift giving twenty or thirty years after their graduation. This enables the selective schools to continue to invest in the undergraduates whose tuition does not cover the full cost of their education—despite the misleading sticker price associated with the university.

I want to address how, if at all, the new technology of online, digital learning influences the component of the university that makes it truly great: the research that leads to discoveries and practical applications that change people's lives and form the foundation of our nation's new economy. This is almost never discussed when we talk about how MOOCs will transform the university. Although these technologies may help us rethink aspects of undergraduate education and possibly reduce cost by opening a new income stream, digital learning will not bring the walls down of the great universities if for no other reason than that it will not have a huge disruptive effect on the research enterprise. While laboratory life will also be influenced by revolutions in technology, thus far MOOCs do not have a home in the laboratory life that is at the very heart of bricks and mortar and of research. MOOCs will have virtually no influence on the conduct of basic and applied scientific research, social and behavioral science research, or new research in the humanities. They might have some effect on the teaching programs in some of the professional schools, such as law or business, where one can imagine world-class First Amendment scholars creating MOOCs that would be used at multiple universities. But we cannot yet do without the laboratories and spaces for research in the biological or physical sciences. And it is the research discoveries, as I've repeatedly said, that have led our system of higher learning to preeminence.

Where MOOCs and similar technological developments may, in fact, become very disruptive are at the second- and third-tier liberal arts colleges and universities. These institutions don't have the endowment necessary to hire large, disparate faculties, and they may gain a great deal by using the new forms of learning. However, even here some evidence to the contrary exists: While working with one hundred undergraduates at an upstate New York liberal arts college, sociologists Daniel F. Chambliss and Christopher G. Takacs found that what students are looking for in college is quite different from what online learning is offering them. They are concerned with friendships (in fact, they follow friends' advice on course selection more often than the suggestions of advisors), learning from their friends and from a diverse culture, and participating in a variety of activities present on campus. They repeatedly said, "encounters with the right person could make a decisive difference in their college careers."[25] Over the next few decades, clicks and online digital education may well improve our ability to gather information quickly or to get the right answers that we can find at the back of a textbook; but it should not replace the "minds rubbing up against minds" that happens in the campus experience.

Finally, there ought to be many new experiments with online learning at the college level, such as the one begun by Ben Nelson in 2014, called Minerva Schools, at the Keck Graduate Institute in Claremont, California. Based upon the work of prominent cognitive scientists, including Stephen Kosslyn, former dean of Harvard's social sciences, Minerva's curriculum purports to offer a rigorous program the equal to that found at the most selective schools. The courses taken online are designed to reinvent "higher education to prepare future leaders and innovators in a global context. With a pedagogy and curriculum specifically designed to teach in service to the science of learning, Minerva is making higher education more accessible and affordable for the brightest and most motivated student from around the world." The program involves a blend of online learning and personal interaction at a "campus" in San Francisco. It is too early to assess the outcome of this for-profit effort, but its goal is to occupy the space on the World Wide Web similar to what we had in mind for Fathom—the exceptionally able students and graduates who wanted to continue to be educated at a high level. What remains unclear is how well the "seminar" aspect of Minerva will work, since it is predicated on using young, adjunct instructors to shoulder a heavy responsibility.[26]

The great universities of the twenty-first century should construct a quiver of technological platforms that contains multiple arrows to be used for different purposes and that will help to transform the way we teach students. Undergraduate teaching as we know it, with lectures and seminars, has not really changed for 400 years. It is either textbook- or lecture-based, with professors teaching toward getting the "right" answer and repeating in classroom presentations what can be found in that textbook. It assumes students are passive learners who either get it or don't. And it is only after the examination that the instructor has an idea of which students are on top of the material. For some students, the lecture moves too quickly; for others it moves too slowly. Generally, it has all the ingredients conducive for sleep or confusion. In science or mathematics lectures, students try to take notes that will enable them to review materials found on several examinations. Rarely is the lecture experience fun, and often it is used to classify students as able or not. In the social sciences and humanities, lectures often transmit information that students find interesting, but there is little room for discussion or debates, which must wait, if students are fortunate, until they find themselves in small seminar classes. If the students are lucky, they can encounter extraordinary lecturers who discuss material that can't be found in any book or journal (as I did sitting in on lectures by sociologist Robert K. Merton and gifted art historian Meyer Schapiro). At flagship state universities, the lecture halls are filled with hundreds of students; there is often a surface noise due to uninterested students who are reading newspapers or viewing their social media sites. These situations are not conducive to producing better analytic thinking and the raising of questions that increase our ignorance rather than decrease it.[27] George Bernard Shaw, presuming he was exercising his usual wit, said at a dinner honoring Albert Einstein, "Science is always wrong. It never solves a problem without creating ten more."[28]

These technologies can improve the quality of education, but some of them will not be easily created and also reduce costs. There ought to be room for traditional forms of interaction between student and teacher. Close discussion of a Jane Austen or Charles Dickens novel, or a sermon by Jonathan Edwards, or analysis of an image by Breughel, Giotto, Matisse, or Rothko, may not require significantly improved technology. They do require a sense of community and interaction in a secure and small setting. There will be no substitute for the engaging and challenging teacher confronting students with pointed questions that make them think, use the text as evidence, and force them to make an argument that can be debated with fellow students in relatively small sections. No new technology is needed for this important style of education, but perhaps a new technology can be developed that falsifies this belief. And there must be room for the traditional laboratory life—that personal interaction in a laboratory among graduate students, post-doctoral fellows, and their scientific mentor. New technologies will be used to make discoveries, but they will not substitute for the casual and serendipitous interaction that so often leads to new ideas or elaboration of an existing one.

A Third Component of the Morrill III Act: Financial Aid for Families Without Means

> There are talented individuals in every part of the population, but with few exceptions, those without the means of buying higher education go without it. If ability, and not the circumstances of family fortune, determines who shall receive higher education in science, then we shall be assured of constantly improving quality at every level of scientific activity. The Government should provide a reasonable number of undergraduate scholarships and fellowships in order to develop scientific talent in American youth.
>
> —VANNEVAR BUSH, *SCIENCE, THE ENDLESS FRONTIER*

Perhaps only the GI Bill of Rights following World War II matched the Morrill Act in terms of its consequences for higher learning, which, as mentioned, set in motion the creation of some of the world's greatest public universities. Of course, the GI Bill did not create new universities, but it opened up access to higher education to returning soldiers who might never have had the opportunity to receive a college education without the support of the federal government.

Both of these efforts by the federal government represent clear evidence that the national government can pull off amazing feats and produce a positive effect on higher learning and on the potential upward mobility of its citizens. It is now imperative for it to do so again. The federal government needs a plan as bold and ambitious as the Morrill Act and the GI Bill. It ought to create a Morrill III Act for Financial Aid for Needy Americans, which would ensure with the proper incentives for the states and universities that every youngster with ability but without means could obtain a good college education at limited cost. Initially, the act ought to increase substantially the maximum awards associated with Pell Grants (which have eroded due to inflation and an inadequate allocation of further funds to keep up with the cost of living), and it should drop interest rates on any government loan to 1 percent. The Morrill III financial aid grants would be indexed, as is social security, to the rate of inflation. The act should also include a loan forgiveness component for those students who go into public service work or become teachers. These elements would be means tested and progressive in their nature—those students from economically disadvantaged homes would receive more in support than those from wealthy families. Indeed, a wealth threshold should be established above which families would be expected to pay full tuition because their good fortune enabled them to do so. It is important that the federal government's support for student higher education not "buy out the base" of the colleges—that colleges not be permitted to use the additional financial support to simply raise their prices. Colleges and universities ought to demonstrate that their financial aid has not declined as a result of the federal aid, unless they can show that the need of the incoming students has been lowered because of higher family incomes. They should also demonstrate progress toward an increase in the proportion of their students that come from economically disadvantaged backgrounds.

The government would ideally create these Morrill grants, which would replace other forms of financial aid, and guarantee that students from lower-income families will have no undergraduate debt burden. Like today's National Science Foundation (NSF) graduate fellowships for students continuing their education in science and technology fields, the Morrill III financial aid grants should go to the individual—to be used at the college of her or his choice—not to the school. The national payoff for this action would be significant, enabling highly qualified young people from less advantaged backgrounds to attend and graduate from college, demonstrating that their higher-level skills are increasing the nation's overall human capital and bringing in to the middle class those who might otherwise have lost the opportunity for upward social mobility. The federal government should cap these investments in learning to perhaps five years in order to provide incentives for students to finish their degrees within that period. The new Morrill Act should also be predicated on a matching of state financial aid to students that is either equal to or in some proportion to the federal aid. The program could match increased state investments; it could also reduce federal allocations when states reduced support of their public universities and colleges. This effort would be entirely consistent with the imperative articulated more than sixty years ago in Vannevar Bush's *Science, the Endless Frontier.*

State legislators and governors ought to be educated on the impact that excellent institutions of higher learning has on state economies and on the wisdom of investments in their entire educational system, from pre-school to graduate school education. The universities can further streamline themselves financially by improving the way new technology can reduce costs of administrative services, if not of teaching; by making choices about the types of amenities that they believe are required to attract the types of students they wish to recruit, and by closing poorly performing or obsolete programs. The creation of academic leagues, which I discuss in Chapter 7, is another way of potentially increasing quality while cutting costs. Many colleges and universities should experiment with online learning, with a new model for the relationship between lectures and seminars, and should create several types of coexisting degrees—some based primarily on off-campus, online learning mixed with experiences on campus; others that use technology and new media primarily to enhance quality rather than to cut costs. Each of these efforts is achievable; and some along these lines have already begun. All of these methods of achieving cost savings are predicated on the belief that the world of higher learning is multifaceted and requires different solutions for different types of institutions.

One concrete example of what might be possible will suffice. Born in 1935 in Woodburn, Kentucky, Harry B. Gray was always fascinated by the question of what produced differences in colors. As a youngster, he was drawn to chemistry—and much of the rest is history. A tall, lean, bespectacled man, Gray would become one of the world's leading chemists. His contributions to science are legendary—having worked at Columbia University and for many years at the California Institute of Technology—both in terms of his research discoveries and his mentoring of students who went on to highly distinguished careers. One of his most recent efforts speaks to the possibility of enlisting students of all ages in a massive, critically important and extremely complex scientific problem.

As George B. Kauffman, one of Gray's longtime colleagues and coauthors, puts it:

One of the great challenges of 21st-century chemistry is how to convert abundant energy-poor molecules to energy-rich molecules by using the power of the sun as the energy source. More energy from sunlight strikes the earth in one hour than all the energy consumed on the planet in one year! We need to replace fossil fuels with solar fuels as hydrogen from water or methanol from water and carbon dioxide. Solar fuels could be used around the clock.[29]

The chemistry to do this is extremely difficult. Multidisciplinary efforts are needed, and a huge amount of experimentation is required to find the right metal-oxide mixture catalysts to help turn sunlight and water into hydrogen. In contemplating this effort, Gray went back to the periodic table and realized that the number of combinations that would need to be tried was extraordinarily large. Loving students and lacking the people and resources to take on the task in his own laboratory, Gray formed his own solar army of students. There were at least two motives in Gray's overall strategy. First, he wanted to solve the problem, and to do so he needed many hands. Second, he sought to make chemistry fun for students of all ages and wanted them to become active participants in the very large project. Gray built the Solar Hydrogen Activity Research Kit (SHArK), funded by the NSF, that students could use to test "metal-oxide combinations that they could prepare in their own classrooms and laboratories for use with the solar fuel cell."[30] Today, SHArKs are used by students at more than eleven universities and by corporations such as Dow Chemical and 3M. But more interesting for us is that "the real foot soldiers in the war to power our planet are the more than 400 high school and college student volunteers across the United States and Germany."[31]

In a recent talk on the project at the American Philosophical Society, Gray spoke about the members of his army who are in middle schools—down to the eighth grade—and who work with mentors to examine many metal-oxide combinations. Their emails and other communications to Gray voice their incredible enthusiasm for being part of this grand project. Believing that the current teaching of science in most middle schools and high schools is dreadfully boring, Gray thinks that if we can get these young students engaged in real and meaningful projects, we can stimulate a much greater interest than previously in STEM subjects and begin to recruit a new generation of college and graduate students into these important fields.

This type of work could be done at the various laboratory schools created under the Morrill III Act and extended to other middle and high schools in the United States and abroad. In fact, as noted, Gray has students in Germany in his brigade, but surely students in other countries could also join his army. His reach is global because his work requires talented people wherever they may be found. For Gray, age and grade level do not matter. Enthusiasm and guided learning by doing, although potentially producing very promising results, can transform a daunting problem into a manageable one. At the same time, students are not limited by a strict curriculum for their particular grade level. If they have the interest, the will to do hard work, and the values to contribute to the solution of a truly important scientific problem, they can join Harry Gray's army, where there are no artificial borders to scientific research. There is no reason why Gray's approach could not be replicated for other problems of great complexity that need to enlist an "army of foot soldiers."

Advertisements for Ourselves

Every major industry in the United States tries to construct a message and bring it to the attention of the public as well as legislators and opinion leaders. We are bombarded with these advertisements in every media to which we are tethered. Even hospitals have begun to place advertisements in the media. One only has to examine the extremely effective ads that New York Presbyterian Hospital runs to witness what can be done. Universities seem willing to advertise themselves only when they are part of NCAA athletic programs or they are searching for students to fill places available in their schools. But the prestigious research universities rarely, if ever, toot their own horns. The public does not know how universities have changed their lives for the better or of the discoveries and technological breakthroughs that have been born at our great research universities. Nor have we explained in simple language what the *real* cost of attending a particular university or college is for students who enroll and their families. Universities must get over their pristine aversion to advertising their great accomplishments and the true cost of educating their students. We should no longer think that public messages about ourselves and what we do degrades our values or mission.

The goals are worthy: to publicize why students should not fear enrolling in universities that offer incredibly generous financial aid packages, or the value of earning a college degree, or the kind of experiences that students can have at a major research university or exceptional liberal arts college that will positively affect the rest of their lives. Leading advocates for research universities, such as the Association of American Universities, ought to spearhead a campaign to properly frame these messages so that they are proven to be effective. Famous graduates of these universities, including scientists, writers, artists, actors and actresses, filmmakers, and leading political figures, ought to be enlisted to speak briefly about their experiences.

I can imagine such a professionally run campaign, using someone like Berkeley's Professor of Cognitive Psychology George Lakoff, a master at framing, who would film present and former students drawn from both private and public universities—students from all types of backgrounds, each with different experiences and emphases in college. Perhaps with the familiar school songs softly playing in the background, we hear the students' compelling testimony. The content would not only include what some of these former students have achieved after college but also information of the following kind presented in their own words. For example, here is fifty-year-old Jennifer (already a world-renowned scientist) speaking:

> I received one of the best college educations in the world at [name of university]. My professors transformed the way I think about my country and the world and they produced my interest in X. What is even more amazing is that I spent four years at Y and did not pay a cent for tuition and fees. I graduated with a college debt of $10,000, which I've paid off at 1% interest over the years. But as a computer programmer working at Z when it was a young start-up company, I expect that my lifetime earnings will be greater than $1.5 million more than if I had not gone to college. After attending Berkeley for graduate school and Harvard after that, I started working on a cure for [a disease] and discovered a cure for it in 2015. You can't imagine my joy when we found a way to save thousands of lives.
>
> When I was growing up as a kid in L.A. in a family where no one had ever gone to college, I thought I would work in a factory for limited wages. All that changed with my college education. I love my country and feel that I can contribute better to it now. Besides, I continue to have a thirst for learning. I'm living the American Dream.

This campaign would not only focus on the value of a college education for all students, but it would also advertise the transformational discoveries made at these universities that have changed the lives of the people watching the ad.

Clearly there is no easy remedy to the quality-versus-affordability problem at American colleges and universities. But there are steps that ought to be taken that will attenuate the problem. First, universities must realize that they are, in fact, partly responsible for the problem—and that includes the most selective of the nation's schools. They have expanded their administrative staffs far too rapidly, in response to competition and to the pressures of various constituencies. That growth ought to stop and, in fact, be reversed. Fifty years ago, the teaching and research faculties of these great universities exceeded the number of administrators. That is no longer true. In addition, universities and colleges cannot be plush clubs catering to every growing pain that students and their parents identify. There are areas that needed real growth, such as attention to students' mental health, but much of the expansion has been excessive.

Second, the federal and state governments have placed undue burdens on universities, as a way of controlling their internal behavior, that also need to be reversed. As I'll discuss in Chapter 9, mandated federal regulations require funds to be used for some important and some useless control over university research and education—money that could otherwise be used to improve student education or to hold down increases in tuition. Moreover, changes in government policies that have greatly burdened research universities but represent unfunded mandates that have unintentionally increased college costs ought to be rolled back where the policies have simply not worked. For the past decade, the states have squeezed the colleges and universities by reducing dramatically their annual appropriations to their universities. The result has been a betrayal of the core mission of educating youngsters born and living in their state.

Some state legislators and governors argue that state appropriations for education have never been higher as a percentage of state budgets, but this overlooks the number of students that are being educated by the state schools and the desire by the state to point to the excellence of their universities. It also overlooks the enormous local economic returns to having great universities and colleges within a state. For example, the University of North Carolina demonstrated that in 2012–2013, the $9.0 billion "in payroll and operations spending of UNC universities and the affiliated medical institutions, together with their construction spending and the spending of their students, visitors, alumni, and start-up companies, created $27.9 billion in added state income."[32] We have already noted the huge economic returns demonstrated by universities in California and in Massachusetts. The same, I'm sure, would be the case in most states. In short, there is a price for excellence and access, but there are also huge returns. Some imaginative governors are beginning to propose various forms of taxation (other than increases in the marginal tax rates) to support education in an earmarked way.[33] This kind of creative thinking ought to be encouraged if increases in the marginal tax rate remain unpalatable to the state's population.

The private colleges and universities that are without large endowments to cover much of the cost of education through grant aid ought also to limit the growth of administrative costs, reduce the number of adjunct professors, and consider forms of collaboration with other similarly situated institutions in order to reduce costs. The most selective schools ought to examine the possibilities of extending education to those who cannot attend these great universities (through high-quality online education) and to consider expanding the size of their student bodies in order to allow a higher percentage of the very qualified students to take advantage of the education that they offer.

Finally, the need for a well-educated population—for access for both the poor and the middle class—and the need for these young people to complete their degrees are in the national interest. Therefore, the federal government ought to become directly or indirectly involved in financial aid (beyond Pell-type grants) that ensures that students with the ability can attend state colleges and universities. The key to the Morrill III Act that I propose here is that the federal government create incentives for the states to contribute to the cost of higher education. We know from the experiences of the large systems in New York and California that it is possible for students who attend the state (or city) universities to obtain degrees without paying almost any tuition. That is an excellent deal, given the economic and social returns from higher education over a lifetime. However, the federal government must not allow, under any circumstance, the states to substitute federal money for their own. Through a combination of mechanisms, the cost of higher education can be contained—even if that includes growth slightly above the rate of inflation.

CHAPTER SEVEN

Creating New Academic Leagues and Knowledge Communities

...blind skyscrapers use
Their full height to proclaim
The strength of Collective Man

—W. H. AUDEN

COMPETITION FOR TALENTED PROFESSORS AND STUDENTS has been a hallmark of American research universities since their inception in the latter part of the nineteenth century. Early leaders of our great universities competed for the best talent, and little has changed a hundred years later except that the competition has become even more fierce and costly in today's era of academic free agency. This contest has also produced intense loyalty to one's own university (although not necessarily among the "free agents") and a sense of individual university identity.

The competitive spirit was an important part of the process leading to our preeminence because it required large-scale investments in the infrastructure that was necessary to conduct cutting-edge research. Although new instruments and machinery were costly, they were, in part, what lured great professors to join new faculties in order to move their work along more rapidly. This was enhanced further if leaders of universities had the prescience to bring in groups of researchers who found great value in collaborating with each other. Two other factors linked to competition propelled the great universities forward: the quality of both the students who would be attracted to learning how to use the cutting-edge technologies, such as recombinant DNA, and the faculty members who led the laboratories; and the willingness of academic leaders to open up novel fields of inquiry that represented spin-offs from more traditional disciplines. The development of molecular biology, biochemistry, and biomechanical engineering are cases in point. These new fields led to an expansion of academic jobs in hot areas of science and technology, as well as in law, medicine, and other professional arenas.

The cost of a university education was affected by such competition, since the dollars required to bring in exceptional talent often far outpaced the national rate of inflation. If the standard for cost control is anything above the consumer price index, then great universities exceeded that number on a regular basis. However, if the return on these investments is measured by major discoveries—many of which have led to new industries and the proliferation of jobs related to those industries—the bang for the buck has been phenomenal. The presence of academic stars also influenced the types of students who chose to attend a specific university, and downstream this often paid off with substantial gifts.

The intense and ubiquitous competition of the twentieth century may turn out to be too much of a good thing for the twenty-first century. The growth of the research enterprise and the way we transmit knowledge have changed; and the need for still-more-extensive collaborations, both national and international, requires new structural relationships that may challenge the idea of institutional autonomy. Competition should not end, but a rebalancing ought to take place between competition and collaboration. Therefore, the distinguished research university of 2040 ought to look quite different from what we are familiar with today.

How ought this to be accomplished? We might begin by trying to think of any American industry in the past century that has not had numerous joint ventures as well as mergers and acquisitions. Almost all have consolidated in various ways. Those that have refused to consider change have often vanished—just take a look at the current versus the original companies that make up the Dow Jones Industrial Average.

Academic institutions, especially those that have been of high quality and are part of the older eastern group of esteemed universities, have not thought about combining their strengths in novel ways. There have been few mergers, for example, even de facto combinations. The university closures and mergers that have taken place almost invariably involved second- or third-tier institutions.[1]

When the Ivy League began to admit women in the late 1960s and early 1970s, there were discussions of mergers between prestigious women's colleges (a few of the so-called Seven Sisters) and Ivy League schools.[2] For example, there was talk of merging Vassar with Yale. Most of the great state universities

continued to expand their number of campuses as their needs to support growing populations of students increased and political pressure from geographic
constituencies called for the building of campuses in their districts. The idea
of merging campuses was not within their leaders' consciousness. Some joint
programs have emerged between universities, generally crafted by two business schools in different locations—including some in the United States and
other nations. I cannot, in fact, think of a single large-scale merger of any portion of two great universities in the past twenty-five years other than attempts
to merge university-affiliated or university-owned hospitals. Almost all of those
attempts have failed.

During the period of great expansion of research universities, academic leaders didn't need to consider alternative organizational structures to improve
the quality of their schools. Demand for higher education was increasing rapidly before World War II and after it with the G.I. Bill of Rights. Until the late
1960s and 1970s, science could still be done within relatively small, campus-
based laboratories. Big Science was beginning to affect the way science and engineering was done; but the cost of doing science had not yet exploded, and
the federal government was playing an increasing role in paying the bills. But the
social and economic conditions affecting both graduate and undergraduate
education, including the cost of running great universities, was changing, requiring these seats of learning to consider new alliances.

The leagues or associations that have grown up around America's best universities have been based almost entirely on athletics. Even the Ivy League had
its origins as a football league. Throughout the United States, athletic conferences like the Big 10, the Pac-12, the ACC, and the Big East, among many
others, compete with each other and share revenues from television and other
contractual arrangements while also competing with nonconference schools.
Perhaps not surprisingly, then, when I was provost at Columbia, the university's
board of trustees spent more time discussing athletics (which, at Columbia,
could hardly be considered a growth industry) than existing or proposed academic programs at the university.

The academic library is the one feature of academic organization at the distinguished universities that has flourished after partnerships have been
formed. Not only have some groups of universities merged their holdings in
state-of-the-art remote storage facilities (such as the one we created among Columbia, Princeton, and the New York Public Library), but cross-library bor-
rowing has also been highly successful over the past thirty years. The merging

of collections has allowed universities to reduce the number of serial titles that they subscribe to, which lowers costs without limiting access to the tens of thousands of journals to which these libraries have traditionally subscribed. The emergence of online archives, such as JSTOR, an academic archive of journals, books, and other primary sources, has made individual university subscriptions to many publications obsolete. But combining collections in remote storage facilities or subscribing to JSTOR is one thing; de facto mergers of academic programs are another. There have also been informal arrangements between and among institutions to share, for example, the teaching of "exotic" languages; and the faculty members in certain graduate departments at different universities teach students from another university.

In the next twenty-five or thirty years, we ought to shift our glance away from intercollegiate athletics associations to academic associations, de facto mergers, and new combinations. These would *not* be formal de jure mergers. We need to create "academic leagues" that will enhance the capabilities of great universities and, at least potentially, lower costs of education. If some universities want to form athletic academies, let them. But for those that aspire to greatness for the content of their ideas and the quality of the education offered, athletics should not be the basis of association.[3] The most fundamental principle in moving forward with this idea, which I'll describe momentarily, is that academic leagues must be built "strength on strength"; otherwise, they will never work. The units of merger can and should differ and will vary enormously across the great universities. They can be based on complex academic problems, such as sustainability, or on academic disciplines, or schools—and, on rare occasions, entire universities or liberal arts colleges within universities.

These academic leagues, or conferences, should, where possible, be international entities. There is no reason to restrict their architecture by national boundaries. In fact, the opposite ought to be true, but we should not create false alliances when we link great programs or departments in the United States with struggling or weak units either here or in China, India, Korea, Japan, or in European nations.

There are important administrative activities that need to become part of the movement toward academic league de facto mergers and partnerships. For example, there are a growing number of offices that specialize in identifying university discoveries that have commercial potential and for which the university would like to seek patent rights. Does every great university need to reinvent the wheel on how to do this properly? Isn't it possible that a single office of technology transfer can be developed that can be used by a league of great universities? Some combinations of this kind have already begun—for example, between the University of Pennsylvania and Arizona State. Other universities, such as Stanford, Berkeley, and Columbia, could emerge as the network node for partnerships in growing the returns to universities from their intellectual property.

Faculty members at the major universities have often been a step or two ahead of their academic leaders in moving toward new combinations and de facto mergers. In part, this is a result of the growth of "invisible colleges,"[4] networks of scientists around the world who communicate with each other, collaborate on scientific and technical papers, and meet informally at conferences to discuss their research efforts. Some of these networks have been institutionalized in formal arrangements, such as the Gordon Conferences, at which leading biologists come together to hear about the latest and most significant advances in the various biological sciences. If the invisible colleges are research centered, there have also been faculty efforts to produce quasi-mergers for teaching purposes. For example, the philosophy departments at universities in or near New York City are very strong. They have, in fact, competed with each other for talent for some time—with the university that turns out to be the winner gaining prestige, while the loser feels remorse and weaker. But what has been won or lost for the students in these programs if a professor moves from Columbia to NYU, or the reverse happens? There is no real gain for higher learning. The philosophers who work at these departments are aware of this and have taken it upon themselves to forge relationships that allow graduate students at Columbia to take courses for credit with NYU, Rutgers, or City University of New York professors of philosophy. They can also have these professors as mentors who participate in their doctoral dissertation defense. But there is, as far as I know, no formal arrangement for this kind of multi-university use of exceptional talent.[5]

There is apt to be faculty resistance to such attempts to construct new organizational configurations, as one example makes clear. While I was provost, I discussed with my counterpart at another Ivy League university a possible de facto merger of two of our institutions' strongest departments—both arguably among the top five in the nation. Each department had roughly sixty members. The professors represented a wide array of academic specialties. A joint venture, where each university admitted its own graduate students, determined its Ph.D. requirements, and offered its own degrees, would have created overnight the finest faculty and program in the world. At the time, the idea was limited to graduate students because they could potentially travel to take courses at the other institution, although that would not have been easy.

Today, new technology would open these intellectual resources up to both graduate and undergraduate students. Using live streaming technology or massive open online courses, graduate and undergraduate students at one institution could benefit from the knowledge obtained from a professor at the other university.[6] Ph.D. students would be permitted to take courses and work on their dissertations with any member of either department. Moreover, faculty members at one institution could (with prior arrangement) occasionally live and teach at the other university. For example, a Pulitzer Prize–winning professor and acclaimed teacher of undergraduates could teach a course on the Civil War and Reconstruction for students at the two universities. In this case, the unit of cooperation would be the departments. With an online platform developed specifically for history courses, any student whose university was part of "the history league" could take the course. The home university would administer examinations and confer grades and degrees, but the course would be offered (at least the lecture portion of it) by someone who might well be at another institution in the knowledge network. After consulting with participating faculty, each university would offer small, highly interactive seminars related to the larger questions raised by the lecturer. Professors would staff the seminar-type discussions and offer feedback to the lecturing professor that might be incorporated in later iterations of the course. In fact, it is now possible for students at the several participating universities to interact with each other in real time during the discussion sessions.

When I raised this idea with my fellow provost, he was intrigued and spoke to the president of his university, who suggested that it be brought to the department's faculty, who almost instantly turned the idea down. We did not pursue the reasons for this rejection. Perhaps it was because it was a "top-down proposal" or was perceived as a threat to the autonomy of the department and its future prerogatives, such as making faculty appointments. I have little doubt that the reception would have been similar at Columbia. There are several "laws" about academic life, one of which is a very strong "status quo" bias.[7] Nonetheless, in the future, regardless of initial faculty skepticism, de facto mergers and new combinations of programs ought to be part of the university landscape—part of the creation of academic leagues that share faculty and student talent and change the way we transmit and grow knowledge. Several additional examples should suffice to give an idea of what I have in mind.

Suppose that Columbia's distinguished economist and director of its Earth Institute, Professor Jeffrey Sachs, puts together a consortium of fifteen to twenty universities that are concerned with problems of sustainability. Only a few of these programs have a significant number of faculty members working on the issue; but many who do participate are of the first rank, come from different disciplinary backgrounds, and are doing important research on the multiple problems involved in attempting to address sustainability. Student interest at each of the universities is high. Sachs initiates an informal online consortium where experts lecture or hold seminars in their area of expertise for students at affiliated universities. Together, the faculty has produced a single course; and, in real time, students at each of these universities can sign up, take the course, and become certified as having mastered the course material through some form of examination. The lectures are also videotaped, stored, and can be referred to whenever students wish to access them when studying for exams. Within a short period of time, small faculties become larger and more knowledgeable; the potential for interaction across universities and continents materializes; students and faculty become conversant about contested facts and why there is no consensus on them; a development of a research and action agenda emerges out of the interaction; scholars from each of these universities become closer colleagues and potential collaborators; and students reinforce their interest in solving the problems posed in the seminar. No additional faculty members have to be hired at any of the universities except to replace those who retire and those who move to other settings—or to acquire faculty who offer a new kind of expertise. An informal agreement is carved out that allows students to take these courses and faculty members at the various locations to teach them. We have just created a de facto merger without any formal agreement.[8] Yet strong programs on sustainability become stronger, and strength is joined with strength. The program takes on an international flavor and begins to approach what can truly be called a global program.

Another type of de facto merger could involve academic departments. Suppose we decide to merge the departments of music at Harvard, Yale, UCLA, Indiana University, the University of Chicago, and Princeton—strong programs with somewhat differing traditions and strengths. Plainly, other universities could be considered in the same league and might be participants in the new group, although it is important to remember that the complexity in running these programs grows exponentially as we add members. But combinations of different sizes, in which various schools add different types of strength to the whole, ought to be tried. And if we add to the mix schools with units of music composition and conservatory type schools like Juilliard, the complexity becomes still greater; but so does the potential strength. In each of these cases, the individual universities would continue to use their own admissions and certification criteria and control the awarding of degrees. What opens up is the potential of students and faculty benefiting from the points of view of a large number of very smart people, including students, who are located in various parts of the globe. It should be possible for some liberal arts colleges to tap into these new combinations—extending what they can offer their students without expanding their size greatly, if at all. In fact, a small liberal arts college that may have only three or four faculty members could now benefit from perhaps more than a hundred members of the faculty. Highly selective liberal arts colleges that have very small but excellent departments would be particularly wise to try to create these kinds of mergers. For example, few of these places have many art historians, yet those who teach at a Swarthmore or Amherst may be excellent teachers and scholars. Why not join forces with Williams, Oberlin, and Bard, to name just a few, and create an "art history league"? This arrangement might enhance the quality of education, expand options for interested students, and prove particularly cost-effective for liberal arts colleges that do not have large endowments and where tuition and related costs are becoming problematic for applicants to the school.

If de facto mergers could take place in music departments, there is no reason why other departments in the humanities and social and behavioral sciences, as well as professional schools, could not pursue similar types of new combinations. The point of departure for thinking about these leagues could be the current athletic leagues that already exist. And research leagues should also be formed. The growth of new technology that will allow easy, high-quality reproduction of lectures and essentially movie-quality integration of voice and video (and easy use on social media) make the possibilities of offering courses for undergraduates almost as straightforward as for graduate students. These lectures would be seen on large-panel television or computer screens and would have a resolution that is far better than is currently available through technologies like Skype.[9] Large-scale lectures, and even smaller lectures, can be given by the teaching stars of the day. There ought to be no room for mediocre lecturers in these new leagues, although there might be two or three video-recorded lecturers offering the same course because they provide different points of view on the same subject. Students would view these lectures, which would, as noted, depart from the traditional standup lecturer with a lectern, using a chalkboard, a microphone, some PowerPoint slides, and little else.

Just a decade ago, I thought that academic research combinations and de facto mergers would be near impossible. In some fields, that is still true and will remain so for a period of time. And it may be quite a while before we can give up the casual interactions and serendipity that often come from being in the same physical space. But I've become increasingly bullish on the possibilities of research leagues as well as instructional leagues.

Some research de facto mergers, which are not referred to as such, are the result of the growth of knowledge itself. For example, the development of experimental high-energy particle physics now requires massive instruments to test theoretical ideas. The Large Hadron Collider in Switzerland, built by the European Organization for Nuclear Research (CERN), was constructed for this purpose. It took years to construct and test. Hundreds if not thousands of physicists and technicians from around the world went there in search of the Higgs Boson, for example, and CERN became their home away from home. Although each of these individuals was a member of a physics department at a university elsewhere, most of the work was done collaboratively (through groups) at the CERN location—or if they worked from home, the work was done remotely with colleagues from around the world.[10] In effect, an academic league naturally grew up from the needs of the scientists. The nature of international collaborations and their sharp rise over the past decade suggest clearly that these global networks or leagues already exist—in the minds and activities of faculty members as well as in the granting agencies. But even on a smaller scale, I see no reason why we ought not to create research leagues among various universities. Let me provide an example that began to convince me of the possibility for research leagues.

A few years ago, I was talking to a distinguished physicist about his work in building new molecules from individual atoms in the field of nanoscience (where scientists work with physical or biological structures that range from one to one hundred nanometers).[11] He worked on a computer screen that might as well have been a Hollywood backdrop. With the instrumentation in hand, he moved a single atom into a particular place in the molecule. This in itself seemed fascinating, but I was even more amazed when he fed me the kicker: "When I moved that single atom into place," he said, "I was at Columbia, but I was moving the atom into place in a Berkeley laboratory." That's when I realized that research leagues could be created from the informal arrangements that already existed.

These new academic leagues should come in a wide variety of forms. The networks will vary from simple partnerships between two universities to complex collaborations, teaching mechanisms, and interrelationships. We ought to codify what is already beginning to happen because of the way knowledge is now growing. We ought to be thinking about optimal-size networks of associations and what the structural features of those associations should be. These leagues provide real opportunities for scholars, scientists, and engineers to join forces in more efficient ways than in the past. In fact, within a limited range, these academic leagues could include a number of top industrial laboratories, such as the former Bell Laboratories, or labs where there is great latitude to pursue basic research questions that are not tied directly to immediate economic results.

There is one other potential feature of de facto mergers that ought to hold great potential. In addition to creating academic leagues, top universities ought to be devising novel ways of learning that extend beyond the university itself to form alliances that can be called knowledge communities—a form of academic village. These knowledge communities would include a set of great universities, as well as participating art and science museums, film forums, and excellent libraries. Although students could use the "campuses" of the participants of these communities, most of the materials would be presented online and would occupy a specific space on the Internet devoted to high-level, certified knowledge and to open, and yet unanswered, questions. The new campuses ought to reimagine and reconstruct the boundary between the campus and the community by using the entrance level of the campus to bring people in rather than to exclude them. The university becomes, in a sense, a museum for the interested public.

Like the San Francisco Exploratorium,[12] these new urban campuses ought to provide iterative, animated, and visual media that represent learning centers. They might focus on some of the research that is being conducted at the universities in the floors above the ground level; and they might offer access to campus exhibits and to film libraries. These communities could include institutions in a single city or combine massive learning opportunities provided by the vast array of cultural institutions within a city. If, for example, Columbia were to join forces with other universities in New York and Oxford, Cambridge, and Imperial College London, to name just a few, while including museums such as the Metropolitan Museum of Art, the Museum of Modern Art, the British Museum, the Tate and Tate Modern, the Barnes Collection, the Getty Museum, the Guggenheim Museum, the New York Public Library, and the Victoria and Albert Museum (all of which have their own educational programs), the potential online offerings to the attentive public and to students and faculty at each of these institutions would be beyond qualitative measure. (And think of the kind of "quasi-endowments" that would be created.) If this consortium of institutions were to create online courses using each institution's resources as well as technology to bring these materials to interested people in a speedy way, then the caliber of the universities and the other institutions could be enhanced greatly. Finally, the combinations could increase the level of social cohesion among the people working at the various institutions. If staff members at the museums or major libraries could take courses at the university, for example, and scholars and students could use the museums' facilities for free, the social fabric of the city's cultural institutions would be enhanced.[13]

One open question is: Would there be exchanges in payments among members of these leagues and knowledge communities? As part of the Passport to New York initiative that I constructed, the leaders of the other cultural institutions agreed to take an inventory of use for two or three years. If no strong imbalance in usage obtained, we would allow free traffic among all members of the consortium. It turned out that there was no imbalance of any significance; and to this day, I don't believe that funds change hands among members of the group. The same operating tallies could be done with academic leagues. If there is a strong imbalance in the "attendance" in the courses of one university compared to another, arrangements for a balance of payments could be made between pairs of schools.

These new academic leagues will pose a host of significant organizational and leadership challenges that we should be able to address successfully. In fact, new governance structures may well need to be formed. For example, some professors are fabulous in lecture-type settings; others are far better with smaller groups and seminars. But the choice of what to teach, which is now to a significant degree left up to faculty members, will have to yield to a principle of maximizing the use of the teaching talents of the professors and may need to involve faculty committees and administrators.[14]

Will de facto mergers, which imply greater cooperation and less direct competition, have an adverse affect on the level of excellence of the overall system of American higher learning? I imagine that the opposite would be true. Quality would be improved by extending the number and caliber of options open to students and faculty. Competition for resources and superior faculty will still exist in many areas. However, competition may shift from individual schools to de facto leagues or knowledge communities. Furthermore, since so many different forms of de facto mergers ought to take place among universities, the leagues that will be formed will be based on differing goals. Units may be designed, for example, to enlarge the number of great programs in studies of the environment, economic development, history, or parts of the geological sciences or physics. These are some of the natural ways that globalization is and ought to take place in the academic community.[15]

These various forms of academic leagues would present enormous opportunities to extend the reach of universities, enabling them to become more powerful entities in furthering some of their research and teaching agenda. They offer the potential of increasing the quality of teaching and possibly of lowering the cost of higher learning, since the leagues will allow universities to find an alternative to "the infinite growth" model that has dominated the psychology of great university faculty and their leaders over the past generation. In principle, great universities could set up de facto mergers of many academic teaching and research programs, and there ought not to be any intrinsic limit on the types and numbers of such arrangements—as long as they are predicated on the already mentioned principle of merging strength with existing strength, at home or abroad.

The idea of academic leagues is based, in part, on the view that collective intelligence is more apt to solve difficult problems (both fundamental and practical ones) more rapidly than relying on the work of an individual or several individuals, especially if they have similar types of intelligence. Whether it comes under the name of crowd sourcing or the power of diversity in decision-making, there is a growing literature that suggests that certain combinations of intelligences and personality traits (often in large numbers) lead to solutions to problems more rapidly and more efficiently than do individuals working alone or together with people who are very much like themselves. It is a bit like placing people representing multiple intelligences in a room and asking them to solve a problem compared to placing in that same room a group of people with high IQs or the same kind of intelligence. Academic leagues and knowledge communities allow for a greater level of diversity brought to bear on thorny problems.[16] This is part of the logic behind the d.school at Stanford.

Academic leagues or knowledge communities should open up the potential of using online digital technologies to reach millions of people around the globe who have little hope of attending places like Cambridge University or Harvard—people like Jima Ngei, whose experiences I described in Chapter 6. The knowledge communities will transmit ideas that are being worked on in laboratories and libraries and at museums and art galleries. In principle, these quasi-mergers ought to lead to the production of courses with high-quality content that can be used by people anywhere who have access to high-speed Internet providers and the computer capacity to handle the content.[17] If we add to the university's stock of knowledge the cultural materials available at institutions outside of the university that are in these knowledge communities, then people can continue their education throughout their lives.

The creation of a new balance between cooperative and competitive strategies in higher learning ought to make our teaching and research programs still stronger and ought to produce higher probabilities that major discoveries and innovations will be made by our research universities. Although it remains to be seen whether such new alliances would result in reduced costs to higher education, that is not the primary purpose of creating academic leagues and knowledge communities. What is gained and what is lost by forming these new combinations? In such configurations, which leave some of our "old school" identities behind in order to create better and more innovative structures for discovery and learning, the goal is to improve the quality of the work produced by students and faculty members at our research universities—and to combine those talents with those that exist at major cultural institutions. This will not be easily accomplished—especially with alumni with great attachment to their individual school—but it is where we ought to be heading under some bold and persuasive leadership.

CHAPTER EIGHT

Reimagining the University Campus

The American campus is a world in itself, a temporary paradise, a gracious
stage of life.

—LE CORBUSIER

RY TO IMAGINE AN IDEAL UNIVERSITY CAMPUS that meets the
nation's needs for the transmission and creation of new knowledge in
the twenty-first century. Would it look similar to the campuses of
today?[1] What are some of the features of a campus that would signal to faculty,
students, and guests that they are surrounded by a college or university and
are in the company of women and men studying and discovering? How do the
problems of building new campuses differ in cities as compared to rural areas?
What do we do with "old" campuses that are, in effect, relics, or have been
viewed by some as "ruins"? Most students of higher learning have not thought
much about these questions, yet the physicality of the campus has a great deal
to do with fulfilling a university's missions.

Almost nothing has been written about the American campus except for a
few books and publications by architects discussing the campus buildings that
they have produced.[2] The term "campus" itself, first used in reference to Princeton University, originally referred to a "green," which morphed over centuries
into the open space between or around the buildings of a college or university
and including the buildings themselves. Far more has been written about urbanism and the place of universities in redevelopment projects and on their impact on the city and surrounding communities.

When reflecting on the quintessential college or university campus, we may
think of some of their prominent features: for example, the magnificent quadrangles of the Oxford and Cambridge colleges; the church or cathedral at the

center of a campus; or the physical landmarks modeled after Rome's domes, such as the golden dome at Notre Dame. Limiting our gaze to America's great universities, we may think of Thomas Jefferson's extraordinary 1817 architectural plan for the University of Virginia—and the continuing effort to be faithful to his idea of an academical village. Then there are the prototypical architectural features of campuses like Harvard or Yale, with their residential houses and college system with their internal quadrangles—cloistered by our standards, but more open to the public than the Oxbridge schools that essentially created barriers to public access to college spaces—resulting in a true town-gown divide. Centuries ago, it was the provost who was empowered to keep the boys in and the villagers out of the Oxford and Cambridge colleges.

There are urban and rural or suburban campuses. Perhaps the quintessential urban design for a major research university campus was McKim, Mead, and White's late nineteenth-century Beaux-Arts master plan for Columbia University. Princeton, Cornell, Stanford, Wisconsin, and Berkeley all have distinct campus styles, but they have in common a plan and feel that differs significantly from those of urban campuses. Walking through these tree-lined sites with their large open spaces surrounded by relatively low horizontal buildings, we can image how Jefferson's academical village is indeed conceptualized as a self-contained community. Although there are many important similarities among all of these institutions, the newer, rural universities are, of course, far more bucolic and open, often spectacularly beautiful in their use of land and the physicality of their academic buildings. Visitors to these campuses have an immediate sense of what the academic culture is apt to be like.[3]

Although the American college system had its origins in the physical structures created in England, our universities departed dramatically from the earlier model in several ways.[4] For one, the British universities clustered colleges together, even if they had independent governance. And, of course, they had varying levels of prestige and wealth associated with them. American universities and colleges separated themselves—so we don't have, for example, Harvard and MIT on a single campus—and they tended to seek out locations removed from central metropolitan areas. In both the United States and Britain, universities and colleges were fundamentally horizontal structures that mixed the housing of students (which had its own evolution) at the college alongside that of the resident professors who also lived within the quadrangles. In Europe, especially in France and Germany, the university was embedded more directly in city life.

These traditional campus designs had their origins when universities were small entities that focused almost exclusively on undergraduate education. The expansion of campuses toward the end of the nineteenth and early twentieth century began to take into account the growth of research and graduate faculties—led by the rise of specific disciplines, such as physics, chemistry, engineering, and medicine, as well as traditional humanities departments and a growing number of social and behavioral science disciplines. In fact, most modern research universities expand their footprint by about one million square feet per decade—and some more than that.[5]

If the concept of a university changed with the emergence of the research university, it was not accompanied by any effort to redefine the fundamental physical structures and configurations that had existed during the time when these universities were essentially small colleges. Additional campus space was needed; universities expanded exponentially; dormitories and libraries were built; and laboratory buildings were constructed for individual disciplinary study. There was a physics building, a philosophy building, and so on. Each tended to have carved in granite or stone the discipline housed in the building, such as "Mathematics" or "Philosophy Hall." These were the silos that were being built to dig deeply into specific subjects.

This campus design reinforced the idea, put forth succinctly by Clark Kerr, the chancellor of the University of California, Berkeley, of the modern research university as a "multiversity," a loosely held together organism where the independent parts were more than the whole. As brilliant as Kerr's analysis was in 1963, it is now, I believe, largely obsolete. The great transformation that ought to take place will in fact replace the multiversity with a set of structures that are far more integrated and that suggest enormous linkages between and among disciplines.

The physical structures that define both the exterior overall campus plan and the interior design of the spaces are reflective of the larger value system in the country and the way in which higher education is viewed. It is hardly surprising, therefore, that in the archetypical campus, the cathedral or the site of religious worship and lectures was the dominant structure. With the development of the research university, at least in its early phases, the monumental library became the symbol of learning and the focal point of many campuses. If one was too dense to recognize that the large building was a repository of great books, the architects and educational leaders made it obvious by carving into the granite façade the names of the great Greek and Roman philosophers, poets, playwrights, and scientists. A rather crude demonstration of this method of identification can be seen in Columbia's Butler Library, which was constructed in the early 1930s.

As the idea of the university evolved into a place for science and technology as well as the humanities, even the historic libraries became less of the focal point of the campus design. And, as we entered the digital age, the need for vast storage facilities was no longer essential in many fields. The materials could be found online and downloaded to individual computers as needed. American research universities created an extraordinary value system that guided their development for more than seventy-five years. The value system that will dominate the campus architecture of 2040 should continue to place a heavy emphasis on that which has served us so well for the past one hundred years; and that is the subject of Chapter 9.

Science, engineering, and medical centers may well be the focal points of the new campus, since so much emphasis is being placed on excellence in these particular academic areas within the broader society. But there ought to be physical changes as well that elaborate on this narrower vision of the university and include prominent places for the arts, humanities, and professional schools unrelated to science and technology. The model to be designed, which would include these nonscience forms of knowledge, should betray the observation by Kerr of his multiversity. But today there are intellectual and social mechanisms that can be used to bring together these multiple cultures through physical space. For example, buildings housing humanists, outside of their cloistered departments, can bring them together with scientists to work on major problems, from neuroscience and art to ethical and moral problems related to new forms of biological and physical science discoveries. There will be a growing need for humanists to deal with similar questions posed because of dramatic advances in engineering and technology. Surely, the curriculum of undergraduates and graduate students should reflect this closer association.

The rise to preeminence of America's great universities took place within separate structures. They were low, horizontal buildings—regardless of the amount of space that a university had access to. Buildings representing a cluster in the humanities, or the sciences, were often placed in proximity to one another; but they were unconnected physically (except perhaps by underground tunnels), and the people working in these structures rarely interacted. An ideology developed that suggested that campuses could realize their objectives of community only in lower, horizontal buildings. In fact, there were a few studies by social scientists that suggested that individuals, whether they were faculty or students, were willing to walk considerable distances on a horizontal plane but would not be willing to climb a flight of stairs to visit a colleague. As of 2015, the tallest academic building in the United States, indeed in the Western Hemisphere, is the Cathedral of Learning, which has forty-two floors and was built at the University of Pittsburgh during the Great Depression.[6] The idea of the horizontal campus worked for generations. But it also became so axiomatic that it has rarely been questioned seriously over the last fifty years, when it is arguable that imaginative physical structures and a new organization of the internal campus community is required—especially in densely populated cities, found not only in the United States but in places like China, Japan, Brazil, and Mexico, among other nations.

Can we begin to conceive of academic corridors in cities like New York, which might run from Columbia's Medical School campus at 168th Street and Broadway alongside Riverside Park down to 105th Street, where the buildings for the Morningside Heights campus now end? Linked with the corridor would be the academic buildings of other collaborating universities, such as City College, which is part of the City University of New York. Can we envision a superuniversity corridor that combines campus buildings for instruction and research with residence halls for students, housing for faculty, university-linked public schools, and childcare and daycare centers for both university and community children? Can we foresee fifty- or sixty-story buildings that are occupied by researchers or by residents of this new academical village? Can these physical structures be linked to the larger city and the parks and the Hudson River directly to the west of the corridor?

These academic corridors may already be evolving. But can we guide that evolution in a way that makes for the wisest outcomes in terms of the growth of knowledge and discovery and the education of a broader public? All of this is anchored by the existing, but to be upgraded, New York subway system that rapidly moves students and faculty from one place to another—if the digital world doesn't make that unnecessary. And why should we necessarily stop at 105th Street? If New York has a financial district, why not an academic superuniversity district—designed to meet educational needs but also that fits neatly into what Rem Koolhaas, the visionary architect and theoretician, has called "delirious New York"?[7]

In the days of Small Science, it was possible to conceive of fitting laboratories into traditional buildings—ones that had far less space than do the modern laboratory buildings of today. For universities to remain great in the twenty-first century, we must rethink the American university campus. Since the reimagination of the campus is an increasingly salient issue for those that are located in cities, I shall concentrate here foremost on the urban campus.

Ironically, most other nations that are building hundreds of new universities are looking at the great American universities of the last one hundred years as their prototypical design model for creating world-class universities. Instead of thinking about what is required for research and teaching in the twenty-first century, these nations are looking backward to an older model that is significantly outdated, if not moribund and fettered. They are looking at the growth of knowledge and its transmission in the twentieth rather than the twenty-first century.

So what should the physicality of the twenty-first century university campus look like—both in terms of its overall design and its internal structures? For many universities that own hundreds of years' worth of unencumbered space, the nature of the overall campus design need not take on a fundamentally different character—although I shall argue that the internal design and organization, as well as the way of thinking about space, ought to be changed. But for those universities with a paucity of space, especially those located in large, densely populated cities, where verticality is as much the norm as horizontal forms (places like Manhattan), a fundamental shift ought to take place in how we conceptualize the campus community and the internal dynamics among its various components. Many campus structures also have historically had a monumental character, expressing certain values by the very size and type of buildings that were, in fact, built.[8] In some cases, universities maintained over decades an integrity to a beautifully thought out larger campus plan. But all too often, the physicality of the university was eclectic and represented architecture that was notable by its poor design features, which betrayed any sense of a concept of what the university was trying to do, its paramount and evolving values, or how built space could be adjusted for alternative uses as the nature of knowledge and the intellectual problems being addressed changed over time.

The Physicality of the New Urban Campus

For decades knowledge grew within disciplines, but that intellectual isolation is a thing of the past. Nonetheless, we have not been guided sufficiently by the speed and the manner in which knowledge is growing or by how it is being used. Let's consider a new campus where knowledge reinforces this pattern of growth rather than inhibits it, where the focus is less on what occurs in a single discipline and more on the type of problem solving that involves collaborators from various disciplines, some located on different campuses. There are now multiple research programs at various great universities that focus on research and teaching about sustainability, from issues of economic development to water resources.

The experts that are involved in these programs are drawn from all over the university. How, then, must we organize them? We need disciplinary spaces that are near each other and reflective of their closeness in the network of scientific and technical knowledge growth or of the overlap of interest among disciplines. Universities should rethink decentralized budget structures that inhibit the development of knowledge without borders. On most of our campuses today, no such structures exist.

Consider Figures 2 and 3, where the proximity of the scientific fields named represent the interconnected network structure of the work in the various disciplines. This arrangement is based on an algorithm that uses co-citations to articles produced in different disciplines to establish the density of the linkages between disciplines as well as the distance between the disciplines.

Note, for example, the thickness of the lines between molecular and cell biology and medicine and neuroscience as well as the smaller connection and linkages between newer fields like medical imaging and orthopedics and the larger fields. We should recognize the substantive scientific and technical problems that are generating these relationships and follow the growth of the knowledge by creating physical structures that enable people in these disciplines to interact with ease.

Several American universities have built such physical structures, such as the Bio-X Center at Stanford University, designed by Foster and Partners in collaboration with MBT Architecture. The goal of Bio-X is stated simply on its website: "The Mission . . . is to catalyze discovery by crossing the boundaries between disciplines, to bring interdisciplinary solutions and to create new knowledge of biological systems, in benefit of human health."

Scholars, scientists, and engineers flow in and out of the structure depending on their participation in the research being carried out at the moment. They don't "own" the laboratories or the offices in which they work. In traditional academic buildings, there are few public spaces. Corridors are lined with rows

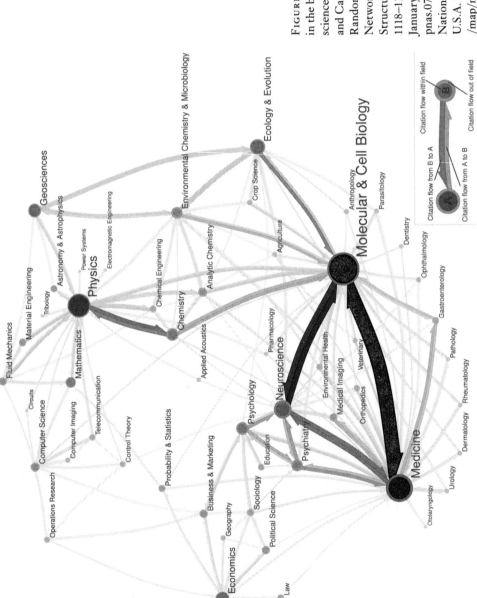

FIGURE 2. Knowledge networks in the biological and biomedical sciences. *Source:* Martin Rosvall and Carl T. Bergstrom, "Maps of Random Walks on Complex Networks Reveal Community Structure," *PNAS* 105, no. 4 (2008): 1118–1123; published ahead of print January 23, 2008, doi:10.1073/pnas.0706851105. Copyright 2008 National Academy of Sciences, U.S.A. http://www.eigenfactor.org /map/maps.php.

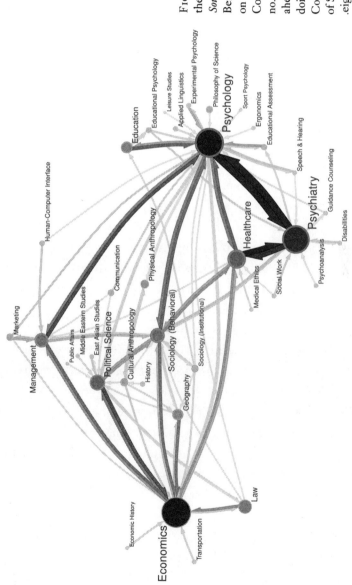

FIGURE 3. Knowledge networks for the social and behavioral sciences. *Source*: Martin Rosvall and Carl T. Bergstrom, "Maps of Random Walks on Complex Networks Reveal Community Structure," *PNAS* 105, no. 4 (2008): 1118–1123; published ahead of print January 23, 2008, doi:10.1073/pnas.0706851105. Copyright 2008 National Academy of Sciences, U.S.A. http://www .eigenfactor.org/map/maps.php.

of offices with often-closed doors that don't invite interaction. Laboratories allow for interaction among its members but are not designed to foster chance encounters that could lead to conversation and new ideas. The structure of Bio-X-type buildings, on the other hand, tends not to be monumental and is designed to be flexible enough to be reconfigured as needed. The shared technological facilities encourage efficient use of scientific equipment and offer the ability to link laboratories with others working anywhere in the world, while also permitting easy interaction—almost inevitable interaction—among those working in the physical space itself. Bio-X also produces educational events for those who participate in the Center and for the general public to discuss "social and ethical issues connected with scientific advances."[9] This signals Stanford's interest in reaching out to the local community—at least to those who are interested in the issues addressed by scientists at the Center.

Two other institutions have similar underpinnings to those of Bio-X. One is the renowned MIT Media Lab (the Lab), which offers space to master's and Ph.D. students along with faculty from a host of disciplines. The building in which the Lab is housed was designed by I. M. Pei and is known simply as the E-15 building. The media lab places a premium on "blue sky" research; the goal is to focus on "technologies that promise to fundamentally transform our most basic notions of human capabilities." The mix of people working in the Lab is also prescient, since it emphasizes bringing together people with very different skill sets and backgrounds. The Lab is "unconstrained by traditional disciplines, Lab designers, engineers, artists, and scientists work atelier-style, conducting more than 350 projects that range from neuroengineering, to how children learn, to developing the city car of the future." Frank Moss was the director of the Media Lab when the Tokyo-based architectural firm Maki and Associates designed a building that was integrated with the original Wiesner Building (E-15), by Pei (producing 163,000 square feet of laboratory, office, and meeting space). Moss described the space in these terms: "An essential ingredient in the lab's distinctive approach to 'open innovation' has been its exploitation of open physical spaces.... The abundance of such spaces in the new building will be a perfect setting for expanding our research agenda into exciting new realms such as robots that learn from people, and bionics, for taking ideas beyond the demonstration stage to working prototypes, and finally for strengthening our ties with corporate sponsors."[10] Reminiscent of John Dewey's progressive educational philosophy, MIT's Media Lab's researchers foster a culture of play and experiential learning.

The other establishment with underpinnings similar to those of Bio-X is the experimental Biodesign Institute at Arizona State University. This institute focuses on solving practical problems related to biology and medicine through the integration of researchers from many disciplines at the university and the recruitment of faculty members who are attracted to the open, interdisciplinary approach fostered there. The site design consists of four interconnected buildings totaling almost 800,000 square feet of laboratories, offices, and common spaces. Only two of the buildings have been constructed thus far; and they house more than 600 faculty, staff, and students in eleven research centers, including Bioelectronics and Biosensors, Evolutionary Medicine and Informatics, and Single Molecule Biophysics.

These ASU buildings, designed for the desert climate in which they are located, are distinctly nonmonumental although built to the highest "green standards" possible today. ASU's president, Michael Crow, has a pragmatic approach to these structures. He believes that if knowledge grows in unexpected ways that make these facilities obsolete in thirty or forty years, they would be reconfigured, if possible, or torn down and replaced by buildings that facilitate the solution of problems of that day. Crow is on to something here; our focus needs to shift from creating those monumental buildings to those that are more versatile and designed to meet specific needs in the growth of knowledge while still being architecturally innovative and beautifully designed. Moreover, all structures on American campuses should be built to the highest possible "green" standards; and state and the federal government ought to provide incentives for these environmentally friendly buildings.

Although the above examples point the way to how research ought to be physically organized in the future, there are, of course, antecedent practices that are suggestive of what changes we might wish to see on campus. For example, the Rockefeller University has never been organized by disciplinary physical structures. Rather, the laboratory associated with particular researchers is the fundamental physical and intellectual unit of analysis. A small but exquisite place, Rockefeller has produced, pound for pound, as many Nobel Prize winners as any university—yet because of its size and level of specialization, it is not apt to be found among the top ten research universities in the standard assessments that have become commonplace. It only demonstrates how those evaluations are flawed in this one way.

In England, there is also substantial interest today in architecture for multidisciplinary research. The Francis Crick Institute[11] being constructed in London will be organized much like the Rockefeller University, as 120 groups of researchers, each with its own research agenda. The Institute will partner—in effect, will become part of a de facto academic league—with researchers at University College London, Imperial College London, and King's College London, as well as the Wellcome Trust Sanger Institute (which is becoming analogous to the Howard Hughes Foundation, which supports great young talent in the biological sciences). As a 2013 editorial in *Science* magazine put it: "Architecturally, the institute has been designed to resemble a chromosome, with four arms meeting at a 'centromere' that facilitates informal encounters and exchanges. The largely open-plan laboratories will juxtapose groups with different interests and encourage their mixing.... Rather than traditional departments, Crick investigators will self-organize into interest groups focused around research questions or technical approaches. Researchers will be free to join as many or as few of these as they wish, and the groups will come and go as science develops."[12] Of course, these scientists, with their multi-interest portfolios, have been extremely well trained in their disciplinary area. The physical structure designed for the Crick Institute is built on disciplinary excellence and the belief that complex scientific and social problems need physical spaces that will allow multidisciplinary collaborations. Designs of the kind described here ought to give us clues about how to organize research over the next twenty-five or thirty years.

Finally, Columbia University's new Mind Brain Behavior Initiative, designed by Renzo Piano, will bring together a group of scientists about as large as those who populate the entire Rockefeller University. Lee Bollinger, Columbia's president, said of the new structure: "The Mind Brain Behavior Initiative has two functions. It's the initiative in the Greene Building in Manhattanville, and it's the link for the work there to every other part of the University."[13] And the co-director of the Initiative, the Professor Thomas Jessell, described the architectural goal this way: "Renzo and his architects have thought very hard about how you populate that building with a thousand scientists and maintain interactions that range from a small, impromptu group of three or four people who want to discuss an idea all the way through more formal presentations that attract 150 to 200."[14] Perhaps of equal interest is the attempt by Piano to link the new campus site with the city surrounding it. He said: "The great challenge is to make the various requirements coexist without renouncing dialog between public and private space."[15]

When reimagining the campus that has limited expansion space available, we must avoid the temptation to build structures for which we can at the moment obtain significant funding rather than considering what structures are needed or where they should be sited on campus. There is an understandable impulse for academic leaders to be opportunistic—to take the money and run. But this often leads to the juxtaposition of enterprises that don't need interaction with each other. Putting great amounts of capital into these diverse structures without an overall strategic plan can lead to the creation of empty castles: investments in infrastructure and neglect of the people who will actually occupy the buildings. We ought to construct a "knowledge-determined campus" with enough flexibility so that it can be altered as knowledge relationships inevitably change over relatively short periods.

The Academic Skyscraper and a Hybrid Campus Design

I want to challenge the view that campuses must be horizontal physical structures and propose that, depending on their function, campus designs in the future ought to mix both vertical and horizontal structures. These conditions are, of course, most likely to occur in highly populated urban environments where other large structures already exist. Consider, as an example, the expansion of the Columbia University campus that is currently taking place in upper Manhattan. For years, Columbia had acquired small commercial buildings and larger sparsely or unused factory structures in a seventeen-acre area north of 125th Street that moves up to 131st Street from Broadway toward the Hudson River. There were virtually no people living in the area and relatively few working there. Columbia's Morningside Heights campus is quite spectacular for an urban setting and largely consistent with the original master plan created by McKim more than a century ago. The buildings, which were constructed over time, between 114th Street between Broadway and Amsterdam Avenues move north to 120th Street, where Columbia's Teachers College begins. The tallest research and teaching structure is the thirteen-story physics building, Pupin Hall, in which a dozen Nobel Prize–winning scientific discoveries were made. Most of the buildings are typically five or six floors in height. One residence hall is somewhat taller, as is a more modern fifteen-story building (which was not part of the original McKim plan) that is located on the east side of Amsterdam Avenue, housing the School of International and Public Affairs and a few social science departments.

Those structures, many quite striking, were built according to the original plan in the most quintessential vertical city in America. And for a long time, the campus had adequate space. But by the 1970s, physical constraints had led Columbia to serious competitive disadvantages when trying to recruit distinguished faculty and graduate students. It seems striking that on the new seventeen-acre Manhattanville campus Columbia would not entertain seriously building structures that would be perhaps fifty or sixty stories in height. Had Columbia chosen to go for broke (since obtaining zoning changes would have been difficult but not impossible) and decided to create a new vertical campus with multiple interdisciplinary structures, such as Bio-X, it could have constructed buildings with some of the most spectacular views of the Hudson River imaginable, while creating more square footage for research, teaching, and public activities.

The idea of building an academic skyscraper in a city like New York almost always elicits skepticism among academics. One initial question is: "How would we know that this is an academic building rather than commercial real estate housing tenants, as in any other skyscraper?" This would be an easy fix. Research universities ought to create markers or symbols, perhaps not as obvious as planting the names of Plato and others on a frieze of the building, that indicate one is entering a structure dedicated to a certain set of values and goals.

Other initial questions are "Wouldn't it be impossible to form a sense of community in a building of that size?" and "How would you move traffic around in such large vertical spaces?" These are legitimate concerns, but a creative architect should be able to devise a remarkable academic structure on a large vertical scale. In fact, we could learn a good deal about what is possible by examining what has been achieved in commercial buildings in major cities as well as in the laboratories that were created at places like Bell Labs or at the Watson Labs at IBM, which were designed by Eero Saarinen, as well as by considering new forms of exterior designs, use of materials, and even explicit references to those who beyond the Greek and Romans were notable for the discoveries that they made at research universities.[16]

The older parts of the campus would continue to be horizontally oriented, of course. But some of the newer buildings—connected conceptually to the large research towers—could also have lower-rising buildings used for special purposes, such as seminar rooms and studio spaces. This could alleviate the problems caused by the movement of large numbers of people via elevators or escalators in short periods of time. In keeping with my earlier proposition, an exceptional secondary school, possibly horizontally shaped, could be located on the campus adjacent to the much taller academic and research buildings. Perhaps much of the undergraduate instruction would continue to be done within the older quadrangular forms and buildings that we have come to associate with the university campus. Newer research buildings, perhaps in combination with residences on the upper floors, would be built with a vertical framework in mind. The academic skyscraper has the advantage, as well, of being able to relocate transdisciplinary groups working on the same set of problems to the same or nearby floors—reducing the need for faculty members to march across campus to obtain advice from a colleague in a different discipline.[17]

The challenge is to overcome the belief that tall vertical structures are impersonal and lack a sense of community.[18] Two techniques that are typically used to foster interaction are the creation of multiple eating locations on different floors (where people eat, they talk) or the design of open spaces that allow for casual, and often unanticipated, interactions. A visit to the Bloomberg building in New York City reinforces the idea that through clever planning, productive interactions can take place in vertical spaces. The flow of faculty, students, and staff presents a major but surmountable challenge. If a campus complex involves traveling distances that cannot easily be traversed by walking, architects should create ways to move people from one campus to another. And campuses should not separate undergraduate from more advanced education. We know, for example, that one of the most meaningful experiences an undergraduate can have is to work on a research project of one of his or her professors. On the new reimagined campus, opportunities for undergraduate research in major laboratories should not be limited by a design that places strong barriers between teaching and research activities.

I've referred to the Bloomberg building because it tries to maximize a strong current value—community and serendipitous discovery through chance conversations. But other examples exist, such as the Seattle Public Library designed by Rem Koolhaas and Joshua Prince-Ramus of OMA, which combines a variety of dimensions of community, openness, and modern technology in a moderately sized building. Koolhaas explained his intention in constructing the library:

Basically the Books Spiral was kind of for us an architectural way of undoing some of the sadness of the typical library, where it kind of really divided in a number of compartments that have very dull-sounding names like "humanity," "sciences," blah, blah, blah . . . we felt that one of the points of a library was that there are accidents and that you find yourself in areas where

you didn't expect to be and where you kind of look at books that are not necessarily the books that you're aiming for. So it was to create a kind of almost
arbitrariness—or to create a kind of walking experience, an almost kind of
urban walk.[19]

This kind of thinking, mediated by knowledgeable academics along with a
novel set of materials, may well be appropriate for new urban campuses. One
should not minimize the role of materials in eliciting the imagery conjured
up by the built structures. If ivy-covered brick buildings signified academic
structures for generations, other materials may be one way for us to construct
a novel sense of what it is to be on a campus.

The Seattle Public Library is not a tall building, but there are examples
where horizontal and vertical buildings coexist as part of a new campus design. Take, for example, the relationship between the academic and living spaces
built by the Juilliard School of Music, which combines relatively horizontal
structures with a strong tower that overlooks Lincoln Center. In these buildings, one finds classrooms, libraries, performance spaces, residence facilities,
places to dine, and public theaters. If strong vertical towers are built on new
urban campuses, one could imagine research towers, residential towers merged
with shorter buildings that could be used for multidisciplinary research and
instruction, physical spaces that house faculty offices and contain new media
studios, and modern, flexible classroom facilities as well as theaters and public
spaces.

Perhaps the most notable recent attempt to build a vertical structure to house
academic activities is the Kohn, Peterson, and Fox Associates design for
CUNY's Baruch College. The seventeen-story building takes up a block in the
Manhattan grid from 24th and 25th Street between Lexington and Third Avenues in a part of the city where skyscrapers are commonplace. The 800,000-
square-foot Baruch complex is dubbed the "vertical campus" and represents an
effort at new architectural design. The building has a glass curtain wall that
faces Baruch's Information and Technology Building to the north and three
atria of varying heights, one of which has a glass curtain that presents dramatic
views of southern Manhattan. A great deal of sunlight enters the building, which
houses state-of-the-art instructional technology; a mix of classrooms and research spaces; and many open areas and cul-de-sacs that are designed for casual conversation, reading, and simply hanging out between classes. There are
theatre and recital spaces, laboratories, a five-hundred-seat auditorium, con-

ference rooms, 375 faculty offices, and offices for the staff and administration. Athletic facilities exist below ground and include a fitness center, a gymnasium, a racquetball court, a pool, and locker rooms. Elevator banks exist as substitutes for walks across campus from one activity to another. In short, many different functions are loaded into the one vertical building at a total cost of $319 million, and most agree that it has been a successful building.[20]

The Value of Ruins

If buildings such as Baruch's structure show what is possible, even if it is far less vertical than some of the structures I have in mind, what is to be done with our "old" campuses whose edifices are outdated in terms of current research and teaching needs?[21] We ought to keep these buildings because they continue to fulfill important functions moving forward—particularly for undergraduate education. They can be reconfigured, of course, in order to use them more effectively. Butler Library, for example, which is directly opposite Low Memorial Library on the Columbia campus, has become a humanities library, but more importantly, a place for social interaction for the school's undergraduates. The vast majority of books, periodicals, and government data sets and records have been placed online or are being stored with greater care for preservation at the modern storage facility at Princeton, which is shared by Columbia, Princeton, and the New York Public Library (obtainable on their desks the day after a request).

Huge library facilities are of course not the only "ruins" on our campuses. Take the offices available to historians and English professors. Many are large rooms where faculty used to store as many as 3,000 books and hold seminars. Today, they are simply vast spaces in search of an appropriate function.

Although there continues to be a place for these resuscitated ruins on our campuses, let's realize what they represent and what was the glue that held the buildings together. There is nothing quite like the fabulous large set of steps leading from the street level to Low Memorial Library, where students drape themselves, relax, and talk at the first sign of spring. The equivalent on many campuses is the campus green, where seminar classes are held when the weather permits. If glass facades represent the symbolic feature of the modern skyscraper, the old-style campus was held together by bricks and ivy—and of course the idea of exclusiveness and class by an American style of aristocracy. It was the campus of Emerson and the transcendentalists, not the campus of modern science, technology, and the interface between the university, industry, and the government. We should preserve some of these spaces because they are beautiful and symbolize a past way of organizing and growing knowledge—they are an appropriate reminder of our history. But this acknowledgment of our past should not prevent us from making a clean break from it when we reimagine a new American campus.

Transmitting Knowledge in New Campus Spaces

I've discussed briefly here the need to reimagine a good deal of research space to maximize interaction and collaboration. But what about teaching and learning space? I believe, as do many others, that the extremely large lecture in the five-hundred- or one-thousand-seat auditorium is, with rare exceptions, a relic of the past. As discussed, online lectures to large groups delivered by the renowned lecturers ought to become the norm. This obviates building classrooms or lecture halls of this size on the reimagined campus.

Simply put, great universities should not be constructing large lecture halls, nor should they be viewing the library as the central axis to a campus, since the nature of libraries has already changed and ought to continue to evolve. Library content will be entirely digitized, and access to books and other materials will be obtained easily online from anywhere in the world. The storage of books and periodicals, to the extent that they require storage, should be done in remote facilities. Today, the vast majority of students and most scientists and scholars access materials almost exclusively online—and they expect that the works they seek to reference will be available there. Although convenient, what is potentially lost is the serendipity, or the eureka moment, of unexpectedly finding a work of importance simply by browsing in the section of the library where other related materials are located. But as web browsers continue to evolve and improve, the new campus will permit a great deal of "browsing" to be done through online search engines. In short, in the future, serendipity ought to be possible online.

It is easy to see why academics, particularly those who are older and less familiar than young scholars with the new technology, would like to destroy the new technology in Luddite fashion. Those of us who used the stacks of libraries frequently for browsing tend to think of those days nostalgically. We forget how often the books we were looking for were missing or had pages torn out of them. On the other hand, we should not believe that the work of great universities can be done entirely online or without places to interact. The new technology, if it is used creatively and is designed well, should offer rapid opportunities to access sources that we never had before. There ought to be computer scientists working with architects, social scientists, and humanists to construct virtual libraries that maximize opportunities for obtaining required sources and for serendipitous searching for materials.

If library resources become available on all forms of new media, this will represent a radical shift in one of the past metrics of a great university: the extent of the holdings in its library collection. Universities used to be ranked by the number of books housed in their libraries or the number of serial titles to which they subscribed. These numbers really have no meaning now and ought to have less meaning in the future. However, available special collections, such as oral history libraries and rare books and manuscripts, or collections of papers of distinguished people, should continue to be important parts of great libraries at universities. The metric will become ease of access and training in the use of universally held collections except for rare books and manuscripts that will continue to be housed in physical storage sites.

In place of the large lecture halls, we ought to be creating high-technology video and sound studios that can be used to record multimedia presentations of lectures that are stored in digital form and are easily accessible to any student taking the lecture course. This will benefit both students who reside on campus and those who retrieve these lectures as part of remote online learning experiences. The kinds of radio and television studios that one finds in the news and entertainment industry ought to become the standard for great universities. Also, we ought to create meeting spaces for students to explore together the ideas that are articulated in the digital lectures. These ought to be flexible spaces with access to high-end technology where demonstrations can take place.

In order for us to create substantial interactions among students and faculty physically located on different campuses, we ought to create seminar rooms that are replicated on each of the campuses that are participating in the course. Businesses that have offices in countries around the world have already created these kinds of spaces. As already noted, they are set up with exactly the same design and technology so that video conferencing occurs with the sense that everyone is located around the same table with access to the same equipment.

Similarly, as we begin to collaborate and form de facto mergers across universities and national borders, we ought to replicate laboratories in each location with a fair amount of similitude. Imagine Chinese researchers collaborating on aspects of neuroscience with their former mentors in the United States. They can work in the "same" lab, even if they are not physically present. They can communicate through technology that allows them to discuss the research in real time. It also allows for the itinerant researcher who moves from one laboratory to another to enjoy the same laboratory conditions needed for experimentation. And it sets these laboratories in other countries on a roughly equal footing with those in the United States.

In many fields, even newer ones, we won't be replacing traditional laboratory work with virtual laboratories. Thomas Jessell claims that even twenty-five or thirty years from now the neurosciences will require new laboratory spaces that improve the types and intensity of social interaction in many ways as well as the interaction among scientists toiling in connected fields whose work is necessary for breakthrough discoveries.[22] But the laboratory environment will continue to exist. It is important that in trying to create new physical structures we don't produce unanticipated consequences that actually impede the development of knowledge rather than facilitate it. Plainly, new physical configurations for their own sake are not what ought to be envisioned. The alterations in the physical entities of the new campus must be reflective of and must facilitate the way knowledge is growing in a field.

It must also be granted that different problems and disciplines require varying forms of physical spaces. No high-energy experimental particle physicist could even think about trying to find new fundamental particles, such as the Higgs Boson, in a campus building. Huge multinational efforts, such as was achieved at CERN, are needed for this type of research, involving hundreds if not thousands of collaborating physicists. Experimental particle research no longer can be performed in a place like Columbia's Pupin Hall. Nor would any single building in a place like New York be adequate to carry out major research efforts in astrophysics or astronomy. These too require collaborative efforts to build large land-based telescopes in places like Chile or in space telescopes, like NASA's Hubble Space Telescope—now one of many different types of telescopes making observations of the universe from space. Other scientific fields may, for the next several generations, be able to work in more traditional laboratory buildings—albeit that are far more flexible and built on the knowledge of how serendipity best occurs in science.

Interior physical spaces ought to be rethought in terms of the goals and mission of what is taught in those spaces. Where the goal of a program is to try to find innovative solutions to practical problems by bringing together individuals from a host of different backgrounds and disciplines, the classroom can have the texture that we see today in the d.school at Stanford, with open configurations and chairs, tables, couches, computers of all kinds, and chalkboards all mixed into a single space trying to create an optimal capacity to foster interaction and innovation. There is a high level of density in these learning centers, creating a great deal of potential for interaction and elaboration of ideas.

Given the strong interest in 2015 in multidisciplinary research that can attack complex research problems, it should not surprise us that the laboratories that are being built at extraordinary universities and research institutes embrace spatial configurations that attempt to promote seamless cross-disciplinary interaction. Although these configurations of common space are currently the rage, we should not neglect spaces designed for contemplation and for small-scale, quiet conversation—discussions that are not carried out in densely populated open spaces. Buildings that are devoted to humanistic disciplines, which are not connected to scientific or social scientific activities, will require such spaces. Faculty members and students should not be compelled to interact at all times. We need areas designed for different types of individuals and various activities.

In the reimagined campus, the structures should represent the functions of the university and the mechanisms by which knowledge is growing. The British quandrangular design and the Harvard and Yale quadrangles were appropriate for colleges or universities where little fundamental or applied research was carried out—where the emphasis was on undergraduate education, even the production of the next generation of ministers. But that all changed with the opening of Johns Hopkins, and we have been very slow to adapt the campus to the basic missions of the institutions that both transmit knowledge and create it. Today, the functions of the university are vastly different from those of the mid-nineteenth century and earlier.

The Campus and the City

If there has been a paucity of notable works on the campus, scholars have had far more to say about the relationship between urban universities and the cities in which they are embedded. Such universities have certain distinct advantages in building complex campuses—if we view, as did Joshua Lederberg, the former president of the Rockefeller University and Nobel Laureate in biology, the city as an aggregation of cultural and educational nodes that could be interconnected. Upon assuming the presidency of Rockefeller in 1978, Lederberg expressed this theme:

> New York played a special role in my scientific career. It was, and is, a communications network. New York is a superuniversity. Evolutionists will tell you that you get the most rapid diversification of species where you have an archipelago—where you have islands that are not totally isolated from one another but have sufficient isolation so that each can develop its distinctive flavor and sufficient communication so that there is some gene flow between them. That's how I would characterize the intellectual environment of the city.[23]

Unfortunately, few university presidents, too often caught up in a competitive strategy, thought of the city as that archipelago. Faculty members were more apt to develop collaborations among the cultural institutions than were their universities. I created the Passport to New York Program at Columbia, which I described in Chapter 7, with a vision of building a knowledge community within New York City.[24] It is now possible to translate such a network to connections among educational institutions, libraries, museums, galleries, and arts centers on an international scale. We did this in New York City, and we tried to do more in creating Fathom. This was an effort to create academic villages. There is no reason why the "campus" of tomorrow cannot include such villages.

All of this leaves a set of unanswered questions and problems that city-based universities encounter. Great research universities are, in many ways, special places—set apart from much else that is found in urban centers. The research that is carried out there requires highly specialized knowledge, which is not held by the general public. When we walk through the iron gates on 116th Street and Broadway onto the Columbia Morningside Heights campus, we know that we are in such a special place. The same is true when we walk through the gates to Harvard Yard. The same can be said for the urban campus of the University of Pennsylvania, or of Brown, or Yale University—and of places like Berkeley and UCLA, and other great public universities. These have been walled-off enclaves (some more extremely, like Columbia, than others)—places apart from their larger surroundings that we are now trying to reform. We want to bring "the city" closer and more accessible to the campus and, correlatively, the campus more permeable with the city. What does this, in fact, mean? What are we trying to comingle and change? In principle, we are trying to open up the university as a more public sphere, but setting boundaries is difficult.

In fact, it is unclear what those boundaries and edges of the new campus should look like. New York University, located in the heart of Greenwich Village, has expanded and improved its quality greatly over the past twenty-five years and does not have a "natural campus." How do we know where the campus begins, where its boundaries are, what is going on inside of its buildings? NYU has cleverly marked out its domain through flags and signage, but it often is unclear to those who walk the streets of Greenwich Village where the NYU campus is. The historian Thomas Bender fears that excessively merging the campus with the city without even the semicloistered heterogeneity that Joshua Lederberg was referring to when he spoke of New York as a super-university will lead to "the university ... increasingly having qualities in common with the suburbs.... There is a great danger in this suburbanization of the intellect. Both vitality and relevance are at risk. [Heterogeneity] is threatened by compartmentalization marked by firmer and firmer and less permeable boundaries. One cannot but fear scholasticism and self-referentiality."[25] Bender believes that the city and the university construct different forms of knowledge. "The university is best at producing abstract, highly focused, rigorous and internally consistent forms of knowledge, while the city is more likely to produce descriptive, concrete, but also less tightly focused and more immediately useful knowledge, whether this is generated by businessmen, journalists, or professional practitioners."[26]

Other American cities, perhaps most notably Chicago with its deep commitment to outstanding architecture, have produced urban campuses with highly predetermined principles of the relationship between physicality and the academic goals of universities. The evolution in Chicago's campuses might begin with Jane Adams and Ellen Starr's Hull House, of course a famous settlement house, not a university, which by 1911 had thirteen buildings. With the founding of the University of Chicago in 1892, a new campus grew up in Hyde Park on the south side of Chicago. Campus architect Henry Ives Cobb "designed a hierarchical group of campus quads in the Gothic Revival mode"[27] in the decade after the university opened its doors. The campus was viewed by the university's first president, William Rainey Harper, and by its other founders as "a city of learning." The symbolically important ceremonial and spiritual centerpiece of the campus, the grand Gothic-style Rockefeller Chapel, was not completed until 1928, but it had a huge impact on the physical development of the university—with its surrounding horizontal buildings in the center of the university's space as well as those resulting from physical creep beyond the Midway Plaisance.

If that represents the more traditional campus of greater Chicago, then the construction of a new downtown campus for the University of Illinois at Chicago Circle (UICC), changing its location from the Navy Pier (from 1946), represents an effort to use principles of the relationship between a campus and urban redevelopment to express both the values of the university and a new relationship between the campus and an external community, or what it advertises itself as "the comprehensive urban research university."[28] The chief architect for the new UICC campus was Skidmore, Owings & Merrill's Walter Netsch. The model that he developed had "three architectural building types—high rise, low-rise linear buildings, and large low-rise buildings with interior courtyards—all connected by pedestrian pathways that organize loose exterior courtyard spaces."[29] According to Sharon Haar, professor of architecture at the University of Illinois at Chicago, the design was one of the first in the United States to shun the organization of buildings by disciplines and departmental structures and was instead far more interested in fostering interdisciplinary work and interaction through the location of its buildings. At the time of its construction, UICC was essentially known as an undergraduate institution (before it consolidated with the health science schools); and its relationship to student traffic took on particular importance. There was no staff or student housing in the design, nor special facilities for the handicapped; but there was a central academic core of buildings that shared infrastructure, which was surrounded by facilities used for the physical plant as well as for physical education. Flexibility was also of particular importance. Classrooms were constructed with the idea that they could be used for many purposes. There were values and ideas behind the configuration of physical spaces. For example, the humanities would be centrally located, as would the one central library and lecture center. Netsch described his idea as "a drop of water scheme," with a series of ripples or rings emanating from the central core of shared physical spaces.[30] It remained unclear whether the guiding principle of the design was based on academic affinities or the idea of having shared infrastructure. But the decision to situate the new campus in its current location, which was deeply contested at the time, reflected the facts that it was first a commuting school for those in or near Chicago that required nearby access to public transportation (achieved) and a location that could also provide a stimulus for urban renewal, which Mayor Daley and business leaders were keenly interested in.[31]

If we are to take seriously the need to link great academic institutions to their context—the local and extended city community—then a plethora of questions related to these new relationships need to be addressed. For example, if the campus becomes a public space open to all comers, have we changed the very meaning of a campus? What are the limits on campuses to members of the community who do not work or study there? What is the glue that holds this new campus together? What are the reference points or the iconographic symbols that announce the presence of such a place? What is the nature of the edges between campus and community life; and what mechanisms, architecturally and otherwise, do we use to let the community into and be part of the campus? Should the campus contain public spaces with exhibits about the scholarly or scientific work that is done on the campus and use multimedia platforms to inform the public about the goals of this research and the potential outcomes of success? Should the campus contain public auditoriums for lectures by university faculty or by other notable figures in the city? Should there be public places to dine and to view films and art exhibits that are curated by the faculty and graduate students at the university? Should there be public pathways that are inviting and public greens for those not affiliated with the university to use? Should there be strict limits on the ability of the public to use the actual teaching and research space on the new campus? How much of these public spaces can universities afford to build without public financial or private philanthropic support? If land is scarce, then the university ought to devote most of the space to the planned expansion of the academic work of the university; but what effect does that have on the perception of the university within the adjacent and larger community?[32]

How ought this new physicality to be constructed? Traditionally, private universities built on "spec." If they constructed a research building, they depended on research grants and contract support to offset the cost of the structure. However, over decades, the government has backed off of its policy of reimbursing universities for the full cost of government-sponsored research and have placed caps on the funds they will provide for facilities and other costs. This has resulted in universities either having to find donors to pay for the cost of construction and the ongoing expenses of the research, financing construction through the issuance of public bonds, or cross-subsidizing the research enterprise with tuition dollars. On rare occasions, universities can compete for federal facilities dollars to help offset the cost of construction; and even more rarely, some private foundations will support construction of new research or classroom facilities. The simple fact is that the major federal agencies that support basic and targeted research have miniscule budgets for facilities construction. For the welfare of the nation, this ought to change over the coming decades.

The situation faced by public universities is even more complex. Different states have very different policies toward financing facilities at expanding universities—and the policies suggest what value the states place on research and teaching at these universities. On the one hand, Arizona does not budget building projects as part of its normal capital budget. Special pleading occasionally wins significant funding to produce buildings, but that only happens after major lobbying efforts by university leaders. On the other hand, California, even in times when the state's operating budget was in substantial deficit, created a capital budget that involved the financing of targeted university expansion. Since legislators and governors rarely talk about a state's capital budget, the public is usually unaware of these expenses. Those states that have helped finance campus expansion actually have a strategic advantage over the private universities, since state allocations can set a course of action that can lead to major strategic developments of a campus that would take far longer at private universities. In fact, the rapid building of the University of California, San Diego, into a world-class science university was a result, at least in part, of California's recognition of the value of a research campus oriented toward the biological sciences that could be jump-started by state financing.

In the future, if the federal government really believes that higher education is the key to our economic and social welfare as well as to our national security, then it needs to allocate far more federal resources than it does today for the construction of buildings on the newly conceptualized university campus. If the United States is to compete in the twenty-first century for highly technical jobs, university campuses will have to reflect investments in the physical facilities required for novel discoveries—and those structures will have to be built far more rapidly than in the past.[33]

Finally, the growing relationship between research universities of the first rank and industry must be recognized. These relationships and their physical manifestations have become increasingly important as much of the "research" in the R&D development process has fallen to the universities. The relationship between the research university and industry is being pushed with increasing intensity by political figures who see the fruits of research as instrumental in the continuing strength of the U.S. economy in the twenty-first century. A substantial amount of research in engineering, computer science, and medicine will have direct or indirect value for the larger economy. Consequently, the new campus ought to include physical spaces that facilitate the growth of incubator and start-up companies without encroaching on the interior community of research scholars. Many of these enterprises will be financed by venture capital, but there is great value to be had from physical proximity of such companies to the scientists and engineers who are making discoveries that have potential practical value. Efforts like the one in New York City on Roosevelt Island, in which Cornell University is collaborating with Israel's Institute for Technology, Technion (a public research university in Haifa with a remarkable record for discoveries), would be better served if they were aligned with multiple universities in New York City, just as Silicon Valley has always been extremely closely aligned with Stanford University and with the University of California, San Francisco Medical School. If Hewlett-Packard was started in a garage on Stanford's campus, there is no reason why we cannot build opportunities for innovative research to grow in spaces adjacent to or within our new campuses.[34]

CHAPTER NINE

The Central Dogma of a Great University

These pages need not be burdened with proof, based on the testimony of a cloud
of impressive witnesses, of the dependence of a free society on free universities.
This means the exclusion of governmental intervention in the intellectual life of
a university. It matters little whether such intervention occurs avowedly or
through action that inevitably tends to check the ardor and fearlessness of scholars, qualities at once so fragile and so indispensable for fruitful academic labor.

—FELIX FRANKFURTER, *SWEEZY V. NEW HAMPSHIRE*,
354 U.S. 234 (1957)

A T THE CENTER OF ANY GREAT UNIVERSITY lies a set of core values
that are essential to its being and without which true excellence is
virtually impossible to achieve. A great university's social structures
and relationships should be designed to maximize the fulfillment of these core
values. Earlier in these pages I enumerated a baker's dozen of these values, which
I also explored in *The Great American University*.[1] Here, I extend the number to
include the values of trust; diversity of intelligences, talents, interests, and backgrounds; and support of the blue-sky thinking that counters prevailing-dogma
research. We could call these values, metaphorically, the soul of the university.

Although their ordering and degree of centrality to the university's mission
may remain an open and contested question, there is, I believe, a hierarchy to
these values—some are more essential than others, and three are absolutely
fundamental to the full realization of the others: trust, academic freedom, and
free inquiry. Also, since universities are dependent on and embedded in the
state, since they are often the vehicles by which university members criticize
the state and other existing social arrangements, and since the state ultimately
controls the use of power, there will always be a delicate relationship (often
fraught with tension) between the state and educational institutions of true
distinction—especially those in the university with the courage to speak out
against the state.

This uneasy compact results in both a formal set of tacit agreements and an
unusual, but accepted, level of trust between what often can only be called

protagonists. As Emile Durkheim, the nineteenth-century French sociologist, suggested, there is more to trust than can be codified in formal contractual agreements. In fact, trust lies in what Durkheim called the noncontractual elements in the contract. When trust breaks down, the other values and all that is built on them are in peril. At that point, the state, with its ability to exercise social control and various forms of repression, begins to use these powers over its universities.

From time to time, indeed in almost every decade from the research university's inception, the United States has witnessed (in varying degrees) a breakdown in trust. In most developing nations, of course, the protection and autonomy of universities from state power simply doesn't exist. Today, we are at a time when trust between the two partners has eroded significantly. In addition, assaults on academic freedom have been associated with elevated levels of anti-intellectualism and, perhaps more often, with times of perceived external threats (such as our recent obsession with, and fear of, terrorism).

The quality of teaching and research at our colleges and universities has suffered when trust and academic freedom are attacked, as they were, to cite only two examples, during the Lochner era[2] at the turn of the twentieth century (when employers had enormous power to fire employees arbitrarily) and around World War I when American fears of anarchism and Bolshevism ran high. Later, in the 1940s and during the McCarthy period, the government questioned faculty and student loyalty (requiring the signing of loyalty oaths, among other forms of constraint) and the motives behind a faculty member's associations and tried to control what professors taught in their courses. Ever-resourceful in shifting its tactics, the government today has held on to some older well-tuned methods of attacking free inquiry, but it also has turned to alternative and less visible means of limiting the freedom of universities: the powers of the purse and the use of its regulatory authority. If nothing else, this intrusion damages universities' abilities to teach young people to become better and more active citizens; to produce novel ideas and discoveries; and to educate students in a large number of specialized professions. If trust between universities and the government is waning, it will be difficult, but necessary, to reverse the trend if our universities are to remain preeminent. In order to rebuild the value of trust, we need to take stock of what lies in the hierarchy of academic values and what the unintended (or perhaps intended) consequences could be if commitment to those values erodes.

A Hierarchy of the Core Academic Values

In thinking about academic values for the evolving research universities of the twenty-first century, let us consider them as part of a hierarchy divided into three levels. Level 1 represents *fundamental, enabling values,* without which other values that underpin great universities would not be even minimally realized; Level 2 includes *essential values* needed for research universities to fulfill their mission and the terms of their compact with American society; and in Level 3, we find *desirable values,* but ones that might not be essential for greatness. This hierarchy is represented in Figure 4. The levels within the hierarchy should not be examined as weights (where the heaviest falls to the bottom), but in terms of their lexicographical priority. When two values come into conflict— and each occupies a different "level"—the value that is most fundamental should always, in the end, trump the one from a higher level. Thus, fundamental values always trump even essential ones when two or more from different levels are conflicting with each other.

Let me describe, in blueprint form, each of the values represented in Figure 4.

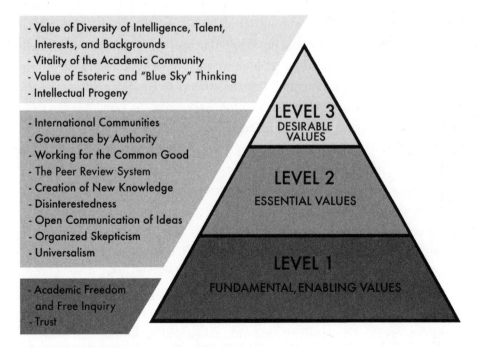

- Value of Diversity of Intelligence, Talent, Interests, and Backgrounds
- Vitality of the Academic Community
- Value of Esoteric and "Blue Sky" Thinking
- Intellectual Progeny

- International Communities
- Governance by Authority
- Working for the Common Good
- The Peer Review System
- Creation of New Knowledge
- Disinterestedness
- Open Communication of Ideas
- Organized Skepticism
- Universalism

- Academic Freedom and Free Inquiry
- Trust

LEVEL 3
DESIRABLE
VALUES

LEVEL 2
ESSENTIAL VALUES

LEVEL 1
FUNDAMENTAL, ENABLING VALUES

FIGURE 4. Hierarchy of fifteen academic values.

Level 1: Fundamental, Enabling Values

Academic freedom and free inquiry, along with trust, are unique values and may be given priority over others because they are *enabling* values. I don't know of any great university where academic freedom and freedom of inquiry are not placed in the foreground of the prevailing value system, because they enable the pursuit of the *other* values in the hierarchy and therefore cannot be weighed on the same scale as the values they enable. As an enabling value, academic freedom allows, for example, the value of universalism or meritocracy or the other second-level values to be realized at our great universities.[3] As I've suggested, even academic freedom and free inquiry are predicated on the value of "trust." Without fundamental trust that faculty members and students will carry out their roles and obligations without continual oversight, even freedom of inquiry would be jeopardized. The value is, therefore, placed on the same level as academic freedom. In referring to John Dewey—one of the founders of the American Association of University Professors, from which the doctrine of academic freedom came—Richard Rorty, the philosopher, conjectures: "Dewey, I think, would say that if it should ever come down to a choice between the practices and traditions which make up academic freedom and antirepresentationalist theories of truth and knowledge, we should go for academic freedom. We should put first things first."[4] This position in the hierarchy is stated axiomatically and without proof, and that is why I would say that it "arguably" represents this central position in the value system of the academy.

In fact, academic freedom and the protection of free inquiry differ from the value, also held by faculty members, of free expression. As Louis Menand, the Harvard literary critic, has said, academic freedom is

the key legitimizing concept of the entire [academic] enterprise. It is the underlying basis of the mechanism that establishes who alone may, with any justification, have control and authority over the critical decisions of the university. It places in the hands of highly trained, competent professors, who have met standards set by the disciplines, the power to create criteria for entrance into the profession, to set standards for admissions, to establish what is and what is not valued or labeled as "high quality work," to determine standards for hiring and promotion to coveted positions, to construct the examinations, and to determine what will or will not be taught in classes run by those professors.[5]

This view is consistent with the views articulated by Robert Post, dean of the Yale Law School, who insists that the origins and history of academic freedom lie in the differentiated roles and rights of the faculty that exist as part of the division of labor at a university, part of the implicit contractual arrangement for the stewardship of the larger enterprise between faculty and the academic administration and trustees.

Truly creative scholarship and criticism can only take place in an atmosphere in which talented people are given latitude to consider contested ideas, to push against orthodoxy, and to explore the unknown. Fear of interference by internal or external forces compromises these possibilities. This enabling value sets universities apart from most other institutions, where political, religious, or social constraints can more easily restrict the introduction of new ideas.

Trust, like academic freedom, is a sine qua non of elite research universities. Its formal meaning suggests a confidence in, or reliance on, some quality of individuals or institutions (such as honesty, effectiveness, character, and ability) that they will fulfill the obligations that they have taken on.[6] As Jon Elster, the political theorist, has pointed out, trust is often said to be the lubricant of society. In defining trust behaviorally, he said: "to trust someone is to lower one's guard to *refrain from taking precautions against an interaction partner*, even when the other, because of opportunism or incompetence, could act in a way that might seem to justify precautions.[7] It could be as simple as trusting a chemist to meet her classes and teach chemistry rather than economics or politics; it might mean that an institution will see to it that when it takes on government research grants and contracts it will monitor honestly how those funds are used and in ways that prevent fraud or conflicts of interest. Research universities could not work with external partners or with their own faculty members and students without trusting that they will internalize and perform their various roles with integrity. Faculty members must also be able to trust that their university will be permitted to explore unknown scholarly and scientific territory, as well as express crucial opinions about the state, without reprisals or sanctions, as long as they are acting within the basic rules that frame the university's larger mission. Without trust, even academic freedom and free inquiry cannot be realized.

Diego Gambetta, the Italian sociologist who has spent a good part of his academic career at Cambridge and Oxford studying various aspects of trust, has opined: "The importance of trust pervades the most diverse situations where cooperation is at one and the same time a vital and fragile commodity: from marriage to economic development, from buying a second-hand car to international affairs, from the minutiae of social life to the continuation of life on earth."[8] We can now add to this array the research university and its relationship with its various partners.[9]

Level 2: Essential Values

Universalism or Meritocracy. Universalism is the belief that new truth claims and discoveries, innovations, or concepts as assertions of fact ought to be evaluated using established impersonal criteria, not the personal or social attributes of the individual making the claim. Such declarations within a university ought to be assessed and rewarded on the basis of merit established by peers and not on criteria such as religion, social class, race, gender, ethnicity, sexual orientation, or personal politics.[10] The growth of knowledge will be impeded to the extent that this value is abridged, and universities will become particularistic in their choices rather than meritocratic. Without universalism, universities cannot establish a just and trustworthy reward system for faculty members and students.

As we look forward, we ought to embrace what I call "conditional meritocracy or universalism." In this form, extraneous criteria such as those noted above must continue to be excluded from consideration in the reward and recognition process—and nothing ought to change about the evaluation of truth claims. But it recognizes that there are time-budget constraints on members of the scientific community. Although it used to be that women were almost always the organizers and caretakers of their families, in the future men and women will be sharing these roles. Therefore, the reward system must emphasize that research quality trumps sheer quantity and that there are circumstances that can slow down the rate of scholarly or scientific productivity without damaging the quality of that research output.[11] So, for example, whether we are considering women or men who have multiple family obligations when their children are young, they ought to have extra time before being reviewed for promotion or tenure.[12]

Organized Skepticism. This critically important value enjoins members of the academic community to hold a skeptical view of almost anything proposed as fact or dogma, applying appropriately rigorous methodological criteria to claims of discovery or truth. Universities are places that at once should explore the most novel and even radical ideas but simultaneously must hold them to the most rigorous standards of proof.

Open Communication of Ideas. For knowledge to grow, it must occupy a public space. It becomes common property, placed freely in the marketplace of ideas for review, criticism, correction, and further development. It ought to contain all of the elements necessary for others to replicate, as far as possible, the findings presented in professional publications and in the media. The data from experiments and observations, wherever feasible, should be stored in publically available places for others to access. This should be done at the time that research papers or books are published.[13] Secrecy impedes the growth of knowledge. Only in the most extreme situations, and there are but a handful that hold any weight, should the methods of an experiment be withheld from its readers. Science and scholarship simply cannot advance without free and open communication of research results. The academic community should remain vigilant in opposition to government attempts to limit publication of scientific results for reasons of "national security." This was attempted after 9/11 and was vigorously, but probably not adequately, opposed by members of the National Academy of Sciences. Prior restraint on communication not only is counter to the spirit of the academic community but is also largely ineffective, since restrictions by one country do not bind other countries from publishing the same results, including censored materials.

Disinterestedness. Disinterestedness, which has been referred to as communism (in the sense of community, not political ideology), enjoins faculty members from profiting financially from their discoveries. It ought not to be confused with altruism or lack of personal ambition. As is well known, the race to be first in discovery has a long history, some of which gets rather sordid. This value has eroded more than any other in the past twenty-five years, which is ironic since it stems from Congress's passage of the Bayh-Dole Act of 1980, which gave universities the ownership of intellectual property (IP) derived from government-sponsored research. As a result, university IP policies were designed not only to move discoveries more rapidly from the university to the marketplace, but also to incentivize individual scientists to make potentially profitable discoveries (as a new stream of revenue for the university). Part of the incentive system, of course, involved giving to individual discoverers some fraction of the returns on intellectual property (whether in the form of some share of the equity in startup companies or of the return from licensing agreements). Gone are the days when scientists, engineers, and other scholars rejected personal gains that derive from their inventions and discoveries.[14] With the development of software technology, universities are creating policies, similar to those that exist for the sciences, engineering, and biomedical disciplines, which carve up the returns from the software that is produced by their faculty members.[15] Universities must have strict oversight of faculty-generated companies and software production to avoid either real or perceived conflicts of interest.

Creation of New Knowledge. The primary currency in the academic world is the production of new knowledge. Whether it is measured by publication of high-impact books and papers, by honors and awards for exceptional discoveries and scholarship, by research dollars obtained through a competitive process, or by the quality of library holdings and information services available, the prestige and quality of research universities are largely determined by these factors—not by the less-easily-measured quality of teaching or other forms by which knowledge is transmitted. Top universities not only try to foster the spirit of discovery, but they try to grow it and enhance the possibilities for future unfettered research. Again, without the fundamental enabling value of academic freedom and free inquiry, little of this would be possible.

The Peer Review System. The peer review system is based on the logical notion that the only people who are qualified to provide in-depth critiques of the proposed work of scholars and scientists are peers—those with a high level of understanding of a field or specialty. This system lies at the heart of the process of assessment, promotion, and recognition within the research university—and from World War II on has figured prominently in the distribution of research resources to universities and colleges, including those from the National Institutes of Health and the National Science Foundation.

The peer review system has been continually under attack from members of Congress as representing an "old boy network" where scientists essentially scratch each other's backs ("I'll give you a high score for your grant proposal if you give me one as well"), as being biased and favoring the well-heeled and more famous universities over those less well-known (and generally not on either coast), and as making frivolous awards for projects of little value (as William Proxmire, an otherwise liberal senator, suggested in initiating his "Golden Fleece of the Month" award for supposedly worthless grants).

Empirical studies have shown that these criticisms of the peer review system have little basis in fact. The system as it stands today does, however, have serious shortcomings that ought to be rectified. The most egregious problem is that it has a strong conservative bias—it tends to fund work with a high probability of some payoff but a low likelihood of leading to pathbreaking discoveries. It has such a low rate of success of funded proposals that faculty members have already done half the work intended before submitting a grant application; correlatively, the system rarely supports high-risk, high-payoff research proposals and it does not adequately fund younger scholars and scientists, preferring to take the less risky path of remunerating those who already have substantial track records. Despite its limits, peer review is essential and should be improved upon. As Winston Churchill once famously said in referring to democracy, it "is the worst form of government, except for all those other forms that have been tried from time to time." So, too, with the peer review system.

Working for the Common Good. As part of the social compact between universities and their larger communities, there is a strong value placed on creating knowledge that will benefit a broader audience and discoveries that can change the nation and the world. The value is realized by producing students who work for the larger good after graduation, as well as faculty members who toil to make discoveries that will have a practical impact and solve societal problems. In principle, the value also enjoins members of the university community to instill ideals and knowledge in their students so that they will become more civic minded and will engage more fully and knowledgeably in the democratic process. Finally, universities ought to be increasingly enmeshed in their local communities rather than purposefully estranged from them. Many have begun to do this through efforts to improve local public school systems; by creating programs that incorporate local citizens into the activities of the university; and ultimately, by allowing them to partake in a form of continuing education through online learning.

Governance by Authority. For the last century, universities have not been run by the imposition of sheer power by an authoritarian president, a board of trustees, or regents. Today, research universities are largely governed through authority, which is distinguishable from power in that it relies on the consent of the governed in order to facilitate or activate change. There is an inevitable tension here, since more often than not faculty members are conservative when it comes to organizational changes to their institutions; and presidents and provosts, who may want to eliminate or add particular structures, are hesitant to take any action that produces significant alterations that might not meet with the approval of the faculty (and to a lesser extent the students). This leads to a strong "status quo bias."[16] This value is evolving through increased discussions within universities about the appropriate roles of the central academic figures. When initiatives are in their blueprint phase of development, who should have the primary responsibility for constructing new ways to organize and grow knowledge—or to transmit it to students? This has been a faculty prerogative for decades. What role should an informed board and its academic officers play in transforming the structures of the university without the consent of the governed? That is an open and debated question, but one that ought to be resolved in a way that gives the central academic authorities more weight in the process than they have had in recent decades. Without this happening, it is difficult to envision major and relatively rapid change taking place at these institutions.[17]

International Communities. This value enjoins leaders and faculty members to think of their research university as a place without borders. Extraordinary research universities have no national boundaries and search for the best minds, both of faculty members and of students, from wherever they may be found. In fact, this holds increasingly true for leaders of universities. Those with strong track records at universities in other nations—particularly Britain—are increasingly candidates for presidencies of major research universities in the United States; perhaps even more common today is the American academic who is asked to lead a foreign university of stature. The ability of American universities to reinforce this value has resulted in many foreign nationals winning the most prestigious awards and prizes while working at universities in the United States and many foreign students becoming intellectual leaders here or, if they return home, leading their nations in a variety of capacities or becoming academic stars there.

Level 3: Desirable Values

Intellectual Progeny. Teaching and training the next generation of students and professionals, as well as national leaders in their selected field, is, along with research, an essential role for faculty members at our universities. The goal is not to teach substance per se but to instruct young people in how to think independently and how to internalize many of the other values: to refine their level of skepticism; to know how to ask profound, yet unanswered, questions; to move to the heart of an argument; to have intellectual courage; to know how to work in groups to produce better outcomes than one could obtain alone. Renowned scientists take great pride in producing minds that they believe are superior to their own and that are capable of moving knowledge forward in the academy or elsewhere.

Esoteric and "Blue Sky" Thinking. Most universities do not set aside enough places for blue-sky thinking—thought that is creative, unfettered by convention, and not necessarily grounded in what is generally considered reality.[18] Unconventional thinking that questions existing orthodoxies must be supported through institutional resources. There has to be more room at our great universities for those individuals, like Stanley Prusiner, who challenged the long-standing belief that proteins could not cause disease. Prusiner found it difficult to get resources for his laboratory; but some at the University of California, San Francisco, believed in the possibility that he was right—that prions could cause a variety of neurodegenerative diseases—and that a scientific breakthrough was possible by following his out-of-the-box thinking and experiments. This is one of the new values that ought to be internalized in the future great university, even if it may not be necessary for the creation of a distinguished institution. Great universities ought to be taking prudent risks on people and ideas that seem esoteric because they do not fit into the standard dogma of a field. In keeping with the value of skepticism, however, those researchers who are blue-sky thinkers ought to be required to produce solid evidence before others accept their novel ideas.

Vitality of the Academic Community. This value requires universities, as individual institutions and as a system, to renew themselves and to enhance their quality from one generation to another. The community needs to recruit some of the most talented and creative young minds to enter the professoriate. Then it needs to nurture and reward these people in ways that produce an intellectual and social environment that is conducive to the emergence of major new discoveries and technologies as well as novel ways of practicing and thinking about the humanities and the professions. The norm is to support and promote talent that will ensure that the nation's research universities retain and improve on their existing quality.

Diversity of Intelligence, Talent, Interests, and Backgrounds. This value suggests that great universities ought to represent virtually every form of diversity that will benefit the quality of the academic community and increase the chances for significant research and teaching experiences. Diversity applies not only to one's race, gender, nationality, or other ascribed characteristics, although we ought to increase the life chances for members of these groups and reap the benefits of their intellects; it also includes one's talents and interests. A university that mixes people of various types of intelligence ought to be a more interesting and productive place. Although this value is surely a desirable one, it is not sufficient for greatness.

Although I have ordered these values hierarchically, any inspection of them suggests that many are interrelated. More importantly, perhaps, is that many of them are dependent on the most fundamental values of free inquiry and academic freedom. Although I have not discussed it here or placed it within the hierarchy of academic values, one might argue that free expression is also one of the fundamental values of any distinguished university.[19] I've omitted it because it is a basic constitutional right, which is safeguarded by the First Amendment and is there to protect the speech of every citizen of the United States.

Academic Freedom Today

In a variety of insidious ways, academic freedom and free inquiry are under attack today—as they have been over the decades. Consider a few examples. In 2014, Senator Tom Coburn (R-OK) attached a rider to a budget bill to fund the National Science Foundation that ordered the NSF to refrain from funding any political science research "except for research projects that the [NSF director] certifies as promoting national security or the economic interests of the United States."[20] Not since former president Ronald Reagan's effort to eliminate all social science funding by the NSF, which he largely achieved, has there been such a blatant attack by Congress (except for legislation initiated from the White House after 9/11) on free inquiry and research judged as superior by members of the NSF panels of experts. The ambivalence toward freedom of inquiry and the honored principle of following the argument wherever it leads, regardless of whether the results are politically palatable to a majority of political leaders, continues to exist in Congress.

In an episode involving the National Endowment for the Humanities (NEH), often a favorite target for members of Congress, Senator Jeff Sessions (R-AL) questioned the peer review process. "I affirm the value of the humanities, but we all recognize that care and discipline must be exercised by any government agency that decides to favor certain projects over others," Sessions wrote in a letter to NEH Acting Chairman Carol Watson. "Recent NEH expenditures raise questions about whether the endowment is meeting this requirement."[21] There is no reason why such a question can't be asked by a senator, nor is it an interference with the peer review system. But when it pertains to the quality of grants that have gone through peer review on the basis of their subject matter, then it is encroaching on free inquiry. And that is really what Senator Sessions had in mind. In the letter sent on October 23, 2013, Senator Sessions asked for confidential information, "regarding the grant process at her [Watson's] agency, as well as the expenditure of public funds to distribute books related to Islam to 900 libraries across the country."[22] He went on to question, among other aspects of peer review, the process behind NEH's "Bridging Cultures Bookshelf Administration" grants program, and particularly a grant titled "Muslim Journeys." "One would think that the NEH takes a fair and balanced approach to promoting culture," Sessions wrote, and then he asked for an "itemized list" covering the prior five years "of all spending related to Christianity (e.g., Protestantism—Baptist, Methodist, Episcopal—or Catholicism) or Judaism where books or forums promoting one point of view were provided to libraries, etc." Sessions is undermining the peer review process because he is, implicitly, worried that *his* point of view is not sufficiently represented in the outcome of the process.

Still further, boards of regents are dismissing chancellors and presidents of universities because of an academic leader's views about the place of the university within their states. This has happened in Texas and elsewhere. Faculty members who speak out on topics related to scientific matters, such as global climate change and the environment, are under attack. Congressional members are trying to control the peer review grant system on grounds of ideology rather than merit. Wisconsin's governor, Scott Walker, even if he backtracked a bit in 2015 after a great deal of opposition from around the state, threatened to eviscerate the Wisconsin Idea by withholding an additional $300 million (a 13 percent cut in state aid) in funding for the University of Wisconsin because he questions its mission. He wants to transform it from a world-class research university, as it has been for about one hundred years, into a trade school ("to meet the state's work-force needs"). Most critics of the Walker proposal believe that the subtext of the idea is to rid the state of the "bastions of liberal academics that do not prepare students for work and are a burden on the taxpayer.... One scientist at the university, Andreas Fodor, said he had been lured to Madison from his native Hungary by its reputation as a top research institution. 'In my field, it is one of the best universities.... That reputation is a terrible thing to destroy.'"[23] The trustees of Cooper Union offered up the president's head if the attorney general halted his investigation into possible violations of their fiduciary responsibilities.[24] Then there are scores of individual cases, such as that of Professor Steven Salaita, who was offered a position at the prestigious University of Illinois, Urbana–Champaign, only to have his offer rescinded by the university and its board of regents because Salaita had tweeted several comments highly critical of the State of Israel's current policies toward the Palestinians.[25]

What is equally troubling is the abridgment of free inquiry and academic freedom at universities around the globe. The organization Scholars at Risk (SAR) champions the cause of academic freedom and identifies egregious violations of it in many countries outside of the United States, cataloging not only the incidence but also the outcomes of these cases, while trying to provide some form of safe haven for these targeted scholars. And the types of violations make those in the United States pale in comparison. SAR identifies murders, imprisonments, and various other forms of extreme sanctions that are found at universities around the world.[26] China is imprisoning scholars who wish to teach cultural history among the Uyghur ethnic population (2014); it is denying access to schools to those who criticize Chinese government policies; it is "reassigning" professors at prestigious universities for criticism of the government.[27] The situation in African universities is probably worse at this time than in Asia. Decrying the state of academic freedom in South Africa today, John Higgins, professor of English at the University of Cape Town and a member of South Africa's Academy of Sciences, doesn't paint a pretty picture.[28] With obvious regret, Higgins notes "that the African National Congress (ANC) in power seemed to be reproducing the Afrikaner reduction of the universities to instruments of state policy in ways that meant the 'English' conception of academic freedom—struggled for during the apartheid years—was an inconvenient ideal."[29]

As our great universities become increasing international, either through collaborations among faculty members, through the construction of campuses in other nations, or through research agreements, we will need to be more attentive to the way those nations treat their faculty members and their scholars, as well as ours.[30] We will have to embrace efforts to see that free inquiry and academic freedom become increasingly a fundamental value in those partner nations. And it will remain an open question as to whether we want to be in bed with partners who disregard the most fundamental value of America's greatest research universities.

In the long historical fight to retain academic freedom and free inquiry in the United States, there has been no greater champion for it than Robert Maynard Hutchins[31] and the longer list of University of Chicago presidents, including Edward Levi, Hanna Holborn Gray, and Robert Zimmer, who followed Hutchins in making academic freedom part of the DNA of that seat of higher learning. Much in keeping with the views of Hutchins, Hanna Holborn Gray notes: "Education should not be intended to make people comfortable, it is meant to make them think. Universities should be expected to provide the conditions within which hard thought, and therefore, strong disagreement, independent judgment, and the questioning of stubborn assumptions, can flourish in an environment of the greatest freedom."[32] And if the University of Chicago faces challenges about the reach of academic freedom and free inquiry today, it surely is an exemplar of how it ought to be defended. This is why I consider it the American university that comes closest to approximating the ideal of a meritocracy of ideas.

In a recent essay, Robert Zimmer, the University of Chicago's current president, wrote about the now-famous Kalven Committee Report (1967) and its reinforcement of these basic principles of the university.[33] That report, written in the midst of the social and political turmoil during the Vietnam War, has the most succinct statement of how a university can reinforce the idea of academic freedom and free inquiry. I quote it at some length because I could not articulate the principles better or more succinctly.

After acknowledging Hutchins's role in defending the university during the McCarthy period, when Illinois was trying to pass laws that would repress those who held communist ideas and who were located at Illinois schools, particularly at the University of Chicago, the Kalven Committee notes the following: (1) "A university has a great and unique role to play in fostering the development of social and political values in a society.... It is a role for the long term"; (2) "The mission of the university is the discovery, improvement, and dissemination of knowledge. Its domain of inquiry and scrutiny includes all aspects and values of society. A university faithful to its mission will provide enduring challenges to social values, policies, practices, and institutions. By design and by effect, it is the institution which creates discontent with the existing social arrangements and proposes new ones. In brief, a good university, like Socrates, will be upsetting"; (3) "The instrument of dissent and criticism is the individual faculty member or the individual student. The university is the home and sponsor of critics: it is not the critic itself.... To perform its mission in the society, a university must sustain an extraordinary environment of freedom of inquiry and maintain an independence from political fashion, passions, and pressures. A university, if it is to be true to its faith in intellectual inquiry, must embrace, be hospitable to, and encourage the widest diversity of views within its own community. It is a community but only for the limited, albeit great, purposes of teaching and research"; (4) "There is no mechanism by which it can reach a collective position without inhibiting that full freedom of dissent on which it thrives.... In brief, it is a community which cannot resort to majority vote to reach positions on public issues. The neutrality of the university as an institution arises then not from a lack of courage nor out of indifference and insensitivity. It arises out of respect for free inquiry and the obligation to cherish a diversity of view-points."[34] In short, no one, not its president, provost, trustees, or faculty and students, speaks for the university.

Although I might be considered a fundamentalist on matters of academic freedom—one who sees few boundaries to it and who agrees strongly with the Chicago view that no one speaks for the university for fear of stifling minority opinion—this view of free inquiry is a contested one. This is especially so when it comes to the matter of whether, for example, a university president or pro-vost ought to speak out against existing social arrangements, such as South Af-rican apartheid, or an endowment portfolio of stocks that includes investments in gun manufacturers, which may be linked to actions that are abhorrent to a majority of the faculty and students. Nonetheless, I see in the Kalven Committee Report a model for what great universities in the future ought to embrace, whether in the United States or in other nations.

The principles of academic freedom and free inquiry had their formal ori-gins in the United States with the formation of the American Association of University Professors (AAUP) and its 1915 *Declaration of Principles on Academic Freedom and Academic Tenure*.[35] Although dogma about free expression has evolved greatly in the law since 1915, until recently there has been little discussion (ex-cept when universities had to defend the value against external attacks) of the principles and the reach of this most fundamental of values. There had been some good historical work on the subject; and a few contemporary scholars, such as Robert Post and Joan W. Scott, would write on the subject—trying to dis-tinguish it from free expression or to locate it in the law, or even to describe potential limits to the idea. But today, there is an energetic debate on such topics as what academic freedom is for; how it might be used as a political weapon; how it can be abused; how it has limits that should be acknowledged; and how it conflicts with other academic values. Indeed, there are discussions of aspects of academic "unfreedom," which looks within the academy for ways in which free inquiry is constrained through dogmatic practices within the uni-versity. Interestingly, however, there continues to be very little empirical work on the subject. Let's now look at an effort to expand the empirical basis of our knowledge.

A Pilot Study of Faculty Views

The overwhelming majority of faculty members at America's leading colleges or universities would fully embrace the concepts of academic freedom and free inquiry. The same is apt to be true for faculty members throughout the nation's more than 4,000 colleges and universities. But if you were to ask the same faculty members what academic freedom was, or how it differed from "freedom of expression," or if you were to ask them what academic freedom was for, they might pause before formulating an answer, and their answers might be highly varied.

Most empirical research on university and college faculty members has focused on their political views, not on academic freedom. The best known of those earlier inquiries was *The Academic Mind*, which was published more than fifty years ago by Columbia sociologists Paul F. Lazarsfeld and Wagner Thielens Jr. The authors examined the behavior and levels of apprehension of more than 2,400 social scientists who worked at colleges and universities during the witch hunts of the McCarthy era.[36]

Far more recently, two sociologists, Neil Gross and Solon Simmons, examined faculty political views. Their 2006 survey also reproduced Lazarsfeld's questions related to academic freedom. Remarkably, the two studies, separated by a half-century, show roughly the same level of faculty apprehension (21 percent) about intrusive outsiders undermining academic freedom. Using different sampling methods and drawing on more universities than the earlier study, Gross and Simmons concluded: "Although the samples are not strictly comparable ... we can still reasonably say that social scientists today perceive as much if not more of a threat to academic freedom than during the McCarthy era."[37] Although a substantial proportion of faculty members then and now are apprehensive about threats to their academic freedom, only about a quarter claimed to feel personally threatened.

In 2012, I surveyed Columbia University's 1,610 full-time faculty members in the arts and sciences disciplines and its professional schools, as well as a sample of faculty in the biomedical sciences departments at the medical school campus. The clinical faculty was omitted from the study. Because this was a pilot study, no effort was made to sample faculty members at other universities for comparative purposes. In an attempt to avoid normative responses, the survey never used the term "free inquiry" and never mentioned academic freedom explicitly—since academic freedom is like motherhood and apple pie to an academic scholar. Rather than ask directly whether faculty members believe in academic freedom or if it was being threatened at Columbia, I presented them with fourteen short hypothetical vignettes and asked them to assess the action taken by the professors, administrators, and outside actors portrayed in each situation, all of which were based on actual academic cases. These vignettes ranged from actions involving congressional interference with research on HIV/AIDS among street workers, treatment of students in class, and appropriate subjects to discuss in class to the role of institutional review boards (IRBs) in limiting research,[38] actions taken by faculty members outside of the university, and the appropriate treatment of faculty members whose research does not conform to the existing paradigm of the field. I also asked the respondents a set of general questions about the idea of a university, a few questions about their own values and politics, and for some demographic information.[39]

The aim was to obtain faculty opinions about academic freedom and free inquiry when that value conflicted with others that the faculty member might hold. I was interested in whether the faculty members thought that the actions represented in the vignettes were justified or not and whether they should be protected or not. If they felt the action was inappropriate, they were asked whether the administration should administer a "soft" or "hard" sanction, or do nothing. Soft sanctions might include a request not to repeat the behavior or a freeze of the professor's salary for a year or two; hard sanctions might include temporary suspension, a formal reprimand, or action to dismiss the professor from the university. Faculty members had the opportunity to write their own suggestions for appropriate action in each case.

Because the full description of the results can be read elsewhere, here I discuss only three of the vignettes.[40] All of the vignettes presented to the faculty members were based on actual cases. In one a tenured professor in a university with a speech code is dismissive and disdainful of an African American student's question in a social science class. The student complained to the dean after the teacher said that he/she "is a product of affirmative action and really doesn't belong at the college." Almost no faculty members thought that the speech code was relevant to actions that should be taken in the case. Only 6 percent of the faculty said that the university should do nothing, while 35 percent thought the university should apply either soft or hard sanctions (roughly equally divided between the two). Fully 41 percent "punted," that is, they said they would leave it up to a faculty committee to decide what to do. Here is a sample of responses from the forty-four faculty members who did not believe any of the categories described their beliefs, which ranged from rather informal to more dramatic action:

> Have someone talk to the faculty member privately about proper treatment of students both minority and nonminority.

Another faculty member said:

> [The] faculty member should be "brought up on charges" with an attempt to carefully evaluate whether and how this incident reflects her/his usual behavior. In other words, it should be handled with the utmost seriousness, but not necessarily with the intent of immediate dismissal. [The] faculty member should be reminded of university policy and should accept responsibility for wrongdoing. Additional violations will result in "harder" sanctions including possible dismissal.

Two other faculty members had varied responses. The first said:

> No sanctions should be taken without faculty review. A formal warning is the strongest reasonable sanction for a first offense.

The second was more emphatic:

> Dismissal is appropriate for unequivocally racist speech in the classroom.

In another vignette, an undergraduate at a highly prestigious university worked on a senior thesis that involved performance art. Her advisor approved the project, which consisted of the student repeatedly inseminating herself with donated sperm and inducing abortions by using herbs. The display of her project featured a large cube wrapped in sheets covered with blood from the abortions, as well as video images of her inducing the procedures. Word of the project got out and there was substantial public outrage, including angry letters from scores of alumni criticizing the university for allowing the project to be done and then possibly displaying the results publicly. The dean of the undergraduate college was "appalled" by the project and decided not to allow the project to be shown, while promising to reexamine what constitutes an appropriate senior art project.

The question put to the faculty receiving the survey was: "What ought to be done about this project?" The responses to this vignette varied greatly. Twenty-eight percent thought that the administration should do nothing, since it was not their business "to determine what 'appropriate' art is even if it does offend the community." A quarter of the responding faculty agreed with what the dean did; another 11 percent not only agreed with the dean's action but also would "publicly sanction the advisor of the student." Thirteen percent would have referred the case to a faculty committee to decide; another 15 percent offered qualitative responses because their responses did not fit into any of the given categories; and about 6 percent of the faculty said: "I don't know what should be done."

One faculty member said:

I am disgusted by the performance, even though I am not against abortion per se. I do agree that they should reassess what constitutes an appropriate senior art project, but given that the student was approved for this project, she cannot be reprimanded now. I would recommend engaging a discussion between the faculty mentor and the administration, as well as other faculty members.

Another put it slightly differently:

I believe the Dean's public statement was appropriate, but not the decision to prohibit the performance. "Appalling" does not mean illegal.

Yet another expressed somewhat different concerns:

I may not agree with the dean's handling of the situation or even the verdict (a committee of faculty members would be the appropriate mechanism), but the university has the obligation and right to determine what is in the interest of the university, its educational mission, and reputation. In this case . . . the student is using university property and resources to produce potentially deeply offensive art.

It remains, of course, an open question how far this faculty member would be willing to go to allow the university administration to define for the faculty what is in the "interest of the university" and "its educational mission, and reputation."

The student's health was another theme raised in the qualitative responses. For example:

> In general, the administration of a university should avoid any censorship of students' creative work. I therefore tend to agree most with the first option ["do nothing"]: The administration should not determine what "appropriate" art is even if it does offend the community.... In this instance, however, the situation is complicated by the fact that the student's work ... is very likely dangerous to her health. There's also the question of whether the university is liable to prosecution for sanctioning or turning a blind eye to such a quasi-medical procedure.... [T]he administration would need to take legal advice to ensure that it is fulfilling its duty of care to its student, and that it is not exposing itself to legal risk by allowing the student to go ahead with her project. A competent advisor would bring these questions before his/her supervisor as soon as he/she learned about the project.

And finally, another faculty member tersely said:

> Get the poor kid some help.

In the actual case, extreme pressure was placed on the student to withdraw the project from public view and to admit, as it turns out, that the abortions were simulated. Under protest and possibly some threat, the student went public and revealed these facts.

Finally, let's look at a situation involving the legitimacy of an institutional review board's (IRB) intervention into the research of a team of anthropologists and geneticists. There has been a good deal of controversy surrounding the role of IRBs, especially among social scientists and members of professional schools who do research that clearly poses minimal, if any, risk to human subjects, and among those whose research is not supported by the federal government. In the survey situation presented to the faculty, the researchers were studying "a rare but deadly hereditary disease in Venezuela." There was a very high incidence of the disease in a small fishing town where there was significant intermarriage within the deeply Catholic community. The researchers, who had been working there for more than twenty years, would provide villagers with birth control information, but only on request. The IRB, in reviewing a grant proposal from the group, told the researchers that they "cannot carry out the research unless they have mandatory sessions explaining the heritability of the disease and how birth control methods could reduce the incidence in the community." The researchers, who had made major genetic discoveries about the disease through their prior research (including the discovery of the gene that caused the disease), refused to comply with the IRB requirement, claiming that the IRB was being insensitive to the religious beliefs of the community and that the IRB's rejection of the proposal was violating their rights of free inquiry. The responses of the faculty to this scenario showed considerable variation: 49 percent of the faculty agreed with the researchers that the IRB was interfering with the right to free inquiry, but 37 percent supported the position of the IRB. (Fourteen percent of the faculty had qualitative responses to the situation since they did not feel that the two response categories captured their views.)

Here is an unsystematic sample of these views. One professor said:

The IRB system is a mandatory requirement of the US Federal medical funding system created to prevent exploitation of human research subjects. A common criticism of the IRB system is that it was designed to handle medical research in US hospitals and that its rules are unsuited for other types of research, especially social science research abroad.... This is a good argument for social science professional societies working towards changing the rules. However, until that time, the university has no legal option but to follow the advice of its IRB. Any student of academic bureaucracies knows that a review board will issue ridiculous ruling[s] in at least a small percentage of cases. Get used to it!

Another faculty member expressed a somewhat different point of view:

It seems to me that the researchers have an obligation to share their results, but in a way that is culturally sensitive and assessed by them rather than imposed by the IRB.

Yet another faculty member thought some form of compromise was appropriate:

The university institutional official should work with the IRB and the PI [principal investigator] and move toward a middle ground—explaining the heritability of the disease may be done without needing to jump to prescribing birth control for all; disentangle these two steps. This is complex. As a former IRB chair, I believe it warrants the university's attention and problem solving.

Another faculty member was inclined to look at the situation in terms of risk assessment:

The key is that the intervention of the researchers does not increase risk to community members. If the rest of their research does not expose community members to increased risk, I don't see why the researchers must hold sessions on the impact of birth control.

And another, who was weighing the response in terms of the relative importance of two values:

I don't know. IRB's job is to weigh ethical concerns against one another, so in principle I support the position of the IRB as the proper arbiter to these issues, but I don't want to select that because it would suggest that I reflexively think reproductive rights obviously trump respect for religious traditions, which is a different question and would require more details.

And, finally, the not infrequent response:

What is an IRB?

Consider a few tentative observations about how the faculty responded to the various vignettes. For most of them, academic freedom is associated with freedom of expression. There was a higher level of consensus among the faculty when they considered basic freedom-of-speech vignettes—with the overwhelming majority favoring doing nothing to hinder open discourse and expression of opinions by faculty members, even when the subject of their speech was a highly controversial topic.[41] However, one of the objectives in creating these vignettes was to place the faculty members in situations where they might find themselves having to evaluate conflicting norms.[42] For example, faculty members might support the right of a colleague to say anything in class, but they might also believe strongly that political statements should be limited to courses about political subjects or should be articulated outside the classroom. The reactions to free speech vignettes were more varied when we introduced what some might feel were inappropriate settings for the speech. So, we found less faculty consensus when a chemistry professor was using his or her chemistry class to discuss a political subject. In situations involving conflicting norms, the level of consensus went down substantially.

The faculty responses were also varied when the vignettes turned to the conduct of research under conditions of potentially conflicting norms. When the government attempted to intervene in research projects that had been funded through the peer-review process of federal granting agencies, the faculty objected strongly and almost without dissent. But when other conditions were added, such as whether it was acceptable to have prior review and prior restraint on publications that could, hypothetically, help terrorists create biological weapons, the faculty members were far more divided in their opinions. When vignettes posed questions about the appropriate role of IRBs at the university, opinions also varied widely. The norm to support the IRB is based on the idea that it exists to ensure that human subjects are protected from harm as a result of a federally sponsored research project. This conflicts with the potential gains to be obtained from the genetic and anthropological work being done and the respect for local cultural norms in a highly Catholic setting.[43]

Faculty members were almost exactly equally divided on the question of whether students had the right to picket and boycott a class because they believed the professor was presenting a biased point of view. Here, the conflicting norms involved the right of students to protest against the norm that faculty autonomy in the classroom is sacred and that the faculty and students are not on equal footing: Faculty members determine what is on a reading list, how a class is organized, and how the discourse takes place inside the classroom. Furthermore, since these protests took place outside the classroom, without the permission of the dean, the action violated the accepted norm of *where* protest can take place on campus, as well as the institutional processes required for such dissent. The responses to the vignettes not only varied but suggest that there may be different types of actions by professors that elicit various responses among their peers in terms of the limits or boundaries of academic freedom.

Faculty members seem cautious about imposing strong sanctions against professors whose actions they disapprove of. The respondents who thought a colleague had acted inappropriately tended to begin by trying to persuade the culprit to desist, and only when he/she did not would they be willing to apply sanctions. Rarely would they apply strong sanctions for actions they deemed wrong or hurtful. They were much more likely to accept the idea of applying soft sanctions rather than considering reprimands or dismissals.

If an erosion of the norms of academic freedom and free inquiry has taken place at American universities and colleges, it may well be the result of abridgements of the freedom of speech that we have seen on campuses over the past several decades. The restrictive nature of speech codes, the willingness to forbid speakers to talk at universities because their speech might offend some members of the community, the efforts by students to have their university or college rescind invitations to recipients of honorary degrees or class speakers at graduation, and the hundreds of cases of curtailments of free speech on campus that have been chronicled by scholars like David Bromwich, Cass Sunstein, Kent Greenawalt, and Greg Lukianoff may have led the faculty to devalue academic freedom compared with other core values of the university. In fact, the reluctance to accept the idea that speakers have a right to offend others' sensibilities may lead faculty members to think of academic freedom and free inquiry as just another value of the university and not a preeminent one. This devaluation, if confirmed by additional research, could have dangerous consequences for the university, including a greater willingness among faculty and students to limit free discourse and free research inquiry.

It also seems to be true that relatively few faculty members, even at a place like Columbia, have given much thought to the consequences of restraints on academic freedom despite the repercussions they may have for free inquiry at the university. In our survey, this becomes most apparent in the situation involving the IRB's actions. We can be reasonably certain that the vast majority of faculty do not view the IRB as a form of licensing that involves prior restraint on speech and research.[44]

If we are to enhance further our great universities, we should continue the debate about the parameters of what we mean by the value of academic freedom and its place at great universities. But while we are in contested territory, let's not forget the basic ideas associated with academic freedom outlined in the Kalven Committee Report. These principles remain fundamental to the creation and maintenance of great universities. Any compromise must be resisted, and all constituents within the university community ought to forge an alliance that defends these principles. Without being vigilant in the defense of academic freedom and to see it as, in fact, a fundamental, enabling value of great universities, the quality of our most distinguished institutions of higher learning will surely erode over the next several decades. This defense will take courage, which is in too short supply these days within the academy. As we see continuing efforts to undermine this value from many quarters, our courage will be tested; and if we fail that test, we will surely regret the consequences for our universities and our country.

CHAPTER TEN

Reconstructing the University-Government Compact

How do we increase…scientific capital? First, we must have plenty of men and women trained in science, for upon them depends both the creation of new knowledge and its application to practical purposes. Second, we must strengthen the centers of basic research which are principally the colleges, universities, and research institutes. These institutions provide the environment which is most conducive to the creation of new scientific knowledge and least under pressure for immediate, tangible results.

—VANNEVAR BUSH, *SCIENCE, THE ENDLESS FRONTIER*

SCIENCE AND TECHNOLOGY did not win World War II, but they made mighty contributions to the Allied victory. The leaders of the Manhattan Project, of the Radiation Laboratory at MIT, and of other large scientific facilities elsewhere in the country improved radar, discovered antisubmarine detection techniques, developed further antibiotics, and were responsible for other scientific and technological breakthroughs. The heads of these missions became national heroes. People whom we know, like Vannevar Bush, J. Robert Oppenheimer, and James B. Conant, found their faces on the cover of both *Life* and *Time* magazines—some more than once. While Senator Joseph McCarthy was trying to track down nonexistent subversives at research universities, the country was simultaneously having a love affair with the emerging national system of innovation and discovery.

On December 7, 1945, a *New York Times* editorial praised the development of the atomic bomb, calling it "the most stupendous military and scientific achievement of our times" and perhaps "the most stupendous ever made in the history of science and technology." The scientists responsible for the bomb were less effusive than the paper of record. The *Times* called for a continuation of American support for science.

What we witnessed after the war was the construction of the great transformational compact between the American federal government and our research universities. We know the bargain. The federal government would appropriate taxpayer dollars for the advancement of science and technology; it would outsource this effort to American research universities after grant proposals were peer reviewed by the newly created National Science Foundation (NSF) or the reconfigured National Institutes of Health (NIH); and it would grant the universities substantial autonomy in pursuing new knowledge.[1] For their part, the universities committed themselves to making important new discoveries that would ensure continued American military superiority; would improve the health of the nation; would increase the skills and knowledge (the human capital) of their graduates; would link teaching with research, especially at the graduate and postdoctoral laboratory levels; and would operate with integrity and accountability for their work.

Although formal arrangements were made, and auditing of grant funds was part of the compact, there was an assumption that universities and the government would stick to the bargain and would act in the best interest of the nation.[2] The original compact had its formal side, but the cooperation that was assumed suggested a very high level of trust between the two institutions.

While Big Science was in its neonatal state of development, the transformation of the American research university was significantly dependent on the successful operation of this compact. It was a different era, of course. In 1970, after what some have dubbed "the Golden Age" of American science, the federal budget was about $200 billion; today, it stands at roughly $3.5 trillion.

As the amount of funding from federal sources (well more than twenty separate funding agencies today) grew dramatically and more players entered the game, the proper use of federal dollars became a source of interest—especially to the federal agencies and Congress. President Reagan questioned the value of federal agencies funding the social and behavioral sciences at all. He largely succeeded in eliminating this funding, cutting over half of the budgets dedicated to these areas of research. Congress began to question the peer review system as an old boys' network, and the original element in the compact—that the universities would recover the full, audited cost of conducting research, both personnel costs and facilities costs—was questioned. Finally, in 1991, the federal government took the step of placing a strict cap of 26 percent on administrative costs in the Facilities and Administrative Cost[3] recovered under the Office of Management and Budget (OMB) Circular A-21, regardless of what they might actually be (previously, the audited costs to run scientific projects and maintain adequate laboratory facilities, which might run to 60 or 80 percent [and in some cases higher] of direct costs for people working on the research project, were paid by the government).[4] Consequently, universities had to find ways to support basic and goal-oriented research with funds that did not come from the federal government. In most cases, that source was student tuition and fees.[5] At the same time, research universities, which were becoming huge institutions as well—with annual budgets exceeding $2 or $3 billion a year—were becoming lax in monitoring and sanctioning transgressions of fundamental scientific norms and values.

In short, after 1970 we began to see a gradual, but very notable, erosion of the fundamental value of trust that was part of the original compact. Parts of the government were questioning how federal dollars were actually being spent—and whether there were inappropriate charges made to federal research projects.[6] As trust erodes, the parties to the agreements begin to introduce formal legislation and administrative regulations that restrain purportedly widespread unsavory behavior. That erosion has continued until today and represents a breakdown that threatens the nation's leadership in producing the world's most significant research.

As societies become as complex as ours, there inevitably will be many laws and regulations that control our behavior. Many of them, although often cumbersome, are ways of protecting us from risks to our health, safety, basic rights, and the environment.[7] In short, there is a need for some government regulation whose importance cannot be minimized. The laws and regulations that are directed toward universities are not dissimilar from those imposed on other institutions. They have increased rapidly over the past half-century. Unfortunately, many of them create heavy costs for these institutions without producing much benefit. So as the government imposes still more regulations and reporting requirements on universities while simultaneously refusing to pay for these unfunded mandates, it is exacerbating the very problems of cost and accountability that it supposedly wants to ameliorate. Compliance becomes more a matter of skilled legal and staff work plus professorial ingenuity than of principled adherence to a set of basic values. This is reflected at universities in the increasingly central role played by compliance officers and lawyers, including the general counsel, in decision making. A culture of risk aversion begins to pervade our universities when they ought to be pushing back against bad ideas and costly regulations of unproven value.[8]

Let me paint the picture of growing distrust and the substitution of legal and regulatory means for what had been the trust component of the compact between universities and the government. Today there are more than 4,000 federal regulations of research done at our universities, and by some estimates more than six hundred of these place a serious administrative burden on university staff. (The height of the paperwork is beginning to rival the size and complexity of the tax code.)[9] One estimate, from the 2012 Faculty Workload Survey of the Federal Demonstration Partnership, suggests that 42 percent of scientists' time on research grants is spent on compliance with federal regulations.[10] Other estimates suggest that somewhere between 8 and 10 percent of a university's total expenditures go toward compliance.[11] Audits today by the federal IGs (inspectors generals) of university research tend to proceed with the following null hypothesis: There is malfeasance, corruption, negligence, and even felony behavior going on at universities, and it is our responsibility to ferret it out and report it to Congress. Now, the universities are asked to prove that this is *not* true—to overturn the null hypothesis. The mind-set of auditors is not one of "we're in this together to help universities produce important new discoveries," but "we will act as if grants are procurement contracts that we are auditing for misbehavior." What is so disconcerting to the universities is illustrated by the supposed overcharges claimed by an NSF inspector general in an audit of a grant to a major research university. Initially, the questioned costs amounted to $6,325,483, which included supposed overcharges for faculty and other summer salaries, inappropriate cost transfers into NSF awards, indirect cost overcharges, and, among other things, the inappropriate use of almost $200,000 of remaining fellowship funds for nonaward purposes. After these claims were questioned by the university and reexamined by the NSF's Cost Analysis and Audit Resolution Branch, the final disallowance was $43,551—a figure, unlike the initial sum, that was not conveyed to the public until months after the original claim of misuse of funds.[12] In another 2015 effort to ferret out misbehavior at a world-renowned public university, the inspector general's office questioned $2,358,380 in charges by grantees of one federal agency. After further review and resolution of these charges, the auditors disallowed $130,469.

All parties can be implicated in this breakdown of trust. Universities have not done what they could by way of self-policing or as self-regulating institutions. In fact, here is the typical pattern of behaviors that lead to federal regulations: A bad actor at a university conducts research in an inappropriate way that leads to some catastrophic event(s) and a scandal.[13] This can be misuse of animals, misuse of human subjects, a novel experiment that leads to one or more deaths of the experiments' subjects, or a conflict of interest influencing trial outcomes due to inappropriate relationships between the trial's industrial sponsors and the professors' financial well-being. Then the university fails to take prompt action to investigate the transgression and, where appropriate, sanction the researcher(s). Some institutions try to sweep the incident under the rug for fear of bad publicity; others are simply inept; and worst of all, some don't think that a major transgression of the basic research norms is wrong. After the bad actor commits his or her sin, not only does the university fail to swiftly take action (again, where the evidence is clear), but it also does not provide any information about the rate at which such bad behavior occurs. This triggers a cascading set of consequences. Like scientific fraud, these incidents of bad behavior represent a tiny fraction of all scientific activities at our preeminent universities—but that doesn't seem to matter. Someone informs or leaks the information of the incident to the media. Since the media often doesn't know how to place the action into some larger context of noncompliance, they tend to sensationalize the incident and make the public feel that the bad behavior is rampant within the academic community. Now the politicians spring into action. Voicing their abhorrence, they publically vilify both the individual researcher and the university where he or she works. The next step is the insistence that there need to be regulations or legislation to ensure that this kind of behavior will not occur again—even if it is impossible for any institution to stamp out all bad actors through a formal process of regulation. Legislation or regulations are drafted, put into effect, and are added to the pile of more than 4,000 others. Importantly, the regulation is *not* limited to any single or set of institutions; it now applies to every researcher at the nation's universities and colleges.

Among the problems with this method of triggering the explosion of regulation is that the new rules are not based on any systematic collection or analysis of data—they are often based on single cases. When the regulation is put into effect, there is no "sunset" clause that would force the administrative agency at some point to take stock of the value of the regulation and whether it ought to be maintained, streamlined, or eliminated. Thus, the burden increases on the research universities. All of these added regulations are done in the name of accountability—as if universities lack accountability when they are, in fact, among the most accountable institutions in the nation.

But there are other perverse, sometimes unintended, outcomes of this process. For example, instead of scientists working on their science (for which the initial grant was intended), and, hopefully, coming up with cures for disease and new fundamental discoveries and innovations, they are spending almost half of their time filling out government forms, helped by the hundreds of compliance officers that the university has hired to deal with these rules. Then the regulations lead many scientists to opt out of fields that require inordinate amounts of documented compliance—for example, working with animals, especially primates, to test vaccines or other potentially highly beneficial discoveries. Given the number of federal agencies that make grants for research, there is a level of unnecessary redundancy and slight difference in reporting requirements that dramatically increases the time needed to demonstrate compliance.

Of course, there are hundreds of other regulations (and legislation) that affect universities beyond their mission as research centers. Many affect students and faculty behavior, hiring and promotion, the workplace environment, and a host of other aspects of our universities. Nonetheless, at the largest and most distinguished research universities that do hundreds of millions of dollars of federally funded research each year, almost all of these regulations represented "unfunded mandates" by the government. The cap on administrative costs produces this new cost structure—one that universities understandably oppose. These unfunded mandates often result, probably without intention, in the universities' difficulty in complying with other requests from the government. For example, if the cost of compliance is 8 percent or more of a university's budget, and the government, donors, or other third parties will not cover those costs, then universities, in order to balance their budgets, can either cut the number of faculty members, defer maintenance on their facilities, drop productive academic activities or other administrative units, or increase tuition. They generally will increase tuition, angering members of Congress and the Executive branch that are pressuring them to hold down tuition increases. Finally, there are some regulations that may well be unconstitutional but have not been challenged by universities. We'll look at one example below.

What we are left with is a state of extreme distrust. And although the public distrusts Congress and other government agencies more than they do universities, the level of distrust between these partners threatens our ability to ensure that our great research universities remain the best in the world. We must begin to think of mechanisms that will reverse this trend and bring some level of renewed cooperation, a sense of common interests, and trust back to this vital partnership. And the worst of it is that many potentially important discoveries that could be used to save lives or to create new industries are never made because of brilliant faculty members opting out of the effort due to the burdens of government regulations, potential sanctions of their work by their university, or public humiliation, which adversely affects their careers through bad publicity.[14]

Before suggesting a few such mechanisms, I want to provide examples of where changes in government policies, coupled with university actions, could improve the probability that our universities will retain their preeminence and become better places for learning and discovery in the future.

I've alluded to a number of these laws and regulations throughout this book. Now I want to suggest what the government ought to do administratively and legally to reduce the unnecessary burdens on our great universities while keeping some important regulations in place. Many of my suggestions have implications for the broader society as well. In fact, these briefs for the university could be made for other institutions, too.

Immigration Law

The American immigration system is broken. Almost everyone in the nation, including its political leaders, acknowledges this, but there seems to be no consensus on how to reform the system. Changes in the nation's immigration laws seem clearly necessary and of particular importance for enhancing still further the standing of our great universities.[15] Both Presidents Bush and Obama proposed comprehensive overhauls of the current system only to be rebuffed by Congress. Contrary to the idea that we are moving toward the existence of global universities, we are virtually there. In 2000, when I was provost at Columbia, 40 percent of the tenured arts and sciences faculty were born or received their academic training in other countries. I'm sure that the percentage is no less today. In fact, a record number of undergraduates as well as graduate students, 886,052, came to the United States in 2013–2014 to study at our exceptional universities and colleges.[16] This number has grown by 72 percent since 2000. Without the presence of foreign-born scholars, there would be a dearth of first-rate graduate students in a number of STEM fields. We are not engaged in altruism; we are filling gaps where we need talent. At the undergraduate level, many of these foreign students supply a significant part of the tuition income stream necessary for the survival of those institutions.[17]

Since we are a magnet for the world's academic talent (which will not last forever), the federal government ought to enact a comprehensive immigration reform act that includes a section specifically tailored to the highly skilled talent who want to do advanced studies in the United States, who want to teach and do research here, and who have families who work in other occupations. Even if the Ph.D. students or postdoctoral fellows are granted "green cards," they may turn down the opportunity because other members of their immediate family are forced to leave the United States. We cannot lose this talent until we are capable of replacing it with our own, which at best will be attained some decades in the future. These changes in immigration laws ought to make it reasonably easy for extremely talented individuals and their families to migrate to the United States as permanent residents or as citizens. To train these people and then refuse to have them become full members of our society not only goes against our historical openness to talented immigrants but is also counterproductive and economically wasteful. We train these young people in ways that make them highly qualified for skilled jobs, and then we let other nations reap the rewards of their economic productivity. While having American-educated leaders in foreign countries may reinforce social cohesion between the United States and those nations, it does not solve our immediate need to open our borders to exceptionally talented women and men with the idea of placing them in the mainstream of American society. Furthermore, the national funding agencies for science, engineering, and other forms of scholarship should support foreigners who do not hold formal citizenship but who work at our universities and colleges. They should not have to seek out bogus "principal investigators" to front for their laboratories and research grants. Finally, we should not place a quota on the number of people in these categories who can move toward full citizenship. These people are not "taking away jobs" from highly qualified Americans. They are exceptional talents who want to remain in the United States and whose expertise we need. In fact, their work often creates many new jobs in the longer run because of their discoveries or innovations that lead to new businesses.

Financial Aid and "Overlap"

All undergraduate financial aid, if possible, should be based on demonstrated need; and admissions should be independent of that need. We ought to construct a financial aid system that mimics what has been in place at the highly selective colleges and universities in the nation (see Chapter 4). As much as possible, available resources, including government financial aid grants, should be used for the truly needy.[18] Those who come from wealthy backgrounds ought to pay more for their college education than those who come from backgrounds of financial hardship, and they should stop thinking of this as a form of mandated charity. This basic principle ought to prevail at state universities as well as private institutions of higher learning.

This full-need principle was dealt a severe blow in 1991 when the Justice Department alleged that the Ivy League universities plus a few other distinguished institutions of higher learning conspired to restrain trade and committed antitrust violations by meeting annually as a group to establish the appropriate level of aid for students admitted to more than one school in the group. The "overlap" group analyzed each case to determine an appropriate and collectively agreed-upon level of financial aid.[19] This practice was undoubtedly a restraint on competition (as the intention was to avoid having bidding wars over students) and by any strict interpretation of the antitrust laws was an antitrust violation. Overlap was designed to have students make choices based on their interest in the academic programs of schools, as well as other factors, but not on the basis of the amount of financial aid offered. The government's assertion was correct: Overlap was, in effect, fixing the price of a college education for students admitted to more than one school and consequently making it impossible for their families to "negotiate" the best deal.

That is, in fact, what the Third Circuit Court found. Rather than appeal that decision, the Ivy League group entered into a consent decree with the Justice Department that ended overlap and forbade for ten years representatives of these schools from uttering a word to each other about their financial aid policies. As provost at Columbia at the time, I thought that the group should appeal this ruling since it struck at the heart of a deeply held value within our institutions of not competing for students on the basis of how much money we could offer them. MIT took the principled position and fought the government. The institution argued that financial aid was a form of charity and exempt from antitrust law and that dismantling the "overlap agreement" would create a bidding war among wealthy schools for students from wealthy families. Since the students who tended to be the highest achievers through secondary school had gone to the best schools, which were supported by families with a good deal of money, there would be less financial aid available for highly qualified students from lower socioeconomic backgrounds. After a protracted, expensive battle, MIT "won" its case in 1993. A federal appeals court ordered that a new trial be held, saying that the district court had failed to sufficiently debate MIT's position.

Following MIT's victory, Congress took up the matter when it passed the Improving America's Schools Act of 1994. Section 568 of the act stated that it was not unlawful or a violation of the antitrust law for schools (in cases where students were admitted to at least two need-blind universities or colleges) to attempt to agree that they would base financial aid on need; that they could use common principles of analysis for determining need and a common application form; and that they could engage in a one-time exchange of certain pre-award financial aid data for students admitted to more than one school in the group. The schools that bought into this set of criteria became known as the "568 Group," which included almost all of the major elite private universities and colleges.

Winning and losing the antitrust case was less important than the principles on which MIT won. In such antitrust matters, the courts should weigh the anticompetitive consequences of the universities' overlap meetings against another important principle, which is the "social welfare justifications" proffered by MIT and held by the universities that had previously capitulated to government power. The attempt to spread financial aid dollars as broadly as possible to include the talented economically disadvantaged was more important than competition for the so-called "best" students, who almost invariably turned out also to be from the wealthiest families.

Under the Section 568 provisions there was, however, no guarantee that two or more schools would offer the same financial aid package to the individual who was admitted into these schools. The institutions could compare data and use a common methodology, but they could not agree on a strict formula that would determine that all of the financial aid packages offered the students would be the same. The law ought to be extended to reinstate the overlap concept that would settle on the amount that any given student should expect to come from his or her parents' contribution to his or her education. Financial aid for students in need is at least as worthy of antitrust exemption as is American baseball.

Faculty Retirement Laws

Every generation or two, the university must be "reborn" with new minds that have different angles of vision from their predecessors and the vitality to build research teams and work with many graduate and undergraduate students. When this process is impeded, two harmful things happen: Brilliant scholars and scientists are unable to obtain positions at top universities, and fewer talented people elect to enter the professoriate since it seems devoid of attractive opportunities. A limited number of legal changes could easily rectify this situation. Much of this rests on the age-discrimination statutes. Until a few decades ago, the federal mandatory retirement age for professors was the Bismarckian retirement age of sixty-five. Since our productive lives far exceed those in Bismarck's time, there is no reason to think of sixty-five as a sacred terminus for a productive career.

In fact, in the past the retirement age for professors was moved first to sixty-eight and then to seventy, which prevailed until mandatory retirement for tenured faculty members ended in 1993. But with the amendment to the 1967 Age Discrimination in Employment legislation, which certainly had significant positive social value, professors were omitted from the exempt category, unlike airline pilots, for example.[20] For the future vitality of the academy, Congress needs to rethink how it treats aging professors.[21] This is also related to tenure, since a tenured professor can work at major universities and elsewhere well into his or her eighties, or even later if they manage to survive that long. The same is true with the federal judiciary, where tenure plays a similar role—providing a form of independence from ideological and political action that is irrelevant to the person's actual performance. But, as with the academy, the absence of any mandatory retirement age retards change (for better or worse).

Although I believe strongly in the importance of academic tenure, some adjustments ought to be made. Congress ought to set a mandatory retirement age for faculty members at some age, perhaps seventy-five, which would allow individuals to continue productive work until they are close to the actuarial average mortality age for their cohort. This number can be indexed to account for increasing life expectancy over time. But along with the maximum working age, tenure for faculty members should end at the age of seventy, in order for a university to ask unproductive faculty members to step down from their tenured positions. For faculty who wish to work beyond the age of seventy-five, universities ought to institute "Distinguished Scholars" programs by which some of these individuals with a good track record could teach one or two undergraduate courses or mentor younger scholars and students.[22] Their place in the community ought to be preserved, which suggests that they should have many of the same privileges that they held while full-time faculty members. But along with some new mandatory retirement age, there must be protection for professors who lose their tenure and who are targeted for an exit by administrators or colleagues for reasons unrelated to the quality of their current work. External evaluators ought to be used to assess the continuing contributions of the older cohort of faculty members as teachers and researchers. Appropriate appeals processes should also be put into place.

The federal and state governments, as well as the universities, produce legal disincentives against retiring. One change in tax law ought to help fix at least part of this problem. Those faculty members who participate in defined contribution retirement plans, such as the 403(b) TIAA-CREF investment company, can defer paying taxes on their accounts until they have reached seventy and one-half years of age.[23] Then the faculty member or the plan participant must begin to draw down annually their invested funds at a rate determined by actuarial tables or by plan policies, unless they continue to work at the same university that employed them at the time they reached seventy and one-half years. The drawdowns are taxed as ordinary income. In good times, when the markets are growing and funds are accumulating rapidly in these plans, faculty members feel that they can retire and not suffer economically, especially when they add the retirement plan amount to their social security. But when the stock market tanks and professors are invested significantly in equity markets through these funds, they believe that they cannot afford to retire. These faculty members continue working out of necessity rather than out of a sustained commitment to teaching and research.

The government ought to change its tax laws to ameliorate this kind of disincentive. All funds that are contributed over the career of the faculty member—whether by the university or the individual plan participant—could be taxed as ordinary income when withdrawn. But the capital appreciation of the investment, which often makes up at least half of the total value of the retirement plan, could be taxed as capital gains. This is no different from the way the government taxes the distribution of appreciated assets in private equity funds. If more faculty members retired under these conditions, it would increase the vitality of the university faculties by opening up slots for new, younger, and extremely talented minds.

For their part, universities could reduce the number of disincentives that are obstacles to voluntary retirement. Term life insurance policies could be continued after retirement; policies on housing, which are sometimes offered as a recruiting incentive, could be altered so that retiring faculty members don't lose their housing privileges for perhaps five years; and offices could be provided on a part-time basis for faculty who often fear loss of community as much as the loss of their financial position. Offering retired faculty free access to courses that they might like to attend, the opportunity to teach a single course each year, and the chance to use the athletic, library, and information technology facilities after retirement would all help. Each of these incentives has cost implications, but they are not nearly as large, on average, as the cost of replacing a long-term faculty member with a vibrant full-time junior faculty member.

Overregulation

As I've suggested, one result of the breakdown in trust between research universities and local, state, and federal governments is that our universities have been shackled by local, state, and federal regulations—ways by which the government can constrain the autonomy of these great institutions. From the perspective of faculty members and academic leaders, there are some that are more onerous than others. Among the top ten candidates contending for the title of most burdensome regulations are: IRB protocols and compliance and training requirements, Institutional Animal Care and Use Committee (IACUC) protocols and training, training of personnel and students, grant progress report submissions, the absence of uniform guidelines for filing research proposals with different funding agencies, the absence of "just in time" requirements when submitting grant proposals,[24] subcontracting and collaborations, safety planning and monitoring, equipment and supply management, and the accreditation process.[25] Here are a few examples that include some on this list and others that regulate university activities other than research grant support.

Effort and Mandated Reporting. As of 2015, the government requires "effort reporting," meaning that if a researcher commits to spending 50 percent of his or her time on a research grant, he or she must attest to that level of effort and, if called upon, must demonstrate that the reporting is accurate. Academic faculty members don't punch time clocks. Some work a seventy-hour week, others work forty hours, others fall somewhere in between. Because many scientists and engineers hold several grants simultaneously—all related to the same research—it is not always easy for them to allocate precisely how much of their time was spent on one grant rather than another. The research is not parsed in that fashion. Instead, they produce reports that will meet federal requirements even if they are not listing precisely the time they said would be needed as indicated on the grant proposals. Time spent on research projects is what they think about, not their compliance with the time allocated on one or another proposal funding the same work. Because we are not dealing with a particularly stupid set of people, they can easily navigate their way around these formulaic regulations. Researchers almost invariably comply with their commitments, but they don't construct billable hours as lawyers do. When regulations like

this one are put in place, it sets in motion the creation of a university bureaucracy that takes care of the mandated regulatory reporting. An administrative office, with many subgroups, is established—and eventually its staff may
grow to scores of full-time employees. Yet these compliance officers will get
nowhere with actually disclosing those who overreport their effort. They'll
send out multiple memos and threats, but it is not in the administrator's or the
faculty member's interest to file government reports that fail to pass inspection
by some bureaucrat in Washington. If the federal bureaucracy suspects some
hanky-panky at the university, a visit may be scheduled to audit reports. That
costs more money and time. Yet, universities are rarely sanctioned for inadequate
effort put into reports. The regulation promotes deviant behavior since faculty
members do not want to jeopardize grants because their effort falls slightly
short of what they have stated on one proposal and slightly more on another proposal funding the same work. It shifts the focus away from what is most important: the discoveries that might have occurred during the time spent on the grant.

Then there is the government's requirement for what is called "mandated
reporting." A faculty member who sees any activity that might involve violations of human subjects or sexual abuse, along with a host of other behaviors,
is required to report this to administrative officers at the university. This form
of regulation has a chilling effect on research. It is difficult to oversee the fieldwork of others, and researchers will often simply not do the research rather than
play the role of informer on their students or colleagues. Mandated reporting
ought to be stricken from the books, and ethical standards ought to be taught
about how to deal with research subjects.

Affirmative Action Reporting. There is a continuing need for and value in affirmative action policies. Unlike Justice Sandra Day O'Connor, who in the 2003
University of Michigan affirmative action case speculated that these laws would
only be needed for twenty-five years, I'm not sure that is the case.[26] My commitment to affirmative action is not based on the arguments put forward in Supreme Court cases from *Bakke* (1978) to the *Gratz* and *Grutter* cases (2003), most
particularly on the supposedly demonstrated societal benefits of increasing
diversity on campus.[27] Rather, the continuing value of affirmative action lies
principally in the fact that African Americans, Latinos, and women have been
and continue to be subjected to various forms of discrimination—and economic deprivation. If we don't fall prey to the reification of test scores as a
proxy for ability of all kinds, then affirmative action helps us shape a community and a culture of broader understanding. (No one will convince me

that Michael Jordan, who attended the University of North Carolina, or Lebron James, who never attended college, is not as "smart" as some of the winners of Nobel Prizes or presidents of universities.) It helps bring all individuals in our society, regardless of ascribed characteristics or economic misfortune, to the "starting line" with roughly equal weights on their backs. We must do this to further our democratic ideals and to reduce racial, ethnic, and gender-based inequalities.

But realizing true diversity of talents in shaping a class and having those talents grow as a result of a university education cannot be achieved by imposing either quotas or mandated reporting of the percentage in one group or another—whether students, staff, or faculty members. Of course, these groups need legal protection; and if they feel discriminated against, they should have full recourse to the justice system and an internal review system within the university. But again, formal massive federally imposed regulations are not the best way to achieve these larger goals. Although figures on the composition of the student bodies and faculty members of the university ought to be publicly available, huge bureaucratic efforts mandated by the government to ensure compliance with the law simply don't work.

The real way to shape a class is to recognize how women, people of color, and those with different sexual orientations and from various socioeconomic backgrounds with varying types of talent make the community a more interesting and rewarding place to be. The same is true for athletes—although, as I've said, I believe that there is a surplus of recruited athletes at prestigious universities.

In fact, our finest universities do better than most other American institutions in seeing the merits of affirmative action. Although the rhetoric of their leaders may conform to the stated reasons given by the Supreme Court to uphold affirmative action, they do, at least the overwhelming majority of them, want to see diversity of talents, points of view, and social and racial backgrounds strolling down college walk.

In the 1990s, when I proposed to provide equal housing and other benefits to gay couples at Columbia (long before gay marriage was upheld by the Supreme Court in 2015), everyone I consulted said it was premature and that the trustees would resist this change in policy. Yet after I made the arguments about fairness and justice to the trustees, as well as about the way lack of equal benefits was harming Columbia's academic quality, only one of twenty-four trustees voted against the proposal—allowing us to lead the way for other colleges and universities to provide similar benefits to gay couples. This was not achieved because of government regulations or mandates; it was achieved because of a set of values about injustice that were broadly held at the university.

This is not the way things tend to work at universities today. Every university has an office to monitor affirmative action goals and achievements as well as equal employment opportunities. But if faculty members at the university wish to circumvent these regulations, it is not difficult to do so. They know the applicant pool for jobs; and they do the interviewing, set the criteria for offers, and evaluate the relative merits of the applicants. They are supposedly experts in their field; so if they claim that a minority candidate was passed over for a white applicant because the minority candidate was less qualified for the position there is no one who can do much about it. This is especially true in faculty hiring and promotions. Creating elaborate affirmative action reports for the government rarely produces the results one might want and is designed to place the university in compliance whether or not a good faith effort has been made to hire underrepresented minorities and women. The government regulations will not produce change; only changes in the quality of the actual pool of eligible candidates, in the university's culture, in faculty attitudes, and in the attitudes of academic leaders, such as deans of schools and chairs of departments, will bring greater diversity to the institutions of higher learning.

In fact, if university academic leaders began to question seriously the need to recruit in some specialty areas rather than others, we might find more rapid inclusion of members of minority groups. For example, almost every English and Comparative Literature department believes it needs one or two scholars to cover most of the literature in each century going back at least to the Enlightenment. Suppose that an academic administrator looking for a good but just fight said: "No, this round of recruitment we are going to shift our focus a bit. We are going to have one more scholar working in African American culture and literature rather than fill the open position with another seventeenth-century scholar." Since there are at most a handful of minority group academics studying seventeenth-century literature and society but far more who are interested in the Harlem Renaissance and African American literature, we would find more qualified minorities in the pool of applicants who might well be offered the position.

If that same courageous administrator were to tell a department that we would forgo another appointment in Roman art history (another important field) for a scholar working in twentieth-century art history, we would have a different composition to the applicant pool and have a far better chance of hiring a minority scholar. And finally, if we were to tell a Near Eastern Studies Department that we want someone who is familiar with the twentieth-century history of the region, we would be apt to receive well-qualified applicants from a range of ethnic groups. Thus, if we tweak just a bit the substantive agenda of the curriculum, we will be more likely to create a more diverse faculty and attract students interested in these areas of knowledge.

Formal Accreditation Processes. In order for colleges and universities to offer any respected degree, whether a B.A. or a J.D., a formal, institutionalized accreditation process is used to determine whether the program's faculty, students, and curriculum meet basic criteria of quality. Regional accrediting societies visit universities in order to determine whether a school ought to be accredited. There are various forms of review, but the major ones take place once every five or ten years; in reality, though, there is always some accrediting team visiting the university to examine one school or another. The members of the accreditation team come from other colleges and universities, and they send their evaluation report to a regional accreditation group for final examination that may lead to no problems or some number of "deficiencies" that need to be addressed before accreditation is granted.

Having standards of quality for universities to meet is, of course, a good idea, but once again this regulation is often carried to absurdity. For example, to prepare for a ten-year accreditation review, many people at the university are assigned various tasks that produce thousands of pages of detailed information about the programs at the university. Hundreds of thousands, if not millions of dollars, are spent by universities preparing for site visits and reviews by accreditation teams. But to require this of the Yale Law School, the Harvard Business School, or the Columbia School of Architecture is ridiculous, and it is even more so when the accrediting agencies require this kind of detail for the entire university. It is simply a waste of valuable time and resources to reach an obvious conclusion. No accrediting agency is going to refuse to accredit the Yale Law School. It would make the accrediting agencies look like a bunch of fools. Instead, the accrediting agencies request a few modifications of existing conditions, which are essentially mandated by the guilds that control these agencies, and then they issue an otherwise glowing report. At Columbia, we have fallen prey more than once to an accrediting agency threatening that they will not accredit our law school, surely among the top in the nation, because we have an insufficient number of actual seats for students in our law library. Today, of course, almost all law students work through the Internet and access library information from digitized sources online, so this particular metric is outdated. For-profit colleges and lesser-quality places need gatekeepers to make sure that their programs are of sufficient quality. But not the Yale School of Law.

So what should be done? The accrediting agencies ought to create a "short form" that can be filled out by universities that have demonstrated several decades of excellence. In fact, those schools that have maintained high quality over decades could be spared the accreditation process altogether, either through exemption or by extending the span of time between accreditation visits. If the statistical indicators fall below some threshold, full accreditation visits could resume. However, there is no need for world-class universities to waste valuable resources and personnel in bogus efforts at compliance with accreditation societies—especially when almost all of these universities run far more rigorous reviews of their schools and departments by visiting committees on a regular three-to-five-year basis independent of accreditation. Keeping mandatory accreditation for universities of varying quality reflects an absence of any form of cost-benefit analysis taking place prior to a review.

Institutional Review Boards to Protect Human Subjects. If we don't want animals mistreated when they are used in biomedical or biological experiments, we surely don't want human subjects harmed during clinical trials or during the course of research. There is a clear need to ensure the safety of participants in research experiments. The government decided to become involved in the protection effort after the infamous Tuskegee Syphilis Study (1932–1972), in which black male participants had not been briefed on how the study was going to be conducted, nor had syphilis researchers received the participants' informed consent after the discovery of penicillin following World War II.[28] Prior to penicillin's discovery, patients in the study were being given minimal care, since that was all that was available to the doctors treating them. Once penicillin was discovered, however, there was an alternative form of treatment for some of the men under the care of these physicians and they were not given information about penicillin. That was unethical and clearly a violation of the doctors' duty. This scandal was magnified still further in the media, and Congress took action to protect human subjects from this kind of negligence. The National Commission for the Protection of Human Subjects of Biomedical and Behavioral Research issued the Belmont Report (which was issued in 1978 and named after the Belmont Conference Center, where the report was drafted).[29] Essentially, the report articulated three fundamental principles:

1. People's autonomy must be respected.
2. People must be treated with respect, which included receiving their informed consent to participate. Biomedical and behavioral science research were prohibited in principle from conducting studies that involved deception.
3. Researchers must "do no harm" and nonexploitative, well-considered, and reasonable procedures be followed.

The National Research Act (Pub. L. 93-348) was signed into law in 1974.[30]

The mechanism for enforcing these principles was established by Congress in 1974: Every university campus had to create an institutional review board, or IRB, consisting of faculty members, administrators, and at least one local community member who reviewed every research protocol that had been funded by federal agencies. The IRB was given wide discretionary power: it could ask for further clarification or changes in the protocols or, at the extreme, could deny permission for researchers to conduct their experiments or research because of their failure to meet the requirements noted above. Although initially the IRBs were to review federal grant proposals, principally in the biomedical sciences, most research universities interpreted the congressional IRB requirement to include any research conducted by faculty members or their students at the university.[31] Additionally, state tort law established liability for universities found guilty of negligence in the conduct of research using human subjects, leading universities to mandate that all research projects must be subject to approval by the IRB. The IRBs became powerful but essentially unregulated bodies on campus. Few people questioned their rationale because they did not want to appear to support studies that had become the symbols of experimental evil, including the Tuskegee study and one designed by respected Yale psychology professor Stanley Milgram to test Hannah Arendt's idea of "the banality of evil."[32]

Milgram's experiment was designed to measure "how far people would go to inflict pain on others" given orders to do so by a researcher. In principle, the experiment was innocuous: It was ostensibly testing people's ability to learn simple facts. The twist was that the subject of the experiment sat at a desk and was told by one of the experimenters to give the person who was answering the questions an electric shock each time an incorrect answer was supplied. For each incorrect answer, the level of the shock became more severe. A ruse was part of the experiment—the person receiving the shocks began to scream and beg not to be given more shocks, even though he was not actually receiving any shocks. The remarkable findings showed that a significant majority of the experimental subjects—ordinary people from New Haven—often egged on by one of the experimenters, would inflict shocks that varied between strong and dangerous levels. By its very nature, the experiment required deception, since Milgram was not going to inflict deadly pain on individuals involved in the experiment. But the subjects did not know this.

The study became famous because of the ensuing debate over the results, which tended to confirm Arendt's idea, and the methods used. Milgram's book *Obedience to Authority: An Experimental View* became a classic work in psychology.[33] The Milgram experiment is now considered to be an example of a study where there was insufficient informed consent and human subjects were abused because of the nature of the experiment. There had been little follow-up by Milgram or others to examine the longer-term emotional consequences of the experiment on those who participated in it. Of course, without the deception, the experiment could not have been done. Did the value of the experiment, which became one of the most heavily cited works in the behavioral sciences over a period of many years, outweigh the potential harm done to the experimental subjects?

Then there is the case of Columbia Professor Nancy Wexler, who for twenty-five years had studied the people of Lake Maracaibo, Venezuela, who have a very high incidence of Huntington's disease.[34] Her collaborative work led to the discovery of the gene that caused this fatal disease. Her efforts, including the collection of blood samples and other highly detailed anthropological data on the family histories of people living on the lake, was funded for years by the NIH. Then the Columbia IRB refused to approve the informed consent feature of the research because Wexler had failed to provide the inhabitants of this lake community with an explicit option to receive birth control information. (It should be noted that this was after Wexler had been awarded, among other prizes, the prestigious Mary Lasker Award for Public Service.) More importantly, one can search for a long time before finding a more compassionate and ethical researcher than Nancy Wexler—something that was widely known. The boat people of Lake Maracaibo are part of a deeply religious Catholic community, and the overwhelming majority did not believe in the use of contraception. Nonetheless, Wexler was not insensitive to this problem and would offer birth control information if asked to do so by any of the study participants. Yet the IRB wanted to mandate that Wexler offer a course on the heritability of Huntington's to the lake people as well as a course on how the use of contraception might prevent the conception of children who would have a 50 percent chance of carrying the dominant Huntington's gene.

Had the IRB gone too far? Had they, in effect, exercised a form of "prior constraint" on Wexler's freedom of inquiry and had they in fact tried to control her research? Had it violated her freedom to conduct ethically responsible research? No one had ever accused her of doing anything unethical, but Wexler was being prevented from conducting further research because the IRB decided it wanted to impose mandated contraceptive advice in the research protocol. Ultimately, Wexler had to appeal to the NIH before obtaining approval to continue her research in the way that she had done previously.

The simple fact is that IRBs can kill faculty research projects, even those that are unfunded, and they have done so. There have been prohibitions on almost all social-psychological studies that involve minimal deception without informing the subjects that deception is part of the experiment. IRBs have prohibited survey research that does not have a section on informed consent, even though those who receive the survey are not required to take it; or, if they dislike what they see, they can press the "delete" button or simply throw the paper copy away. In order to avoid any potential scandal, have the government and the university administrators violated one of the university's core values—freedom of inquiry—and perhaps even an individual's fundamental constitutional rights of free speech? Few IRBs make it clear that there are "tiers" of risk versus potential rewards of doing specific projects and tend to treat projects involving online social surveys much the same way as they examine a clinical trial.

A number of distinguished professors at world-class universities have gone a step further and contend that IRBs have run amok. Columbia law professor Philip Hamburger, for one, believes that the IRB regulations represent a form of licensing of speech and the press on "human subjects research." The IRBs are the instruments for this government licensing, which according to Hamburger harkens back to "the dimly lit past, [when] the Inquisition and the Star Chamber licensed the press and thereby suppressed much scientific and political inquiry.... The licensing of speech and the press, however, has returned on a wider scale than anything imagined by the Inquisition or the Star Chamber.

In response to anxieties about the academic study of human beings . . . the government carries out this licensing through institutional review boards."[35] As Hamburger goes on to say:

> Licensing is consistently dangerous for several reasons. First, it is a means of wholesale suppression. The government ordinarily must enforce laws against speech in retail fashion, proving the danger of each publication, one by one, in a complex court proceeding. In its licensing, however, the government generally bars publications until they get permission, and it thereby suppresses them wholesale, without individual proceedings and other due process in court. Second, licensing in any sphere of speech is profoundly overbroad and disproportionate. In order to prevent harm in some instances, it imposes prior review in all instances, and it thereby suppresses or at least chills much entirely innocent speech. Most seriously, third, licensing requires individuals to get permission from the government before they speak or publish—as if they had not authority on their own to share information and ideas. Licensing in this manner forces the people to be submissive about their words. It makes them acknowledge the government's sovereignty over the very means by which they hold the government to account, and it thereby inverts the relationship of individuals to their government.[36]

Licensing through the IRBs represents a mechanism by which the federal government through legislation not only limits academic freedom and free inquiry but also demonstrates its lack of trust in the ability of universities to conform to the norms of acceptable research practices.[37]

There is another good reason to be concerned about the chilling effects of IRB regulations on academic inquiry and the advancement of knowledge: they may well have unintended perverse consequences of hurting those that researchers (and the rest of us) might want to help. Victoria Phillips, professor of public health at Emory University, notes: "[coronary] bypass fatalities have fallen substantially, but highly disparately. Over the last decade, the rate for white males declined by 33 percent, while that for black males remained stubbornly steady and fell by only 3 percent."[38] Phillips goes on to say that two factors may have been overlooked in trying to explain this difference: "the characteristics of surgeons themselves, where and when they trained, and [the] specific setting in which they operate." Philip Hamburger suggests that another lurking factor may be IRB regulations. In the so-called Common Rule, the Department of Health and Human Services (HHS) sets minimum ethical standards for licensing through the IRBs. Hamburger is aware that there are no rigorous scientific studies that demonstrate with any high level of probability that IRBs "kill" rather than "save lives." However, he argues that provisions of the Common Rule make it more likely that more lives are lost rather than protected because of it. Referring to Professor Phillips's work, Hamburger argues that under the Common Rule, IRBs "should be particularly cognizant of the special problems of research involving vulnerable populations, such as children, prisoners, pregnant women, mentally disabled persons, or economically or educationally disadvantaged persons." Although it doesn't mention blacks explicitly, Hamburger argues that everyone knows that they are of particular importance here because of the Tuskegee study. What Hamburger argues is that because of the particular focus on "vulnerable populations," research that might have been done to deal with specific health problems faced by minorities has not been carried out. As a result, discoveries about certain diseases or conditions that disproportionately occur among minority populations are never researched—leading to more rather than fewer deaths in these subpopulations—just as is the case in the rate of deaths resulting from bypass surgery.[39]

It remains an open question whether courts would find IRBs to be unconstitutional violations of the First Amendment. Whatever the outcome of challenges to their legality, we ought to be balancing better the need for preventing abuses of human subjects with generally permitting faculty members to pursue their research in an unfettered way. One hopes, of course, that by the time young American researchers engage in experiments with human subjects, they are cognizant of the ethical and moral issues that surround the research project and have weighed the costs and benefits in a reasonable way. Even so, universities can also better educate their faculty and students about following ethical standards in conducting research, and when the norm is violated, move swiftly to investigate the transgression, acknowledge it if the evidence is clear, and sanction those who betray the trust that the university and the government have placed in them.

But in today's world of licensing within universities, a journalism student working on a rather pedestrian project of interviewing local storeowners may well have to have his or her research protocol reviewed and signed off on by an IRB. A person who has been funded by the NSF and is working on a survey of public opinion about some aspects of the American political system requires IRB approval. IRB members can fundamentally alter a research project. Simple experiments with human subjects, such as the study carried out at Johns Hopkins University on methods for controlling hospital infections, were pronounced by the HHS to insufficiently protect human subjects. Yet this work, which had already begun by the time the HHS found that the IRB had not properly defined who the human subjects were in this research effort, led to prevention of tens of thousands of deaths annually from hospital infections. Simple checklists were used to produce the dramatic effects, things like the frequency with which hospital employees washed their hands. Billions of dollars were saved, to say nothing of the thousands of lives, which might not have happened had the IRB and HHS been able to prevent this research from taking place—as they were inclined to do.[40]

The IRBs can also try to influence the writing of scholarly or scientific papers resulting from the inquiry—and they have done so. IRBs are not about to be eliminated, but their scope ought to be narrowed and their practices should be streamlined. Place a little bit of power in the hands of a small group, and it will often turn into an effort to exercise excessive control.

This is overregulation, and it does impose a form of licensing on freedom of inquiry—controlled by a group of academics who may know almost nothing about the subject and who require more paperwork than you can possibly imagine. Even when we get into more dicey areas of research with human subjects, turning down a project for insufficient informed consent may have substantial consequences on the probability of important biomedical discoveries. As Hamburger argues, if we were to do a cost-benefit analysis of gains and losses as a result of IRB licensing practices, we might well find that these review boards are doing more harm than good.

The institutionalization of IRBs represents another instance of risk aversion on the part of universities, and an unwillingness of leaders of these institutions of higher learning to push Congress for more reasonable and less burdensome regulations, but clinical trials and medical research in general are not risk free and cannot be made so. All research, whether it is on human subjects or lethal bacteria, has potential risks, even lethal risks. But those risks, if reasonable, should not halt scientific research. More to the point, research by behavioral scientists that has essentially no risk attached to it should probably not even be subjected to IRB review.

As much as I have argued that IRBs can forestall important scientific discoveries, I don't want to attach too much blame to these regulations for their effects on scientific progress and discovery. Scientific work is hard: it is full of false starts, negative results, and hopeful beginnings that turn out to generate more unanswered questions than solutions to the complex problems under study. The difficulty in problem solving and devising appropriate methods, technologies, theories, and experiments are more important factors than IRB regulations (however much this is a burden) in failing to produce more rapid advances in most areas of science. IRB regulations will not change the way science is actually done. But, given how difficult it is to unravel difficult problems, we ought to be giving scientists and social and behavioral scientists the greatest opportunity possible to do scientific work rather than to have that precious time consumed by what are often administrative requirements of little, if any, value.[41]

We ought to rein in the IRB's discretionary power; we must recognize that in most cases they are abridging academic freedom and free inquiry, and that beyond the cost of this oversight work, they are placing constraints on the processes leading to important discoveries. We should do a far better job of educating legislators and regulators that by conducting some forms of research that on their face could not pass IRB inspection, thousands, if not millions, of lives can be saved. That said, we need to regulate research that clearly poses real dangers to the lives of human subjects. Perhaps we can reform IRBs so that their work concentrates on those cases where substantial risk is clearly part of a research project's protocol.

University Responsibilities for Disciplinary Action

Great universities have had, and continue to have, an obligation to reinforce fundamental academic values. When deviant behavior among their students, faculty or staff occurs, these institutions have an obligation to enforce rules of conduct that have been clearly articulated and known by all members of the university community.

This is particularly true for certain types of behavior, such as academic integrity. Those who violate these basic standards ought to be punished, whether it is a faculty member who plagiarizes from another's work or fabricates data in an experiment, or a student who plagiarizes or has someone else write a term paper. Any form of personalized verbal or physical harassment ought to be subject to disciplinary action as well. However, speech codes have no place at great universities. As Benno Schmidt, the former president of Yale, once said in response to a campus reporter's question about some opprobrious speech at

Yale: "The First Amendment protects cowards too." Forms of individual or institutional conflicts of interest should also be subjected to disciplinary or correctional action.

Various forms of campus protests, which should never be prohibited, should follow a set of procedures that have been outlined and accepted by the community. When those processes are followed, the university should allow such expressions of discontent—institutions of higher learning are places where criticism of established practices or current policies should be able to take place without fear of reprisals. However, if the student newspaper publishes an article that is libelous, the student responsible should be held accountable. And if a member of the faculty has a sexual relationship with an undergraduate student who is in or has been in his or her class, and which is explicitly prohibited by the university, that would call for disciplinary action unless the circumstances are truly unusual. In fact, sexual relationships between faculty members and undergraduates ought to be frowned upon in general and ought to be part of an explicit university policy, since it is almost impossible to conceive of a situation where there are not significant power differentials between the two parties—even when the relationship is apparently consensual.

Then, of course, there are instances of poor judgment that should be subject to disciplinary authority. That might include drunkenness and disturbances in residence halls or throwing empty beer bottles out of a twelfth-story window of a dormitory. For a long time universities have had mechanisms for dealing with these violations of basic codes of conduct as well as an established appeals process. Universities should have an obligation to create a safe environment for learning, thinking, and doing creative scholarship and research. But this obligation ought never cease to reinforce their commitment to free expression and academic freedom in the name of creating a safe environment. If students feel offended by certain speech or by certain speakers, they should not find acceptance of an argument that claims that the existence of such speech creates an unsafe environment. As I've said, universities, by their nature, are intended to be unsettling.

There are a few violations of the law that the university has absolutely no business being directly involved in. There are some transgressions that are so severe that any prosecution of a case must assure strict adherence to fundamental procedural rules and to various basic constitutional rights, such as due process of law, equal protection of the law, and the right to legal counsel. For example, a university does not get involved in a murder case that allegedly involves one of its students or faculty members—in part because of the severity of the crime but more importantly because it does not have the authority or the ability to fairly adjudicate such cases—and people's lives are at stake. Similarly, sexual assault is a crime that is not only a heinous felony but is also the type of crime that universities are not best suited to pursue. Yet, there are powerful groups on campus these days that insist that the university must take action, and few leaders of these institutions have the courage to admit that the university is incapable of fairly adjudicating these cases. Students often make the argument that because the criminal justice system is "broken," we need universities to step in to see justice done. Of course, this argument suggests that the students ought to be working to improve the criminal justice system, particularly in those areas where they have complaints. But to assume that universities can act as acceptable substitutes for that system is almost naïve—especially given the way the campus "justice system" is constructed by federal mandate.

Administrative leaders should send the message: If there is a claim of sexual assault, let us help you get in touch with the civil authorities who will hear your case and possibly take action. The reasons that presidents and provosts, and even trustees, shy away from making such statements is their fear of being labeled as "soft on sexual assault" by campus groups for whom sexual assault is a transcendent issue. It is likely that campus marches, placards, and vocal denouncements of the academic administration and the trustees would result from taking such a position. Bad publicity would follow. Yet, it would be the right thing to do. After all, universities are not law enforcement agencies. When they get into that business, they often do a bad job of it—such as the way Duke University jumped to false conclusions, expelled students, and fired the lacrosse coach in the infamous lacrosse team alleged gang rape case. Later, Duke settled the case for some undisclosed sum, but we can believe it was rather large.[42]

Nonetheless, universities today are prevented by government policies, pressure, and actions from taking such a position unless they have the guts to fight against laws and regulations that are popular among highly active groups on campus (and beyond) and that thrust them into the position of having to set up quasi-courts to review these cases and to hand down verdicts. Unfortunately, the president of the United States is not helping to further the distinction between behavioral acts that are and are not the province of university disciplinary systems. By creating a watchlist of eighty-five (as of October 2014) or more universities and colleges that supposedly have not demonstrated that they are taking bold enough preemptive action to prevent sexual assault on campus, the administration is placing a spotlight on schools that may not have any poorer review processes than hundreds not on the list. When the Obama administration publicized such a list, a thousand or more presidents of universities whose institutions did not appear on the list must have breathed a deep sigh of relief and thought: "There but for the grace of God go I." That is because instances of sexual assault on campus, just as in the greater society, are ubiquitous and can happen anywhere, on any campus, regardless of whether or not it has in place serious educational programs to teach young students the hazards of certain types of dating and of binge drinking. Placing some restrictions on students' social behavior outside of the classroom might help reduce the number of assaults, which often happen at fraternity parties or at schools that almost place a premium on being "party schools." Universities and colleges do have a responsibility to educate their students about the conditions under which a person (generally a woman) should think twice about having sex on a date after consuming large amounts of alcohol, as well as about other risky situations that might lead to harm.[43] And, of course, universities should educate young students about the potential medical and emotional consequences to sexual assault (defined here as attempted or real rape but including sexual harassment that universities are in a position to adjudicate, groping, and other forms of sexually inappropriate behavior.)[44] But even these efforts do not always produce adequate results. Youngsters at universities and colleges do a great deal of drinking, and they are far more sexually active than people in older age groups. They often simply will not heed the advice of courses on ways to avoid treacherous situations.

In a major review article on campus and other forms of sexual assaults, Professor Maria Testa and Jennifer A. Livingston, both high-level researchers at the State University of New York (SUNY), Buffalo, characterized these cases, after a vast review of the extant literature, in the following way:

> These studies lead to several conclusions with important implications for prevention. First, a substantial proportion of rapes, particularly among college students, occur as a direct result of the victim being incapacitated by substances and unable to consent or resist. Separating forcible rapes from incapacitated rapes reveals that only a minority of forcible rapes involve victim substance use. Thus, it appears that a substantial proportion of alcohol

consumption–involved sexual assaults are actually instances of incapacitated rape that occurred as a direct result of the victim's heavy drinking. Cognitive impairment resulting from a moderate dose of alcohol may increase women's sexual vulnerability by making it difficult to recognize or respond to risk; however, these data suggest that this mechanism is relevant to only a minority of rapes.

Our review of the literature on women's substance use and sexual victimization points to the conclusion that women's alcohol consumption plays a significant role in a large proportion of sexual assault incidents among young women, particularly college students. Findings clearly point toward women's voluntary heavy episodic drinking within social settings as a key risk factor in sexual victimization and a mechanism to address in prevention efforts.

The conclusion that voluntary heavy episodic drinking (HED) puts college women at risk of alcohol-related sexual assault is not likely to come as a surprise to researchers who have documented the high prevalence of heavy episodic drinking among college students and its associated negative consequences. From the perspective of these researchers, sexual assault is one of a number of negative consequences that are attributable to HED.[45]

There are many reasons why universities are ill suited to the task of making judgments in the case of felonies. The procedures required are quasi-legal at best, and at most universities the tribunal that meets to decide these cases knows next to nothing about the law, criminal procedure, and the nature of evidence. Ninety-nine percent of these "judges" are well-educated people who come to these matters with their own biases and presuppositions, which might be true for any set of jurors, but lawyers and trained judges are not running the show— and in most of these procedures the plaintiff and defendant do not have access to active legal counsel. In addition, these sexual assault cases are often difficult to adjudicate because the vast majority of them involve heavy alcohol consumption by both parties, who have often dated for some time. Moreover, the alleged victims often do not report incidents at all or come forward immediately, but wait months before doing so. Many district attorneys refuse to take these cases because the nature of the evidence is often so unclear. If this is a fault of the criminal justice system, let's try to fix it, not try to produce an alternative and flawed method of adjudicating the cases.

Why are universities required to take action that they are ill suited to carry out with the kind of efficacy that we find in legal institutions? The two basic sources for federal regulations and compliance are Title IX of the Civil Rights Act of 1972 and the Violence Against Women Act, which Congress renewed in 2013.[46] Originally intended to help women get to college and to expand their opportunities, particularly in intercollegiate activities, the expansion of the scope of Title IX is, according to Brett A. Sokolow, president of the National Center for Higher Education Risk Management, "like a pebble in a pond . . . its influence is ever increasing outward in concentric circles." Although the evolution of the meaning of Title IX has taken several decades, today the law is being interpreted "to require colleges to investigate and resolve students' reports of rape, determining whether their classmates are responsible for assault and, if so, what the punishment should be. That is the case whether or not an alleged victim decides to report the incident to the police."[47] And if universities and colleges fail to handle complaints with dispatch (a term not clearly defined), and if they fail to report allegations promptly and fairly, they can be accused by the victim (as they have been) of violating the rights of the alleged victim and thereby creating a hostile learning environment. To make matters worse, in April 2014 the Department of Education sent a fifty-two-point question-and-answer document to all colleges and universities telling them how to conduct an investigation, how to interview witnesses, how to examine evidence, and what they must do on an interim basis to "protect the complainant." Add to this the strict new guidelines issued by the Obama administration on how to "help colleges combat assault." The threat, although never fully acted upon, is the loss of all federal funding to the university or college—or the nuclear option, as one senator referred to it.

Not only are universities required to adjudicate these cases, but they are also doing so using procedures that actually bear little resemblance to the way a grand jury or a court would behave in such cases. Furthermore, the mandated standard of proof is that there exists a "preponderance of evidence," which is the guideline set for civil crimes, not "proof beyond a reasonable doubt," which is the standard in criminal trials. In fact, many colleges and universities use a "clear and convincing" standard in these cases, which is actually a higher standard than the government requires. The alleged victim and the defendant in the case can have one person present as an advisor (who could be a lawyer), but if it is a lawyer, he or she is not permitted to participate in a lawyer-like way that might involve cross-examination or to insist on principles of basic due process.

Creating a set of procedures to hear these complaints is only one of the many unfunded mandates that the government is imposing on universities as part of this social movement to have them become police investigators. The universities "should ensure that officials handling such cases are 'appropriately trained and do not have a conflict of interest or bias [how this is determined remains unspecified] for or against the accuser or accused' and that both parties 'receive simultaneous notification, in writing, of the result of the proceeding and any available appeal procedures."[48] The government is now placing an emphasis on speed at resolving these cases. Efforts by alleged perpetrators' (almost always male students) to increase levels of due process into the proceedings have been resisted. One alleged perpetrator, who was expelled from Auburn University but was not indicted by a grand jury, had this to say about the extant process that he faced: "The way the system is set up, I was guilty automatically." And because of the undeniable fact that most of these cases result from the severe intoxication of both parties, creating a Star Chamber type of "legal process" is regrettable. The police and investigators often eschew taking on these cases just because the evidence is often so ambiguous. However, if the conclusion of the disciplinary process favors the plaintiff and the victim then decides to take the case to the district attorney, all of the proceedings of the university tribunal are "discoverable" by the DA's office and can be used in a criminal trial.

Of course, all university leaders are concerned with campus violence, and particularly rape and date rape—to say nothing about gun assaults on campuses—but these leaders, although almost invariably mute when asked to discuss their problems with the current regulations, are worried about the costs of setting up elaborate training and investigative as well as adjudicative procedures on campus. This is just one more imposed set of costs, requiring millions of dollars, but which pales in comparison to the public spectacle of being accused by advocacy groups of condoning sexual violence on their campus. The costs are also minimal in comparison to the possible loss of hundreds of millions of dollars in federal research funds and financial aid that could be jeopardized by not following the government mandates—to say nothing of the adverse publicity that a university receives from being on the "most wanted list."

In July 2014, Harvard University, which will always be a trendsetter in almost every area of higher education, decided to "hire a team of investigators to deal specifically with sexual harassment and assault complaints."[49] If at least the wealthy universities can afford these new administrative expenses, many smaller colleges and universities cannot unless they find another source of revenue to cover the ever-widening expansion of federally mandated regulations. And for these smaller institutions, creating yet another new compliance office to carry out this work translates almost directly into tuition increases and potentially to increased student debt, another aspect of universities that the government would like to regulate.

If nothing else is done, the federal and state governments need to review the hundreds of laws and regulations imposed on universities and colleges and assess their value against the costs incurred. Many of the regulations are forcing universities to increase their budgets in ways that have little to do with educational or behavioral outcomes, either because universities can easily circumvent the regulations and appear to be in compliance or because the regulations actually make no sense as applied to universities. In the future, great universities ought to fight to reduce these regulations in an effort to focus on the work that they were created to do—transmitting and creating knowledge—while avoiding unnecessary expenses that only create higher costs with little, if any, additional protection for families whose children are attending these houses of intellect.

A Mechanism for Reconstructing the Compact

If the root cause of the proliferation of laws and regulations by the federal and state government is based on distrust and a breakdown in the compact between these necessary partners, then more needs to be done to restore university autonomy and its self-regulation, and to reduce constraints on academic freedom and free inquiry. It remains an open question whether the government is interested in reducing the level of mistrust. It ought to be, because this distrust is adversely affecting the ability of our scientists, engineers, physician-scientists, and behavioral scientists to spend the time needed to make important new discoveries. Distrust is difficult to overcome and virtually impossible if one of the two partners is not interested in efforts to change policy and restore the partnership that once existed. One mechanism that ought to be tried is the creation of a new working body, located in Washington, DC, and possibly linked to the Office of Management and Budget and more particularly to the Office of Information and Regulatory Affairs (OIRA) that works out of the White House. OIRA is charged with investigating whether the cost of regulations outweighs the benefits. The central idea is to talk to one another for extended periods in order to make clear the concerns and fears of each party. All the relevant stakeholders ought to be present, including those representing Congress, the regulatory agencies, and research universities. Perhaps before this new structure is formed, the universities have to examine those incidents that triggered regulations and to be able to demonstrate that they have put in place, by themselves, methods of reducing the probability of such incidents recurring. They must also demonstrate that they are willing to take appropriate action in the form of sanctions against wrongdoers who violate the fundamental and other core values of the university.

Then the government and the universities ought to formulate principles that will enable them to consider how to evaluate regulations on the basis of empirical evidence, to streamline certain regulations, to consider the continuing need for old regulations, to assess proposed new regulations or laws on the basis of experiments done before the regulations go into effect, and to consider introducing "sunset" clauses in all regulations related to the universities. If they select perhaps a dozen burdensome regulations or laws as candidates for scrutiny and discussion of how they might be altered or eliminated, then crafting a new compact (that increases mutual trust and that lifts restrictions on research) may be possible.

Cass Sunstein, professor of law at Harvard University and a former head of OIRA in the Obama administration, has suggested a number of principles that he believes ought to be followed in assessing laws and regulations, some of which affect universities.[50] He strongly argues for simplicity in the regulations within the context of an empirically based assessment of the cost versus the benefits of the regulation under scrutiny. Sunstein says:

> Here is the basic claim: Too much of the time, the government tells people exactly what to do and exactly how to do it. It issues highly prescriptive requirements for schools, teachers, hospitals, and employers, at an absurd level of detail, rather than just describing its general goal and letting human beings use their own creativity and initiative to get there. In a nutshell: Fewer rules and more common sense.... If the government can reduce costs and increase flexibility by granting discretion, and if it can do so without creating uncertainty, evasion, or confusion, it should grant discretion.[51]

It surely is in the national interest and in the interest of maintaining the preeminence of the nation's great universities to try to simplify these regulations and to turn distrust into a more trusting relationship.

CHAPTER ELEVEN

Structural Change

Change is the law of life. And those who look only to the past or present are certain to miss the future.

—JOHN F. KENNEDY

Never believe that a few caring people can't change the world. For, indeed, that's all who ever have.

—MARGARET MEAD

B ORN AT JOHNS HOPKINS almost 150 years ago, but firmly established only after World War II, the American research universities formulated a set of values and norms that represented the foundation on which they could build new educational structures. Although these institutions have flourished, some of their social structures ought to be modified in light of changes both in the universities themselves and the society in which they are embedded.[1]

I've already identified some policy changes that ought to be made. Here I want to highlight structures that ought to be changed or created. The first are structural changes *within* universities; the second, which are perhaps of greater consequence, are structures of governance and leadership at the federal, state, and local levels that ought to be modified if our universities are to maintain their preeminent position.

Increase Differentiation and Decrease the Number of Ph.D. Programs

Although the most distinguished universities have substantial variations in their internal organization, most of them try to be "full-service" enterprises that grow like weeds over time. More disquieting is the effort among them to look alike rather than to try to differentiate themselves from each other. Part of this is a response to public pressure and a quest for prestige, but a good deal of it is the desire for every aspiring university to look as much as possible like Harvard, Stanford, or Berkeley. There are certain fields, such as parts of the biological sciences, that require a formidable presence if a university is going to contribute to the growth of knowledge in ways that will define it as truly superior. But not all fields have to be present at every university. Some of our great universities can be best known for their humanities programs and humanities research that intersects with other disciplines. Others can be the finest in the social and behavioral sciences and link their research to the work of scientists and engineers. Still others can focus on the biological and biomedical sciences, on engineering, and so forth.[2] There has to be a more intense search for individual identity. For example, Columbia has always had New York—to the point where its name is actually Columbia University in the City of New York. And Stanford has an ever-growing tradition of innovation. Despite its excellence in many other fields, its identity is wrapped up in its history of extraordinary support for innovative science and engineering.

If a lack of differentiation among our leading universities is the norm today, we also face the problem of having too many Ph.D.-granting universities. More than three hundred now offer one form of doctorate or another. Yet beyond the top 150, most of the programs are distinctly mediocre, although one can occasionally find a gem of a Ph.D. program at an otherwise unremarkable institution. Over the next twenty-five years, we should reduce the number of Ph.D.-granting programs in the United States. There are a host of reasons to cut back on the number of such programs, including the facts that graduate students in these programs are viewed as cheap labor to teach large numbers of undergraduate students and that the quality of the faculty teaching the graduate students is often mediocre—thus almost always producing disinterested and mediocre students. However, if these students entered graduate school with the intention of deepening the knowledge that they would use to teach students in secondary schools after receiving their doctorate, there might be a justification for the programs.

Because many of these programs can be found at large state universities, if they are cut, who will teach the thousands of undergraduates matriculated at these schools? Many students in first-rate doctoral programs cannot find jobs at places equal in prestige to those where they were trained. In general, these students move down the prestige ladder but up in rank. This is the wealth of untapped scholarly labor that ought to be used, rather than graduate students, to teach the undergraduates at these state and lesser private universities. The problems attached to this idea are, of course, how much this increases cost and that the students receiving their doctorates from top-tier universities are socialized inappropriately to believe that anything less than taking the place of their own professors is an unworthy use of their abilities. We need to change this conception of the academic marketplace. It would be far better for a physics Ph.D. from a top-fifty university to teach at a university not ranked within the top one hundred than to drive a taxicab in New York (as some have done) or to become yet another captive of the high-paying world of Wall Street finance. A high priority for academic institutions is to alter our students' ideas of how a Ph.D. can be used in valuable ways that contribute greatly to the larger society. Furthermore, this need to serve a large body of students may pose opportunities to demonstrate that the use of high quality and specially constructed digital technology allows us to teach students without sacrificing quality and without the need for graduate student instructors in large introductory courses. For example, Arizona State University (ASU), which prides itself on "inclusion" of students with ability but without means to enter its undergraduate colleges, has announced a joint venture with edX to offer online freshman year courses, dubbed the "Global Freshman Academy," in which students' performance will be evaluated and the course credits can be used to fulfill the requirement for a degree (at $200 per credit hour).[3] Part of the experiment is designed to reach students around the world, but also students who do not have access to the ASU campuses. Other universities will undoubtedly follow suit. If this effort is successful and can be demonstrated with empirical evidence, then the need for Ph.D. "bodies" may be replaced by very high-quality teachers who are offering massive open online courses (MOOCs) on platforms such as edX.

Ironically, even if we reduce the number of doctorates produced at our research universities, we do need to produce more Ph.D.'s than we think we need at any given time. Labor markets, for one, rarely follow a prescribed path. There is a need for redundancy in the system because with few exceptions (mostly in fields like mathematics and physics and the other physical sciences, including computing), it is extremely difficult at the point of the Ph.D. to predict who will make seminal contributions in his or her field.[4] We need to be careful about arguing after the fact that, because only 10 percent of the scientific and scholarly community is responsible for 60 to 70 percent of all the literature that has an impact on the world, we can cut back on the number of doctorates produced. If we actually could predict who would be among the 10 percent at the time they enter graduate school, we might be able to cut back significantly on the number of degrees we offer. However, our ability to make that prediction at that age is difficult, except for the rare few. Also, if exceptionally able students do not believe there are academic jobs available for them at the end of the difficult journey to the doctorate, then they will be less likely to consider a career as a scholar or scientist coming out of college. That said, we probably do not need two hundred or so Ph.D. programs in chemistry to ensure that we have a robust community of chemists in the future.

We should consider also changing the requirements for degrees in the humanities. Stanford is experimenting with the idea that published papers can substitute for the doctoral dissertation. We ought to carry out more such experiments. Although we should not be seeking to eliminate book-length manuscripts, we also ought to realize that few young scholars who produce lengthy dissertations on their subject have more than a few publishable chapters in the larger work. Why require students to spend several more postgraduate years working on a dissertation, many of which won't get published—and more often than not will be turned into several articles submitted for publication? Some of the social and behavioral sciences have gone in this direction, and it has not ruined the scholarship in those fields. We ought to be experimenting with the production of humanistic scholarship that fulfills the requirements for publishable written work that might not be as extensive as a book-length manuscript.

Finally, great universities have historically been the parents of outstanding university publishing outlets, both of books and journals. Today there are a fair number of superb university presses, but many others, even at distinguished universities, are suffering from the transformation of the publishing industry as well as the problems associated with publishing exceptionally good specialized books that have limited audiences. A few universities, among them Harvard, Princeton, Stanford, and of course Oxford and Cambridge, have excellent scholarly presses, but many others are barely able to survive.[5] As I indicated, the goal of many Ph.D. and professional school students is to publish books with outstanding presses in order to justify tenure committee decisions rather than to sell copies. It is, in fact, unfortunate that we do not have a reading public that choose to read many of these fine books, but the reality is, and is apt to be, that scholarly monographs don't sell well despite their publication by excellent university presses. Over 90 percent of scholarly monographs sell fewer than around 400 copies, and probably half of those are to libraries. We ought to ensure that a greater number of university presses continue to be able to publish exceptional specialized works that will not have paid back the cost of their publication. One way of helping to do this is for the presses to print copies only on demand rather than to print copies that my have to be stored as part of the inventory of the press. But another way of ensuring that at least several scores of university presses can continue to fulfill their mission is to seek large endowments for these presses from foundations. Several $10 million endowments for each university press could offset a good deal of the cost of publishing these excellent but rarely sold monographs. Foundations like the Andrew Mellon Foundation, which has a long history of being of enormous help to university libraries and has been remarkably creative in furthering new information technologies to be used to store and retrieve scholarly journals or art images online, could help create these endowments. If properly managed, these endowments could grow and serve an important function within great universities.

Governance and Leadership

Dwight Eisenhower once said that leadership is the art of getting someone else to do something you want done because he wants to do it. This concept of leadership is particularly apt for great research universities. Structural reforms are difficult to make at these institutions because they are, as Clark Kerr observed in his classic book *The Uses of the University*, "inherently conservative institutions but with radical functions." Kerr elaborates on this conclusion by noting, "There are so many groups with an interest in the status quo, so many veto groups; yet the university must serve a knowledge explosion and a population explosion simultaneously. The president becomes the central mediator among the values of the past, the prospects for the future and the realities of the present."[6] In models of shared governance the prerogatives of faculty members, academic administrators, and trustees are outlined and have over time become a matter of tradition and culture, rather than of law. The concept of shared governance is an important one and should be maintained, but it has its limits as well as positive functions. In fact, the Supreme Court in *Minnesota State Board for Community Colleges v. Knight* (465 U.S. 271 [1984]) found that at public universities, the faculty has no legal right to participate in academic governance.[7] If this is so, where does the impetus for structural change and reform originate—a question raised by Matthew Goldstein, former chancellor of the City University of New York, in a recent paper on how change is related to the concept of shared governance and academic freedom at the major American universities.[8] Even if there is no legal basis for faculty members at the great state universities having veto power over proposed changes by academic administrators, please don't tell this to the sitting faculties at Berkeley, Wisconsin, or Michigan, among the other great public universities.

The structure of governance and the characteristics of leaders of great universities vary enormously. It is therefore difficult to critically analyze these multiple forms except for certain commonalities that most great universities have in their governance. The major distinction is between public and private institutions. Private universities are formally governed by boards of trustees, public universities by boards of regents or a group carrying a similar title. The fundamental question is: How are board members selected, and what do they know about higher learning? At private universities, boards tend to be self-perpetuating, although best governance practices tend to mandate term and age limits. At public institutions, board members can be elected or appointed by the governor and, occasionally, mayors. These are often political appointees and can represent a form of patronage, but they are also as often appointments made with good intention of individuals with expertise in everything but higher learning and in how universities are structured and run.

The appropriate size of a private university board is probably around fifteen to twenty members, and certainly no more than thirty. A board larger than this does not allow for detailed discussion of crucial issues or for the trustees to feel that they really have a hand in shaping and evaluating policies, strategic opportunities, and failures. One of the functions of these boards is to raise large sums of money for a variety of essential purposes. Given that the university needs benefactors, and these individuals often want places on the board before opening their pockets, there is a tendency to expand boards to forty members or more. This produces several problems along with the benefits: It makes many members of the board feel like outsiders and turns the board meetings into "show-and-tell" episodes rather than serious discussions of university policies. What ought to be done is to restrict the board membership to around twenty while creating a parallel group of overseers who are directly involved in specific school policymaking—generally regarding the institutions that these members graduated from or have special interests in. These overseers should have substantial prestige within the university community and some real influence on shaping the future plans for the school. When boards grow beyond twenty-five or thirty members, an executive committee of the board is formed and tends to have almost all of the power.[9] Certainly, boards of regents that "oversee" public universities do not need more than fifteen members.

Because trustees at a private university tend to know very little about the university that they have ultimate authority to govern, they leave the governance to the operating officers of the university unless they call for the dismissal of the president, or more frequently, the football coach. Most well-meaning and often well-heeled trustees receive virtually all of their information about the university from the president and his or her staff; the information flows in one direction and often is highly screened before presentation to trustees.

On a daily basis, the president, provosts, deans, and vice presidents of the various schools and major units of the university, such as an executive vice president of "the health sciences," department chairs, faculty, and students (or equivalent titles), actually run the university. Individuals who occupy these positions have fiefdoms they control, and various roles and responsibilities. A large university is usually divided into two major sections: the academic side and the financial and purely administrative side of operations. Many of these institutions also have either a faculty senate or a composite senate that has elected representatives from the various constituencies within the university. Where the university's senate represents all constituencies, it rarely has any real impact on the university because it represents too many conflicting interests. Consequently, university senates or councils should be representative of the faculty. Other formal groups can represent other interest groups within the university.

There are, of course, varying types of relationships between board members and the top administrative officers of the university. Some board chairs are incessant micromanagers, while others feel the need for close oversight without interference with the university's decision-making structures. The typical distinguished, full-service research university may have as many as fifteen or more schools and hundreds of administrative offices that deal with a very wide range of issues, from the school and budgets to legal issues and compliance with government laws and regulations, student psychological counseling, athletic programs, and student placement to community relations, government relations, libraries and information technology, development and fund-raising, maintenance, assistance for faculty, human resources, and so forth. The operating budgets for these institutions, as I've said, may exceed $3 billion or $4 billion per year. The architecture of this house is intricate, and few of those who live in it (students) and work in it (faculty members and staff) day-to-day are really knowledgeable about what are in the house's various rooms or how it is run. Consequently, most boards simply rubber-stamp almost all of the policy decisions made by the top academic management—though their role should be substantially greater than that of quiet assenters.

Even many university presidents do not have detailed knowledge of how budgets are constructed; they come to these positions with little training in managing large enterprises; and there is no course of study or career path toward becoming an academic leader. Yes, a few universities give summer courses in academic administration, but few attend them and their value is questionable. There is no toolkit of skills or well-articulated set of attributes that one looks for in a search for a president. Trustees, faculty, students, and one or two alums carry out the search; and the winner of the race is often the individual who is either "good at lunch" or has proven his or her value by being sought after by another university. So, if a candidate comes in "second" in the Princeton or Stanford search, the assumption is that he or she must be good enough for some other great university. There is no probationary period of testing for the leadership of a university and, more often than not, the search committees place enormous emphasis on attributes of the individual candidate rather than on whether or not the individual fits into the existing culture of the university. In other words, presidents are selected for their personalities, their quick intelligence, and to a limited degree on their track record at another institution. But that track record goes largely unexamined, and it may involve work done at a totally different type of institution. Often presidential search committees, which are invariably led by a trustee at a private university, fail to look for candidates who fit well with the highly successful structure that is already in place. If a great university has a structure where there is a clear division of labor, for example, between the president and the provost—and there is a long-standing record of this division working well—the search committee should not adopt a cult of personality, but should be sure that the new president is comfortable with the prevailing division of labor. Many universities allow presidents to determine the structure of academic leadership rather than look for candidates who will do well within a well-functioning and historically proven structure.

Furthermore, individual trustees often have undue weight in the selection process, and the students and faculty on the search committee rarely know enough about what it takes to be a superb president to offer much valuable input. They may have good intuition, and surely they have good intentions, but

STRUCTURAL CHANGE [281]

that does not make them qualified to make good decisions. Thus, we have a system where we have candidates who often do not fit the position, whose skills are largely unknown but who look good on paper or in interview situations, and a set of individuals on the search committee who know even less about what the university needs. Of course, the great universities with long histories and large endowments can run on autopilot for a while, but poor selections of presidents can damage the institution for some time.

We need to make academic administration a true career path. We ought to be searching for individuals who are imaginative, interested in governing, and have the ability to do so. Then, we ought to train them in what is required of these positions, particularly in terms of thinking innovatively and leading a faculty that is often at odds with the administration on what new initiatives are worthwhile. That effort needs to be matched by the training of members of search committees in how they can recognize the person who is the best fit for a university. Ideally, there would be many more internal track promotions—the movement of an individual from a faculty position, to the head of a department or fairly large institute, to dean of a school, and finally to provost and president. Of course, some individuals are "made" to be provosts rather than presidents, and others find being president far more rewarding than guiding the academic side of a university. But moving up the chain of command rarely occurs these days. More often than not search committee members view the pastures somewhere else as greener, despite their knowing virtually nothing about the person they are about to select. There tends to be bias against internal candidates because their weaknesses are better known; and in the course of having to say "no" to many good ideas, they tend to build up resentment in some quarters of the university. There ought to be a conscious effort to change the way academic leaders are chosen. Because leaders of universities govern by authority, most university presidents are risk averse and play "defense" very well. And that defensive thought process might characterize most of their tenure in office.

Finally, there are entirely inadequate mechanisms for boards to evaluate the performance of the leadership of universities. As I've said, almost all the information that board members receive is highly filtered through these leaders, and the materials that they might want to see are rarely offered to them. Boards ought to use modern social and behavioral science techniques for evaluating the leaders of universities. For one, there ought to be a detailed self-evaluation by the president and provost in answer to specific questions formulated by the board with the assistance of outside consultants. In addition, there ought to be surveys done of faculty, staff, students, and outsiders about the quality of the experiences of these constituencies that probe into the strengths and weaknesses of the leadership of the university, and that ask them to assess what it is like to work at the university. These surveys can also obtain evaluations of the progress made in the strategic initiatives that are part of larger plans for the future of the university. A far clearer picture of what is actually going on would emerge from these new sources of information.

Boards of universities should be less reluctant to change presidents if it is clear that the leader does not have what it takes to effect changes in quality, to recruit better faculty, to work well with faculty and students, and to take risks on new components of the university and new areas of knowledge development. Governance can go from bad to worse when boards add to already sunk costs by keeping on truly ineffective executives because they consider them indicators of their lack of wisdom in selecting these executives in the first place. There are few presidents or provosts who are late bloomers. After the first five years a board should be able to make an informed assessment of whether it is time to change leadership. Of course, this kind of action by boards of trustees is predicated on their having a sophisticated knowledge of the university; a board that is fundamentally ignorant of how the institution works is in no position to make big decisions, and one must be careful that the decisions are not based purely on ideology or politics but on the quality of performance agreed upon between the board and the top academic leaders of the university.

Role Relationships

It is time for us to reconsider the governance authority of the various players at the research university. We operate today under the principle of shared governance, but we ought to rethink how these responsibilities should be shared. Faculty members must retain their authority over the recruitment and selection of faculty members, subject to rigorous review beyond the department level. They also must shape the curriculum in their fields and be responsible for selecting postdoctoral and graduate students who enter their programs. They should, as proposed, play a far greater role in shaping a class of undergraduates. There are, of course, many other faculty prerogatives that I need not mention here. But when it comes to changes in the direction of the university, in its allocation of resources and in the creation of new and different structures for growth, how does the understandable conservatism of the faculty members, along with their ideological biases and presuppositions, fetter that change? Indeed, given the procrustean rate of change at most of the established universities, is any evolution greater than at a snail's pace possible without redefining the relationships among the various stakeholders?

One great midwestern private university has been engaged over the past several years in a serious discussion of the boundaries of responsibilities between faculty members and the academic leaders of the university—initiated after the resistance of some faculty to a series of decisions by the president and trustees to accept a large gift to help build a new research enterprise on campus. Although ideally academic leaders and faculty members will work in concert with one another, when inertia settles in or strong disagreements persist, what is to be done and who is to do it? We need extremely able and enlightened leaders (especially those who can work with the faculty to articulate the reasons for proposed changes and why they are justified) to carry more of the water in matters of institutional and structural change. The university community has some good individual leaders who represent models of how to achieve ordered change. Although faculty members should have and want a say in almost all decisions that the university makes, they tend not to want to make the final, difficult choices, especially when they involve contentious disputes among various factions of the faculty and among the students. But giving greater authority to academic leaders and ultimately a board to make these difficult choices is predicated on having knowledgeable and able presidents, provosts, and trustees. Unfortunately, too many presidents lack creative imaginations; they will too often follow fads or imitate what they see other major universities doing in initiating changes about which they know little; and they often are not particularly good at implementing the changes in an integrated way that will, in fact, improve the potential for novel discoveries, innovations, and new forms of teaching. Consequently, it is imperative in the future that we create a cadre of exceptionally able academic leaders and overseers. And we do have a cadre of extremely effective presidents and provosts of our research universities, although this is hardly the norm.

Too many presidents of the leading research universities are people of exceptional intelligence and goodwill who are strong advocates for small incremental changes; they are too often wedded to their institution's time-honored traditions and structures. These leaders turn out to be extremely effective managers of the status quo. The principle of shared governance has produced a set of useful checks and balances at our great universities, but it can also produce ossification and stagnation. And that is what I fear is beginning to happen—an absence of a sense of what our institutions can and must become.

Nonetheless, somebody has to steer the huge ship, as slow as it may be moving, and occasionally change its direction. For decisions about new enterprises and structures, primary responsibility ought to fall to the top academic leadership of the university, with faculty and certainly trustee involvement in the final decision making. Trustees have final authority in approving plans for change and growth or for cuts in programs. The faculty should be consulted throughout these processes, but the final decisions about creating or eliminating structures must rest with the leadership of the university and its trustees or regents.

What ought we to expect from board members, aside from their fiduciary responsibilities? Though it is a quasi-independent body, the board ought to work closely with the president, provost, or chancellor on the fundamental issues confronting research universities. For instance, as discussed, board members must be educated in the nature of universities before they can exercise their responsibilities. This requires something that is often scarce among them: time and deep interest. Many universities offer brief tutorials in the nature of the university, but these sessions are too few and too brief for trustees to get a thorough grasp of how the university operates and what it ought to be aspiring to. There ought to be seasoned, independent educators on the board who have had extensive experience with and knowledge of institutions of higher learning.[10]

By far the most important person on these boards is its chairman. In fact, the chair should understand the nature of universities, but that is not always necessary. When Robert Maynard Hutchins was publicly fighting the Broyles' Commission bills in the Illinois legislature (bills that would have put restrictions on anyone who espoused Communist ideas), the chair of the University of Chicago board became a powerful voice supporting Hutchins and helping to kill the bills. The former president of Princeton, William Bowen, speaks to the importance of the board chair in a recent discussion of his experiences at Princeton:

Absolutely central to effective governance is the relationship between the president and the leader of the board of trustees (usually the chair). These two individuals must see themselves as partners in leading a complicated enterprise, and they must enjoy an excellent working relationship based on a high degree of mutual respect. They have complementary roles to play in organizing and managing the work of the board (a major responsibility of the chair) and in providing executive leadership on all fronts (a major responsibility of the president). This relationship is so important that, in my view, it is essential that the president be comfortable with whoever is chosen to chair the board.... My strong belief in the notion of "partnership" notwithstanding, I never forgot that I worked for the board—the board does not work for the president.[11]

Bowen implies here that *he* did not choose who the chair of the board would be. Although technically the board selects its chair, in many instances the president either "suggests" who the next board chair should be or actually has a determinative voice in that choice. That bodes ill for the university because it places too much power in the hands of a person who owes his or her appointment to the president of the university.[12]

Public universities ought to have a strong, active board; private universities ought to have boards where members feel that their greatest responsibility is to the welfare of the institution, not to the welfare of the academic officers. Trustees and regents ought to have independent access to information about the university, but they cannot, nor should they, set up independent structures and groups to find and report that information to them. But they should help determine what the benchmarks for success are for the university; they ought to be engaged in a fundamental discussion of the purpose of the particular university that they are helping to manage; and they ought to be in a position where they can raise relevant questions about the movement of the university toward its strategic goals, which they ought to have a role in developing. Here they must be supportive of those in charge of implementing change—the president, provost, and other academic officers of the institution. They must decide "why" this university is here and what its purpose is, independent of a comparison with other research universities. They must help decide how and in which ways they wish to be great—not by imitation, but by reasoning about the purpose and needs of the institution. Perhaps most important of all, they must help to empower the academic leaders, particularly the president of the university. They should collaborate with the president to produce a set of objectives for the research university that defines its raison d'être and then empowers the leadership of the institution (after proper consultation with faculty, students, and alumni) to move forward toward achieving the goals set for the institution.

One of the best examples of this is the job that Benno C. Schmidt Jr. has done at the City University of New York. Schmidt, of course, had a great deal of academic administrative experience under his belt as former dean of the Columbia School of Law and as president of Yale University. He not only was the key author behind *An Institution Adrift*—an assessment of the City University of New York (CUNY) system[13]—but was instrumental in recruiting Chancellor Matthew Goldstein, who was enormously effective at transforming the structure of CUNY from an open admissions university with huge remedial responsibilities and very low graduation rates into a model that reversed all of those trends and began to look perhaps more like Clark Kerr's 1960s California Plan than the California system itself. Without the knowledge and leadership of Schmidt, in concert with Goldstein's exceptional ability and strategic and tactical skill, it is extremely unlikely that the new CUNY could have been restructured and put on a path to becoming one of the great public university systems in the United States.[14]

Furthermore, trustees ought to be given a one-year course in "The University in American Life," where they learn not only about the history of higher learning in the United States but also about the evolution of their own university. They must be fully versed in the core values of the institution and why adherence to those values, and a defense of them, is essential to creating or maintaining greatness. In fact, they should learn which factors contribute to a university becoming among the world's best. They ought to learn how decisions are made at universities as opposed to corporations, and how competing claims on resources are adjudicated; they must become knowledgeable about the underpinnings and goals of the undergraduate and graduate curriculum; they must become aware of the nature of federal, state, and local regulations affecting the university and federal research policies; they ought to know about the great discoveries made at their university and what structures facilitated those discoveries; they should learn about the economic impact of the university; and they should learn about failures as well as successes in carrying out a strategic initiative. They should know about the tenure process; they ought to be familiar with how strategic planning is done and carried out; they ought to be informed and consulted about the priorities that the university leaders have set for the next decade or so; they ought to be versed in the resources that are required to improve the university; and they should know about how those resources can be obtained. They must have accurate and clear indicators that measure whether the university is, in fact, improving or losing ground to other similarly situated institutions of higher learning—and relative to those that they aspire to emulate. They should learn about the relationships and competition among universities and how new structures are being built to foster collaboration among universities; and they ought to know the philosophy behind the admission of students in every school in the university. There are other components in this course, which would be taught by a faculty member or a member of the board who has an outstanding track record as a leader of an academic institution. Finally, there must be a communications network within the university that allows the trustees to hear directly from opinion leaders on the faculty, students, and staff about their perceptions of how well the university is pursuing its goals and what might be done to improve its performance.[15] We should no longer rely only on the academic leadership to filter information to the board.

Because trustees are almost invariably extremely busy people without the time to attend a weekly seminar based on my proposal, we should use new, digital technology to help educate them. Universities ought to create a MOOC that focuses on the nature of universities and their role in governance, perhaps called, as I suggested, "The University in American Life," which trustees or regents can take at their leisure, can return to as a refresher, and can follow-up with when questions emerge from their studies. The online course ought to make use of multiple players, including former presidents and trustees, faculty members well versed in higher education, current academic leaders, and faculty and students knowledgeable in how the house is run. Creating such an online preparatory course would allow for greater in-depth conversations of strategic issues at board meetings.

Of course, university trustees are selected for many reasons. At private universities the boards are self-perpetuating and the sitting president of the university has a huge influence on the selection of trustees. In the best of cases, that president has a sense of the value that the board can play in governance without it overly micromanaging the institution and is willing to appoint the best people to take on such responsibilities. Often, however, presidents propose board members who are known to be their supporters and who will pose no threat to their incumbency. Governing boards must not be in place *only* for honorific reasons, or for their giving potential, or for their expertise in a specific business that is relevant to the university's future excellence. Board members have to be willing to learn about universities and to truly help in their governance—and in protecting them from external attacks and abuse. Individual board members are rightfully proud to have been asked to serve as trustees, but they must begin to recognize that their role is more than perfunctory. Just as the University of Chicago board chair eloquently articulated a defense of academic freedom when Robert Hutchins was in a fight about "reds" at the University of Chicago during the McCarthy period, the board members must be knowledgeable and prepared to articulate the reasons why they support a specific course of action by academic leaders. The regents at public universities have a critical role in fighting for the continued support of higher learning in their state. Although they may be picked by a governor or voted in by the public, they must learn about the ambitions of their universities and of their states and become independent advocates with members of the state legislature and the governor for the resources required to move toward their universities' strategic objectives. Finally, like all presidents and provosts, as well as deans and chairs of departments, trustees should have "quitting issues." These are values and principles which, if continually undermined, will lead to their resignation. Too few academic leaders even think about quitting issues.

Budgetary Reform

The most important policy documents at research universities remain their annual operating and capital budgets. If we have the capacity to examine budgets closely and understand their nuances, we can get an unusually detailed sense of the academic priorities of the institution and how they are changing. It is imperative that academic leaders know how to read and analyze budgets and be in control of them; but, as mentioned, many have difficulty since they were never formally trained to do such analytic work. Although every large research organization needs expert financial and budget officers who are not academics, the key allocation decisions must remain with the academic leaders. Over the past several decades most great research universities have moved toward a decentralized budgetary system. What this means is that the revenues generated by the units (generally schools) within the university go directly back to those units. This would include, as examples, tuition, gifts, government grants, and student financial aid from outside sources. The units then pay a tax to the central administration for "common costs," which might include, among other items, the cost of the general counsel's office, various forms of facilities fees, library and information technology expenses, costs for the central administration of the university, and expenses of other offices where it is more efficient to have one unit centrally controlled than a proliferation of such units throughout the university. The units are often asked to contribute more than their allocated share of the common costs (arrived at by an algorithm that is generally based on the size of the unit), so that the central administration has funds to redistribute to its highest priorities. This central tax may, in part, be returned to the unit that contributes to it, or it may be reallocated to other units. The central administration of the university may have revenues that come from central endowments, from intellectual property, and other revenue streams, such as indirect costs that come with government and other grants and contracts.

The rationale for this form of budgeting is that it provides incentives for the units to raise revenue and reduce expenditures in order to yield surpluses that they can reinvest in their academic programs and faculty research efforts. It also has been assumed that placing greater control of resources in the schools enables the university to attract better candidates for deanships because they will have substantial control (subject to annual reviews by the central administration) over their resources. This budgetary system worked reasonably well at many exceptional universities during "the age of disciplinary silos" or the era of the "multiversity." The open question is whether this form of budgeting has become sufficiently dysfunctional and a drag on the growth of collaborations and the eventual discoveries that come from them.

The fundamental problem with decentralized budgeting is that it tends to create arbitrary borders between schools and disciplines, which often inhibit the cross-fertilization among the schools and departments. It tends to weaken the center of the university and to strengthen individual units. It also tends to incentivize academic redundancies. For example, rather than use statistics department faculty to teach basic statistics and pay the department for the faculty member's time, the social science department or business school creates its own course in introductory statistics. The decentralized system also makes it difficult to reallocate resources, since the center tends to be "poor" relative to the schools. Because each school claims poverty relative to its competitive peer institutions, it resists contributing to the center. The school's position is not without reason since, for example, the Columbia School of Business is economically disadvantaged relative to the Harvard Business School; but if we accept each of these assessments and carry each to its logical conclusion, it would be impossible to use resources generated by one school to enhance the quality of another. Inequalities of wealth exist in universities as they do in the larger society, and the rich at universities don't like increases in their taxes any more than the 1 percent do in the United States.

A model that is more centralized may facilitate collaborations across the university and consequently improve the likelihood of important discoveries that are apt to come only from such collaborations. Budgets should not fetter new ideas. When the central administration, with appropriate input from faculty groups that help to set university priorities, has funds that can be used with greater flexibility, the resources can more easily follow and help stimulate the intellectual action. If, as well, all tenure billets come back to the provost's office when an individual leaves the university, retires, or dies, that provides the chief academic officer of the university with more discretion and freedom to restructure and reorganize academic units, including increasing or decreasing the number of new faculty members. This centralization offers the possibility of moving forward on new initiatives more rapidly than if tenure and nontenure lines remain in the hands of their former departments and schools. That static, historical "right" to professorial lines is the way many of our great universities are structured today. Two of the most decentralized great universities, Johns Hopkins and Harvard, could be important exemplars by altering their budget models and by creating cross-school collaborative efforts that allow far easier intellectual free trade. That would set an important precedent for other world-class universities.[16] Even if this involves evolutionary change, which it inevitably would, structural changes—led by the president and the board of governors—would do much to allow these two great institutions far more latitude in developing university-wide programs for faculty and students—and thereby improve the way knowledge develops on these two famous campuses.

Balancing Teaching and Research Roles

At least two decades ago, Derek Bok, who was then president of Harvard, warned the academic community about an insidious infection that was eating away at the integrity of our great universities: the temptation to offer academic stars lighter teaching loads than other professors in order to attract them to one's university. As important a warning as this was, the academic community failed to listen—competitive market forces seemed to prove too powerful. Teaching loads became lighter and lighter, until an economics professor at a major university today is teaching two courses per year. Back in the 1960s, great academic stars, such as Lionel Trilling or Meyer Shapiro, typically would be expected to teach four or five courses, not two. It did not destroy Columbia or these exceptional scholars' writing and research careers to have those teaching loads. It was a part of the job; they did not "shop" themselves around in order to minimize their work with undergraduate students. Professors in the sciences always had lighter teaching loads, in part because they were expected to support graduate student and postdoctoral fellows and staff through their research grants and contracts. This reduction in teaching loads has, of course, an economic impact. The star professors negotiate higher than normal salaries and consume more resources while teaching fewer courses. Must we hire two Trillings in order to obtain what we used to get with one? Although I'm not specifying what the optimal teaching load is, I know that before long we will have a cadre of research professors who have great prestige and the highest salaries but who have never met an undergraduate or graduate student other than their doctoral students and postdoctoral fellows. That would be unfortunate for the university and the students.

Once the genie is out of the bottle, is it possible to get him back in? If not, we ought to offer professors the opportunity to take one or two courses a year as part of professional development, or allow them to have a lighter course load in exchange for developing online courses or for serving on an important committee, such as the admissions committee for undergraduates—assuming that they are highly qualified for the task. Faculty members at the great universities with which I'm familiar work very hard. They are highly self-motivated individuals who seek recognition from their students for excellent teaching, for mentoring postdocs, and for making research discoveries. But there must be structural balance in the system for it to work well; and we are, as Derek Bok warned, rapidly falling out of balance.

Evolution, Revolution, or Stagnation

If we assume that new scientific and behavioral science knowledge will require the collaboration of very high-quality faculty members from several disciplines, then we must consider structural reforms that enhance the chances that these discoveries will be made. The long-standing division of universities into schools and disciplinary departments, which once worked so well, will no longer be sufficient. Depth of knowledge in a disciplinary area will be required, but those who work together on complex problems will need to have a working knowledge of other disciplines. Collaborators will need to learn a set of new "foreign languages" of different disciplines. These conceptualizations of structures that produce a community of knowledge should be translated into physical structures (and campus planning), as discussed, and into new combinations and configurations of disciplinary knowledge that make pathbreaking discoveries more likely.

In order to affect change, let's consider what ought to be done in different types of universities. I envision three Weberian ideal types of structural reform: one that is evolutionary (although pursued at very different rates of evolution); a second that is revolutionary (that attempts to transform the very idea of a university into a new set of structures within the framework of the old set of values); and a third that is represented by stagnation, ossification, and decline.[17] The first two types require a rare combination of unusually sensitive and creative academic leadership, which tends to follow the same 10 percent rule: Roughly 10 percent of the presidents have all of the right stuff to be responsible for about 70 percent of the truly creative work in the academy.

The evolutionary form of structural reorganization ought to be the goal at the older, historically most prestigious research universities. Here, we can find enormous resistance to any form of change, although there is some evidence to the contrary, such as what is happening at Stanford University, which has always been influenced by a scientific and engineering mentality. It seems to be in the DNA of that institution of higher learning to seek systemic structural changes in order to solve problems (e.g., after the discovery of DNA, the institution made the bold move of relocating its medical school from San Francisco to Palo Alto so that it could coexist with those faculty working in the basic biological sciences). The university has a history of bringing units into proximity with the expectation that useful collaborations will take place. It also has a history of leadership that understands that innovation results from the melding of creative minds with different backgrounds. And the school has historically been extremely entrepreneurial. If we examine Stanford today, we see the results of these trends. In part this is due to the fact that Stanford is structurally sound: Its leadership has had clearly defined roles, including the president and provost, for example, since after World War II—and they have stuck with that organizational structure and allowed it to become part of the Stanford culture.

Thus, for example, we witness its leadership creating multidisciplinary structures, such as BioX. Furthermore, not all of Stanford's efforts focus on advanced scientific or technical problems. The d.school, created by David Kelley (who does have an electrical engineering degree from Carnegie Mellon University), is another example of a forward-thinking multidisciplinary and creative enterprise. Kelley was cited in Stanford's one-hundred-year retrospective, which focused on those Stanford faculty members who epitomized its tradition of academic excellence, "the melding of can-do spirit with limitless imagination."

Stanford's effort to create evolving new structures extends to the humanities, where it has one of the larger national programs exploring the "digital humanities." Its scholars use new technologies, such as 3-D mapping, electronic literary analysis, digitization, and advanced visualization techniques, to conduct interdisciplinary research in a host of areas typically attended to by humanists.[18] One project underway is the creation of the Stanford Geospatial Network Model of the Roman World, which "reconstructs the time cost and financial expense associated with different types of travel in antiquity."[19] A good deal of this research is carried out through the Stanford Humanities Center, which brings together faculty members from a variety of fields to work collaboratively on these exploratory projects. Although it may not be clear where the "digital humanities" will lead the disciplines in the future, they represent one more attempt by Stanford to create novel structures that will facilitate new explorations—whether or not the results prove of great value.

Of course, this evolutionary pattern can be seen in many of the older, Eastern research universities as well. Harvard, for example, is making an effort to move beyond its traditional structure toward a place that brings back the "uni" in the idea of the university. A Harvard without borders is not easily achievable, if for no other reason than its endowments are tied so closely to the various schools. But should Harvard succeed in implementing this structural change, it will become an even more attractive university for scholars and students. Other renowned research universities, including many of the best public research universities, are also increasing their efforts to reduce tariffs on free intellectual trade across the university and create new virtual and real physical structures that enhance their capabilities to compete as the best research and teaching institutions in the world. But the pace of change at these older universities tends to be slow. Few structures are eliminated; few new structures are built; and the role of the academic leaders and the faculty in initiating and implementing change has not been clearly defined. New campuses are born or expanded into, yet they are not often knowledge-driven. They are driven instead by expediency and by lack of architectural courage, and they often fail because of faculty resistance to change and leaders' reluctance to confront the issues of restructuring and the natural process of birth and death of parts of the university.

Finally, let's examine briefly the way evolutionary structural change has occurred at one of those top public research universities in the world: the University of California, Berkeley. Although Berkeley is still recognizable in terms of its departmental structure and its institutes, despite difficult fiscal times over the past five or six years, it has evolved into a university far more concerned than ever before with multidisciplinary research that focuses on a number of strategic problems. Consider only two examples. The first is a four-UC-campus multidisciplinary collaboration with Berkeley in the lead called CITRIS, or the Center for Information Technology Research in the Interests of Society. Now more than ten years old, CITRIS has established partnerships between three hundred campus faculty members and thousands of students with more than sixty corporations in the private sector, as well as with government agencies. It uses state-of-the art facilities at the four campuses—Berkeley, Davis, Merced, and Santa Cruz—to produce cutting-edge research in information technology that focuses on some of the most pressing social, environmental, and health care problems faced by the nation, from finding viable, sustainable energy alternatives and simplifying health care delivery to developing better ways of handling electronic medical records that can be used for remote diagnostic purposes. These efforts are aimed at increasing economic productivity.[20] What is most impressive about this as a prototypical effort is that the endeavor is creating structures within new physical spaces that allow students to rub minds with each other and with some of the great scholars and scientists at these universities. These are not students passively sitting in lecture rooms, nor are they studying in isolation, or taking courses in discrete departments that are never connected with each other. It is an "academic league" within the UC system that is leveraging intellectual and physical resources to help students think about how to use their imaginations. By introducing semester-long courses where the objective is for students to develop software applications that can be entered into a league-wide competition, Berkeley and its partners are making undergraduate education active, participatory, collaborative, challenging, and fun.

Another example is Berkeley's Institute for Data Science (BIDS), which "brings together data-gathering and data-analysis scholars from throughout the campus, [including] mathematical and physical sciences; engineering (all subfields); social sciences; humanities; and more."[21] This effort is also one that collaborates with other universities outside the California system. All of the Berkeley programs of the CITRIS and BIDS type, and there are many, involved significant investments in building appropriate new facilities for these activities or renovating and repurposing older buildings. Berkeley and its partners are evolving into a different kind of university from the one that Clark Kerr described more than fifty years ago, and Berkeley and the other great universities that I've used as illustrations here are evolving into knowledge and teaching networks of varying complexities. Some are entirely "in-house" and link various disciplines and schools with each other; but many others go far beyond those linkages into more complex structures involving the faculty and students at multiple universities working with many industrial and government partners to identify key problems, to find novel and innovative solutions, and where appropriate, to bring the results to those businesses that will translate the work into ongoing enterprises. Berkeley may not be undergoing revolutionary changes in its physical structure—it still has all of the schools that existed decades ago—but it is reshaping its organizational structure in a planned evolutionary way. It is not giving up on the knowledge brought forward by the silos of disciplines in the past, but it is combining that deep knowledge with the discoveries made in other schools and disciplines in a way that motivates students and faculty and that will drive discovery and innovation in the future.[22] That is what all great universities ought to be striving to achieve.

Given the structure of shared governance of these universities, there are few leaders who are willing to be bold and imaginative for fear of alienating the traditionally oriented faculty. Consequently, these leaders are not able to collaborate with the faculty toward a new vision for their institutions. They fail to make faculty members believe that they have not only been heard, but they have a stake in change. And since these universities currently are the most prestigious in the world, there is no urgency to move forward in sharply new directions with novel structures. These universities build and hold onto their reputations by use of traditional metrics: how difficult it is to gain admission to the university; how difficult it is to gain tenure at the university; how well the faculty are treated in terms of the entire range of rewards, from faculty salaries, to academic space, to housing, and to retirement benefits. If important technological changes present themselves, academic leaders and regents will jump on the bandwagon, such as joining groups to produce MOOCs or participating in efforts to build joint computing centers, or shared equipment facilities, or virtual information and library storage facilities. These leaders fear not having a first-mover advantage, so they jump aboard the latest initiative that they are told will become a disruptive technology that is apt to undermine their basic educational economic model, or they are told that this is the silver bullet that will solve their problem with escalating costs. These patterns of leadership behavior are hardly unexpected, but their adoption results in a slow, evolutionary means for incremental gains in quality.

If most of our older distinguished universities follow an evolutionary path toward structural change and reorganization, some of our newer public universities have taken a more revolutionary path; perhaps the quintessential example is Arizona State University.

Two decades ago, ASU was a backwater university that was expanding its number of undergraduate students. The State of Arizona and Phoenix, in particular, experienced such a breathtaking population growth that today the city of Phoenix has a larger population than Philadelphia. Despite this growth, the university always took a back seat to its sister institution in Tucson, the University of Arizona, and it could barely be classified as an intensive research university.

This pattern of sleepiness obtained until the arrival in 2002 of a new, highly ambitious president, Michael Crow.[23] If most university presidents play defense, then a few, like Michael Crow, play offense—and they play it well, like a great hitter in baseball. He is not risk averse and knows that a career batting average of .300 and a hefty number of home runs will get you into the Hall of Fame—if you have not used performance-enhancing drugs. But this is not Crow's goal; rather, it is to create a new type of university. After working in administration at Iowa State University and then for a decade at Columbia, where he was an increasingly important member of the policy-governing group as its executive vice provost, Crow had developed many innovative ideas about how a new type of American research university ought to be structured.[24] Arriving at ASU with Herculean energy, Michael Crow began a process of transformation that after a decade has taken ASU to a dramatically higher level of excellence.[25] Today, it educates more than 75,000 students and anticipates that number should reach 90,000 or 100,000 within a decade. Simultaneously, Crow launched an honors college that attracts extremely competitive students nationally and that allows them to live in residence halls together and to experience learning without significant borders, including the possibility of conducting innovative research as undergraduates. At the same time, ASU has become a national leader in online education, providing options for students seeking different types of educational environments (some out of pure choice, others out of economic necessity).

One of its three campuses, located in downtown Phoenix, is the result of a cooperative public and private redevelopment effort.[26] Scores of new buildings there are housing research and teaching programs. All of this was done without any annual capital allocation from the State of Arizona, not that President Crow hasn't used his considerable persuasive powers to have the state make special appropriations to help build some of these new structures.

Furthermore, the university prides itself on serving Native American, Latino, and African American students from poorer socioeconomic backgrounds who are often the first in their families to attend college. Despite taking on what others might term high-risk students, ASU's goal, not yet fully achieved, is to graduate 90 percent of its students. Simultaneously, ASU's research budget has grown enormously as the school has won many national peer-reviewed competitions for resources. Its research expenditures grew to almost $350 million in 2010, placing it among the top ten American universities in terms of expenditures for universities without a medical school. To reach such numbers, its faculty has had to be competitively strong, and there has been an expansion of the number of faculty and especially faculty drawn to the university because of its radically new orientation—much like the early days at Johns Hopkins. Simultaneously, ASU has forged collaborations with other impressive entities that want a presence in Phoenix and an affiliation with solid university programs. Recently, ASU has partnered with the famed Mayo Clinic, but it can also boast linkages with major high technology businesses in the region. It is now a leading force in areas of developing intellectual property.

In efforts to bring together faculty from a variety of disciplines to attack practical problems, Crow created the Biodesign Institute, discussed earlier. He has also realigned the structures of many traditional departments and schools in an effort to reorient their focus toward dealing with practical problems. For example, the political science department in the College of Liberal Arts was merged with the School of Global Studies to form a new structural entity, the School of Government, Politics and Global Studies. The Department of Mathematics and Statistics was transformed into the School of Mathematical and Statistical Sciences, with more than one hundred faculty members—again to use the deep knowledge in these disciplines to help create more useful knowledge. The School of Transformation grew out of the merger of the Justice and

Social Inquiry and Women's Studies departments, plus programs in African and African American Studies and Asian-Pacific American Studies. These efforts are designed to foster collaboration between intellectual affinity groups.

Of course, some are critical of Michael Crow's revolutionary efforts. But whether one disagrees with his ideas about how to create a revolution in the desert, or believes that he has embarked on too risky a project, no one would deny that he is incredibly innovative, smart, and willing to take risks, some of which will undoubtedly fail but from which we may learn how to organize teaching and research efforts more effectively than has been done in the past. In many ways the effort at ASU is not so revolutionary. For one, the university embraces the core values that we have spoken about; but it has been willing to experiment with new structures built on that value system.

Clearly, the prototype of the New American University at ASU would not fit the model of development found at the older, more traditional, prestigious research universities in America. And it remains an open question as to what features of this newer model will actually work. ASU will have to produce some case studies of how the restructured ASU can outperform universities using older models of organization. Nonetheless, ASU is an interesting example of an institution undergoing revolutionary structural change. How was this all accomplished in a little more than a decade?

When Michael Crow became president of ASU, it was ripe for change. It's unlikely that Crow would have survived five years at one of the Ivy League or great state universities because of faculty resistance to the "top-down" management style that he employed to foster structural change.[27] In all likelihood he would have had to move because of faculty pressure. So, Crow chose the right place at the right time to begin his experiment.

We should not think, however, that Michael Crow is a lone ranger who works independently of his board or his faculty. Rather, he spends innumerable hours with his board and faculty members discussing the fundamental objectives of ASU, and what it would take for him to create a different type of great institution—one, as he says, that is not measured against the more established private universities, but that will meet the needs of his state and graduate 25,000 students a year while expending roughly $700 million a year on significant research efforts.

Michael Crow possesses an unusual set of traits—ones that Max Weber, the renowned sociologist of the late nineteenth and early twentieth centuries, characterized as part of "charismatic authority." It is by virtue of the strength of

Crow's ideas and personality that many are willing to join in his efforts. He is extremely persuasive with almost all of the powerful constituencies interested in the university, including the state legislature and the board of regents, local Phoenix political leaders, and captains of industry. He is also persuasive with the most research-oriented and active faculty members, who were just waiting for a Michael Crow to come along. He also has another rare attribute: He thinks like an engineer or an architect and is willing to tolerate a reasonable (others would say a high) level of risk in order to implement his ideas. Beyond all of this, Crow has a rare ability to honestly convey to both the university community and those beyond it what his ideas are for a new American university. He is the rare leader who has both a set of ideas and the ability to see them to fruition.

Let me give you one more example in addition to his recent partnership with edX to offer a freshman online degree program. On June 15, 2014, the *New York Times* online edition ran a front-page story on an agreement ironed out between Starbucks, which has been known to look out for its employees, and ASU. Starbucks would pay for the online college education of any of its more than 135,000 employees in the United States, so that they could earn a college degree and potentially become more socially mobile. They would, of course, have to meet ASU's entrance requirements for online programs; but for those who could, this represented a unique opportunity and a model for other companies to follow. Moreover, Starbucks would pay for those employees who earned degrees but had moved on to other jobs during their course of study. How did it come to pass? Crow became friendly with Howard D. Schultz, Starbucks' chairman and chief executive officer, and together they worked out this plan to offer educational opportunities to the relatively lower-paid service workers. This was not a cynical move by ASU to generate more income, although it might do that. It was an effort to implement part of its larger strategy: to be an inclusive rather than an exclusive club. Few presidents of universities in the United States would have thought of the idea, recognized that it could set an example for other institutions to follow, or been able to work well with industry to implement the novel plan.[28]

In a recent speech, Richard Levin, the Yale economist and its former president, who in 2014 became CEO of the online higher education company Coursera, predicted: "In 10 or 20 years, when we judge the great universities, it will not just be on their research but on the reach of their teaching."[29] Perhaps the operative word in this sentence is "just," since pathbreaking research discoveries will remain the most fundamental determinant of greatness. But Levin's ambitions for teaching and its scope are quite apt. Whether it is through the worldwide democratization of educational content that brings opportunities to those who could not otherwise afford to get a degree, or educating our own young Americans, such as the employees of Starbucks, the ability to teach these students well and to enhance their basic knowledge and critical reasoning skills (as well as their social and economic prospects) will be far more measurable then it is today and will become *one* of the components by which we measure the greatness of institutions of higher learning.

One big challenge remains in Crow's effort to transform ASU at a revolutionary pace: effecting the transition that Weber discusses from those individuals who "rule" by charismatic authority to those who govern through more traditional, bureaucratic mechanisms. The question on everyone's lips at ASU as they watched buildings go up, light-rail systems being built to transport students from one campus to another, Nobel Prize faculty or their equivalent coming to Tempe as new faculty recruits, and new research initiatives being formed is: What happens to ASU when Crow leaves it? Was the model sustainable, and could it be institutionalized without him? In fact, Crow is aware of this problem and has tried, mostly through the new faculty and those who rose up through the ranks, to create a new "culture" at ASU—one that incorporates his vision, but could be taken as a given after he leaves the presidency.

If Michael Crow is trying to transform ASU in a revolutionary way, there are institutions that have moved innovatively at speeds somewhere between those found among the older, prestigious universities and new research universities like ASU. One institution that illustrates this middle ground is the University of California, San Diego. Consider its unofficial mission statement: "UC San Diego is an academic powerhouse and economic engine, recognized as one of the top 10 public universities by *U.S. News and World Report*. Innovation is central to who we are and what we do. Here, students learn that knowledge isn't just acquired in the classroom—life is their laboratory."[30]

In fact, Arizona State University is technically older than UC San Diego. ASU was established in 1885 as a Territorial Normal School at Tempe to train teachers for the Arizona Territory. UC San Diego came into being because the local population was concerned about the proximity of a military rifle range to their local La Jolla neighborhood and wanted something else there. In 1955, the San Diego City Council offered the University of California land for free to train professional engineers, and the University of California Regents established what was to become the Scripps Institution of Oceanography (which became part of UC San Diego). Virtually from its outset, UC San Diego became noted for its oceanographic research, particularly the now-famous Keeling Curve for measuring carbon dioxide levels in the atmosphere. UC San Diego did not offer humanities courses until the early 1960s, about the time that President Kennedy turned over four hundred acres of Camp Matthews (the former rifle range) to the University of California system. Over the following forty years, San Diego, with a series of innovative moves, particularly related to biological research, built a campus and set of programs that today make it one of the leading research universities in the world. From a small engineering program, focused principally on climate issues and the ocean, it evolved rapidly into a new multipurpose university (it had one of the best philosophy departments for years) with a strong emphasis on research and teaching at all levels. Strong academic leadership, particularly during the tenure of Richard Atkinson, provided the impetus for growth. Access to funds from California's capital budget allowed the new university to construct world-class research facilities comparatively rapidly. This university was able to take bold initiatives because it did not have to transform itself; it had to build itself from scratch into a world-class enterprise, and it did so because its leaders were prescient about what would turn out to be important areas of research as well as about how the research enterprise ought to be organized—plus they were able to recruit world-class faculty members. The lesson to be learned from both the ASU and UC San Diego experiences is that with extremely good leadership, proper use of resources, and a willingness to see which way the knowledge winds are blowing, it is possible to create a world-class university in a relatively short period. The correlative is also true; neglect of these institutions of higher learning can lead to rapid atrophy.

This brings me to the third type of structural reform. Whether it is complacency, blindness, or inertia, some of our universities are not able to adapt to the changing environment. They will proclaim a golden past rather than embrace an uncertain, but perhaps even more glorious, future. These universities may survive for some time, but their relevance to the system of higher learning and scholarship will surely diminish. No university has an intrinsic *right* to exist. We have hundreds of places where education and research are carried out, but we have thousands of colleges and universities that generate very little new knowledge. Among the latter, many provide real additional value for their students and new forms of opportunities. But not all of these institutions will

exist twenty-five or thirty years from now. That will not necessarily be a tragedy. Either these universities and colleges adapt to new needs, either they take
some risks and try to be innovative in a variety of ways, or they should fall by
the wayside. The first American college, which preceded the founding of Harvard in 1636, did not survive. Located in Virginia, it was named Henrico. No
one is mourning that loss today. To do what is necessary to change, many of
these lesser institutions will need to demonstrate that their raison d'être is worth
preserving—and that students and faculty can obtain something there that they
can't get at other institutions. It will be sad if truly innovative, adaptive institutions that have a great deal to offer students and faculty are eliminated for
purely financial reasons—reasons that they simply cannot respond to as much
as they may try. But let's not forget how much can be done to adapt, such as
what has been accomplished at ASU and at UC San Diego.

Many state systems confront another great challenge, especially if they are
characterized by a structure that is divided, as in California or New York, by
two or three tiers that include community colleges, senior colleges, and graduate schools. At CUNY, for example, a large percentage of its undergraduates
begin in the community college system, where the dropout rate is very high.
Because the system is predicated on the ability to move seamlessly from one
tier to another, it is imperative that structures exist that allow this to happen.
This includes agreed-upon curricula at the community colleges that will be
accepted by the senior colleges upon the transfer of students. What can be done
about the very high dropout rate? With the exception of mental health services,
many of the offices for teenage growing pains can be downsized or eliminated
and those resources allocated for teaching and mentoring these undergraduates.
If this is handholding for youngsters who are the first in their families to attend
college, then so be it. There is a need for these students to have continual access to trained mentors who can guide them through the system and toward
graduation. Without this mentoring system, all of the funds that these youngsters spend to receive college degrees get wasted when they fail to graduate.
But CUNY has put into place an elaborate support and preparatory system for
its community college students—and it seems to have a positive effect. Graduation rates, as many educators have said, are as important as the number of
students initially attending college and its cost.

Part of the graduation-rate problem at community colleges can be positively
influenced by President Obama's call for tuition-free community college edu-
cations. But the problem of dropout rates goes beyond tuition assistance. Many

of the students need some form of remedial assistance, and only the college or university system can develop and implement it. Moreover, although it may be hard enough to obtain federal support for community college attendance, the need for federal financial support goes well beyond those colleges. As I've suggested, there is a need for a comprehensive Morrill III Act that provides federal support to needy students, regardless of whether or not they are in community colleges.[31]

Necessary Structural Reform at the State and Federal Levels

We obviously cannot build or maintain great universities without resources. The best private research universities built up endowments, gifts that could be spent down (unlike endowments where roughly 5 percent of the corpus is spent each year and the rest, if there is a yield greater than that, is put back into the endowment for future growth, spendable gifts can be used in their entirety at the discretion of the president, provost, or dean of a school); federal, state, and private research support; and other streams of income to enable them to achieve greatness. The top state universities were products of many of the same resource streams (and increasingly so), but with the critical difference that they were dependent on state financing for the education of in-state college and graduate students. Of course, the federal government played a critical role in their development in the way it structured the funding of research. If structural changes are needed within our great universities, it is equally important that structural change takes place in the governments that influence the universities' performance and research productivity.

I've emphasized throughout this book that the actual preferences of state governments in their allocation of funds for higher learning betray the rhetoric used by their leaders. State financing of their universities has plummeted over the past two decades. As I've said, look at budgets and you have a sense of a university's academic priorities; look at state budgets and you'll get a sense of the state's priorities. In a fundamental way, many states have violated the trust that was placed in them when they took the land allocated to them by the Morrill Act of 1862, which many sold and then used the proceeds to build the land-grant college and university systems and agricultural and home economics research stations.[32] The intent of that act was for the states to support these new institutions, which today educate about 80 percent of today's undergraduate students. Yet, while in the past the states supported students going to college, that support has essentially evaporated. That surely was not the intent of those who voted to pass the Morrill Act. If great universities are to be held accountable for how they spend their money, so should the states that have built universities that date back to the act.[33] Congress ought to declare that those states that fail to support their universities with at least 30 percent of their operating budgets ought to be put on notice that they can lose federal financial aid. They have a choice: increase their support of higher learning (while auditing expenses of the universities) or risk withdrawal of federal funds. In fact, we ought to go still further and mandate that states that lower their support of their public universities and colleges to less than 10 percent forfeit the right to maintain them as state institutions.[34] The universities—which must increase the number of out-of-state students who are willing to pay three or four times what an in-state student pays—have become, in order to balance their budgets, essentially private institutions operating under the state's education laws. Those institutions should have the option at some threshold level of limited state support (perhaps three consecutive years of less than 20 percent of the budget for financial aid and the cost of faculty and facilities) to declare themselves as private universities. This would be called "the opt-out clause," and would be exercised by a vote of an independent board of overseers and the academic administration and faculty of the university. If the state insists that these institutions pay off the cost of the campus buildings or similar types of state investments, the universities should be able to use the present-day value of the funds that the state received from the Morrill Act (and subsequent federal support) to offset the amount of money that is due the state. Given the funds that each state received under the Morrill Act of 1862 and subsequent inflation, it might well be that universities would not have to pay the states a penny. States have a choice, just as they have a choice with the Affordable Care Act. They can refuse to participate and give up substantial additional Medicare funds. Here they can refuse to finance their universities and pay the penalty of lost federal government funds.

Of course, it would be extremely unfortunate if even one great university had to exercise this option. State universities have a public mission, and to have to abandon that identity would be tragic for aspiring students as well as for the institutions that contemplate taking the "poison pill." But the states should not be able to have it both ways: They cannot castigate the universities for being spendthrifts and ignoring costs while they withdraw their support of the universities, thus causing the educational institutions to take draconian actions such as increasing the number of full-paying out-of-state and foreign students who would love the opportunity to attend one of the United States' great public universities. I realize how unlikely it is that Congress would adopt this proposal regarding the fiduciary responsibility of state governments to their universities under the terms of the Morrill Act. However, even an open discussion of the issue in Congress and forcing a vote on the matter in a statewide referendum would shed light on how hypocritical state governments can be.

Structural Reforms in Federal Support of Higher Education and Research: Further Elements in the Morrill III Act

Big Science research is costly. It requires not only funding the faculty members who are the principal investigators on the research project but also the postdoctoral fellows and graduate students and technicians who often do the lion's share of the bench work, not to mention, among other things, the facilities and equipment needed for the research. For decades, the compact between the federal government and our universities was largely adhered to. To be sure, there were moments when the government questioned the value of some of this research (remember Wisconsin's Senator William Proxmire's "Golden Fleece of the Month Award")[35] or got caught up in its political implications (remember efforts during the second Bush administration to muzzle the climatologist James Hansen's observations about man's impact on global warming). But the cost of scientific research pales in comparison with the savings on the cost of disease. Consider the thoughts of Nobel laureate and discoverer of prions, Stanley Prusiner, on the allocation of resources in cases like Alzheimer's disease:

> The economics of Alzheimer's do not make sense. We spend nearly $200 billion annually caring for Alzheimer's victims, a colossal sum that includes the lost productivity both of patients and caregivers. Moreover, Alzheimer's victims occupy half of all nursing home beds in America. Yet we devote less than half a billion dollars a year to research, so we spend four hundred times more on care than on research directed at stopping this curse.[36]

American ambivalence toward scientific and scholarly expertise has begun to erode aspects of the compact between our preeminent universities and the government policymakers in Congress. One of the first features of Vannevar Bush's plan was the full reimbursement of the audited cost of research (often referred to as indirect cost recovery, or ICR).[37] Over several decades following the War, the level of this reimbursement by the government was a product of negotiation, often so detailed and complex in terms of auditing that at least one full-time government employee was permanently located on the university campus to monitor research costs. Then, slowly the government began to cut back on its reimbursements for audited research expenses. Finally, it put a cap on the reimbursement it would make for facilities charges. By compromising the pact, the federal government was actually making universities pay for government grants and contracts as well as having the universities build new research in anticipation of adding government grants that would at least pay for the cost of conducting research in those buildings. The problem was compounded by the fact that most private foundations that supported research, as well as industrial companies, would refuse to reimburse the universities for the full cost of doing this research.[38] Some foundations would not provide indirect costs at all. Contrary to existing beliefs both inside and outside the university, research that was in the national interest and was judged to be of high potential quality was not being fully funded. In fact, it was costing the universities money to do it.

This had cascading consequences for our universities. In order to meet the full costs of doing research and of competing for the best researchers (which often required strong economic incentives in the form of state-of-the art laboratory space and equipment, guaranteed support for a number of postdoctoral students, laboratory technicians, and other support staff), universities had to find dollars within their budgets to cross-subsidize potentially pathbreaking research. Two sources were clearly available: tuition dollars, and gifts from donors who saw great value in the research. Ironically, some of the increasing cost of tuition for undergraduates, which so often reaches the media and evokes criticism from public officials, including the president of the United States, is a result of the federal government not living up to the terms of the compact made decades ago.

There are other ways in which the government has produced unpredictable policies that haunt our finest university research efforts. For example, it is extremely difficult to know what funding increases or cuts will be contained in each federal budget cycle; if restrictions will be placed on the types of work that can be funded, such as stem cell research; or if Congress will try, as mentioned, to mandate that the only political science projects to be funded by the National Science Foundation (NSF), despite its processes of peer review, are those that deal with national security issues. Government policies toward student loans and eligibility for those grants or loans are ambiguous and often restrictive. Research is part of the "discretionary" budget and is often looked to for "savings," when it is, in fact, in the interest of the nation to support both fundamental as well as more pointed research that might lead to effective treatments or cures for diseases.

If we have strayed so far from the concept of federal financing of American research, then we ought to rethink aspects of the social compact between government and the universities. Consider a few possibilities based upon the widely held view that investments in our research—its people and its infrastructure—are no less important than investments in military preparedness, because the consequences of those investments create an economy that can retain its international leadership.[39]

Vannevar Bush was a staunch advocate for fundamental scientific research. He believed in stockpiling basic knowledge and was confident that those discoveries would lead to new applications that would create highly skilled jobs and a flourishing national economy. He feared that the support of scientific research would become a political football that would be misused by people who knew little about research and its effects on the nation. He proposed a quasi-independent body, a National Research Foundation, which would be given a sum of money and would oversee the conduct of American research. That became a practical impossibility, as neither the Congress nor President Truman was willing to cede control over the purse that supported science. Although this could be expected, over the years, the level of scientific and technological literacy in Congress has become abysmally low and troubling for the long-term needs of the scientific community and for the nation's economy.[40] As Congressman Rush Holt, who has a Ph.D. in physics and served in Congress until 2014, said upon announcing his departure from Congress after around fifteen years: The level of scientific discourse "has not gotten better, let's put it that way. There are still people who read popular science articles, and most members of Congress say they value science and respect scientists. But I don't see more scientific thinking—evidence-based, critical thinking."[41] He was being polite to his colleagues.

We now need to look at some alternative models for the financing of the national research effort in order to stabilize the flow of funds to science for numerous years—since science so often involves multiyear investigations. And we need to place knowledgeable people in charge of the accountability of science and its activities. Looking back on Bush's proposed model, it was clearly utopian.

It is not likely that the Congress and the executive branch of the federal government will relinquish control of the spigot from which funds flow. An alternative model, however, could be constructed. This new body would not replace the current roles of those agencies within the federal government that currently fund scientific research. And it is emphatically not intended to take funds away from any of those academic research funding agencies. It would be designed to meet other existing needs that the nation has in maintaining the superiority of its research universities and the discoveries that will influence our international power and standing in the future. This body would have some independent funding authority, but a good deal of its effort would be spent on advising Congress on emerging fields, novel strategies for conquering disease, new scholarship that ought to be supported, evaluating what federal regulations are impeding the growth of knowledge or ought to be streamlined or eliminated, and what the rate of growth in the overall budget ought to be. This new organizational structure, a National Foundation for Science, Technology, and Scholarship, would act much as the Howard Hughes Medical Institute (HHMI) has functioned in the field of biomedical research—allowing exceptionally talented scientists and engineers the freedom to work on highly significant problems without fear of losing their funding. To date, seventeen Nobel laureates and more than 170 members of the National Academy of Sciences have been funded by the HHMI program. The new Foundation would also encourage and fund groups of investigators, as the HHMI does, "to undertake projects that are new and so large in scope that they require a team with a range of expertise."[42] Further, this Foundation would provide these kinds of funds to exceptionally gifted behavioral science researchers and for scholarship of importance in the humanities. If necessary, it would call on the expertise of outside people to assist in assessing the potential of the proposed or ongoing work. The individuals or groups funded would be accountable to the Foundation's leaders to demonstrate their progress toward their goal every three to five years. The Foundation's board of governors, along with its advisors, would, as part of its mission, try to fund young scientists and innovators with enormous promise. It would also suggest policies to the various federal funding agencies involved in biomedical research on how to lower significantly the age at which younger scientists can establish their own laboratories with RO-1 grants (which today are typically not made until a scientist is in his or her early forties).

In short, we ought to create a quasi-independent, nonpolitical body to oversee science, engineering, behavioral sciences, and the humanities that would recommend a five-year funding stream for researchers. This would *not* be an effort at central planning. Rather, this group of experts would come from the scientific and academic communities and elsewhere and would be selected for their knowledge in the areas funded. Much as members of the Federal Reserve System are appointed, these individuals would be nominated by the president with the majority consent of the Senate.[43] The Foundation's board of governors would comprise seven or nine members who would make final decisions about recommended areas of funding and would review the progress made in those fields as well as the efficacy of the peer review system. These governors would hold terms of six years, renewable once, in order to allow turnover; and their selection would be staggered in order to ensure continuity. The board would not only recommend amounts to be allocated to the various science agencies, including the NSF and the National Institutes of Health, but would examine the types of science and technology that are being done in order to assess their progress as well as to recommend the level of funding for higher risk "blue sky" programs. This body would not be a redundancy for the President's Council of Advisers on Science and Technology (PCAST) which, along with the National Academies of Science, advises the president. PCAST has had a very checkered history depending upon who the sitting president is and his (perhaps "her" in the not-too-distant future) interest in matters of science and technology. It has been dormant or very active, but it has not had the formative role of recommending funding levels for the various fields covered by government grants and contracts, nor has it been directly involved in funding exceptional scientists and scholars. Once confirmed by the Senate, these board members would act as independent agents who view themselves as serving the people of the nation, not any individual or political party. The Foundation would report annually to Congress and to the Office of Management and Budget on the progress made by its funded research and would produce a set of proposals for the funding of the national system of innovation and academic research.

Where would this Foundation obtain the resources that are needed to do its creative job of ferreting out innovative, exceptionally qualified, younger scientists and scholars? We return to the provisions of the new Morrill III Act. In addition to providing for the laboratory schools, federal financial aid program, and support for state universities, the act would specify that the Foundation will receive three allocations of $4 billion a year for five years, giving it an initial endowment of roughly $20 billion. In terms of assets, this would make the Foundation one of largest in the United States.[44] And if well-to-do private citizens wished to contribute to the endowment of the Foundation to set up programs, it could easily become one of the wealthiest foundations in the nation. This endowment would be invested in a variety of financial instruments that would be expected to produce total annual returns of about 9 percent. The bank would establish, as do universities, a spending rule that targets a payout of roughly 5 percent of the corpus for its operating purposes. The remainder of the growth would be reinvested in the Foundation's portfolio. The usable funds would support exceptional people and extraordinary science, technology, and scholarship. A National Fellows Program would be created, and the awarding of grants for an initial five years would rapidly become highly prestigious. The grants would cover much of the cost of a laboratory or a group of scholars or humanists and innovative collaborative groups. The funded scholars and scientists would work at universities—the funds would go to the universities to support research there, rather than be kept for intramural research.

Two other features of the Foundation are important. First, individuals with exceptional wealth could contribute funds to set up specialized, but not overly specialized, National Fellows Programs in specific areas, such as "mind, brain science," or "the study of a sustainable planet," or "the study of social groups," or "development economics," or "the study of how individuals learn."[45] Instead of placing their wealth while living or upon their death into private, self-perpetuating foundations—which over time often reflect the interests of the current leaders of the Foundation rather than the original intent of the donor—they could contribute to the national welfare by giving at least a portion of their assets to the Foundation as part of a national trust fund for scientific and scholarly research. These contributions would receive appropriate tax incentives in terms of gift and inheritance taxes and would be part of a growing endowment dedicated to the goals of American society. The donor's name would be associated with a specific program endowment.

Second, intellectual property that might emerge from discoveries made by the Fellows would belong to the federal government; but the proceeds from patents, licenses, and start-up companies would be split between the researchers and the Foundation. For example, the scientists might obtain 25 percent of the returns but no more than a 10 percent equity stake in a start-up company, and the Foundation would receive the rest of the returns on the intellectual property. The proceeds from the intellectual property would be returned to the endowment in order for it to grow still further. It is quite likely that over time the initial investment by the government would be repaid many times over. In *The*

Great American University, I suggested that those who have accumulated enormous wealth would be better off investing in universities than in private foundations. Although I still believe that is the case, this would provide another vehicle that could be used for the public good and place the shepherding of truly original ideas in the hands of proven experts. Much of the success in the HHMI is due to this type of funding structure—without the additional means of growing the original endowment.

The Foundation would not only support cutting-edge research, but it would also establish strong linkages to industry that would benefit potentially from the work of the faculty supported by the Foundation. The effect would be to develop new businesses and methods for treating and curing disease; innovative technologies for creating new industries; and novel methods for addressing social and economic problems that would ultimately save hundreds of millions of dollars and improve the quality of life of millions of people around the world. Industrial contributions to the Foundation would also be welcome.

The objective of the Foundation would be to support particularly innovative work on the campuses of the great universities, pay for the full cost of that research, and create what over time would become the largest endowment for science and scholarship in the world. The Foundation's various fellows programs would be governed by the same board as the entire Foundation, but like the Nobel Prize Committee, the Foundation would have a small fund to be spent on actual operations, selection of new fellows, and renewal of continuing fellows, while overseeing the quality of the work being done. A renowned academic administrator would act as its director or president and would report to the board of governors, which would report to both the Congress and executive branches of the federal government.

There would be one final feature of the Morrill III Act. The legislation that brought the Foundation into existence would provide the Foundation with a set of government airwaves for the creation of a new multimedia educational broadcasting company. The mission of this noncommercial, nonprofit public media company would be to teach the American public about education from preschool to the advanced achievements of scientists and scholars at our great universities (and what scientists and scholars are working on). It would also promote work to produce a more informed citizenry. Because a significant segment of the American population does not understand a great deal about our educational system and its enemies, this network would promote useful knowledge. There is a great need in the United States for a better understanding of why education matters for individuals and the nation. The new network (born out of the Morrill III Act) could produce shows on all aspects of education. The United States does not currently have a nonprofit broadcasting network. The nation ought to have one that examines education and its social and economic consequences,[46] educational opportunities, theories, and practices related to preschool education or lifelong learning courses. It should address current problems challenging the American educational system, and, finally, the programs should also focus on the process of discovery and innovation with an emphasis on conversations with men and women who have made those discoveries. We have not demonstrated to the public the power of the intellect, which is often located at our great educational institutions. This national educational broadcasting network would use older and newer forms of communication, from radio, television, social media, and educational platforms, including MOOCs, to educate the American people about how education has and can change for the better their lives and the world we live in. Its ambition would also be to help people, through education, to live more enjoyable lives by exposing them to ideas and themes that may well capture their imaginations.

It is logical to ask how we might finance the Morrill III Act. This large-scale commitment to education includes, to reiterate, an extensive financial aid program designed to help students attain a college education with minimal debt. It also sets up 100 secondary schools that are located at major research universities, where there would be permeability between work done in the secondary school and the associated university. It creates an organization that advises the Congress and the executive branch on the increases in funding required to make substantial scientific progress in important areas of research; it is designed to fund brilliant young scientists in a way that gives them the maximum amount of freedom to pursue science without administrative burdens; and it creates a public outreach program by creating a national educational broadcasting network. Here are just a few of the ways that we could finance this new set of initiatives. For one, we could reallocate resources from other areas to education, although there are other important new needs that also must be financed, such as renewing America's infrastructure. Perhaps we ought to look at imposing a special tax on the offshore earnings of American corporations that circumvent the tax system by relocating their enterprises in lower-tax locations outside of the United States. We could also raise the marginal tax rates on individuals with earnings that place them in the top 1 percent or higher of the income distribution of the nation.

Finally, consider that the Congressional Budget Office, which is a nonpartisan group advising members of Congress, has estimated that over the next decade the U.S. government will raise approximately $165 billion in *profits* from students who take out federal loans. This is an unconscionable windfall, especially when the federal government charges approximately 5–6 percent interest on student loans but charges banks only about 1 percent on loans. It should not escape anyone's attention that while these profits are being accrued by the federal government, the very same bodies are browbeating colleges and universities for the level of debt carried by their graduates. If the federal government ran a not-for-profit student loan "business" and lowered the interest on those loans to the level offered banks, student debt would suddenly drop precipitously.[47] As part of the Morrill III Act, the federal government ought to reduce the interest rates on student loans to the cost of administering the program, but not higher than the rate charged large banks.[48]

Creating a Federal Institute for Disease Prevention and Vaccine Production

Recent research on disease and potential pandemics caused by bacteria and viruses suggests that there is a need to create an ongoing organization that can respond quickly and steadily to potential lethal bacterial, viral, or prion diseases. We currently have no highly institutionalized way of addressing these health risks. To depend on private enterprise to move swiftly into action to produce vaccines for a potential pandemic is difficult because a business has to gamble on whether or not the disease is apt to spread and becomes one that kills thousands, if not hundreds of thousands, of people around the world. Because businesses exist to make money, and in most cases creating vaccines or antidotes for *potential* pandemics is not profitable, it is hard for the nation to count on the private sector to protect the nation against an Ebola or bird flu epidemic, for example, or from other forms of bacteria or viruses that could be lethal and spread rapidly. As one example, Trudie Lang, professor of global health research at Oxford, said of the bureaucratic delays that made it difficult to pursue treatments and vaccines for Ebola:

> Despite the lack of a proven treatment for Ebola, our efforts and those of other researchers over the past year will have been worth it if they help to ensure that, next time, the global community is better prepared.... An international,

neutral body needs to be put in charge of outbreak research. Before the next outbreak, such a body could hammer out the details of crisis trial staffing and contracts. Most importantly, this organization could set the research priorities during an epidemic and ensure that adequate numbers of sites and patients are allocated to the different teams involved.[49]

Perhaps this new institute could be an international one, but we ought to be taking our own precautions against the possibilities of pandemics far more contagious than Ebola. Therefore, the federal government ought to create an institute for disease prevention and vaccine production that is linked to the Centers for Disease Control (CDC). Although this mechanism for combating pandemics will not always be cost-efficient, it will provide potentially far more protection for the world's population, and particularly the American population, than what currently exists. The institute would have an important defense role as well—producing vaccines or antidotes for bacteria or viruses that might get into the hands of groups trying to use bioterrorism to harm the American people. In addition, the same institute might well play a role in helping private enterprise produce better drugs to address the symptoms and causes of a variety of diseases that affect millions of Americans every year—such as a host of prion-related neurodegenerative diseases. Currently, private pharmaceutical companies are marketing products that have little or no efficacy while spending more on advertising these products than on research and development. This new institute would help develop sound research on which efficacious drugs should be produced. Some of the Institute's work would be done internally, but some of it would function as a granting agency that funded work on vaccines and antidotes, or methods of controlling pandemics, at our nation's great universities.

The Nexus Between Industry and Our Great Universities

If the partnership between the federal and state governments and the universities ought to be reconstructed, the relationship between universities and industry needs to be strengthened still further. Here are several ways that we ought to encourage greater interaction for mutual benefit between our businesses and our research universities. We ought to facilitate cooperative agreements between the two, both for the continuing education of those who work for industry and to facilitate the development of ideas that could create new businesses or industries. Over the past several decades, we know that an increasing proportion of research that leads to innovative new business ventures is produced at universities. Universities are best positioned to produce novel ideas; industry is far better equipped to develop these ideas into viable business ventures. Consequently, we ought to incentivize businesses to work collaboratively with universities to develop intellectual property. Many universities have incubator facilities where faculty can begin to develop ideas that have potential practical value. However, not enough has been done yet to create continuing and closer bonds between these institutions.

Silicon Valley is, of course, a location where many ideas that were spawned at universities in California have been built into hugely successful businesses. Similar results have obtained in Massachusetts, near MIT in Cambridge. More recently, the state of New York is creating a partnership between Cornell and Technion–Israel Institute of Technology and Industry by building a campus on New York's Roosevelt Island devoted to the transfer of university discoveries into business possibilities. And, as mentioned in Chapter 8, the Research Triangle Park in Durham, North Carolina, is another example of close partnerships between new business and the state's research universities. We need many more of our distinguished universities to create locations near their flagship campuses for industry to find a home and to work with universities to develop the ideas of brilliant faculty members. We can do far more than we have thus far in connecting the business community to our great universities—and we ought to develop mechanisms, including financial incentives for both parties, to enter into a more closely knit relationship. Hundreds of thousands of highly skilled jobs can be generated through these relationships. The creation of innovative knowledge can be shared with industry in a way that produces entirely new businesses—types of businesses that we may not even be able to imagine today.

Businesses should also make greater use of universities to develop their workforce while they are on the job. There is no reason why the advanced knowledge created at our universities can't be shared with many businesses through the use of online teaching and learning. This effort has already begun by universities such as Georgia Tech, among others. We ought to be expanding these efforts significantly over the next several decades. Businesses that have a workforce that is not highly skilled should use university programs to improve the human capital of its workers—even if it leads to some of them moving on to better-paying jobs with greater responsibilities. In short, there is a huge untapped potential for the partnership between universities and industry, and the

American economy and its workers will be the beneficiaries. States should be committed to providing the financial glue that helps to create and sustain the linkage.

Our model for great universities worked exceptionally well for almost seventy-five years, but environmental conditions that surround these universities have changed. In order for us to grow, adapt to these changes, and move closer to our full potential as a colossal force in the creation and transmission of knowledge, we ought to think of various ways to alter the structure of universities in order to make these things happen. Those who adapt, who take some prudent risks, and who acknowledge that new conditions in the way knowledge grows create the need for new or reformed university structures, will be among the great research universities of the world in twenty-five or thirty years, and U.S. research universities will remain the envy of the world.

A United States That Can
Accommodate Great Universities in 2040

Strong values enable us to live in harmony with one another. Without trust, there can be no harmony, nor can there be a strong economy. Inequality in America is degrading our trust. For our own sake, and for the sake of future generations, it's time to start rebuilding it. That this even requires pointing out shows how far we have to go.

—JOSEPH E. STIGLITZ, NOBEL PRIZE WINNER IN ECONOMICS

IT HAS NOT ESCAPED my attention that many of the ideas that I propose in this book would have a questionable fate if we were to put them to a vote, or in the hands of today's policymakers at many of our great universities, or in the U.S. Congress and state governments. Attitudes and behavior both in the nation at large and within universities will have to change if we are to maximize our great universities' full potential. Levels of trust among us and between institutions will have to increase. When I suggest how we ought to change our system of admissions to college or our emphasis within the undergraduate curriculum, for example, I am implicitly saying something about what our society ought to look like twenty-five or thirty years from now. Who we admit into our finest institutions of higher learning tells us something about what our nation values and the types of leaders we want to develop in all walks of life. Consider some features of what that society ought to look like if it is to produce the kinds of universities that I have been describing in these pages.

As discussed, the executive branch of government seems to have little respect for the Madisonian idea of transparency of government. Much of the information that the people need to make reasonable decisions is now classified, and the executive branch continues to hide behind the implausible argument that national security is risked by disclosure of this information. And yet the judiciary, the Congress, and the public refuse to question these activities. Perhaps equally disturbing is the absence of any sense among a majority of members of Congress that they are working for the welfare of the people. The idea of a "common good" seems to have disappeared from our national government. Even cries for change that a vast majority of Americans seem to want, such as some form of gun control and a reduction of the inequality of wealth, seem to fall on the deaf ears of their elected representatives. The power of money and individuals of great wealth to determine the outcome of elections—even the choice of candidates—has been exacerbated by Supreme Court decisions like *Citizens United v. Federal Election Commission.*[1] Within the next generation or two, I expect that reforms in Congress will take place so that it regains some modicum of public trust and allows meaningful legislation to be passed without constant gridlock. Aside from substantive civil rights legislation, major legislation that recognizes the value of educational training and research will pass Congress and set the stage for an era of enormous growth in the creation and transmission of knowledge.

In addition, over the next decade there will be a greater recognition by state governments of the value of universities as well as a better understanding of the ways that these institutions help shape the social organization and economic well-being of the states. Supporting access and excellence in higher learning, as well as in K–12 education, is not a matter of real discretion. It is far more important than spending tens of millions of dollars on things like border security or the "war on drugs" that we have clearly lost. In fact, I envision states becoming active partners with universities in creating better schools and universities and attracting new industries to their borders—partly drawn there because of the exceptional human capital that the state has to offer those businesses.

And in the next several decades, I assume that we will improve the level of equality of educational opportunity. This is an extremely complex and difficult problem. The mechanisms for achieving better outcomes for those from poorer economic backgrounds are not clear to economists or other social scientists. The future will depend on solving this most vexing issue, which is as much a family problem as it is a schooling problem. We are witnessing in the United States the process of "the accumulation of advantage." It is much in keeping with the biblical words of St. Matthew (25:29 King James Version): "For unto every one that hath shall be given, and he shall have abundance: but from him that hath not shall be taken away even that which he hath." The sociologist Keith Stanovich has employed the idea of the Matthew Effect in education, noting that early, successful readers tend to read more and become more knowledgeable, in contrast with slower learners of reading who tend not to read and fall farther behind in attaining verbal and other skills.[2] How do we break out of this pattern to provide real opportunities for those demographic groups from disadvantaged backgrounds that are a growing portion of our society?

I envision new solutions based upon a far better cadre of teachers, better relationships between teachers unions and educational boards, and an end to the commodification of the educational system. The testing craze will have run its course, and we will turn to substantive-based curricula and measures of competence rather than test results. Our universities will play a larger role in improving local community schools. We will completely change the way we teach science and math so that young people, regardless of gender or race, become truly excited about scientific and engineering careers. We will honor our teachers through increases in compensation and prestige to the point that they will compete with physicians and other professionals for standing in the community.[3] An increasing number of Ph.D. scholars and scientists will turn to precollege education and transform the quality of the teaching body in our K–12 schools. Teachers unions will be reformed; will increasingly accept the idea of merit-based rewards; and, along with school boards, will take a more active role in setting a curriculum agenda and developing new measures of students' mastery of the curriculum.

The inequality of educational opportunity is related, of course, to perhaps the greatest issue facing the United States today: the growing inequality of wealth. The "rich are getting richer and the richest of the rich are getting still richer, the poor are becoming poorer and more numerous, and the middle class is being hollowed out."[4] Writing in 2012, Nobel Prize–winning economist Joseph E. Stigliz concluded that "we became a society that was so unequal, with opportunity so diminished," that the consequences for our social and economic welfare were huge. Stiglitz puts it starkly: "The top 1 percent get in one week 40 percent more than the bottom fifth receive in a year; the top 0.1 percent received in a day and a half about what the bottom 90 percent received in a year, and the richest 20 percent of income earners earn in total *after* tax more than the bottom 80 percent combined."[5] Think of the consequences of these levels of growing inequality in America. The rich and very rich send their children to expensive and superior elementary and secondary schools and to the most prestigious colleges and universities without having to worry about cost. But the overwhelming majority of Americans can't afford to send their children to first-rate institutions of higher learning without substantial financial aid—and when they choose to do so, they or their children accrue huge debt or, even worse, forgo necessary medical and other forms of care in order to pay for that education. This is not only a problem faced by those from the most disadvantaged groups in the nation but also by the middle class with family incomes that are quite respectable—in fact, high enough that they often do not qualify for much financial aid.

Stiglitz places these contrasts in bold relief:

> There are two visions for America a half century from now. One is of a society more divided between the haves and the have-nots, a country in which the rich live in gated communities, send their children to expensive schools, and have access to first-rate medical care.... The other vision is of a society where the gap between the haves and the have-nots has been narrowed, where there is a sense of shared destiny, a common commitment to opportunity and fairness, where the words "liberty and justice for *all*" actually mean what they seem to mean, where we take seriously the Universal Declaration of Human Rights, which emphasizes the importance not just of civil rights but of economic rights, and not just the rights of property but the economic rights of ordinary citizens. In this vision, we have an increasingly vibrant political system far different from the one in which 80 percent of the young are so alienated that they don't even bother to vote.[6]

Part of the solution might be found in tax reform, but the vast majority of Americans have a knee-jerk reaction against any tax increases and most do not understand the concept of marginal tax rates.[7] They incorrectly believe that the higher marginal tax rates have a direct connection with growth in the GDP per capita. Between 1955 and 1970, the highest marginal tax rate was, averaged over those years, 82.3 percent. That rate fell to 70 percent during the 1970s, and today the highest marginal tax rate is only 39.3 percent. In 2013, the members of Congress argued over the consequences of having the highest bracket of 39.5 percent kick in at an income level above $250,000 or $400,000, while no action was taken to treat income derived from private equity and venture capital sources as capital gains, which in 2013 were taxed at 15 percent. (Never mind the use of corporate tax loopholes and other means of avoiding taxes for the very rich.) So even if we can justify that the pay for top managers of huge corporations, private equity funds, and leaders of large banks should be in the millions of dollars annually, there is no reason why the income beyond a certain threshold shouldn't be taxed at a higher marginal rate—allowing for meaningful redistribution of wealth in society. Unless Americans come to grips with the rising inequality of income and wealth among our citizens, we will fail to have the resources necessary for providing opportunity and access to higher education for many children of middle-class families. This is at least as true for the states as it is for our federal government. Without confronting tax issues, states that faced fiscal constraints simply cut their allocations to institutions of higher learning. The drop in state subsidies of education lead directly to higher costs for families sending their children to these universities.

We ought to be attacking the problem of income and wealth inequality with much greater focus and determination than we seem to be currently demonstrating. Yet the Congress of 2015 seems to refuse to acknowledge income inequality as a serious problem. We need to evolve into a society in which there is an acceptance of higher marginal tax rates on the fabulously wealthy. Economists Thomas Piketty and Emmanuel Saez conclude after extensive study that we will need a marginal tax rate of roughly 70 percent if we wish to halt the widening difference in wealth and income in the United States.[8] Americans need to understand that higher marginal taxes on the very rich and better distribution throughout the society does not hurt economic growth, but it does lower the levels of inequality of income and wealth and provides the middle class with resources to spend on education and other forms of goods and services.

The problem of growing inequality is as much a problem of a breakdown in governance at the national level as it is of core economic instability. As the preeminent Columbia University economist Jeffrey Sachs has put it:

We are living through a new Gilded Age exceeding the gaudy excesses of the 1870s and the 1920s. The extent of riches at the top of the income and wealth distributions is unimaginable to most Americans, especially at a time when one in eight Americans depends on food stamps.... Our challenges lie not so much in our productivity, technology, or natural resources but in our ability to cooperate on an honest basis. Can we make the political system work to solve a growing list of problems?... Will the super-rich finally own up to their responsibilities to the rest of society? These are questions about our attitudes, emotions, and openness to collective actions more than about the death of productivity or the depletion of resources.[9]

In the society that ought to prevail in 2040, Americans will recognize that there is a role for government and a role for free markets, but that free markets without constraint can produce skewed and dysfunctional economic and social outcomes. Americans must come to appreciate that there is no free lunch—there is a price that we have to pay for the things that we want. Almost all polls of the American people have demonstrated the distinction between their reaction to a general rubric, such as "welfare" (bad), and each of the elements in welfare policies (good). Framing makes a difference. Americans are in favor of the various elements in a social welfare policy. Similarly, our citizens react viscerally and negatively to the idea of big government, which they see as taking their money and misspending it; but they support increases in military budgets, huge increased allocations of resources to protect national security, government expenditures to limit drug traffic, and fences to keep illegal foreigners out of the United States. A majority is currently opposed to universal health care. That I think will change over time as they see the great benefits of legislation like the Affordable Care Act. Fortunately, the voting public will not tolerate political efforts to dismantle New Deal programs such as Social Security and Great Society programs like Medicare, despite persistent efforts by politicians in Washington to cut the benefits that are attached to these programs.

The states, not the federal government, provide the bulk of resources for education. If states are willing to spend more on incarceration than on higher education and if they are unwilling to tax property, income, or wealth in such a way as to generate resources for higher education, their universities will fail to achieve greatness or will slowly, if not precipitously, fall from their prior lofty standing. Of course, the great driver of our economy has been technological and scientific growth—and much of the resources for pure discoveries and for research on health and welfare come from the federal budget. If we don't view education and discovery as one of our highest values, then the system of higher education, both public and private, will suffer dramatic negative consequences. We tend to be our own worst enemy.

What I've proposed as changes in higher learning should provide an idea of my hopes for the United States over the next several generations. I trust that our society will move closer to a true meritocracy for minorities, for women, for people with different sexual orientations. I trust that we will begin to appreciate difference more than we do today. We will have greater appreciation for cultural artifacts, for humanistic and creative thinking. Simultaneously, we will renew our belief in the "common," and that those who have been most fortunate in our society need to help those whose lives have been less so. I expect that we will reduce our level of anti-intellectualism and that we will value products of our imagination, especially those that are embodied in the arts and sciences. None of these ends are easily reached, but they are possible and desirable. We will have to respect diverse cultures and form uneasy partnerships. But, if our great research universities begin to truly approximate their maximum potential, it will indicate that the United States has also moved toward being a more just, curious, and creative society.

Acknowledgments

In many ways, this book is the result of my thinking about and experience with students, teachers, and academic administrators at research universities over many years and discussions with each of these groups about how to ensure that the United States maintains its preeminent research universities, and how to develop them still further so that they may maximize their full potential. Over the course of those years many friends, faculty members, presidents, and provosts of our leading American universities, and my students and family members, have discussed ideas with me about what makes a research university great and what kinds of changes are in order for them to increase their quality—both in terms of the transmission and the production of new knowledge. I can't possibly acknowledge all of those individuals who have contributed to my thinking, but here are a few who have influenced my thinking on this subject and contributed to the development of ideas in this book.

My interest in the fabric, values, and structure of a research university come initially from my early efforts with Robert K. Merton, Harriet Zuckerman, and my brother Stephen to develop a small, and at the time, virtually unrecognized specialty—the sociology of science. The values that were part of the growth and institutionalization of science in the seventeenth century can be traced through to the inception of research universities. Many historians and philosophers of science, such as Peter Galison, Gerald Holton, Thomas Kuhn, and Derek J. de Solla Price, as well as many sociologists of science, such as my friends and colleagues Bernard and Elinor Barber, had written about science and scientists in a way that captured some aspects of how creative work was done and discoveries made. That experience with science and the growth of knowledge led me to a sustained interest in academic administration.

Many presidents and provosts of our great universities, past and present, have contributed to my thinking on this subject. Among those who I've learned a great deal from are: Richard Atkinson (University of California, San Diego and the California system), Derek Bok (Harvard University), William G. Bowen (Princeton University and Mellon Foundation), Robert Brown (MIT and Boston University), Gerhard Casper (University of Chicago and Stanford University), David Cohen (Columbia University), Michael Crow (Arizona State University), Ronald Daniels (Johns Hopkins University), Nicholas Dirks (University of California, Berkeley), James Duderstadt (University of Michigan), John W. Etchemendy (Stanford University), the late A. Bartlett Giamatti (Yale University), Matthew Goldstein (City University of New York), Patricia Graham (Harvard University), Hanna Holborn Gray (University of Chicago), Vartan Gregorian (Brown University and the Carnegie Corporation), Amy Guttman (University of Pennsylvania), John L. Hennessy (Stanford University), Pat McPherson (Bryn Mawr College), the late Martin Meyerson (University of Pennsylvania), Jerry Ostriker (Princeton University), Hunter Rawlings III (Cornell University), Frank Rhodes (Cornell University), Alison Richard (Yale University and Cambridge University), Neil L. Rudenstine (Harvard University), Benno C. Schmidt Jr., Claude Steele (Columbia, Stanford, and Berkeley), Geoffrey Stone (University of Chicago), Shirley M. Tilghman (Princeton University), Charles Vest (MIT), Robert Zimmer (University of Chicago), and, of course, Columbia's own Michael Sovern, George Rupp, and Lee Bollinger, under whom I served first as their vice president of arts and sciences and then as provost and dean of faculties from 1989 to 2003. There are too many faculty members at Columbia and elsewhere who have been particularly helpful in listening and responding to some of my ideas that are contained in this book, but I want to thank particularly Richard Axel, Bonnie Bassler, Peter Bearman, Akeel Bilgrami, David Bromwich, Craig Calhoun, Andrew Delbanco, Richard A. DeMillo, Jon Elster, Stuart Firestein, David Freedberg, Howard Gardiner, Henry Louis Gates Jr., Brian Greene, Philip Hamburger, Ben Heineman, Thomas Jessell, Eric Kandel, Robert Post, Jeffrey Sachs, Joan Scott, Richard Shweder, Neil Smelser, Gabrielle Spiegel, Nancy Wexler, and the late Edward Said, whose works and our personal conversations continue to influence my thought. I also want to thank my former colleague and close friend, Herbert Pardes, who has taught me as much as anyone about leadership and has been a continual collaborator in discovering how universities, medical schools, and hospitals can become great institutions. Many other friends have helped shape a number of my ideas. Two who have been particularly willing to listen to me and discuss issues found in the book are Susan Reiger and David Denby. Then there is the summer crowd on Martha's Vineyard, like Ken and Jill Iscol, Anne and Paul Grand, Jerry and Kathy Kauf, Carol Rocamora, and James Katowitz, among many others, who have listened to countless renditions of my proposals for the great university of the future.

I've learned a great deal from my students in classes, both in the Department of Sociology, Columbia School of Law, and in the Columbia School of Architecture, Planning and Preservation, where I've taught seminars and studios dealing with the university in American life. These were remarkably analytic and creative students who helped me think through many of my own ideas and respond to many of theirs. Of particular note is the fantastic colleague and teacher, Professor Laurie Hawkinson, with whom I co-taught two advanced architectural studios and seminars; and in a combined seminar and studio, Laurie and Reinhold Martin. Each of the students in these studios, along with Laurie and Reinhold's penetrating questions and suggestions, helped me think through a variety of problems in reimagining the research university campus. I also want to thank the jurors who critiqued student projects on aspects of a new-style university campus, especially Columbia's new dean of the School of Architecture, Amale Andraos.

There have been a number of national committees of which I've been a member that have taught me a great deal about different aspects of university life. Particularly important have been the American Academy of Arts and Sciences Lincoln Project, which has been ably led by Robert Birgeneau, former chancellor of the University of California, Berkeley, and Mary Sue Coleman, former president of the University of Michigan. More recently, the members of the National Academy's Committee on Federal Regulations and Reporting Requirements: A New Framework for Research in the 21st Century, under the leadership of Larry R. Faulkner and Harriet Rabb, have taught me a great deal about the increasing role that federal regulations have had on the work carried out at our research intensive universities.

Once again, I want to thank my literary agent, Kathy Robbins, for her continuing belief in this project and her support and invariably good suggestions about the manuscript. Peter Osnos, who is responsible for the creation of

PublicAffairs, is the quintessential example of an individual who truly cares about publishing books on important contemporary subjects. He has also been invaluable in discussing how to best tell the story for an audience of both academics and the educated public. I also want to thank Clive Priddle of PublicAffairs for his astute suggestions about ways to cut an overly long manuscript into a more readable one, and for his guidance of the project from its inception to its conclusion. I've also been blessed to work again with a wonderful old-style editor, Mindy Werner, who read the manuscript as often as I did and had keen suggestions for reorganization, editorial cuts, and inserts, and who through detailed conversation helped shape this manuscript. Her contributions were more than an author can hope for. Thanks also to Melissa Raymond and Katherine Haigler of PublicAffairs, who oversaw the production process, and John Donohue and Jill Uhlfelder of Westchester Publishing Services for their editorial work during the final editing phase of the book.

Over the years of gestation, I've been very fortunate to have two extremely able assistants, Sarah Hospelhorn and Danielle Burgos, who have kept everything in order, have helped search for documents and materials, have done the heavy lifting in receiving permissions, and have tended to the needs of my students. Their technical skills have also helped me produce the drafts of the manuscript.

Over the decades I have received generous support from the National Science Foundation (NSF) and from the Macy and Ford foundations to support parts of my work. I could not have done this project on research universities without their financial support. As those who have read both my prior books and this one will know, without research support, especially from federal agencies like the NSF, American scientists and scholars could not possibly have made the advances in knowledge that we have seen over the past sixty-five years. I therefore want to thank both the program directors and the peer reviewers, who work tirelessly to identify promising scientific work.

Finally, I want to acknowledge the love and support that I've received from the members of my family who have heard probably more than they cared to about research universities. Thanks to Daniel and Nick, to Susanna (Nonnie) and Gabriel, and to my grandchildren, Lydia and Charlotte, who might have had to forgo some stories that I might have read to them if I hadn't been working on this book. I've also been very fortunate to have a mother, though no longer alive, who always encouraged me to live the life of an academic, especially if baseball was no longer an option. My in-laws, Joan Lewis and her late husband George (who was like a father to me), always showed great interest in my work over the years and supported my family in many ways. Finally, my wife Joanna has been willing to listen more often than anyone to my thoughts on research universities and can probably tell you more about what is in this book than anyone else. Most wonderful!

In this book, more than any other that I've written, all those who I have acknowledged hold no responsibility for any errors or opinions that are found in it. The faults are mine alone.

Notes

Preface

1. C. P. Snow, *The Two Cultures and the Scientific Revolution* (Cambridge: Cambridge University Press, 1959). The original essay had the title listed above. In some subsequent editions, the book was simply called *The Two Cultures.*

2. There were other factors, of course, that drove many of us into graduate school and eventually an academic career, perhaps most notably our unwillingness to serve in the Vietnam War.

3. Quoted in Jon Marcus, "New Analysis Shows Problematic Boom in Higher Ed Administrators," *The New England Center for Investigative Reporting*, February 6, 2014, necir.org/2014/02 /06/new-analysis-shows-problematic-boom-in-higher-ed-administrators/. The Delta Project, from which these data were obtained, is located at American Institutes for Research and focuses on helping scholars and others interested in higher education make sense "of higher education revenues, spending, and outcomes." Source: www.deltacostproject.org.

4. Here is just a sampling of the offices that now exist at Columbia to deal with administrative tasks, many of which did not exist thirty years ago: hundreds of administrators whose job it is to oversee compliance with government regulations (e.g., conflict of interest; affirmative action; effort reporting; institutional review boards [IRBs] that review every research project for the safety of human subjects; officers now required to deal with sexual assault on campus) that have come into being because they are triggered by some university event and that never go away, regardless of whether or not the initial problem has been remedied. There are government and community relations offices; staff members devoted to parent and alumni relations, industrial relations, and foundation relations; and lobbyists who try to persuade Congress to pass laws that benefit the financial aid of students or increase funding for basic and medical research—and equally as often to prevent unwise, restrictive, and counterproductive constraints on the work of the university. There's an ombudsman's office and an office of the university chaplain, which oversees religious activities on campus.

5. The Office of the General Counsel also deals with cases ranging from race, gender, or age discrimination to suits involving rights to the intellectual property produced from the

discoveries of faculty members associated with the university. Indeed, there are offices of growing size that deal with university patents and licenses. There is a growing group of savvy individuals who deal with new media and information technology; there are teaching centers where faculty can go to learn how to present course materials in a more palatable way. Title IX of the Civil Rights Act of 1964 mandated gender equality in athletics, leading to a huge increase in the number of athletic teams and their coaches. Then there are offices that deal with the housing of new and current faculty, which is particularly important in the recruitment process in a high-cost city like New York or Palo Alto. Faculty members insist that their children have opportunities to attend good primary and secondary schools, which has led to placement offices or to the building of university-affiliated primary and secondary schools.

6. There is a substantial literature on how poor experts are at predicting future events. To cite just two, see Philip E. Tetlock, *Expert Political Judgment: How Good Is It? How Can We Know?* (Princeton, NJ: Princeton University Press, 2005) and Robyn Dawes, *House of Cards: Psychology and Psychotherapy Built on Myth* (New York: Free Press, 1994).

Introduction

1. I devote a third of *The Great American University*, specifically the stories in part II, to describing the unique performance of our finest universities in producing novel discoveries, inventions, and widely used concepts. After briefly discussing the national system of innovation in the United States, I present examples of great and life-changing discoveries in the biological, physical, social, and behavioral sciences, as well as in the humanities.

2. The prestige and renown of research universities is more dependent on their discoveries and innovations than on the quality of their teaching. Although excellence in teaching is an essential feature of any great research university, it is not the strongest determinant of its international or national standing.

3. A substantial number of books and essays have been written on the current state of the university—most, as is typical, focusing on undergraduate education at state universities or at reasonable or highly selective colleges and universities. What I provide is a point of departure; hardly an exhaustive list of worthwhile books on the subject. Anyone who wishes to obtain a good view of the situation at America's research universities ought to begin with the works of William G. Bowen, Derek Bok, James Duderstadt, Henry Rosovsky, A. Bartlett Giamatti, Clark Kerr, Jacques Barzun, Frank Rhodes, Charles Vest, Richard Atkinson, Edward Levi, Harold Shapiro, Charles Vest, Richard C. Levin, and David Holinger, and the excellent work of Roger L. Geiger, among those who have been writing on the subject over the past fifty years. Many have written from the point of view of former university presidents. For earlier publications by prominent academic leaders and observers, one should also read some of the works of Robert Hutchins, Thorstein Veblen, José Ortega y Gasset, Abraham Flexner, and other early founders of the American research university. Other recent books are worth examining. Most of these works have not been authored by former leaders of research universities. For a sample of books to read that have been published since the publication of my own *The Great American University: Its Rise to Preeminence, Its Indispensable National Role, and Why It Must Be Protected* (New York: PublicAffairs, 2009), see Hanna Holborn Gray, *Searching for Utopia: Universities and Their Histories* (Berkeley: University of California Press, 2012); Andrew Delbanco, *College: What It Was, Is, and Should Be* (Princeton, NJ: Princeton University Press, 2012); William Deresiewicz, *Excellent Sheep: The Miseducation of the American Elite and the Way to a Meaningful Life* (New York: Free Press, 2014); Benjamin Ginsberg, *The*

Fall of the Faculty: The Rise of the All-Administrative University and Why It Matters (New York: Oxford University Press, 2011); Peter Brooks, ed., with Hilary Jewitt, *The Humanities and Public Life* (New York: Fordham University Press, 2014); Charles T. Clotfelter, *Buying the Best: Cost Escalation in Elite Higher Education* (Princeton, NJ: Princeton University Press, 1996); Michael M. Crow and William B. Dabars, *Designing the New American University* (Baltimore, MD: Johns Hopkins University Press, 2015); David F. Chambliss and Christopher G. Takacs, *How College Works* (Cambridge, MA: Harvard University Press, 2014); Fareed Zakaria, *In Defense of a Liberal Education* (New York: W. W. Norton, 2015); Danielle Allen and Rob Reich, eds., *Education, Justice, and Democracy* (Chicago: University of Chicago Press, 2013); Michael S. Roth, *Beyond the University: Why Liberal Education Matters* (New Haven, CT: Yale University Press, 2014); Goldie Blumenstyk, *American Higher Education in Crisis? What Everyone Needs to Know* (New York: Oxford University Press, 2015); and Richard A. DeMillo, *Abelard to Apple: The Fate of American Colleges and Universities* (Cambridge, MA: MIT Press, 2011). Many other books and essays of interest will be referenced in each chapter.

4. In the winter of 2015, Governor Scott Walker of Wisconsin proposed reducing the budget of the University of Wisconsin, Madison, by $300 million annually. He also suggested transforming the state's flagship university into a form of trade school, moving it away from the Wisconsin Idea and its position as one of the nation's most distinguished places for discovery and invention to a place "to meet the state's workforce needs." Not only did Walker seek to transform the central mission of the University of Wisconsin from "the search for truth" to "training the workforce," he also attacked professorial tenure and the collective bargaining rights of graduate students and staff. If realized, these changes would transform one of the world's great universities into a second-tier institution. Under attack at home, Walker claimed that this proposal was the result of a "drafting error." Source: Julie Bosman, "2016 Ambitions Seen in Walker's Push for University Cuts in Wisconsin," *New York Times*, February 16, 2015. See also, Andy Thomason, "A Brief History of Scott Walker's War over Higher Education," *Chronicle of Higher Education*, July 13, 2015; David J. Vanness, "The Withering of a Once-Great State University," *Chronicle of Higher Education*, July 13, 2015.

5. We should be careful, of course, to distinguish between the ideal and the actual. In its early days, the University of Virginia hardly approximated Jefferson's ideal. The university was probably known more for the drunken students and debauchery than for the exceptional learning produced in that idealized "village." Nonetheless, these extraordinary national leaders did have an idea: They honored learning for its own sake and for the nation's sake, and even if their idea was not approximated in the early period, their proposals had enormous impact on the nation's thinking about higher learning.

6. Among those leaders were Hopkins's Daniel Coit Gilman, Columbia's Nicholas Murray Butler, Chicago's William Rainey Harper, Harvard's Charles Eliot, Cornell's Andrew Dixon White, and the Carnegie Foundation's Abraham Flexner (who would be instrumental in forming the Institute for Advanced Study at Princeton), as well as many educational philosophers, such as Arthur Lovejoy and John Dewey and societal critics such as Upton Sinclair.

7. The second generation of university presidents who opined on the structure of research universities included Chicago's Robert Hutchins and Harvard's James B. Conant; MIT's Vannevar Bush; the University of California's Clark Kerr; Stanford's provost, Frederick E. Terman; and Columbia's Jacques Barzun.

8. For more details on the forces that led to the preeminence of American universities, see part I of Cole, *The Great American University*. There are many histories of higher learning in the United States. You will find many references to other sources in this book.

9. We can associate particular individuals with the institutionalization and defense of some of these values. For example, Robert Hutchins became the greatest champion of the value of academic freedom and free inquiry and defended the University of Chicago (and indirectly all of the other great neonatal research universities) against external efforts to debase that value. Similarly, James Conant introduced policies at Harvard that furthered greatly the idea of meritocracy and brought greater universalism to the students and faculties at that extraordinary institution. And, finally, Clark Kerr extended the idea of meritocracy to the state university system with his (and his colleagues) ideas formulated as part of the California Plan of 1960. For a more detailed discussion of these people and their influence, see part I of Cole, *The Great American University*. Among the core values that represent the foundation of our system of higher learning, which will be discussed in greater detail below, are: universalism or meritocracy, academic freedom and free inquiry, open communication of ideas, disinterestedness (not profiting from one's discoveries), creation of new knowledge, governance by authority rather than by power, organized skepticism, and renewal of the vitality of the community. I also suggest that a few new values ought to be institutionalized into the culture of our finest universities.

10. The act, named after Representative Justin Smith Morrill from Vermont, had failed to be passed before (it actually passed in Congress in 1859 but was vetoed by President James Buchanan), but once the Civil War began, it could be passed without the Southern states presence in Congress to obstruct it and with Lincoln as the nation's president. Of course, none of the Southern rebellious states were eligible for this federal gift of land. Under the Act, which was later followed by a second Morrill Act of 1890, the federal government gave each state 30,000 acres of federal land to create agricultural colleges. Overall, the Act allocated more than 17 million acres of land to the states for this purpose. During the same period, Congress also established the National Academy of Sciences to help members of Congress and the Executive branch obtain expert opinions on scientific matters. President Lincoln also signed this bill during the Civil War. The impact of the federal government's entrance into the realm of higher education cannot be minimized. Many of the greatest public universities in the nation, those that educate the vast majority of our nation's students today, came into existence because of the federal government's role in enabling their creation. It is worth noting that not all of the great state universities had their origins in the Morrill Act of 1862.

11. Yale and Harvard had established schools of science by the middle of the nineteenth century; and the Social Darwinist views of Herbert Spencer gained a strong foothold in the United States, especially among those who represented the Gilded Age. In fact, many of the great philanthropists of higher learning embraced Social Darwinism as a narrative that justified their own wealth. But more generally, American society was beginning to believe in the fruits and potential of science and technology. The characteristics of the nation's experts shifted from the clergy as opinion leaders toward university leaders, scientists, and social and behavioral science experts.

12. The individuals who were prescient enough to leave Germany and other countries taken by the Nazis before it was too late form nothing short of an all-star list. (It was not only the German scientific community that was decimated by the acts that purged Jews and others from civil service positions, which included university employment.) Among those who left were Leo Szilard, the remarkable physicist; Max Delbrück, another physicist who became the putative father of molecular biology; and the physicists Hans Bethe, Enrico Fermi, and Wolfgang Pauli. Fully 50 percent of Germany's theoretical physicists and 25 percent of the entire physics com-

munity that existed in January 1933 left for safe havens in Britain and the United States. Social scientist Paul Lazarsfeld, architect Mies van der Rohe, composer Béla Bartók, and novelist Thomas Mann, as well as latecomers Sigmund and Anna Freud, also emigrated. Theodor Adorno wrote *The Authoritarian Personality* while in the United States, although he returned to Europe after the war. They all gave up the attachment to the lost Weimar Republic that had once been so attractive to them. There was a second wave of émigrés as well, and we should not forget how the children of these groups populated major universities and occupied other leading positions in the American occupational structure following World War II.

13. There were others, many of whom held somewhat different views from Vannevar Bush, who were deeply concerned with America's postwar scientific efforts. Most notable among them was Senator Harvey Kilgore, who embraced certain aspects of the Bush Report and rejected others for his own alternatives. What emerged from the extended congressional debate with President Truman was a workable compromise that produced a restructuring of the National Institutes of Health and the creation of the National Science Foundation, among other things. While Europe was recovering from the war, the United States began to pour significant dollars into both pure and more practically oriented science; and the media, such as the *New York Times*, were all for it. For the best brief summary of the Bush efforts, see Daniel Kevles's introduction to the fiftieth anniversary edition of Vannevar Bush's report *Science, the Endless Frontier* (Washington, DC: National Science Board, 1995).

14. Bush's report had several objectives. Among them was to maintain America's military superiority after the war, to create a system that would significantly improve the nation's health, and to develop a system that would educate a new generation that would be prepared to work in a more technologically advanced world—to raise the level of human capital in America.

15. In terms of student access to higher education, the G.I. Bill of Rights opened up higher learning to millions of former members of the military who might not have had the opportunity to attend universities and colleges. But certainly of equal significance for the rise of American universities was the science policy put into place after World War II.

16. Although Vannevar Bush was an engineer through and through, who had patented several important ideas and was a major figure in developing disciplines in engineering, he was a staunch advocate of what we now call the linear model. In 1997, Princeton's Donald Stokes offered an alternative to the linear model in *Pasteur's Quadrant* (Washington, DC: The Brookings Institution, 1997), which has garnered a great deal of support within the scientific and academic communities. Stokes uses Pasteur as the quintessential example of a scientist who was interested simultaneously in basic knowledge and research and in solving practical problems that would be of great use to society. In fact, he managed to do just that in his work.

17. When the European star émigré scientists came to the United States, they often commented on the democracy of the American laboratory and the spirited give-and-take between students and their professors—quite different from their prior, far more hierarchical, experience.

18. In *The Great American University*, I identified a baker's dozen of factors that would be required for producing a truly distinguished university. They included: (1) faculty research productivity; (2) quality and impact of research; (3) grant and contract support; (4) honorific awards; (5) access to highly qualified students; (6) excellence in teaching; (7) physical facilities and advanced information technologies; (8) large endowments and plentiful resources; (9) large academic departments; (10) academic freedom and free inquiry; (11) location; (12) contributions to the public good; and (13) excellent leadership.

19. This entrepreneurial focus paid off handsomely for Stanford. In a review of the Silicon Valley 150 in 2013, Stanford reported that faculty members, students, and alumni entrepreneurs had founded more than 2,400 companies—a subset included Cisco Systems, Nike, Sun Microsystems, Yahoo!, and Google. These and other companies generated revenues of $2.7 trillion annually and created 5.4 million jobs. This would rank Stanford as the tenth-largest world economy. Of course, not all of the Silicon Valley 150 had their origins at Stanford, but enough did that have led to many significant gifts to Stanford in one form or another. MIT has had a similar record, if a somewhat different approach to generating innovative companies. That institution has tended to take equity shares in startups rather than rely on proceeds from the patents and licenses that were created by their innovative faculty members.

20. I elaborate on these values and how they have changed over time, and what ought to be reinforced or added to this set of strong institutional beliefs in Chapter 9, which deals with the hierarchy of values and the erosion of some of them in the academy today.

21. Hunter Rawlings III, "The Lion in the Path: Research Universities Confront Society's New Expectations," paper presented at the symposium "Institutional Conflicts of Interest in Research Universities," Petrie-Flom Center for Health Law Policy, Biotechnology, and Bioethics and Edmond J. Safra Center for Ethics, Harvard Law School, November 2, 2012. This quote is taken from page 19 of a summary of papers delivered at the symposium.

22. In an April 22, 2015, *New York Times* opinion piece, Newt Gingrich argued for another large government investment in science. He notes that since the doubling of its budget in the late 1990s, the science budget at the National Institutes of Health "has effectively been reduced by more than 20 percent.... The Institutes awarded 12.5 percent fewer grants last year than in 2003 [while] grant applications, over the same period, increased by almost 50 percent.... As a conservative myself, I'm often skeptical of government 'investments.' But when it comes to breakthroughs that could cure—not just treat—the most expensive diseases, government is unique. It alone can bring the necessary resources to bear." Gingrich then names a score of diseases where the cost of treatment far exceeds what we invest for research to find cures for these diseases.

23. Unlike *The Great American University*, this book does not focus predominantly on the research mission of the university. It takes up other issues without avoiding discussion of how research activity ought to change. In that sense alone, this book is linked to the earlier book. Together, I hope they offer a history of how American universities became the most dominant in the world as of 2015 and what we ought to do to ensure that the system retains that position.

Chapter 1: Getting In

1. The American path to college admissions in 2015 is also vastly different from the ones found in European and Asian societies. In most other nations, there is almost total reliance on standardized national examinations—and the anxiety goes way up as students prepare for these exams that will largely determine their future. (Although I don't know of anyone who has tried to measure student anxiety comparatively, my hunch is that it is actually far less in the United States than in China, where about 1 percent of the high school students are admitted into the university of their choice.) Because students in these other countries apply to specialized programs, such as law or architecture, once they are admitted to a university, there are few ways of changing their focus of interest if they decide that they want to study, for example, physics. Switching "majors" in mid-stream is nearly impossible. In these countries, how you test is who you are. That is why the junior year in China, for example, is called the "black year," as stu-

dents prepare to see if they represent part of the 1 percent or so who will be offered positions in universities and colleges based on their scores on national examinations. In Europe, which fifty years ago offered places at their universities to less than 10 percent of its high school graduates, the hierarchical structure of the academic system (and the relatively few professorial faculty members) has not caught up with the policy of admitting all students who pass the national examination. In France, the *baccalauréat*, or *le bac*, introduced into French society by Napoleon in 1808, is taken after completion of the *lycée* and represents the qualifying examination for university study. Of course, the competition to be admitted to the most prestigious French *grandes écoles* is fierce and the most desirable outcome for the French elite and upper middle class. In 2007 and 2008, more than 80 percent of the mainland French lycée seniors who sat for the baccalauréat exam passed it. By law, they are eligible for admission to any university in France in their chosen subject. Similar situations exist throughout Europe. In England, where students sit for what are called A-level examinations, the process of admissions to particular universities is more refined and rigorous.

2. Richard Arum and Josipa Roksa, *Academically Adrift: Limited Learning on College Campuses* (Chicago: University of Chicago Press, 2011).

3. Ibid., 69.

4. A significant rise in applications to these schools is a result, in part, of what is known as "the Common Application." High school students no longer have to fill out separate forms when applying to different schools. There tends to be one basic required essay, and different schools require other "supplemental" essays. One result is that high school seniors apply to many more schools than in the past, not only because it is now far easier to apply but also because the chances of being admitted to the very top schools have gotten so low.

5. On April 10, 2013, Stanford University reported admission of 2,210 potential members of the Class of 2017. They were selected from an already highly self-selected group of 38,828 applicants, or an admissions percentage of 5.69 percent, perhaps the lowest in the nation that year. Harvard posted the second-lowest of 5.79 percent. This amounts to a lottery. Source: The April 10, 2013, edition of The Loop, a monthly email newsletter sent to alumni and friends of Stanford University.

6. Roughly 20 to 25 percent of the applicants are admitted early through policies of "early decision" (which is binding for those that accept) and "early action" (which is not binding). An institution such as Columbia accepts almost half of its class early decision because it wants students who really are committed to coming to the university and who do not want to view their position there as a second choice. Of course, this involves a game theoretical decision: Such students have to estimate the chances of getting into one school or another before they apply for early decision. Harvard, Yale, and Princeton have the "luxury" of not having to do this, because when students are accepted to these schools as well as to other Ivies, they tend to choose either Harvard, Yale, or Princeton.

7. In fact, a study by Princeton economists Alan B. Krueger and Stacy Berg Dale showed that the variable with the highest correlation with future earnings of college graduates was the amount of tuition that was paid at the college from which the student graduated. See Stacy Berg Dale and Alan B. Krueger, "Estimating the Payoff to Attending a More Selective College: An Application of Selection on Observables and Unobservables," *Quarterly Journal of Economics* (November 2002): 1491–1527; Alan B. Krueger and Stacy Berg Dale, "Estimating the Return to College Selectivity over the Career Using Adminstrative Earning Data," Princeton University Industrial Relations Section, Working Paper 563, February 16, 2011.

8. In contrast, the faculty is deeply involved with deciding which students to admit to Ph.D. programs. Admissions officers, not faculty members, are largely responsible for admissions decisions to professional schools—with medicine being an important exception.

9. Patricia Conley, "Local Justice in the Allocation of College Admissions: A Statistical Study of Beliefs Versus Practice," *Social Justice Research* 9, no. 3 (1996): 239–258. The same disjunction between beliefs of program officers who determine who receives grants from the National Science Foundation and what actually determines the decision has been shown to exist in a prior study that I conducted with Stephen Cole. While program officers like to think they had a great deal of discretion in making decisions, the determinants of the actual funding decision correlated very highly with the peer review scores that the grant proposal received.

10. In fact, there is increasing evidence that minority students who would be qualified for admission at the most selective colleges don't apply, either because they are never counseled to do so or because they assume that they have no chance of admissions. They have restricted "effective scope" in what opportunities are open to them.

11. This figure does not include totals for Columbia's sister institution, Barnard College, or for its undergraduate school for nontraditional students, General Studies.

12. Melvin Lerner and Carolyn Simmons, "Observer's Reaction to the 'Innocent Victim': Compassion or Rejection?," *Journal of Personality and Social Psychology* 4, no. 2 (1966): 203–210. Other articles along similar lines are Melvin J. Lerner and D. T. Miller, "Just World Research and the Attribution Process: Looking Back and Ahead," *Psychological Bulletin* 85, no. 5 (1978): 1030–1051, and Melvin Lerner, *The Belief in a Just World: A Fundamental Delusion* (New York: Plenum, 1980).

13. This percentage reached a high of greater than 20 percent at some of these schools during the late 1990s and early 2000s, but this percentage has decreased recently because these schools have increased the size of their undergraduate student bodies without increasing concomitantly the number of their athletic teams.

14. Bowen also coauthored a second policy-oriented book on athletics at top-tier colleges and universities. Bowen and his collaborators have studied this matter in detail by collecting a tremendous amount of data and subjecting them to detailed analysis—testing all manner of hypotheses about the athletes and how they do in college and beyond. He followed several different graduating classes at these schools—one from 1976, another from 1989, and a final group that graduated in 1999. See James L. Shulman and William G. Bowen, *The Game of Life: College Sports and Educational Values* (Princeton, NJ: Princeton University Press, 2001); William G. Bowen and Sarah A. Levin, *Reclaiming the Game: College Sports and Educational Values* (Princeton, NJ: Princeton University Press, 2005).

15. Tamar Lewin, "At Many Top Public Universities Intercollegiate Sports Come at an Academic Price," *New York Times*, January 16, 2013.

16. Shulman and Bowen, *The Game of Life*, chaps. 10–11.

17. Delta Cost Project at American Institutes for Research, http://www.deltacostproject.org/.

18. Tamar Lewin, "At Many Top Public Universities, Intercollegiate Sports Come at an Academic Price," *New York Times*, January 16, 2013. A version of this article appeared also in the January 17, 2013, print edition of the *Times*, on page A14. The quote from Terry Hartle appears in these news stories.

19. Ibid.

20. Ibid.

21. With the commodification of intercollegiate athletics and NCAA rules that permit athletes to leave school after their first year, there is enormous pressure to engage in what can only be called "deviant behavior." This behavior takes many forms. In the continuing scandal at the great public university, The University of North Carolina at Chapel Hill, we see athletes who have been given relatively high grades for courses that were never given or for individual projects with professors who are part of the scandal. This harms the students at least as much as the professors who are engaging in unethical behavior. There have been notorious scandals at Pennsylvania State University involving unethical behavior of coaches; there has been unethical behavior by district attorneys who delay or refuse to conduct serious inquiries into alleged cases of sexual misconduct. Moreover, the NCAA is itself a big business, negotiating billion-dollar television contracts with the various media while creating rules that restrict athletes from even having a coach obtain a cold medicine for a sick athlete. The bulk of NCAA rules and regulations are almost as extensive as the tax code. For two good discussions of the role of athletics at some of our better public and private universities (published after the two books by Bowen and his colleagues cited above), see Jay M. Smith and Mary Willingham, *Cheated: The UNC Scandal, the Education of Athletes, and the Future of Big-Time College Sports* (Lincoln, NE: Potomac Books, 2015); Stuart Taylor and K. C. Johnson, *Until Proven Innocent: Political Correctness and the Shameful Injustices of the Duke Lacrosse Rape Case* (New York: Thomas Dunne Books, 2007).

22. Ivy League coaches will tell you that reducing the number of recruited athletes, especially in sports like football (where most of the recruited players never play, are not on the traveling squad, and often quit the team before their senior year), would save the universities a considerable sum of money and make the teams far more competitive. It is also obvious that the fact that Stanford and Duke have athletic scholarships as well as full-need financial aid policies does not hurt their prestige or international reputation.

23. I want to thank Stanford's vice provost, Harry J. Elam, for describing the way the financial aid program at Stanford works. Any errors that may have slipped into this description are mine.

24. The NCAA may of course be forced to change its fundamental stance toward athletes. The lawsuit against the NCAA by several groups who claim that the universities are using them to make large sums of money (mostly through television contracts) without compensation for the players is still in play. The results of these legal challenges could change some of the fundamental ways intercollegiate athletics are organized. For one, *Edward O'Bannon, Jr. v. NCAA*, U.S. Court of Appeals for the Ninth Circuit (http://www.ca9.uscourts.gov/content/view.php?pk_id =0000000757), is an antitrust class action suit filed by former UCLA basketball player Ed O'Bannon challenging the use of its former student athletes' images for commercial purposes without compensating the athletes. In another action, Northwestern University football players voted to unionize. As Kain Colter, a former Northwestern quarterback, said: "We're one step closer to a world where college athletes are not stuck with sports-related medical bills, do not lose their scholarships when they are injured, are not subject to unnecessary brain trauma, and are given better opportunities to complete their degrees." Source: "NU Players Cast Secret Ballots," ESPN.com news, April 26, 2014, http://espn.go.com/college-football/story/_/id /10837584/northwestern-wildcats-players-vote-whether-form-first-union-college-athletes. On August 17, 2015, the National Labor Relations Board voted 5 to 0 that the athletes did not have the right to unionize. Source: Ben Strauss, "N.L.R.B. Rejects Northwestern Football Players' Union Bid," *New York Times*, August 17, 2015. As Strauss writes: "The board did not rule directly on the central question in the case—whether the players, who spend long hours on

football and help generate millions of dollars for Northwestern, are university employees. Instead, it found that the novelty of the petition and its potentially wide-ranging impacts on college sports would not have promoted 'stability in labor relations.'" The fight continues, but clearly the NCAA won this battle.

25. Howard Gardner, *Multiple Intelligences: New Horizons* (1993; reprint, New York: Basic Books, 2006), chap. 1.

26. Many of the elite universities have faculty committees that supposedly play a role in admissions, but in fact they have very little to do with the actual process.

27. The decisions of the university's admissions committee ought to be reviewed independently every three to five years to determine what kind of success rate the admissions process has had, who are the successes and failures and in retrospect what is correlated with these outcomes, and what value added has the shape of the class had on the individuals who are admitted. How has it altered their intellectual and social experience, how has it changed their view of society and the world, and what can they do when graduating that they simple could not do upon entry into the great university or college? Equally important is to create longitudinal studies of the graduates of these universities to understand their career trajectories and how they contribute to the larger society. A second ongoing experiment should also be undertaken: The results of the faculty committee model ought to be compared with the results obtained using young administrators to determine admissions. There is no guarantee that "experts" will prove better at this job than less experienced, nonfaculty members; but if they do not, it will provide us with some important information about the structure of university decision making.

28. The decisions by the group of administrators would be subjected to sampling to see if the criteria that the faculty have articulated are being followed. Performance standards for these administrators would be based on how closely they follow the criteria.

29. Scott E. Page, *The Difference: How the Power of Diversity Creates Better Groups, Firms, Schools, and Societies* (Princeton, NJ: Princeton University Press, 2007), chaps. 1–6.

30. Source: http://www.juilliard.edu/apply-audition/application-audition-requirements.

31. The North Carolina school, which was founded in 1980, led the way in state-supported secondary boarding schools for top-achieving students.

32. The basis on which students will be selected for the school will lead to those with exceptional intelligence—multiple intelligences—being selected for the school, but there will be a strong effort to have a wide diversity of talents, socioeconomic backgrounds, genders, and races and ethnicities at the school.

33. Michel Foucault, *Discipline and Punish: The Birth of the Prison* (New York: Pantheon, 1977), 184–185, 192.

34. The idea that families and social class make as much of a difference in status attainment of young people is an old one. James S. Coleman, in his classic 1966 work *The Equality of Educational Opportunity* (Washington, DC: U.S. Department of Health, Education, and Welfare, Office of Education), demonstrated this empirically, showing that family effects were greater than school effects on academic achievement. Since the Coleman study, hundreds of works have examined this issue. Social class and early family advantages have been shown to continue to make larger differences than the difference among schools. For a similar recent argument, see Peter W. Cookson Jr.'s *Class Rules: Exposing Inequality in American High Schools* (New York: Teachers College Press, 2013).

35. As quoted in Nicholas Lemann, *The Big Test: The Secret History of American Meritocracy* (New York: Farrar, Straus and Giroux, 1999), 69.

36. This situation is even more dramatic in Europe and Asia, where performance on one examination can determine the future of an individual. It is hardly surprising that the children of teachers and professional parents in France have children with a much higher probability of being accepted into the *grandes écoles* than children from economically and educationally deprived backgrounds. The same pattern is found in China, Korea, and Japan.

37. See, among his many other books, Howard Gardner, *Frames of Mind: The Theory of Multiple Intelligences* (New York: Basic Books, 1983, with multiple later editions) and *Multiple Intelligences* (cited above). What is most disheartening about the reliance on variations of the standard IQ tests is that the results have been accepted, virtually without question, as accurate and legitimate indicators of the ability of individuals. The testing mentality, as it exists, has been culturally internalized and self-reinforcing. Gardner has challenged this orthodoxy. He originally identified seven forms of intelligence: Musical Intelligence, Bodily-Kinesthetic Intelligence, Logical-Mathematical Intelligence, Linguistic Intelligence, Spatial Intelligence, Interpersonal Intelligence, and Intrapersonal Intelligence.

38. James J. Heckman, *Giving Kids a Fair Chance (A Strategy That Works)* (Cambridge, MA: MIT Press, 2013), 4–5.

39. Carol Dweck, *Mindset: The New Psychology of Success—How We Can Learn to Fulfill Our Potential* (New York: Random House, 2006), chaps. 1 and 2.

40. The association is probably more robust than reported because of the truncation of the variance in scores among those who are selected because of their high scores. In short, because students are selected to a significant degree based on their College Board or other examination scores, those who are admitted all have relatively high scores. Consequently, the differences in scores are apt to explain less variance in first-year grades than otherwise, because the test is not that precise a predictor when considering limited differences.

41. Here is a sentence-completion question quoted by Barzun:

If we cannot make the wind blow when and where we wish it to blow, we can at least make use of its _____.

(A) source   (B) heat   (C) direction   (D) force   (E) atmosphere

Most of the people to whom I show this question immediately view (C) and (D) as possible answers. On reflection, they realize that (B) is also a possible answer. If they are of a literary turn of mind, they at first see little merit in answer (A); but when I point out that to scientists the phrase "the source of wind" implies the combination of the heat of the sun and the rotation of the earth, they look on (A) with renewed interest and often agree that it may well be the best answer. Answer (E) seems impossible: We do not usually talk of the wind's atmosphere. Yet with a little poetic license we might, and then (E) would be a strong contender. Let us not become poetic, though. These questions are hard enough when we remain prosaic. Even without (E), there are four promising candidates.

The examiner happens to want answer (D), but unfortunately he gives no reasons for his choice. I wonder whether he notices that the presence of the word "where" suggests (C) rather than (D), even though force has both magnitude and direction; or that it is possible to see in the phrase "at least" a further suggestion that (C) is preferable to (D), and this despite the fact that we cannot use the wind's "direction" without to some extent using its "force."

The presence of the phrase "at least" raises many problems. The sentence would have a sharper focus were "at least" deleted, especially if the first word were changed from "If" to "Although"; and I think the sense of the sentence would not be substantially affected by the change. Why, then, was "at least" inserted? Was it intended as a clue? If so, it is an obscure one, for the precise significance of "at least" in the sentence is tantalizingly elusive.

I submit that there is here substantial prima facie evidence for the proposition that the College Board tests should be viewed with concern, but that if this concern is justified in the case of products of the Educational Testing Service, which is acknowledged to be outstanding in its field, then one can tentatively assume that similar tests made by other organizations should be viewed with concern. See Jacques Barzun, *The House of Intellect: How Intellect, the Prime Force in Western Civilization, Is Being Destroyed by Our Culture in the Name of Art, Science and Philanthropy* (New York: Harper & Brothers, 1959), 266–267.

42. It turns out that the School at Columbia is extraordinarily diverse in terms of ethnic, racial, and socioeconomic characteristic—and that the graduates of grade 8 are admitted to New York's top high schools.

43. This was, of course, Alfred Binet's original intention when he formulated his first set of tests of intelligence. We have strayed a long way from that original intention.

44. Diane Ravitch, the education historian who was, much to her own chagrin, one of the architects of the testing movements and partially responsible for the No Child Left Behind movement, makes this point after having a distinct change in her beliefs about the value of these tests. She says, "Our schools will not improve if we rely exclusively on tests as the means of deciding the fate of students, teachers, principals, and schools. When tests are the primary means of evaluation and accountability, everyone feels pressure to raise the scores, by hook or by crook." See Diane Ravitch, *The Death and Life of the Great American School System* (New York: Basic Books, 2010), 226. Ravitch now sees the public school problem as being far more related to families and poverty than to a lack of skills produced by the schools.

45. Today, this early form of progressive education has evolved into constructivist theories, among others, but it is a form of experiential learning, and at places like the Bank Street School for Children or the University of Chicago Laboratory School, you can see it in operation in a highly successful way.

46. The case for experience-based learning and the liberal arts goes back, of course, to Thomas Jefferson's plea for a liberal arts rather than a vocational form of education. William James also argued near the turn of the twentieth century for teaching that focused on learning by doing. Perhaps Jane Addams had the greatest influence on Dewey's thinking about education. Within the black community there was a lively debate between advocates for more practical training, such as Booker T. Washington and W. E. B. Du Bois, who opined: "The function of the university is not simply to teach bread-winning, or to furnish teachers for the public schools, or to be a centre of polite society; it is, above all, to be the organ of that fine adjustment between real life and the growing knowledge of life, an adjustment which forms the secret of civilization" (Du Bois, *The Souls of Black Folk*, ed. Henry Louis Gates and Terri Hume Oliver [New York: W. W. Norton, 1999], chap. V). Du Bois wanted to identify what he called "the Talented Tenth," who would not only achieve great things themselves but have as well the responsibility to improve the life chances of others by working for the welfare of those not in the talented tenth. Dewey was, of course, very active in setting up the famous University of Chicago Laboratory School, which still exists and has become a model for many other university laboratory schools. Dewey's influ-

ence today goes beyond the K–12 school years and has been reinvented again, often without reference to the original Dewey ideas, in efforts to emphasize group learning through experience. And there continues to be great early childhood education that takes this form, notably in schools like the Bank Street College of Education and its School for Children, which has existed for roughly one hundred years. See, for a discussion of these ideas, Douglas Thomas (professor at the Annenberg School of Communications of the University of Southern California) and John Seely Brown (who had been chief scientist of the Xerox Corporation), *A New Culture of Learning: Cultivating the Imagination for a World of Constant Change* (self-published, but easily obtainable, in 2011). They say: "In the new culture of learning, the classroom as a model is replaced by learning environments in which digital media *within* those environments are integral to the results….A second difference is that the teaching-based approach focuses on teaching us about the world, while the new culture of learning focuses on learning through engagement within the world" (p. 38).

Chapter 2: Thoughts on Undergraduate Education and Its Future

1. COFHE is an acronym for Consortium of Financing Higher Education. It consists of thirty-one highly selective private colleges and universities, including all of the Ivy League universities, Rice, women's colleges, as well as other liberal arts colleges such as Amherst, Williams, Swarthmore, Oberlin, and Pomona College. The Consortium, which is financed by the member schools, concentrates on collecting data, research, and policy analysis as these data are related to admissions, financial aid, and other problems with financing a college education.

2. These data were obtained directly from COHFE and were approved to be included in this book.

3. When I was provost at Columbia, I looked at the proportion of undergraduate courses with student enrollments of varying sizes. It turned out that roughly 80 percent of Columbia College courses had fewer than twenty-two students. Teaching a small number of students, the professor is apt to have a better opportunity to get to know each student—a very different situation than if he or she is teaching one hundred or more students in a class. This is the nature of boutique education in the most selective colleges and universities. And this does not approach the situation in many Oxford and Cambridge colleges, where there are individual tutorials that represent the foundation of the curriculum.

4. J. Hillis Miller, "What Ought Humanists to Do?," *Daedalus* (Winter 2014): 31.

5. William G. Bowen, Matthew M. Chingos, and Michael S. McPherson, *Crossing the Finish Line: Completing College at America's Public Universities* (Princeton, NJ: Princeton University Press, 2009). See chap. 5 and p. 198 of that work for a discussion of "overmatching."

6. Caroline Hoxby and Christopher Avery, "The Missing 'One-Offs': The Hidden Supply of High-Achieving, Low-Income Students," *Brookings Papers on Economic Activity* (Spring 2013).

7. Andrew Delbanco, *College: What It Was, Is, and Should Be* (Princeton, NJ: Princeton University Press, 2012), 3.

8. Discussion by Howard Gardner in William G. Bowen, *Higher Education in the Digital Age* (Princeton, NJ: Princeton University Press, 2013), 100–101.

9. Hanna Holborn Gray, *Searching for Utopia: Universities and Their Histories* (Berkeley: University of California Press, 2012), 43.

10. Christopher Clark, *The Sleepwalkers: How Europe Went to War in 1914* (New York: HarperCollins, 2013), Location: 243, 263, 265 out of 17098 (Kindle Edition).

11. *Report on the University's Role in Political and Social Action*, a report of a faculty committee, under the chairmanship of Harry Kalven, Jr., committee appointed by President George W. Beadle, published in the *Record* 1, no. 1, November 11, 1967.

12. In a brief essay in the *New York Times* (January 20, 2012), former Harvard University president Lawrence H. Summers speculated about how he hoped higher education's curriculum would change over the course of the next several decades to reflect the very rapid societal changes that we are witnessing. His "guesses" and "hopes" were captured succinctly in six points. He believed that (1) "Education will be more about how to process and use information and less about imparting it"; (2) "An inevitable consequence of the knowledge explosion is that tasks will be carried out with far more collaboration"; (3) "New technologies will profoundly alter the way knowledge is conveyed ... it makes sense for students to watch video of the clearest calculus teacher or the most lucid analyst of the Revolutionary War rather than having thousands of separate efforts. Professors will have more time for direct discussion with students—not to mention the cost savings— and the material will be better presented"; (4) "As articulated by the Nobel Prize winner Daniel Kahneman in *Thinking, Fast and Slow*, we understand the processes of human thought much better than we once did.... Not everyone learns most effectively in the same way. And yet, in the face of all evidence, we rely almost entirely on passive learning ... with the capacity of modern information technology, there is much more that can be done to promote dynamic learning"; (5) "The world is much more open, and events abroad affect the lives of Americans more than ever before. This makes it essential that the educational experience breed cosmopolitanism—that students have international experiences"; (6) "Course of study will place much more emphasis on the analysis of data." I'm truncating and quoting from Summers's piece here. He reinforces the thoughts of those scholars I've alluded to in the body of the text. He makes one other point that is worth noting: "A paradox of American higher education is this: The expectations of leading universities do much to define what secondary schools teach, and much to establish a template for what it means to be an educated man or woman. College campuses are seen as the source for the newest thinking and for the generation of new ideas, as society's cutting edge."

13. I speak here of books or texts. I think new media and film ought to be included in the discussion of the humanities and undergraduate curriculum as well, because young students are at least as familiar with these sources and forms as the books we place on our reading lists. In short, there ought to be a "viewing list" as well as a reading list. The point is that every author or director, if they are any good, is trying to convince the reader or viewer of the value of his or her point of view, or of the authenticity of his or her argument. This occurs in film as much as it does in great novels and we ought to use film more often in teaching this major feature of skeptical thinking. For a good discussion of the current conflicts over the nature of the curriculum and the use of new media, see David Bromwich, "Trapped in the Virtual Classroom," *The New York Review of Books*, July 9, 2015, 14–16.

14. For two good discussions of "trigger warnings" on the content of the curriculum and student protests over the content of books assigned by the faculty, see Todd Gitlin, "You Are Here to Be Disturbed," *Chronicle of Higher Education*, The Chronicle Review, May 11, 2015; Mike Vilensky, "School's Out at Columbia, but a Debate over Trigger Warnings Continues," *Wall Street Journal*, July 1, 2015.

15. For a list of all of the texts that have been offered in the humanities core class, see http://www.college.columbia.edu/core/1937.php.

16. John W. Boyer, *"Teaching at a University of a Certain Sort": Education at the University of Chicago over the Past Century* (Chicago: University of Chicago Press, 2011), 187–188.

17. Gray, *In Search of Utopias*, 10. The original thoughts of Hutchins can be found in expanded form in his book *The Higher Learning in America*, 2nd ed. (New Haven, CT: Yale University Press, 1962).

18. Source: news.harvard.edu/gazette/story/2011/12/gen-ed-connects-the-dots-of-life/. See also Louis Menand, *The Marketplace of Ideas: Reform and Resistance in the American University (Issues of Our Times)* (New York: W. W. Norton, 2010).

19. This summary is taken from Dan Berrett, "Stanford Remakes Curriculum, Following Trend to Focus on Critical Thinking vs. Disciplinary Content," *Chronicle of Higher Education*, January 26, 2012.

20. Source: http://www.registrar.fas.harvard.edu/courses-exams/course-catalog/philosophy -232r-art-living-graduate-seminar-general-education-new.

21. Jonathan R. Cole, "Two Cultures Revisited," *The Bridge* (National Academy of Engineering) 26, no. 3–4 (Fall/Winter 1996): 16–21.

22. For an example of this sense of despair see Mark C. Taylor, *Crisis on Campus: A Bold Plan for Reforming Our Colleges and Universities* (New York: Alfred A. Knopf, 2010).

23. George Santayana, "Why I Am Not a Marxist," *Modern Monthly Review* 9 (April 1935): 77–79.

Chapter 3: A House Built on a Firm Foundation

1. These questions and Professor Spiegel's responses to them are taken from an unpublished talk that she gave at UCLA and in 2010 to a Johns Hopkins University advisory board on the subject of why the humanities are relevant today. Although the talk has not been formally published, it contains a superb argument for how the humanities are relevant for intrinsic reasons and why humanists are missing opportunities to make their case to the broader public about their continued importance at great universities. I will quote and cite this unpublished work several times in this section. Copies should be obtained from the author. I want to thank Professor Spiegel for sharing a copy of this talk with me.

2. Commission on the Humanities and Social Sciences, American Academy of Arts and Sciences, *The Heart of the Matter: The Humanities and Social Sciences for a Vibrant, Competitive, and Secure Nation* (Cambridge, MA, 2013). This commission, which included leaders in higher education, business, and the arts, made a set of recommendations that focus on greater support for the humanities because of the crucial role that these subjects play in producing a more knowledgeable public and a better-functioning set of institutions within the United States. I'll have more to say about this report below as it relates to the role of the humanities in the great university of the future.

3. Each of these general prescriptions has a set of subcategories that are discussed at some length in the Report.

4. My principal focus here is on undergraduate humanities courses, but there is an entirely different and equally important problem related to the doctoral education in the humanities. This subject has been treated with sophistication in Ronald G. Ehrenberg, Harriet Zukerman, Jeffrey A. Groen, and Sharon M. Brucker, *Educating Scholars: Doctoral Education in the Humanities* (Princeton, NJ: Princeton University Press, 2010). Prior to reading this book, which focuses on an effort by the Andrew W. Mellon Foundation to transform doctoral education in the humanities along two important dimensions—reducing both the attrition rate of graduate students and the time they take to obtain their degree—one should read the excellent set of essays in Alvin

Kernan, ed., *What's Happened to the Humanities?* (Princeton, NJ: Princeton University Press, 1997). Finally, as background to my comments, see David A. Hollinger, ed., *The Humanities and the Dynamics of Inclusion Since World War II* (Baltimore, MD: Johns Hopkins University Press, 2006).

5. Of course, Snow, in the second edition of *The Two Cultures and the Scientific Revolution* (Cambridge: Cambridge University Press, 1964), envisioned the emergence of a third culture that would close the communications gap between scientists and literary intellectuals. It is unclear whether this third culture has come to pass; but it ought to, and a mechanism for producing this exchange between the humanities and sciences as a normal interaction requires that the disciplines work on intellectual problems together. That can be achieved, in part, by recognizing that the sciences increasingly need the humanities and that the humanists have a role to play in the development of scientific practice and its presentation to public audiences. Until now, scientists—at least a limited number of them—have been public intellectuals. Individuals like the string theorist Brian Greene and, previously, the biologist Stephen Jay Gould and the neuroscientist Eric Kandel, and a number of physicists, have spoken directly to the public through books, television appearances, and essay writing. If we find it difficult to penetrate the membranes between fields in the humanities and sciences, we ought to think of mechanisms that make it easier for us to do so. One way that works is for great universities to create schools for children of their faculty members and for some non-university youngsters. Since children do not sort themselves by discipline, and since friendships often result from patterns of interaction with parents whose kids are in the same primary school class, this is a natural way for these faculty members to meet, to interact, and to become friends to the point that they actually know what each other is doing.

6. David A. Hollinger, "The Wedge Driving Academe's Two Families Apart: Can STEM and the Humanities Get Along?," *Chronicle of Higher Education*, The Chronicle Review, October 14, 2013.

7. Of course, the methods of science, engineering, mathematics, and statistics also play a formidable role in developing critical thinking. In fact, I would argue that a person who is ignorant of basic concepts in probability and statistics will have a difficult time navigating complex information that she or he is asked to assimilate and critique.

8. In a 2014 Gallup poll, 70 percent of adult Americans could not name a single living American scientist. Of the 30 percent who could name someone, the top vote getter by far was the English cosmologist Stephen Hawking and a few others who were known from the portrayal of these scientists in the movies or on television. Although hardly the best indicator of knowledge, this poll suggests that Americans are simply ignorant of those who make the most important discoveries that influence their lives.

9. "The American Revolution: Who Cares? Americans Are Yearning to Learn, Failing to Know," http://www.prnewswire.com/news-releases/83-percent-of-us-adults-fail-test-on-nations-founding-78325412.html.

10. Kathleen Hall Jamieson, Director, The Annenberg Public Policy Center of the University of Pennsylvania, "Public Understanding of and Support for the Courts," 2007, www.annenbergpublicpolicycenter.org.

11. See also a more recent survey conducted in 2012 by FindLaw, "Two-Thirds of Americans Can't Name Any U.S. Supreme Court Justices, Says New FindLaw.com Survey," http://company.findlaw.com/press-center/2012/two-thirds-of-americans-can-t-name-any-u-s-supreme-court-justice.html/.

12. Even a decade ago, the numbers of book monographs sold was depressing. Roughly 90 percent of all scholarly books sell fewer than 400 copies—and many of these books are on

extremely interesting subjects and are very well written. And most of these 400 or fewer sales are to university libraries, not to individuals.

13. Dan Berrett, "'Report Card' on the Humanities Finds Light amid the Gloom," *Chronicle of Higher Education*, September 4, 2013.

14. Dan Berrett, "Harvard Mounts Campaign to Bolster Undergraduate Humanities," *Chronicle of Higher Education*, June 7, 2013.

15. Beckie Supiano, "How Liberal-Arts Majors Fare over the Long Haul," *Chronicle of Higher Education*, January 22, 2014.

16. Martha C. Nussbaum, *Not for Profit: Why Democracy Needs the Humanities* (Princeton, NJ: Princeton University Press, 2010), 47–48.

17. Martha C. Nussbaum, *Cultivating Humanity: A Classical Defense of Reform in Liberal Education* (Cambridge, MA: Harvard University Press, 1997), 85.

18. Ibid., 21–22.

19. Hollinger, *The Humanities and the Dynamics of Inclusion*, 1. In the Hollinger book, the essay by Roger L. Geiger entitled "Demography and Curriculum" (pp. 50–72) is particularly illuminating, as are most of the works of this preeminent historian of higher education. In his essay, he speculates on the rise and fall of interest in the humanities among undergraduate students during the 1960s and 1970s. The pattern is marked by a spectacular rise in interest in the first decade and a precipitous decline during the second—a decline from which the humanities has never fully recovered. Geiger finds no evidence for a gender gap in this rise and fall. He does suggest that the large expansion of higher education during the 1960s, which opened up a career path for many younger scholars who were particularly appealing to young students, as well as a rejection of an older line of scholarly work for the New Criticism, which tended to open up the curriculum to the analysis of more contemporary works, contributed in some undetermined way to the rise in interest. The fall had something to do with the hardening of the American labor market for college graduates, the increased concern with job opportunities in the post-college years, among other factors, well described by Geiger in his chapter.

20. For a book that provides extensive data on the state of Ph.D. education in the humanities, see Ronald G. Ehrenberg and Harriet Zuckerman, *Educating Scholars: Doctoral Education in the Humanities* (Princeton, NJ: Princeton University Press, 2009).

21. Source: http://www.harvard.edu/president/role-university-changing-world.

22. Andrew Delbanco, *College: What It Was, Is, and Should Be* (Princeton, NJ: Princeton University Press, 2012), 3.

23. Quoted in Martha C. Nussbaum, *Cultivating Humanity: A Classical Defense of Reform in Liberal Education* (Cambridge, MA: Harvard University Press, 1997), 85.

24. For a discussion of this and similar points, see Bill Readings, *The University in Ruins* (Cambridge, MA: Harvard University Press, 1996), 172–173.

25. Quoted in John Markoff, "In 1949, He Imagined an Age of Robots," *New York Times*, May 20, 2013.

26. This is a shorter distillation of the actual questions found in the letter as presented by Daniel J. Kevles in "Principles and Politics in Federal R&D Policy, 1945–1990: An Appreciation of the Bush Report." This introductory essay can be found in the fiftieth anniversary edition of *Science, the Endless Frontier*, published by the National Science Foundation, p. ix.

27. Spiegel, unpublished talk.

28. Ibid.

29. I have spoken to many Israelis and Palestinians about this matter, and almost all agree with this general statement. It was an opportunity lost—and one that resulted in institutional conflict, described by the sociologist James S. Coleman in terms of the polarization of views that often begin as minor difference during social conflict. See his book *Community Conflict* (New York: Free Press, 1957).

30. Spiegel, unpublished talk.

31. Ibid.

32. See, among many others, Frances Stonor Saunders, *Who Paid the Piper? The CIA and the Cultural Cold War* (London: Granta Books, 1999); Frances Stonor Saunders, *The Cultural Cold War: The CIA and the World of Arts and Letters* (New York: New Press, 2000); Tim Weiner, *Legacy of Ashes: The History of the CIA* (New York: Anchor, 2008); Steve Coll, *Ghost Wars: The Secret History of the CIA, Afghanistan, and Bin Laden from the Soviet Invasion to September 10, 2001* (New York: Penguin Books, 2004).

33. See Spiegel's short essay for references to the Call to Action.

34. Ibid.

35. During World War II, the military viewed language training in Japanese as critical to the war effort and set up highly successful language training programs for qualified soldiers. Some of the most distinguished East Asian scholars after the war were graduates of these military language programs.

36. At the turn of the twenty-first century, a number of humanistic disciplines that were rapidly losing students to other subjects rethought their programs to make them more appealing to a larger audience. At the great universities and colleges of the nation, classics represents one of those disciplines. Few high school or college students were well-versed in Latin or Greek and therefore were not prepared to read classical literature in the original language. Consequently, except for those classical texts required in core courses (like the humanities course at Columbia and the University of Chicago), they were stymied in going further even if they found the subject of great personal interest. Many classics departments began to offer two pathways toward a major in classical studies: one that involved reading in Greek and Latin, and the other that involved reading the same works in translation. Enrollments began to grow significantly. Other language departments followed a similar course. Some may argue that reading in translation is a bastardized form of learning the classics, but others argue that even reading translations allows students to engage the texts and the substance of issues addressed by the great classical authors.

37. Berrett, "Harvard Mounts Campaign to Bolster Undergraduate Humanities."

38. Commission on the Humanities and Social Sciences, American Academy of Arts and Sciences, *The Heart of the Matter*, 33.

39. The title of the article published by Mt. Sinai Hospital is "Mount Sinai Study Shows that Humanities Students Perform as Well as Pre-Med Students in Medical School." Quoted in the piece, Dr. Nathan Kase, Professor of Obstetrics, Gynecology and Reproductive Science, and Medicine, and Dean Emeritus of the Medical School, said: "The Humanities and Medicine program at Mount Sinai was established to encourage students with a humanities background to consider a medical career when they would not otherwise do so.... These data show that these students are as successful as, and in some cases more successful than, their traditionally educated classmates." Source: http://www.mountsinai.org/about-us/newsroom/press-releases/.

40. The real world of professional work is far more murky than what students might think after taking a course of study in a preprofessional discipline. In fact, in the complex world of solving problems on the job, good analytic thinking is apt to take the student farther than the limited range of subjects studied in a preprofessional education.

41. The effort by the United States during World War II to increase substantially the number of Americans who were fluent and could read Japanese and other foreign languages can act as a guide to what we ought to do in the future.

42. Source: https://www.youtube.com/watch?v=O_hBj8qlp_k.

43. Jon Elster, "Obscurantism and Academic Freedom," in Akeel Bilgrami and Jonathan R. Cole, eds., *Who's Afraid of Academic Freedom?* (New York: Columbia University Press, 2015), 81–96.

44. Akeel Bilgrami, "Truth, Balance, and Freedom," in Bilgrami and Cole, *Who's Afraid of Academic Freedom?*, 20. Bilgrami elaborates on the dogmatism found in economics in this essay, suggesting that many economists at first-rate institutions simply cannot conceive of alternative explanations "downstream" that would falsify their dogmatically held theories.

45. Ibid., 18–19.

46. This is a significant problem when dealing with the concept of academic freedom and free inquiry. I shall refer back to this in Chapter 9, which deals with our universities' core values, including academic freedom.

47. Bilgrami, "Truth, Balance, and Freedom," 20–21.

Chapter 4: The Contours of the University

1. Jonathan R. Cole, *The Great American University: Its Rise to Preeminence, Its Indispensable National Role, and Why It Must Be Protected* (New York: PublicAffairs, 2009), 39.

2. Ibid., 40.

3. Upton Sinclair, *The Goose-Step: A Study of American Education* (Pasadena, CA: Self-published, 1923). This book has been reproduced and published by several different publishers since 2000.

4. Cole, *The Great American University*, 35–44.

5. Here I'm including, among the arts and sciences, the departments of engineering and computer science, as well as the basic biological sciences often located in medical centers at the university.

6. Before suggesting some responses to this question, I should note six axioms that I am building on. First, if the school's curriculum does not produce value added above and beyond what on-the-ground professional training would provide, there is no good rationale for the existence of that school within the university. In short, if you can learn as much with three years of work at a business firm as you can in business school, then the value of the business school is questionable. The same can be said for a program in the arts, social work, public administration or public policy, public health, architecture, or journalism. Second, if most of the value added is achieved within a truncated portion of the years spent getting a degree, serious consideration ought to be given to shortening or transforming the nature of the curriculum or the nature of the degree. Third, if the academic products of the school are not used in the profession, then we should raise questions about what is the value of the scholarship in the professional school. Fourth, if the school is not linked in some way with the core arts and sciences disciplines, and is not to some extent integrated with them, then there are salient questions to be answered about the value of what the students are learning and what the professors are teaching. Fifth, if a professional school is not committed to knowledge without borders, then its place in the university has to be justified on other significant grounds. Sixth, and finally, when schools are controlled largely by professional guilds that fight to exclude the cross-fertilization of knowledge and restrict entry and teaching to those who hold the degree in the school's area of supposed expertise, then the knowledge in that school is going to be of lesser value. In fact,

I will argue that those professional schools that have "imported" or "linked" themselves with core arts and sciences disciplines, as well as with engineering and medical disciplines, have far greater promise of contributing to the distinction of the university. Those that have not need to be changed, or their value as units in the university ought to be questioned.

7. We might think that accreditation groups could do this work, but these groups are often made up of members of the guild who are willing to do this work but who are often not particularly innovative thinkers about what dramatic changes ought to be considered.

8. Columbia eliminated (phased it out over two years beginning in 1990) the School of Library Science, which had only four tenured faculty members at the time, because it refused over many years to reorient itself toward online and newer technologies that would clearly affect library science, and because it refused to become more integrated with departments like computer science. Although the program was small, and some of its subprograms, such as its program to preserve rare books and manuscripts that could be transferred to other universities, were outstanding, the tuition it charged was perhaps five to ten times what it cost to go to equally good state university schools of library science. But after deciding to close the school, I had to spend hundreds of hours over the next several years defending the action against alums and those who believed that closing such a school would seriously damage the greatness of Columbia. The University of Chicago also closed its Graduate Library School (they stopped accepting applications in 1989). But examples of the death of programs, departments, and schools are part of a very short story in the history of American higher learning.

9. David Muller, "Reforming Premedical Education—Out with the Old, In with the New," *New England Journal of Medicine* 368 (April 25, 2013): 1567–1569, http://www.nejm.org/doi/full /10.1056/NEJMp1302259. Here I follow closely the summary provided by Dr. Muller, but there are many other sources that provide details about each of these criticisms.

10. Ibid.

11. Of course, I hope I don't have to make an argument that organic chemistry is an extremely important field and that powerful new discoveries have resulted from the work done by organic chemists. But, except for the very few physicians doing research that requires deep knowledge of organic chemistry, my guess is that few physicians ever use it or remember the content of their premedical course.

12. The waning number interested in pursuing a career in medicine is mostly a result of self-selection. Students who obtain poor grades in subjects such as organic chemistry come to believe they don't have what it takes to be a physician and that they are unlikely to be admitted to medical school. Consequently, they become dropouts from potential careers in medicine.

13. If physicians who are in medical school and those who have been out any length of time were quizzed on the meaning and proper interpretation of the statistical results that they read in the top medical journals, most would be unable to do well on an examination that measured that ability. In fact, it's not clear what the reading habits are of doctors who have been out of medical school for varied periods of time. Consequently, they rely almost entirely on "authority"—the authority of the author(s) affiliation(s) and the quality of the peer-reviewed journal in which articles appear.

14. There is some movement afoot to change some of these prerequisites and to require, in fact, knowledge of statistics; but a thorough reexamination of the curriculum and what types of knowledge lead to becoming an outstanding physician has not, as far as I know, taken place.

15. See Robyn Dawes, *House of Cards: Psychology and Psychotherapy Built on Myth* (New York: Free Press, 1994); Elizabeth Loftus and Katherine Ketcham, *The Myth of Repressed Memory: False Memories and Allegations of Sexual Abuse* (New York: St. Martin's Press, 1994).

16. Muller, "Reforming Premedical Education."

17. Of course, some great universities, like Stanford and the University of Pennsylvania, have their medical schools in close proximity to the other major schools of the university. In fact, it was a bold step indeed when Stanford, under President Sterling during the 1950s and early 1960s, planned and implemented the move of its medical center from San Francisco to Palo Alto, despite substantial resistance. But the move at Stanford was implemented only a few years after Watson and Crick discovered the structure of the DNA molecule. It became obvious to many that we were witnessing the dawn of a new era in science-based medicine, where genetics and the pure biological sciences would lead to medical discoveries.

18. This is a generalization, since many of the faculty members at schools like the University of Chicago believe that their students are fully engaged in the third-year curriculum.

19. I should note that I have no empirical evidence about this emphasis. At best, the evidence is anecdotal; and some of the high-quality law students whom I teach contend that the quality of teaching and the commitment to students is very mixed.

20. Of course, many of the students receive some financial aid, which brings down the sticker price considerably; and there are loan-forgiveness plans at many law schools for those who spend a certain number of years in public service legal jobs.

21. Quoted in Ben W. Heineman Jr., William F. Lee, and David B. Wilkins, "Lawyers as Professionals and as Citizens: Key Roles and Responsibilities in the 21st Century" (Preprint, 2014).

22. The crunch for positions at the top law firms in places like New York City, which was a consequence of the deep recession of 2008, seems to have abated by 2015.

23. To be fair, some of my law school faculty colleagues, especially at places like the University of Chicago, dispute my claim that the third year adds little to the capacity of students to think like lawyers or to become more competent in anticipation of becoming one. I do not doubt that there is significant variation among law schools, especially among those where third-year grades have a greater influence on the job offers they will receive.

24. Many law schools do allow students to take a limited number of courses outside of the law school; and of course, there are joint-degree programs that are offered with other schools; but for the most part, students are not encouraged to take courses beyond the boundaries of the law school. They tend to take some courses by nonlawyers at the law school who have faculty status or are affiliated faculty. But I would be shocked to find out that more than a handful of law students have taken a statistics or biomedical science course while in law school.

25. There is now evidence that a law degree from a leading law school increases lifetime earning of graduates by more than $1 million above what they would earn with a B.A. degree. Also, at least at the leading law schools, the default rate on debt incurred, which is often substantial, is low—around 5 percent. Source: Michael Simkovic and Frank McIntyre, "The Economic Value of a Law Degree," April 13, 2013, Social Science Research Network, http://ssrn.com/abstract=2250585.

26. From the perspective of aspiring law school students and those at elite law schools, there are other aspects of legal education that might be worthy of review in a Flexner-type report. Among these are standards and criteria for admissions, which are very highly dependent at the elite law schools on GPA and LSAT scores, which tend to be only moderately correlated with

first-year law school GPAs. Few law schools are like Yale, where the faculty is significantly involved in the selection of incoming students and tend to pay more attention to essays and other qualitative factors than to the standardized tests and grade-point averages. Students also question the value of the Socratic method for many students who become apprehensive and have a distaste for this kind of learning; the absence of enough time on clinical work; the qualifications of the faculty members themselves, who often have little or no experience practicing the law; and problems with employment opportunities given that about 85 percent of law school students have about $150,000 in debt upon graduation. I thank the law school students in my seminar on "The University in American Life" for pointing out some of these concerns that seem to be widely held by students.

27. See, as one example of Burt's work, *Structural Holes: The Social Structure of Competition* (Cambridge, MA: Harvard University Press, 1995).

28. It is difficult to assess the state of contemporary journalism—which has become far more specialized and requires many more technical skills than in the past—with the quality of investigative reporting, foreign policy reporting, or reporting from subjects like science to fashion relative to journalism in the past. But surely we can say that journalism has experienced the effects of profoundly disruptive technologies and consequently has been forced to rethink how it covers stories in the world of the Internet and almost instant blogging.

29. Some educational graduate schools do attract able students, and some of them turn out to be extraordinary teachers or administrators. Schools that teach a specific approach to educating young people, such as the Bank Street College of Education, do a remarkable job in producing dedicated teachers who remain in the field a long time and who are evaluated as superior teachers. An assessment in 2014 by Stanford's School of Education of Bank Street and its graduates showed that they are an example of a successful, if small, program.

30. There are many books on the effects of superb teaching, but one only has to read Muriel Spark's *The Prime of Miss Jean Brodie* to see how an eccentric, iconoclastic, yet devoted teacher can have lifelong effects on young minds. For a very contemporary look at the work of several extraordinary teachers at public schools, one of which is populated by youngsters from very poor socioeconomic backgrounds, see David Denby, *Lit Up: One Reporter, Three Schools, and Twenty-Four Books That Can Change Lives* (New York: Henry Holt and Co., 2016).

Chapter 5: The Affordability and Value of Higher Education

1. Andrew Hacker and Claudia Dreifus, *Higher Education: How Colleges Are Wasting Our Money and Failing Our Kids—and What We Can Do About It* (New York: Times Books, Henry Holt and Company, 2010), 113.

2. Mark C. Taylor, *Crisis on Campus: A Bold Plan for Reforming Our Colleges and Universities* (New York: Alfred A. Knopf, 2010), 103 (table).

3. I speak here for the first time of the "cost-value proposition," which is a term of art, if you can call that art, that suggests that without examining what students get in value for the price they pay, we are misleading the public. We have to associate the value of the education, in a multidimensional way, with the price before drawing conclusions about whether the cost exceeds the value received.

4. Daniel Kahneman, the Nobel Prize–winning psychologist who won the prize for behavioral economics, has two cognitive decision-making heuristics that make such reified facts difficult to get rid of. One is the availability heuristic. When people think about the cost of

tuition, what comes to mind immediately is this $50,000 price tag. This price also represents what Kahneman and his late collaborator, Amos Tversky, would call an "anchor." It is what individuals hold onto as the basis for their thinking and further calculations about tuition pricing. As Kahneman and Tversky demonstrate through multiple clever experiments, decisions based on availability and anchoring are often wrong.

5. In fact, if we look only at community colleges, the number is closer to 25 percent.

6. Recent 2015 data suggest that colleges and universities without large endowments, such as Sarah Lawrence College and New York University, have moved their sticker prices to well over $60,000 a year. They too provide significant discounts from this figure by taking part of the tuition and applying it to financial aid. But headlines that include only sticker prices give the wrong impression about cost. The real problem lies at institutions that already have high prices and low demand, without large endowments. They are at risk. But one should ask: How many of these colleges and universities really need to exist in the future? Nick Anderson and Danielle Douglas-Gabriel, "Private College Sticker-Price Shock: Past $60,000 a Year," *Washington Post*, March 27, 2015.

7. Of the 4,140 colleges and universities in the United States as of 2013, 629 were public, four-year institutions; 1,845 were private, four-year institutions; 1,070 were public, two-year institutions; and 596 were private, two-year institutions. Most two-year institutions are community colleges that prepare students to graduate to larger four-year institutions. American colleges enrolled roughly 17.5 million students in 2013, of which about 14.5 million were undergraduates, 2.1 million were graduate students, and 300,000 were professional school students. National Center for Education Statistics, *Digest of Educational Statistics*, as of April 28, 2013, https://nces.ed.gov/programs/digest/.

8. The states are remarkably inconsistent in revealing these preferences. Take two examples: California voters in November 2012 approved by a margin of 54 percent to 46 percent a ballot measure strongly supported by Governor Jerry Brown to raise taxes by $6 billion annually over seven years to "save the state's public schools and balance the budget." Norimitsu Onishi, "Californians Back Taxes to Avoid Education Cuts," *New York Times,* November 7, 2012. A year later, Colorado voters rejected by a wide margin a ballot to raise income taxes to fund education in Colorado—66 percent voted against the ballot. Ana Campoy, "Colorado Education-Tax Measure Fails," *Wall Street Journal,* November 6, 2013. In short, there is significant variation over time and among the various states in their revealed preferences for maintaining or creating top-tier schools and institutions of higher learning.

9. Roger L. Geiger, *Knowledge & Money: Research Universities and the Paradox of the Marketplace* (Palo Alto, CA: Stanford University Press, 2004), 33. In this book, Geiger not only examines the trend in college costs but offers a set of explanatory variables that are linked to price increase. He also discusses the "real" cost of higher education over time in a clear and cogent way. The universities in his study include many of the most intensive research universities in the United States—the ones that I'm most concerned with in this book. Geiger notes: "They perform nearly 70 percent of academic research and graduate 68 percent of the doctorates. They also award 28 percent of bachelor's degrees and 34 percent of first professional degrees" (p. 30). I should note that I'll reference a number of data-based studies here that use different samples of universities—not all of which are random samples. Although the general pattern in all of the studies is consistent, the explanation of the causes of the increased tuition and how "real" they are often emphasizes different factors—although most agree about the overall major explanatory variables.

10. Bowen's influential published work on higher education includes discussions of the consequences of affirmative action policy, the nature of graduate education in the United States, the problems with access to higher education by the poor, the cost of higher education, and the effects of the commodification of athletics on the values of higher learning, just to mention a sample of his projects. See among other works William G. Bowen and Neil L. Rudenstine, *In Pursuit of the Ph.D.* (Princeton, NJ: Princeton University Press, 1992); William G. Bowen and Derek Bok, *The Shape of the River: Long-Term Consequences of Considering Race in College and University Admissions* (Princeton, NJ: Princeton University Press, 2000); William G. Bowen, Matthew M. Chingos, and Michael S. McPherson, *Crossing the Finish Line: Completing College at America's Public Universities* (Princeton, NJ: Princeton University Press, 2011), (this is perhaps the best and most readable book on student loans; see especially chaps. 8 and 9); William G. Bowen, *Lessons Learned: Reflections of a University President* (Princeton, NJ: Princeton University Press, 2010); William G. Bowen and James L. Shulman, *The Game of Life: College Sports and Educational Values* (Princeton, NJ: Princeton University Press, 2001); William G. Bowen et al., *Reclaiming the Game: College Sports and Educational Values* (Princeton, NJ: Princeton University Press, 2005). The work that Bowen discusses in his Tanner Lectures about the "cost disease" was developed in collaboration the distinguished Princeton economist William J. Baumol in *Performing Arts: The Economic Dilemma* (New York: Twentieth Century Fund, 1966).

11. William G. Bowen, *Higher Education in the Digital Age* (Princeton, NJ: Princeton University Press, 2013), 2–3. This is taken from the published version of Bowen's 2012 Tanner Lectures that were delivered at Stanford University.

12. Sandy Baum, Charles Kurose, and Michael S. McPherson, "An Overview of Higher Education" (paper presented at the Princeton conference "Future of Children: Postsecondary Education in the United States," April 26–27, 2012). Sandy Baum is a senior fellow at the George Washington University Graduate School of Education and Human Development and professor emerita of economics at Skidmore College; Charles Kurose is an independent consultant to the College Board and a former research associate at the Spencer Foundation, which focuses on educational research; and Michael McPherson is president of the Spencer Foundation and former president of Macalester College. The paper is cited in Bowen, *Higher Education in the Digital Age*. The data presented are based on the Delta Cost Project. As Bowen suggests, the original paper has a wealth of excellent data on costs and perhaps more significantly provides the reader with both an historical perspective on rising costs and state and federal investments in higher education since the 1960s. I should note here, as does Bowen in his Tanner Lectures, that calculating "costs" is often a tricky business because many different indicators are used and aggregated in different ways. Nonetheless, the overall pattern has been remarkably consistent as reported from a variety of sources.

13. Charles T. Clotfelter, *Buying the Best: Cost Escalation in Elite Higher Education* (Princeton, NJ: Princeton University Press, 1996), 1–2. Clotfelter does not claim that his results are based upon a systematic random sample of colleges and universities, but he does provide reasons why the findings are suggestive of real trends in cost. At public four-year colleges, the range was from New Hampshire's tuition and fees that were roughly $14,660 to Wyoming's $4,404 and $5,885 in Alaska.

14. Robert B. Archibald and David H. Feldman, *Why Does College Cost So Much?* (Oxford: Oxford University Press, 2011), 82.

15. Baum, Kurose, and McPherson, "An Overview of Higher Education." Of course, using percentage increases as the indicator of cost escalation, rather than absolute dollars, can be very

misleading; if the starting tuition rate is very low, even a 200 percent increase may still leave the student and her family with a rather low tuition bill.

16. Note that even the sticker price for public colleges and universities is far lower than what is often cited in books like Taylor's or in the media, which concentrate almost exclusively on the private, elite colleges and universities. Since public colleges and universities educate the vast majority of college students, this in itself represents a gross distortion of fact.

17. Douglas Belkin and Caroline Porter, "College Tuition Increases Slow, but Government Aid Falls," *Wall Street Journal*, October 22, 2013. The data reported here for increases in tuition and fees were produced by the College Board; and Sandy Baum, whose paper was quoted earlier, said of this decline: "The news in terms of college price increases is that it does seem the spiral is moderating, not turning around, not ending, but moderating." For substantial statistical data on the cost of higher education at different types of universities and colleges, see the College Board, *Trends in College Pricing 2013*, Trends in Higher Education Series, http://trends .collegeboard.org/sites/default/files/college-pricing-2013-full-report.pdf. As one would expect, there is significant variation among states and private colleges and universities. Also, note that some of these figures are for 2012 or 2013. There is generally a lag of one or two years in the publication of these kinds of aggregated data for colleges and universities.

18. For the year 2013–2014, federal Pell Grant awards for full-time students ranged from $650 to $5,645, based on the level of need calculated by formula in the award application. There are also Federal Supplemental Educational Opportunity Grants (FSEOGs), which are also based on need and range from $100 to $4,000 per year, and a federal work-study program that enables students to work a maximum number of hours at on- and off-campus jobs that are deemed eligible for the program. The cost of these awards is borne by the federal government. There are also a number of larger federal student loan programs, notably the Subsidized Federal Stafford Loan program, which provides long-term, low-interest loans for eligible undergraduate students. Undergraduates who are eligible for these loans may borrow up to $3,500 in their first year of college, up to $4,500 the second year, and up to $5,500 for the third through fifth years. A loan from this program may not exceed $23,000. The Federal Perkins Loan Program offers low-interest loans for both undergraduates and graduate students, with limits of $5,500 for undergraduate students annually and no more than $27,000 for students pursuing a bachelor's degree. Other federal loan programs exist. In California, as in New York, there are state financial aid programs based on financial need. For example, the Cal Grant A Entitlement Awards provide grants that range up to a maximum of $5,472 for undergraduates in 2013–2014 who maintain at least a 3.0 grade point average. The Grant B Entitlement Program offers a living allowance of up to $1,473 for students with at least a 2.0 academic average. This program is independent of the Grant A program. Other states clearly provide assistance to needy students based upon their own state-organized and state-administered program. Source: http://www.calstate.edu/sas/fa_programs.shtml.

19. Beckie Supiano, "Tuition Increases Slow Down, but There's More to College Affordability," *Chronicle of Higher Education*, October 23, 2013. Through tax credits, the federal government provides families and students with about $20 billion annually in savings, which is roughly the equivalent of 60 percent of what the government spends annually on Pell Grants, according to Ms. Supiano.

20. A great deal has rightly been written about the growth and purposes of the University of California system of higher education, which I consider the greatest large system of public higher learning ever constructed. This is particularly true about Clark Kerr's 1960 "Master

Plan for Higher Education in California," http://www.ucop.edu/acadinit/mastplan/mp.htm. Comparatively little has been written of a definitive nature about the components of the CUNY system and its far longer history as one of the great engines of social mobility in America that, for most of its history, could boast a very high-quality faculty and set of students at most of its campuses. There needs to be a detailed history of CUNY and its components written by a first-rate historian.

21. For an excellent empirical book on the relationship between pricing, discount rates, and dropout rates from colleges of varying levels of selectivity and quality, see Bowen, Chingos, and McPherson, *Crossing the Finish Line.* The data necessary to compute accurate dropout rates are not easily acquired. For example, suppose a student begins college at the University of Michigan and transfers to Yale and graduates within four years, this is counted as a dropout from Michigan. That surely makes no sense, yet that is the way most of the data on dropouts have been calculated. Efforts are being made to improve these data.

22. CUNY also will supplement students with need with funds from TAP.

23. Roughly three-quarters of Pell Grant recipients go to community colleges, where they most often are charged by the point, rather than on a semester basis. This leads to higher costs for a full-time program. Consequently, a substantial number of these community college students never register for more than the minimum number of points needed for eligibility for Pell Grants. The perverse result is that it is far harder for these community college students to finish their education in four years. This becomes even more of a problem when the Pell Grant amounts become capped, but tuition continues to rise. Sandy Baum, Kristin Conklin, and Nate Johnson suggest, Congress "could solve this problem by awarding larger grants to students who enrolled for more than 12 credit hours." "Op-Ed: Stop Penalizing Poor College Students," *New York Times*, November 12, 2013. In short, Congress is providing disincentives for students who might want to attend school full-time but can't afford to do so. The authors suggest that this would probably change the way community college students think about full-time programs, leading more to enroll full-time, and consequently increasing the graduation rates.

24. Source: http://www.cuny.edu/about/resources/value/CVFactSheet2013.pdf.

25. Only the State University of New York, which does not match the California system in terms of quality, comes remotely close to matching its size. SUNY has about 465,000 students at its multiple campuses in New York, another 1.1 million adult education students spanning sixty-four campuses in New York, and a total of 88,000 faculty members. SUNY claims to be the largest comprehensive higher educational system in the country.

26. Arizona State University (ASU) has undergone a remarkable growth in quality since Michael Crow became its president in 2002. For 2015–2016 it has a sticker price, for tuition and fees, of roughly $10,500 for full-time students. It estimates the total cost of one year of attendance for a full-time student living on campus at approximately $25,000. Its tuition and fees have gone from less than $5,000 a year in 2006–2007 to the current number. Over the past decade, ASU has seen spectacular growth in the quality of students, using almost any measure, as well as in research dollars. It prides itself on whom it admits, rather than whom it turns away, and in 2014 it had a total of about 67,500 undergraduate and nearly 16,000 graduate students studying at its several campuses—a total of 83,500 students. Its number of National Merit Scholars has grown dramatically, as has the number of Pell Grant recipients, which now numbers about 25,000 of the total student population—the largest number of Pell Grant recipients at one university in the nation and a growth from roughly 3 percent in 1990–1991 to over 40 percent in 2011. This level of access for students from poor socioeconomic backgrounds is

far beyond the average of about 25 percent at "very high research activity universities." As of 2010–2011, the average debt of its students was roughly $25,000 upon graduation in four years; 49 percent had college loan debt; and about $16,000 of this total resulted from federal loans. ASU represents an example of a state that has tuition and fees higher than those at CUNY and in California for in-state students, which illustrates again the range of affordability that exists within the larger system of colleges and university. Source: These data were obtained directly from the Office of the President of ASU.

27. Plainly, I've discussed only two large systems of higher education in only two states. The numbers will differ according to specific state policies regarding in-state student financial aid and how each determines the amount and eligibility of students. Arizona may well differ from both New York and California, and from Florida, Alabama, Ohio, Michigan, Wisconsin, and the other states. These figures on student debt at CUNY and the California public higher educational system do not, of course, include the very substantial debt that might be incurred by these students if they do post-graduate study at a professional school. For those who do go on to law school or business, journalism, architecture, social work, or other graduate programs, substantial additional debt may be incurred because state-based professional schools rarely offer substantial financial aid packages. The focus of the national discussion on the affordability of college is, however, on undergraduate education, and that is what I am considering here.

28. Source: http://www.newamerica.org/education-policy/familiarity-with-financial-aid/.

29. See Rachel Fishman, "2015 College Decisions Survey: Part II, Familiarity with Financial Aid," New America Foundation, http://www.luminafoundation.org/resources/the-college-application-process, 4. The online survey of sixteen- to forty-year-olds who did not have college degrees but were planning to enroll or were recently enrolled was conducted in the fall of 2014 and carried out by the Harris Poll. The sample size was roughly 1,000 and was weighted to match population parameters.

30. In fact, President Obama has proposed that all community college students receive federal financial aid that makes it possible for them to pay zero tuition. However, as of 2015, no federal legislation has been passed to support this proposal.

31. Aside from the Harvard and Princeton endowments in the fiscal year 2012, the others in the top ten include: Yale University ($19.3 billion), Stanford University ($17.03 billion), MIT ($10.1 billion), Columbia University ($7.7 billion), the University of Michigan ($7.6 billion), Texas A&M University ($7.0 billion), the University of Pennsylvania ($6.8 billion), and the University of Notre Dame ($6.4 billion). Interestingly, some of the most prestigious liberal arts colleges have endowments per student that exceed those of many of the major research universities. For example, Amherst College, which may have as many as 2,000 students, has an endowment of 1.6 billion; Williams College's endowment in 2012 is listed as $1.8 billion. Compare these figures with the first truly research university, Johns Hopkins, which has an endowment of $2.6 billion, most of which can be found attached to its medical school. Nonetheless, most private research-intensive universities, such as NYU and Boston University, continue to be extremely dependent on tuition and fees. Sources: en.wikipedia.org/wiki/List_of_colleges_and _universities_in_the_United_States_by_endowment, and www.usnews.com/education/best -colleges/the-short-list-college/articles/2013/10/01/universities-with-the-largest-financial -endowments-colleges-with-the-largest-financial-endowments. These figures can also be found in the the *Chronicle of Higher Education Annual Almanac*, which is published annually. While this may be available by subscription, the source for the annual almanac is http://chronicle.com

/section/Almanac-of-Higher-Education/801. It is a basic source of a wide variety of data on the state of higher education and comparative data among institutions.

32. This means that the average College Board scores (SAT or ACT scores) and high school GPAs for recruited athletes and some legacy children, as well as minority and economically disadvantaged applicants, do not need to be as high as the median of the overall class or applicant pool.

33. An elite liberal arts college, like Williams College, which also has a relatively large endowment, has an average student debt at graduation after four years of $8,369. Although Williams has a sticker price of over $55,000 a year, it is able through scholarships to reduce the average actual cost to $15,360 a year. Here I refer only to the private highly selective colleges at major research universities.

34. Source: https://college.harvard.edu/financial-aid/how-aid-works. The quotes are taken from the website, but not all are located on the page that you will find at this URL.

35. Source: http://www.ticas.org/about.vp.html.

36. The Institute for College Access & Success, *Student Debt and the Class of 2012*, December 2013, ticas.org.

37. The report omits figures of the "for-profit" colleges, since so few of them are willing to report their data. The accuracy of the data ought also to be kept in mind. It is unlikely that the reported numbers are based on very reliable samples of significant size for each college and we don't know what the selectivity bias may be in the reporting of debt by individuals at these colleges and universities. These data were gathered from several sources, but they were not audited or reviewed by any outside entity.

38. In fact, it is remarkable how many Americans object to the idea that if they pay the full-sticker price of tuition, or some limited amount less than that, that they are subsidizing the education of others who receive greater financial aid. This is true at both private and public institutions. There is, for one, no sense that even those who pay the full sticker price are not covering the total cost of their education and there is little sense that the composition of a person's cohort in college can influence a student's experience for the better. To say that among parents and students that there is little altruism or sense that it is just for those with greater means to pay more for the same "product" as those with lesser means would be an understatement. At most private and public universities financial aid dollars are taken from tuition revenues and spent on financial aid. This is often referred to as the "discount rate." The public needs to be educated about the advantages to everyone of having a diverse student body, which would include many students who cannot afford to pay the full price of tuition. See Douglas Belkin, "More Students Subsidize Classmates' Tuition," *Chronicle of Higher Education,* January 9, 2014.

39. When examining the debt of students who graduate from college at, say, age twenty-one or twenty-two, we ought to compare their situation with a comparable age cohort that did not go to college. The latter group is likely to have built up some credit card debt or automobile loan debt, among other forms of debt. If examined properly, we should ask: How much more debt do college graduates have than others of comparable age who did not attend college?

40. In Chapter 11 I suggest how the federal government can improve the graduation rate and the education of those at community colleges, although they are not the real focus of this book.

41. Bruce Watson, "Even in Countries Where Tuition Is Free, College Debt Can Be a Problem." *Daily Finance*, September 11, 2013, www.dailyfinance.com/on/student-loan-debt -countries-free-college-tuition/. I have not discussed the default rates on student loans, but it is not insignificant. As you would expect, the default rate is highest among those students who

come from the least well-off families and who often wind up with lower paying jobs after college. The default rate is particularly high among students who attend for-profit colleges, where the expectation is that most of the revenues (and profits) will be generated by students' receipt of government loans. Roughly 40 percent of the income at for-profit institutions is designated as profit and is taken in by the company that "owns" the school. This has become something of a national scandal since many of these students are told to apply for loans to cover their costs when those advising them know that the student's chance of repaying the loans is slight.

42. John Immerwahr and Jean Johnson with Amber Ott and Jonathan Rochkind, *Squeeze Play 2010: Continued Public Anxiety on Cost, Harsher Judgments on How Colleges Are Run*, a report by Public Agenda for the National Center for Public Policy and Higher Education, 2.

43. Ibid.

44. The pioneering research on the economic returns to education by Columbia professor Jacob Mincer in the 1960s began the discussion of how much earnings were affected by educational attainment. See Mincer, *Schooling, Experience, and Earnings* (National Bureau of Economic Research, 1974). Mincer argued that there was a significant effect and scholars have endeavored for the past forty years to expand on his work and obtain more precise estimates of the value of a college degree. With Chicago professor Gary Becker, Mincer's work led to the theory of "human capital." We will see that there are many different estimates of the value of higher education and the differences in that value based on the college one attended, the major that one pursued, and a host of other factors.

45. Commission on the Future of Higher Education appointed by Secretary of Education Margaret Spellings, *A Test of Leadership: Charting the Future of U.S. Higher Education* (Washington, DC: U.S. Department of Education, September 1, 2006).

46. The Spellings Commission cites as evidence data from the College Board and a paper by Jennifer C. Day and Eric C. Newburger, *The Big Payoff: Educational Attainment and Synthetic Estimates of Work-Life Earnings* (Washington, DC: U.S. Census Bureau, 2002).

47. Katie Zaback, Andy Carlson, and Matt Crellin, *The Economic Benefit of Postsecondary Degrees: A State and National Level Analysis*, a report produced by the State Higher Education Executive Officers and the National Center for Higher Education Management Systems, 2012.

48. Catherine Rampell, "The Return on College, Around the World," *New York Times*, June 28, 2013. Rampell described in the *Times* piece the results of a report by the Organization for Economic Cooperation and Development. The United States did not have the highest relative returns to educational attainment. Chile and Brazil, for example, had far higher returns to increased education than the United States.

49. Scott Carlson, "Is College Worth It? 2 New Reports Say Yes (Mostly)," *Chronicle of Higher Education*, November 4, 2013. A second study reported in this same article appeared in a paper, "The Economics of B.A. Ambivalence: The Case of California Higher Education," by Alan Benson, a professor at the University of Minnesota; Frank S. Levy, an emeritus professor at MIT; and Raimundo Esteva, a former research assistant at MIT. Source: http://www.russellsage.org/economics-ba-ambivalence-case-california-higher-education. They argue that college degrees have substantial value over high school diplomas but that past studies have neglected to consider that many students don't earn their B.A. degrees in four years, instead taking five or six years or longer. Obviously, if a student is in school longer it is apt to affect his or her lifetime earnings. When we examine how different subpopulations perceive the value of higher-education degrees, we find that minorities and other subgroups are actually more optimistic about their value. Fully 70 percent of Hispanic students, 55 percent of blacks,

61 percent of Asians, and 71 percent of nonwhites answered "yes" to a College Board survey question that asked: "Do you think young people today need a four-year college degree in order to be successful, or not?" Source: Ronald Brownstein, "Why Minorities Are More Optimistic About the Value of College," College Board/*National Journal* Poll of 1,232 adults, http://www .nationaljournal.com/next-america/education/why-minorities-are-more-optimistic-about-the -value-of-college-20131107. The margin of error was plus or minus 3.9 percent. Democrats were considerably more likely to respond "yes" to this question (64 percent) compared with Republicans (40 percent), and the responses to the question by different age groups was nonlinear: Those from thirty to sixty-four years of age were more positive about the importance of a college education than were either eighteen-to-twenty-nine-year-olds or those over age sixty-five.

50. Source: www.cfr.org/united-states/us-education-reform-national-security/p27618.

51. Claudia Goldin and Lawrence F. Katz, *The Race Between Education and Technology* (Cambridge, MA: Belknap Press of Harvard University Press, 2008). Of course, Goldin and Katz did not "discover" the role that technology plays in economic growth. That work was done earlier by a number of economists, notably MIT Professor Emeritus Robert Solow, whose work on this subject earned him a Nobel Prize in economics.

52. Caroline Hoxby, "The Return to Attending a More Selective College: 1960 to the Present," in *Forum Features: Exploring the Future of Higher Education*, ed. Maureen Devlin and Joel Meyerson (San Francisco: Jossey-Bass, 2001), 13–42.

53. Andrew Gillen, Jeff Selingo, and Mandy Zatynski, "Degrees of Value: Evaluating the Return on the College Investment," *American Institutes for Research*, May 9, 2013, www .educationsector.org/publications/degrees-value-evaluating-return-college-investment.

54. There are now quite a few books and commentaries on the problem of completion rates. For perhaps the most comprehensive and data-based look at the problem, see Bowen, Chingos, and McPherson, *Crossing the Finish Line*. Bowen has an uncanny ability to identify fundamental problems in higher education and to write books on them with extremely able collaborators. On completion rates, see also John L. Hennessy, "The Real Crisis in Higher Education," *Carnegie Reporter* (Winter 2014, special issue): 35–36.

55. Lindsay Ellis, "Many New Ph.D.'s Emerge Deeper in Debt Than in the Past, Survey Shows," *Chronicle of Higher Education*, December 6, 2013.

56. Audrey Williams June, "The Cost of a Ph.D.: Students Report Hefty Debt Across Many Fields," *Chronicle of Higher Education*, January 16, 2014.

57. Lindsay Ellis, "Many New Ph.D.'s Emerge Deeper in Debt Than in the Past, Survey Shows," *Chronicle of Higher Education*, December 6, 2013, http://chronicle.com/article/Deeper -Debt-Hits-Many/143461/?cid=at&utm_source=at&utm_medium=en.

58. Zero-based budgeting presents other problems for universities, almost all of which follow fund accounting practices. Suppose we have a long-standing endowment for a program and professors in a type of engineering that no longer exists with any degree of importance. The endowment is closely worded in such a way that not to offer courses in this area would lead to a loss of the endowment funds. Although university leaders never prefer this kind of tight-knit control written into endowment gifts, sometimes donors insist on very strong restrictions on fund use. In the case of the obsolete knowledge area, should the university simply eliminate the less-than-useful program and return the endowment, which is now one hundred years old and has appreciated greatly, or should the university continue to offer a program that has little current value? Of course, the university would try to get the heirs of the donors or the courts to loosen the terms of the endowment, but neither these endowments nor endowments received

for faculty professorships in minor areas of enquiry could be "zeroed out" without significant legal work.

59. Source: www.vpcomm.umich.edu/pa/key/understandingtuition.html. Correlatively, under the remarkable leadership of Chancellor Matthew Goldstein and perhaps some enlightened thinking among city and state legislators, the City University of New York has retained city and state support of about 42 percent of its operating budget as of 2013.

60. Eric Kelderman, "State Spending on Higher Education Rebounds in Most States After Years of Decline," *Chronicle of Higher Education,* January 21, 2013.

61. Sandra Baum et al., *Losing Ground: A National Status Report on the Affordability of American Higher Education* (San Jose, CA: The National Center for Public Policy and Higher Education, 2002), 5. A still-longer view shows that UCLA used to receive roughly 70 percent of its operating budget from California; in 2013, it received 12 percent.

62. Data from 2013 suggest that there has been some reversal in the level of state aid for higher education. Although the trend line has flattened and in some states has actually shown a positive slope, the increase in investments do not come close to making up for the cuts in state allocations to higher education over the past decade. There is also some evidence, as of 2014, that many colleges and universities are moderating their annual tuition increases.

63. Mark Keierleber, "U.S. Will Earn $66-Billion from Student Loans of 2007–2012," *Chronicle of Higher Education,* February 3, 2014. The U.S. Government Accountability Office made these estimates based on loans paid out from 2007 through 2012. The same office estimated that the United States will bring in $185 billion in profits on new student loans made in the next decade.

64. William J. Baumol and William G. Bowen first developed the concept of the "cost disease" in their classic 1966 study of the economics of the performing arts. See Baumol and Bowen, *Performing Arts.* See also Bowen, *Higher Education in the Digital Age,* and William J. Baumol, *The Cost Disease: Why Computers Get Cheaper and Health Care Doesn't* (New Haven, CT: Yale University Press, 2012). Many other economists and social scientists have written about the cost disease since its earliest publication.

65. Baumol, *The Cost Disease,* xx–xxi.

66. These quotes can be found in Baumol, *The Cost Disease,* xx–xxi.

67. Joseph E. Stiglitz, *The Price of Inequality: How Today's Divided Society Endangers Our Future* (New York: W. W. Norton, 2012), chap. 1, esp. 3–9.

68. Ibid., 8.

69. Robert B. Archibald and David H. Feldman, *The Anatomy of College Tuition* (Washington, DC: American Council on Education, 2013). These two economists are the coauthors of *Why Does College Cost So Much?,* cited above.

70. Ibid., 5.

71. Ibid., 7.

72. Jonathan R. Cole, *The Great American University: Its Rise to Preeminence, Its Indispensable National Role, and Why It Must Be Protected* (New York: PublicAffairs, 2009).

73. Ibid., 14.

Chapter 6: An Accessible, High-Quality Education for All

1. This group includes not only the economically most disadvantaged families but also those families who make good incomes but cannot afford to optimize their children's life chances because of the cost of tuition and other associated college fees and/or because they have several

children of college age simultaneously. So, for example, a family who has a couple of particularly gifted children—one in the sciences, the other in the arts—may have a combined income of more than $150,000 a year in 2015. If both are admitted to the most selective colleges, where the sticker price for each child is more than $60,000 after taxes (or $120,000 total), sending both of their children to such colleges simultaneously becomes unaffordable. Even after taking into account the financial aid that they might receive, given that their income is significantly above the national mean, the family may still have to pay $60,000 after taxes annually for their children's education.

2. Fareed Zakaria, *In Defense of a Liberal Education* (New York: W. W. Norton, 2015), 124.

3. Hunter Rawlings III, past president of the University of Iowa and Cornell University and current president of the Association of American Universities, spoke at Harvard's 2013 Institutional Conflicts of Interest conference about the humanities and the current pressure to produce MOOCs, stating that "the eventual possibility of a new source of revenue has sent universities scrambling to jump on the MOOC bandwagon, creating a tension between educational and economic imperatives."

4. This effort was led by Michael Crow, who was then the executive vice provost at Columbia and who brought his rare talents to the presidency of Arizona State University, where he has transformed a backwater, but good, university into a major research institution that not only has the highest number of undergraduate students in the nation (more than 70,000 as of 2014) but is also a dynamic and innovative center of higher learning.

5. Stuart Firestein, *Ignorance: How It Drives Science* (New York: Oxford University Press, 2012), 11.

6. Douglas Belkin, "Coursera Names Former Yale President as Its New CEO," *Wall Street Journal*, March 24, 2014. http://www.wsj.com/articles/SB10001424052702304679404579459681722504264.

7. For example, a University of Pennsylvania survey found that roughly 80 percent of those taking MOOCs already had earned a degree of some kind. The highly publicized experiment, which was spearheaded by Governor Jerry Brown of California, to provide online education for credit at San Jose State University has turned out to be a veritable disaster thus far.

8. Danya Perez-Hernandez, "Passive MOOC Students Don't Retain New Knowledge, Study Finds," *Chronicle of Higher Education*, May 1, 2014.

9. Sebastian Thrun, as quoted in Eric Westervelt, "The Online Education Revolution Drifts Off Course," NPR, December 31, 2013, http://www.npr.org/2013/12/31/258420151/the-online-education-revolution-drifts-off-course.

10. For a thoughtful discussion of the role of these new technologies and resistance to them by both research university leaders and current faculty members, see Zakaria, *In Defense of a Liberal Education*.

11. "250 MOOCs and Counting: One Man's Educational Journey," *Chronicle of Higher Education*, April 20, 2015.

12. A Scott Berg, *Wilson* (New York: G. P. Putnam's Sons, 2013), 67.

13. Charles Huckabee, "Princeton Mathematician to Receive the 2014 Abel Prize," *Chronicle of Higher Education*, March 28, 2014.

14. Sherry Turkle, *Alone Together: Why We Expect More from Technology and Less from Each Other* (New York: Basic Books, 2011).

15. Obtained during a personal interview with Brian Greene at Columbia University in 2015.

16. "Prof. Brian Green Launches Elegant Online Physics Course," *Columbia News*, February 26, 2014, http://news.columbia.edu/oncampus/3364.

17. Craig Lambert, "Twilight of the Lecture: The Trend Toward 'Active Learning' May Overthrow the Style of Teaching That Has Ruled Universities for 600 Years," *Harvard Magazine*, March–April 2012, http://harvardmagazine.com/2012/03/twilight-of-the-lecture.

18. Ibid.

19. Ibid.

20. Ibid.

21. Ibid.

22. Ibid.

23. This description of Eric Mazur's experiments with a new form of teaching follows closely the article about him and a few other Harvard faculty members that appeared in "Twilight of the Lecture," cited above.

24. Caroline M. Hoxby, "The Economics of Online Postsecondary Education: MOOCS, Nonselective Education, and Highly Selective Education," National Bureau of Economic Research, Working Paper 19816, January 2014, http://www.nber.org/papers/w19816. Hoxby, who admittedly is stylizing the two forms of postsecondary education that form the basis for her essay, uses the most reliable governmental and nongovernmental sources of data for her analysis.

25. Daniel F. Chambliss and Christopher G. Takacs, *How College Works* (Cambridge, MA: Harvard University Press, 2014), 3.

26. Source: http://about.minervaproject.com.

27. Firestein, *Ignorance*. Firestein argues that contrary to popular belief, working on science is, at least in part, exciting because the search for facts and truths leads to new questions without answers. Consequently, the end result is that the process creates a higher, rather than a lower, level of ignorance—even as we make profound and meaningful discoveries.

28. Quoted in Noson S. Yanofsky, *The Outer Limits of Reason: What Science, Mathematics, and Logic Cannot Tell Us* (Cambridge, MA: MIT Press, 2013), chap. 7, note 20.

29. George B. Kauffman, *Harry Gray's Solar Army*, http://fresnoalliance.com/wordpress/?p=4313.

30. Ibid.

31. Ibid.

32. Economic Modeling Specialists International, "Demonstrating the Collective Economic Value of North Carolina's Higher Education Institutions System," February 2015. A more inclusive analysis of the North Carolina system by EMSI, which included data on thirty-six independent colleges and universities and fifty-eight community colleges, found that in 2012–2013, these educational institutions "created $63.5 billion in additional income to the North Carolina economy." See the Executive Summary of the report.

33. Washington's governor, Jay Inslee, has proposed that taxes imposed on excessive energy use be used for education and transportation. Kirk Johnson, "Washington Governor Puts Focus on Climate Goals, and Less on Debate," *New York Times*, April 4, 2015.

Chapter 7: Creating New Academic Leagues and Knowledge Communities

1. Of the relatively few mergers that have taken place, a significant number have involved small religious schools or stand-alone professional schools merging with a larger university. For example, the California College of Medicine merged with the University of California, Irvine,

in 1940. Some universities have been renamed; private companies have bought others interested in starting for-profit colleges.

2. Of course, Cornell rightly prides itself on having always been coeducational—from 1865 on. So here I'm referring to the seven other Ivy League universities and the Seven Sisters schools. Columbia College was the last of the Ivy League schools to admit women, in 1983; Barnard College remained single sex and continued to have an affiliation agreement with Columbia.

3. A few institutions manage to combine high-quality athletic programs with exceptional academic quality. Stanford University is one such example. It often wins the national award for the best overall athletics program in the nation, while maintaining very high academic standards. Duke University is another school that is in this almost unique position—and within the Ivy League, Princeton does unusually well in competing on the national level in low-profile sports.

4. The idea of invisible colleges dates back at least to science in seventeenth-century England and the formation and development of the Royal Society. Robert Boyle refers to "invisible colleges" in the 1640s before the Royal Society of London was formed. There is a good deal of literature on these invisible colleges that was published as the sociology of science began to take off as a research specialty in the 1960s and 1970s. The most notable of these works was by Diana Crane, *Invisible Colleges: Diffusion of Knowledge in Scientific Communities* (Chicago: University of Chicago Press, 1972), which built on the particularly innovative and imaginative work of Professor of the History of Science Derek J. de Solla Price on citation networks.

5. There also are soft cooperative alliances in the Midwest among the Big 10 universities (and the University of Chicago also participates in some of these alliances) as well as in the University of California system.

6. Graduates of these universities who are in the workforce could also enlist in the leagues' programs and take courses online.

7. In their studies of how people make choices, Daniel Kahneman and Amos Tversky developed the concept of "status quo bias." Their influential work (after Tversky's death, Kahneman won the Nobel Prize in economics for this work) related to assumptions in the neoclassical model in economics. Their research has been extended by dozens of social scientists, and the field of behavioral economics was spawned by their work. For others working with this concept, see the work of Professor Richard Thaler of the University of Chicago.

8. Formal agreements would be drawn up, of course, that would specify the nature of the relationship and the conditions under which students could receive credit for courses taken at a university other than their own. But there would be no legal merger of educational corporations. There would also have to be balance-of-trade agreements that involve sharing some form of exchange, whether it be of monetary or some other form of exchange. The mechanisms for this can be worked out without a great deal of difficulty, as I did when I built relationships between Columbia and the various museums in New York, and with the Juilliard School, which we called "The Passport to New York Program."

9. This type of technology is already available and used by businesses. I've participated in an international exchange at a company located near Silicon Valley in which the broadcasted image was near movie quality and the sound allowed participants to feel almost as if they were sitting in the same room—which was, in fact, configured exactly the same.

10. Moreover, the U.S. federal government funded a substantial amount of the research time at CERN of these physicists through research grants or contracts. Similarly, other nations provided support for physicists working at CERN.

11. Nanoscientists are increasingly working with biological matter like DNA as potential storage material for information. The work started out looking at Buckminsterfullerenes, or buckyballs, which were named after Buckminster Fuller and discovered first by scientists at Rice University in 1985.

12. The San Francisco Exploratorium is, in its own words, "a twenty-first-century learning laboratory, an eye-opening, always changing, playful place to explore and tinker. For more than forty years, we've built creative, thought-provoking exhibits, tools, programs, and experiences that ignite curiosity, encourage exploration, and lead to profound learning." Source: www.exploratorium.edu. What they say is true.

13. Obviously, perhaps, a majority of research universities are not located in major cities. They were conceived of as being on the periphery or outside of the city. But for those in or near cultural centers, opportunities to form knowledge communities (even with institutions not located nearby) are vast.

14. The construction of the curriculum within each league might involve committee members representing the various participants in the league.

15. Globalization through the creation of international knowledge communities does not have to take place only in other nations. The University of California, Berkeley, is planning "The Berkeley Global Campus at Richmond Bay," which is only five miles north of the main campus. Berkeley leaders are in the process of recruiting international and local partners—including universities, businesses, and government agencies—that will join forces in designing "an integrated and genuinely global network of activities, programs and enterprises. The goal of this new campus," say its creators, is "to provide our students, faculty, and staff with an unparalleled global experience and education, as well as to generate and to sponsor global research and entrepreneurship that will benefit both our campus and the entire region of northern California." Source: www.bgc.berkeley.edu.

16. For a discussion of "collective intelligence," see the website at the MIT Center for Collective Intelligence, http://cci.mit.edu. The central question addressed by the MIT Center is: "How can people and computers be connected so that—collectively—they act more intelligently than any person, group, or computer has ever done before?" See also Scott E. Page, *The Difference: How the Power of Diversity Creates Better Groups, Firms, Schools, and Societies* (Princeton, NJ: Princeton University Press, 2007).

17. See Chapter 6 for a full discussion of massive open online courses and other forms of new digital technologies.

Chapter 8: Reimagining the University Campus

1. During the spring 2012 academic year I taught an advanced studio at Columbia's School of Architecture with two extraordinary architects, Professor Laurie Hawkinson and Christian Uhl. The title of the studio was "A New University?" I want to thank Laurie and Christian, as well as a talented group of a dozen students who discussed new ideas for the physicality of the twenty-first century university and who made models of possible new types of structures for it. During the fall 2013 semester I was able to join Professor Hawkinson again in overseeing an advanced studio and, along with Professor Reinhold Martin, to hold a weekly seminar on the idea of a new university with a set of excellent students, which included advanced Columbia architectural students and a number of Ph.D. students in architecture, the social sciences, education, and journalism. My colleagues and the students engaged in lengthy and, for me,

fruitful discussions about the nature of universities and how their physical structures might change. We were also fortunate to have visitors to the seminar, including Professors Bonnie Bassler of Princeton, and Akeel Bilgrami, Andrew Delbanco, and Brian Greene from Columbia.

2. Probably the most extensive discussion of properties of the American college and university campus can be found in Paul Venable Turner, *Campus: An American Planning Tradition*, Architectural History Foundation/MIT Press Series 7 (New York: Architectural History Foundation, 1984). For the post–World War II period from the 1950s to 1970s, which included enormous expansion of the universities in both the United States, Britain, and European countries, a leading source on the idea of a campus that I have found very useful is Stefan Muthesius, *The Postwar University: Utopianist Campus and College* (New Haven, CT: Yale University Press, 2000). A provocative essay is Anthony Vidler, "The Third Typology," in Robert L. Delevoy et al., eds., *Rational Architecture: The Reconstruction of the European City* (Bruxelles: Éditions des Archives d'Architecture Modern, 1978). Also of general interest is Jürgen Habermas, "The Idea of the University: Learning Processes," trans. John R. Blazek, *New German Critique* 41 (Spring/Summer 1987): 2–22, and Thomas A. Gaines, *The Campus as a Work of Art* (New York: Praeger, 1991). A modest number of other books or doctoral dissertations on this topic exist. See, for example, M. Perry Chapman, *American Places: In Search of the Twenty-First Century Campus* (New York: Praeger, 2006); Reinhold Martin, *Utopia's Ghost: Architecture and Postmodernism, Again* (Minneapolis: University of Minnesota Press, 2010). However, individual architects who have designed buildings on a variety of campuses have produced the vast majority of discussions of the campus, at least in the United States. These publications display the architects' work but do not discuss general trends or principles of campus design or its history. See, for example, Robert A. M. Stern, *On Campus* (New York: The Monacelli Press, 2000). See also William J. Mitchell, *Imagining MIT: Designing a Campus for the Twenty-First Century* (with an afterword by Charles M. Vest) (Cambridge, MA: MIT Press, 2007). More limited studies of the campuses of the University of Chicago, Columbia, the University of California, Berkeley, the University of Pennsylvania, the University of Virginia, Harvard University, Princeton University, and Stanford University have been published. As limited as the literature is on the American campus, there are far more discussions of campuses at private than at public universities. In the first decade of the twenty-first century, Arizona State University has published a great deal of interesting material on how its physical space is linked to its academic ambitions. Other useful works that focus on the development of single campuses include Barry Bergdoll, *Mastering McKim's Plan: Columbia's First Century on Morningside Heights* (New York: Miriam and Ira D. Wallach Art Gallery, Columbia University, 1997) and Andrew S. Dolkart, *Morningside Heights: A History of Its Architecture & Development* (New York: Columbia University Press, 1998).

3. The hands and minds of great architects surely have expressed their ideas about campus buildings and the university as a place. Some of the world's best architects and some notable architectural movements are well represented in the history of campus buildings in the United States, Europe, and Asia, and they have designed either campuses or individual buildings for major research universities. It is, in fact, an all-star cast of individuals whose firms have worked on academic buildings. These structures have generated substantial debate because they represent architectural typologies and major architectural movements. A few names in that all-star twentieth-century cast will suffice: Le Corbusier, Eero Saarinen, Walter Gropius (who held the influential position of dean of Harvard's Graduate School of Design), Ludwig Mies van der Rohe, Walter Netsch (probably best known for being the principal architect of the U.S. Air Force

Academy), and other modernist architects, along with Louis Kahn, Robert Venturi, and many of today's leading architects, including Frank Gehry, Rem Koolhaas, Renzo Piano, Zaha Hadid, and Steven Holl. Each has his or her signature on campus buildings. But these architects, for the most part, designed individual buildings (many of which are extraordinarily successful), but they were not asked to rethink a campus from scratch—a modern campus for the twentieth or twenty-first century.

4. Here I follow the work of Turner's book, *Campus*. Many universities have chosen over decades to build new structures that are architecturally consistent with the original design. To some extent that has been true with the University of Virginia campus. Others have tried to harmonize new architectural ideas and theories with the old motifs of the original designs. Still others have chosen at a certain point to make a radical shift from an earlier style, such as the Beaux-Arts architecture of the late nineteenth and early twentieth century, toward far more modern structures. And still others seem totally eclectic without any overarching architectural theme, building new structures that are useful for the current needs in growing knowledge and are designed by exceptional architects.

5. Space becomes a critical commodity in the competition among universities to provide adequate facilities for both research and student learning and housing. As Reinhold Martin, professor of architecture and architectural history at Columbia, suggests in his course "The American University: Architecture and Enlightenment 1750–1959," the earlier development of the university campus is linked to "a discursive field in which knowledge interacts with technology, religion, capital, and the state." Moreover, there was little concern with providing space for public discourse and public participation in the activities of the university. See Reinhold Martin, *The Organizational Complex: Architecture, Media, and Corporate Space* (Cambridge, MA: MIT Press, 2003). In analyzing Saarinen's work on the IBM campus, Martin notes: "For Saarinen this organicity had been provided earlier by the recognizable totality called the university, with its neo-Gothic surfaces and interlinked quadrangles. But as that institution dissolved into the matrices of the military-industrial-academic complex, it had to be submitted to a visual and organizational regime capable of integrating Vannevar Bush's 'endless frontier' of science—the new landscape—into another species of unified totality. This was the mission, indeed the obsession of the organizational complex to which Saarinen was beholden" (p. 206).

6. Of the leading ten or fifteen universities in the United States, Columbia has fewer acres of land than any other—and not by a small margin. It also resides in a city where space is dear and extremely expensive to build on. Leaders at Columbia gave thought to building somewhat more vertical structures, and one representation of that was in the 1960s campus plan produced by I. M Pei. Pei sketched a set of Columbia buildings that would have built two large towers at the center of the campus and expanded the library by creating underground stacks beneath South Field, which is also at the center of the Columbia campus and which had been used in the early part of the twentieth century as a baseball diamond on which the great Lou Gehrig used to skyrocket baseballs into adjacent buildings. Needless to say, the Pei design went nowhere and in fact would have disrupted significantly the original McKim design for the campus.

7. There are precedents for somewhat similar efforts in Chicago around the rebuilding of the loop district, with an emphasis on building colleges for commuting students. The great difference here is that we would be constructing a plan for the great research university of the twenty-first century, not a design for moving students and traffic in and out of the center of a city for undergraduate educational purposes. For a discussion of this effort at urban redesign

that involved an urban college campus, see Sharon Haar, *The City as Campus: Urbanism and Higher Education in Chicago* (Minneapolis: University of Minnesota Press, 2011). Haar's central message is: "I am arguing that the urban campus, far from being a subtype of campuses in general, has developed into a unique spatial type, one that integrates the need to produce new environments for the creation of scholarship, research, and expertise on emerging urban space and on social, cultural, and economic practices, on the one hand, and the need to produce new forms for the encounter of pedagogy, research, and the city, on the other" (p. xxx). For a very different type of discussion from that of the urban environment in which universities are built, see Rem Koolhaas, *Delirious New York: A Retrospective Manifesto for Manhattan* (New York: The Monacelli Press, 1994), especially 81–151 on the skyscraper. The paucity of space for campus expansion in urban centers is not unique, of course, to the United States. Evidence that limited space has become a critical problem for efforts to create world-class universities in 2013 can be found in the densely populated city of Hong Kong. This translates into a reimagining of the campus into a combination of far more strong vertical structures along with more limited numbers of low horizontal buildings. On tall buildings never built, see Charles Linn, stories by James Murdock, "Tall Tales: The Story of a Few Classic Skyscrapers That Were Never Built Tells Us Much About What Motivates Architects, and Their Clients, Too," *Architectural Record: Innovation*, http://archrecord.construction.com/innovation/2_features/0411history.asp. Among the architects discussed briefly in this essay are: Ludwig Mies van der Rohe (1921), Adolf Loos and Eliel Saarinen (1922), I. M. Pei (1956), Frank Lloyd Wright (1956), Paul Rudolf (1989), Paolo Soleri (1996), Adrian D. Smith and William F. Baker Skidmore (1998), Frank O. Gehry (2000), and Ken Yeang (2000).

8. Take as an example Low Memorial Library, the first building constructed on the "new" Morningside Heights campus in the last years of the nineteenth century. It was the original library that looked south over much of Manhattan from the then sparsely populated area of the Columbia campus. It has a neoclassical form and is extremely impressive as it rests upon a height reached by walking up scores of terraced steps. But Low Library became obsolete within three decades as a library. The new Butler Library was built, and students moved the books from Low to Butler on a conveyer belt that sloped down to the new monumental building that would house much of the Columbia collection for another fifty years. But what was Low to be used for after it was obsolete as a library? It basically was an inflexible structure. It was now a national landmark, but of little value as an academic building. The inevitable happened. It became the university's main administrative building housing the offices of the president and provost and other central administrative offices. It became a symbol of administrative power and aloofness during the raucous 1960s student campus protests—and correctly so.

9. These quotes are taken from the website under Bio-X Stanford University, biox.stanford.edu/about/index.html.

10. Source: http://newsoffice.mit.edu/2006/media-lab-building.

11. Recall that Francis Crick was one of the scientists who shared the Nobel Prize in Medicine and Biological Sciences with James Watson for their work on the structure of the DNA molecule.

12. Paul Nurse, Richard Treisman, and Jim Smith, "Building Better Institutions" (editorial), *Science* 341, July 5, 2013.

13. Source: http://news.columbia.edu/mbbi. This is the online edition of Columbia University in the City of New York, *On Campus: News From Across the University*, June 23, 2011.

14. Ibid.

15. Ibid.

16. For an exceptionally informative and original discussion of these laboratories and what they represent, see Reinhold Martin, *The Organizational Complex: Architecture, Media, and Corporate Space* (Cambridge, MA: MIT Press, 2003), chap. 6. Other works that discuss campus laboratories include Bruno Latour and Steve Woolgar, *Laboratory Life: The Construction of Scientific Facts* (Princeton, NJ: Princeton University Press, 1986). See in particular chap. 2, "An Anthropologist Visits the Laboratory," which focuses on discovery at the Salk Institute Laboratories, designed by Louis Kahn. This is a highly controversial work, and while I believe it has many problems in its analysis, it is worth reading. See also Reinhold Martin, *Utopia's Ghost: Architecture and Postmodernism* (Minneapolis: University of Minnesota Press, 2010). See particularly Martin's discussion of the "postmodern" laboratory in chap. 4.

17. There have been multiple efforts by world-class architects to design huge skyscraper buildings, although none that I'm aware of with the purposes of a university in mind. For example, Frank Lloyd Wright designed a mile-high building with a gross area of about 18.5 million square feet, referred to as Mile High Illinois, Illinois Sky-City, or just The Illinois. He describes the building and, of course, offers renderings of it in his book *A Testament* (New York: Horizon Press, 1957). Many other architects have designed extremely tall buildings, even if not quite the size envisioned by Wright. Some have been built around the world in highly populated cities; others have remained in the architect's archives.

18. In the past, studies suggested that people will walk long distances down corridors but won't negotiate one flight of stairs to see a friend or colleague. But there are many ways to change that pattern of behavior, including the use of escalators and incentives to walking a flight of stairs in order to reach a place for coffee or food. Even if this were correct in the typical office building, the challenge is to build physical structures that can be quite tall and yet promote a sense of community. Also, studies from more than fifty years ago, which still have great credibility, such as the housing study by Leon Festinger, Stanley Schacter, and Kurt Back, *Social Pressures in Informal Groups* (New York: Harper & Bros., 1950), show how architectural forms can foster or inhibit social interaction. Propinquity was a major factor in creating interaction within communities. Those housing projects that were shaped like a "u" were far more likely to foster interaction among neighbors than row housing did.

19. Mark Rehner, "Talking with Rem Koolhaas, the Architect Behind the Central Library," *Seattle Times*, September 9, 2008.

20. The physical space of universities should become "communities of education." Increasing opportunities for robust communication between the public and the university needs to be strategically planned so that what the German sociologist and philosopher Jürgen Habermas calls "the public sphere" can be expanded.

21. The Canadian professor of comparative literature Bill Readings, who died before finishing his book, discusses in a somewhat different way the concept of ruins in *The University in Ruins* (Cambridge, MA: Harvard University Press, 1996). Readings juxtaposed the old idea of the university as "the university of culture," which was largely dedicated to the internalization of values and norms from the nation-state, with the newer form of campus—"the university of excellence"—which places a premium on excellence. Readings saw us as being in a period where nation-states lost their hold on academic life; and the purpose of universities, now much more deeply embedded in the military, industrial, and bureaucratic life of the world, placed a sharp

premium on "excellence." Readings's concern with this transformation is the focal point of the book, but for him, the older idea of the university is essentially in "ruins" with all of the multiple meanings of the word.

22. This is based on a conversation I had with Professor Jessell about the new Mind Brain Behavior Initiative and the organization and structure of the building. Conversations with other biologists, such as Professor Bonnie Bassler of Princeton, whom I interviewed in 2015, also suggest that there is an immediacy of interaction between a lead scientist who runs a fairly large laboratory and the postdoctoral fellows, graduate students, and others who work in their labs. Whether that immediacy can be recreated online remains an open question.

23. Thomas Bender, "Scholarship, Local Life, and the Necessity of Worldliness," in Herman van der Wusten, ed., *The Urban University and Its Identity* (Dordrecht, Netherlands: Kluwer Academic Publishers, 1998), 17–28. Bender obtained the quote from a 1978 interview with Lederberg that was published in *The New Yorker* magazine's "Talk of the Town." As Bender points out in his exceptionally provocative essay, Lederberg was hardly the first to think of the city as university. Bender cites Goethe describing similar possibilities in looking at Paris in 1827. On issues of urbanism and campus architecture, see also Thomas Bender, ed., *The University and the City: From Medieval Origins to the Present* (New York: Oxford University Press, 1991), and David C. Perry and Wim Weibel, eds., *The University as Urban Developer: Case Studies and Analysis* (Cambridge, MA: Lincoln Institute of Land Policy, 2005).

24. This program had the effect of increasing the resources in New York City that were available to our students (and later to our faculty, as well as to the staff members of the other cultural organizations that were our partners) and increased enormously Columbia's "virtual endowment." No other university in the United States, after all, could match the combined art collections of the Metropolitan Museum of Art, the Museum of Modern Art, the Guggenheim Museum, the New York Public Library, among other resources. Our link to the Juilliard School enhanced the possibilities of exceptional students to continue their musical development while taking a rich arts and sciences course of study, and correlatively, the possibilities of Juilliard students to benefit from taking Columbia courses. For our faculty, the library resources of New York, when combined, matched any in the nation, if not the world. These types of programs produced great quality for Columbia because we could recruit faculty that otherwise might not have been attracted to the university.

25. Bender, "Scholarship," 19.

26. Ibid.

27. Gaines, *The Campus as a Work of Art*, 50.

28. Here I follow the work by Haar, *The City as Campus*, and discussions of these campuses in our 2013 architectural seminar at Columbia. I use the name University of Illinois Chicago Circle (UICC) throughout this discussion. That was its name during the period of architectural development of which I'm writing here. After that new downtown campus opened in 1965, it eventually was consolidated with the Medical Center, and in 1982 the name was changed to University of Illinois at Chicago (UIC). In the year 2000, the university developed its South Campus, which included increased residential space and research facilities.

29. Haar, *The City as Campus*, 110.

30. Ibid., 113.

31. Haar notes: "Of the four towers Netsch and his team originally proposed, three remain in the final design despite the university's request that there be none.... The tallest, University Hall, contains the offices for the College of Liberal Arts and Sciences, the offices of the hu-

manities faculty, and the offices and functions of the upper administration. This twenty-eight story building locates the campus within the skyline of the city." Haar, *The City as Campus*, 116.

32. We also must remember that just as universities are dynamic organisms, so are cities. Take New York's Harlem. In the 1960s it was a predominantly black and Hispanic neighborhood with a rich history but a rather impoverished present. That part of Harlem borders on the new Columbia Manhattanville campus. But Harlem is rapidly changing into a dynamic and far more integrated community in 2016 than might have been imagined in 1970. It is undergoing rapid gentrification. This raises the question: What city and neighborhood populations are you designing the "new" campus to serve? The nature of the neighborhood bordering on the new Columbia campus will be vastly different in demographic composition, racial and ethnic configuration, and socioeconomic level in 2025 than it was when the expansion of the Columbia campus was conceived of.

33. This echoes the position taken in the recent report by the National Academy of Sciences, *Research Universities and the Future of America: Ten Breakthrough Actions Vital to Our Nation's Prosperity and Security* (Washington, DC: National Research Council of the National Academies, National Academies Press, 2012). See especially recommendation 6.

34. A good example of the planning for interaction between research universities and industry can be found in the Research Triangle Park in Durham, North Carolina. One of the largest research parks with ties to industry, its existence is based on its proximity to Duke University and the University of North Carolina, Chapel Hill, as well as several of the other larger universities in the state. The park describes itself thus: "We are dreamers, believers, planners and creators.... We imagine what the world could be and then roll up our sleeves and make it so." Source: http://www.rtp.org/. The park covers some 7,000 acres. Created in 1959, its creators included state and local governments, local businesses, and nearby universities. Source: https://en.wikipedia.org/wiki/Research_Triangle_Park. Now more than a half-century old, it is beginning to rethink its campus design and how a redesign can allow it to improve its productivity.

Chapter 9: The Central Dogma of a Great University

1. Jonathan R. Cole, *The Great American University: Its Rise to Preeminence, Its Indispensable National Role, and Why It Must Be Protected* (New York: PublicAffairs, 2009), chap. 11.

2. The Lochner age takes its name from the Supreme Court case *Lochner v. New York*, 198 U.S. 45 (1905). The court gave employers a great deal of latitude to hire and fire employees at will. It symbolized the age of contracts. Academic institutions acted like other institutions during this period. Presidents and trustees felt that they could unilaterally fire professors for their political and social views—and they did precisely that. Faculty members had little, if any, power to protect themselves from the arbitrary opinions of the administration and trustees.

3. I have challenged others to offer even an "existence proof" of a great university that does not internalize fully the value of freedom of inquiry and academic freedom. I've yet to hear of a convincing example.

4. Richard Rorty, "Does Academic Freedom Have Philosophical Presuppositions?," in *The Future of Academic Freedom*, ed. Louis Menand (Chicago: University of Chicago Press, 1999), 35.

5. Louis Menand, "The Limits of Academic Freedom," in Menand, *The Future of Academic Freedom*, 4.

6. There are several levels on which "trust" may be studied. Most often, as in this definition, we use it as it is commonly found in the vernacular, as in whether or not "the public trusts

the government." But psychologists, sociologists, and political scientists have worked on the concept in more formal terms: attempting to theorize the concept of trust. Russell Hardin, the political scientist, notes: "In general, trust depends on two quite different dimensions: the motivation of the potentially trusted person to attend to the truster's interests and his or her competence to do so." See Russell Hardin, "Distrust: Manifestations and Management," in *Distrust*, ed. Russell Hardin (New York: Russell Sage Foundation, 2004). Of course, social scientists have studied trust and distrust on the level of individuals and at the organizational and societal level. When I use the idea of a breakdown in trust, I am assuming that at the institutional level the government has begun to question both the interests and the competence of universities to fulfill their part of the compact that was established by the two parties after World War II.

7. Jon Elster, *Explaining Social Behavior*, rev. ed. (Cambridge: Cambridge University Press, 2015), 373. Emphasis in original.

8. Diego Gambetta, ed., *Trust: Making and Breaking Cooperative Relations* (Cambridge: Basil Blackwell, 1988), 4.

9. Trust is increasingly a topic of study among sociologists, particularly those who focus on organizations. We know what can lead to a decline in trust, and we have a good deal of game theory that is related to the concept of trust; but there is still a limited amount of research on how to rebuild trust once it has eroded. For a good introduction to the subject of trust, see the brilliant work of Professor Diego Gambetta and the multiple books in a series of volumes published by the Russell Sage Foundation. See, as examples, Roderick M. Kramer and Karen S. Cook, eds., *Trust and Distrust in Organizations: Dilemmas and Approaches* (New York: Russell Sage Foundation, 2004); Hardin, *Distrust*, footnote 6; and the other volumes in the series, entitled Russell Sage Foundation Series on Trust. There are at least eight volumes in the series.

10. Here I follow the work of Robert K. Merton on the norms of science and my own discussion of core values in *The Great American University*.

11. Stephen Cole and Jonathan R. Cole, "Scientific Output and Recognition: A Study in the Operation of the Reward System in Science," *American Sociological Review* 32, no. 3 (1967): 391–403. In that paper we established that "perfectionist" physicists (those with a high density of published quality papers) were more often highly rewarded than scientists who were "mass producers."

12. This statement may fly in the face of some empirical findings, including a number by me, that showed that married women with children actually were more scientifically productive than unmarried women or those who were married without children. But these studies did not follow the set of events and their consequences for women and men of obligations during the early childhood years, which tend to be the time when scholars and scientists establish the credentials used for promotion and tenure decisions. See, for example, Jonathan R. Cole, *Fair Science: Women in the Scientific Community* (New York: Free Press, 1979); Harriet Zuckerman, John Bruer, and Jonathan R. Cole, eds., *The Outer Circle: Women in the Scientific Community* (New York: W. W. Norton & Sons, 1991), chap. 6. For a typology that examines the relationship between quality and quantity of scientific output as it influences rewards, see Jonathan R. Cole and Stephen Cole, *Social Stratification in Science* (Chicago: University of Chicago Press, 1973); or Cole and Cole, "Scientific Output and Recognition." Paid leaves may not go far enough, since they neglect the multiple obligations of parents during the early childhood years. The scholars and scientists who are given extra time before their work is evaluated should, more often than not, be "perfectionists" (with a high density of quality in their published work) rather than "mass producers" (who may produce exceptional work, some of which is lost in the sheer size of their

output because they believe, incorrectly, that scholars will perish if they don't publish—even if much of what they publish is substandard, thus diluting the overall quality of the corpus of work). Many research universities have policies in place that allow the "tenure clock" to stop for a period of time for parents to care for young children. That should be extended to all research universities.

13. Some disciplines, like astronomy, have strict rules about the amount of time an investigator can have proprietary rights to the data that she or he has collected. Then those data must be placed in the public domain for other scholars to work with and to review in detail. This practice ought to be extended to any discipline where it is possible to archive collected data.

14. In the early part of the twentieth century, when the University of Wisconsin was producing new discoveries, faculty members would conspicuously reject the financial rewards from their discoveries that were being given to other universities, like the Rockefeller Institute (now University). This is well documented. See Cole, *The Great American University*, for examples.

15. In the case of developing courses, such as those that are being built for edX, Coursera, and other online platforms, universities are taking different approaches toward compensating the faculty who produce these courses. In all cases that I'm currently familiar with, the courses are owned by the university. However, there are significant differences in how great teachers are being rewarded for these efforts. This is apt to become a more contentious issue as the economic returns for enrollments in these courses increase.

16. For a discussion of the status quo bias, see Daniel Kahneman, *Thinking, Fast and Slow* (New York: Farrar, Straus and Giroux, 2013), and Richard H. Thaler, *The Winner's Curse: Paradoxes and Anomalies of Economic Life* (Princeton, NJ: Princeton University Press, 1994).

17. Of course, the most clever academic administrators have a plan for change and then work with the faculty in such a way that faculty members consider and support, as their own idea, the plan that lies latent in the mind of these academic leaders. But these institutions cannot be run by sheer power. Moreover, although I believe that American universities are better off than many in Europe, for example, by selecting presidents through a process involving several constituencies within the university rather than through a faculty vote (which tends to politicize the process of selection), the downside of this selection process is that it is left in the hands too often of trustees of good will who don't fully understand the needs of the university and how it ought to be shaped in the future.

18. For at least one definition of blue-sky thinking, see, among many other dictionary entries: http://dictionary.reference.com/browse/blue-sky+thinking. For examples of this kind of thinking, examine Defense Advanced Research Projects Agency (DARPA) projects, where a government agency encourages research on things that seem almost impossible today to contemplate, but much of which has become reality through research. Although DARPA is an arm of the Department of Defense, many of its projects have nondefense, practical applications—if they are realized. It is an agency willing to take big risks on big ideas. For examples of DARPA projects past and present, see http://www.darpa.mil/. For some examples of the most "blue sky" projects, see http://www.wearethemighty.com/weird-darpa-projects-2015-04.

19. In 2014, Robert Zimmer, president of the University of Chicago, asked a small group of faculty members led by Geoffrey Stone, the Harry Kalven Jr. Professor of Law, to develop a statement on the place of free expression at the university. Perhaps it's ironic that the Harry Kalven Jr. Professor of Law produces such a document and that it has some of the same characteristics as the Kalven Committee Report (1967). It is equally brief and to the point, builds on the traditions of free expression at Chicago, and articulates the exceptional value that must

be placed on free expression for the university to meet its goals. It is likely to take its place alongside the Kalven Committee Report as an exemplar of a well-articulated statement of centrality and limits on free expression on university campuses. Interestingly, after the document was approved and made public, Princeton University adopted the policy almost word for word.

20. David Weigel, "The Republican War on Science: They're Winning It," *Slate*, April 30, 2013, http://www.slate.com/articles/news_and_politics/politics/2013/04/national_science _foundation_and_tom_coburn_the_republican_effort_to_cut.html; see also American Psychological Association, Psychological Science Agenda, "Coburn Amendment Restricts NSF Political Science Funding," April 2013, http://www.apa.org/science/about/psa/2013/04/political -science-funding.aspx.

21. U.S. Senate, Committee on the Budget, "Sessions Questions National Endowment for the Humanities over Dubious Expenditures," April 10, 2014, http://www.budget.senate.gov /republican/public/index.cfm/2014/4/sessions-questions-national-endowment-for-the -humanities-over-dubious-expenditures.

22. U.S. Senate, Committee on the Budget, "Sessions Investigates Grant Process, Questionable Use of Funds at National Humanities Endowment," October 23, 2013, http://www.budget .senate.gov/republican/public/index.cfm/active-investigations?ID=4a47b3d2-fa98-43ca-8a56 -37840ff62584.

23. Julie Bosman, "2016 Ambitions Seen in Walker's Push for University Cuts in Wisconsin," *New York Times*, February 16, 2014.

24. In fact, Cooper Union's president, Jamshed Bharucha, and five trustees resigned in June 2015, pushed out by a board of trustees that seemed to be looking for a sacrificial lamb. Bharucha had a distinguished career as an administrator and scholar before coming to Cooper Union. See Mike Vilensky, "Cooper Union President Resigns," *Wall Street Journal*, June 10, 2015.

25. Scores of news articles have appeared about the Salaita case. He is now suing the University of Illinois. One can find multiple articles about the case with a simple Google search of the Internet.

26. Scholars at Risk (SAR) publishes a monthly report called "Scholars at Risk Freedom Media Review," from which I have taken a number of these examples. There are hundreds reported by SAR. For full disclosure, I am a member of the board of SAR. It is extremely difficult to sanction these other nations for their behavior toward university scholars, but SAR does try to cast a light on what is happening and raises funds to help scholars find positions or fellowships to shield them from the oppression that they find in their home countries. SAR is largely supported by universities around the world and by private donations.

27. See Edward Wong, "China Sentences Uighur Scholar to Life," *New York Times*, September 23, 2014, for the quotations on Professor Tohti. Two stories should suffice to capture that larger canvas on which academics work within China today. The first is of a forty-four-year-old professor of economics at the Central Minzu University of Bejing, Ilham Tohti, perhaps the most visible symbol of "peaceful resistance by ethnic Uyghurs [a Turkic ethnic group living in eastern and central China] to Chinese policies" toward this ethnic minority. On or around January 15, 2014, the police raided Professor Tohti's home and confiscated his computers, phones, and passport, as well as his students' essays. He was arrested and reportedly held incommunicado until late June. He was denied access to his family. He was not only fired from his academic position but, even more strikingly, after his two-day trial on charges of organizing and leading a separatist group, was sentenced to life imprisonment. Some critics of the sen-

tence pointed comparatively to the sentence meted out to Liu Xiaobo, a Chinese scholar and the winner of the 2010 Nobel Peace Prize, who was charged with "inciting subversion of state power" and agitated for an end to a single-party rule. He is currently serving an eleven-year prison sentence for subversion. Source: https://en.wikipedia.org/wiki/Liu_Xiaobo; see also http://www.amnestyusa.org/our-work/cases/china-liu-xiaobo.The case of Professor Xia Ye-liang, an economist and advocate for free markets, is of equal interest. Peking University de-cided in October 2013 to fire Professor Xia for his political views. Apparently, Professor Xia's troubles with state and university authorities began when he signed a petition in 2008 urging democratic change. The primary author of that petition, known in academic circles as Charter 08, is the Nobel laureate Liu Xiaobo. In September 2013 Xia Yeliang received a letter from the administration of Peking University informing him that he would face a faculty vote on the future of his appointment at the university. Such votes are apparently quite uncommon at that institution. Professor Xia had just returned from spending a summer as a visiting scholar at Stanford. The letter did not state any formal charges against the economics professor, but he was well known for his liberal political views and for his criticism of the Chinese government. Eventually, after the faculty "voted" to fire Professor Xia, Peking University school officials said, "Xia Yeliang's teaching evaluation scores were for many years in a row the lowest in the entire university." Mr. Xia responded that his evaluation scores were stronger, and in that case the school's dismissal process was a sham based on "no written rule." Source: David Feith, "Xia Ye-liang: The China Americans Don't See: A Peking University Economics Professor Who Was Sacked for His Political Views Explains the Underside of Elite Chinese Higher Education," *Wall Street Journal*, October 25, 2013, http://www.wsj.com/articles/SB10001424127887323308504579 085611270637836.

28. John Higgins, *Academic Freedom in a Democratic South Africa: Essays and Interviews on Higher Education and the Humanities* (Johannesburg: Wits University Press, 2013).

29. Ibid., 45.

30. An effort to empirically measure some aspects of academic freedom in Europe can be found in Klaus Beiter and Terence Karran, "Measuring Academic Freedom in Europe: An Em-prical Analysis," paper presented at SAR Faculty-Researcher Workshop, University of Ge-neva, June 3–5, 2015.

31. The University of Chicago's first president, William Rainey Harper, also was a great be-liever in free expression at the university. He said: "The principle of complete freedom of speech on all subjects has from the beginning been regarded as fundamental in the University of Chi-cago" and "this principle can neither now nor at any future time be called into question."

32. Hanna Holborn Gray, *Searching for Utopia: Universities and Their Histories* (Berkeley: Uni-versity of California Press, 2012).

33. See Robert J. Zimmer, "What Is Academic Freedom For?," in *Who's Afraid of Academic Free-dom?*, ed. Akeel Bilgrami and Jonathan R. Cole (New York: Columbia University Press, 2015), 239–274; see also the essay in the same volume by the noted anthropologist Richard Shweder, "To Follow the Argument Where It Leads: An Antiquarian View of the Aim of Academic Free-dom at the University of Chicago," 190–238. Shweder discusses the pressures at the university to pull back from its earlier, full commitment to the principles of free inquiry and academic free-dom, while realizing that the history at the university in defending these principles is a great one.

34. "Kalven Committee: Report on the University's Role in Political and Social Action." The Report was published in the University of Chicago's *Record* 1, no. 1 (November 11, 1967). Source: https://provost.uchicago.edu/pdfs/KalvenRprt.pdf.

35. Source: http://www.aaup.org/NR/rdonlyres/A6520A9D-0A9A-47B3-B550-C006B5B224E7/0/1915Declaration.pdf.

36. Paul F. Lazarsfeld and Wagner Thielens Jr., *The Academic Mind* (Glencoe, IL: Free Press, 1958).

37. Neil Gross and Solon Simmons, "The Social and Political Views of American Professors," Working Paper, September 24, 2007, http://citeseerx.ist.psu.edu/viewdoc/download?doi=10.1.1.147.6141&rep=rep1&type=pdf.

38. For those unfamiliar with institutional review boards, the federal government instituted a review of the research protocols of all federally sponsored grants and contracts that involved human subjects. This followed the Belmont Report and the Kennedy hearings, which focused on the now-famous Tuskegee syphilis study of African American men. The Kennedy hearings led to the establishment of institutional review boards, located at universities that had the power to deny researchers the right to conduct their research if the review board felt that there was some threat to the human subjects.

39. The Columbia administration supplied us with their most current list of full-time faculty, and we emailed faculty members a request to respond to the survey through an Internet link to an anonymous, web-based survey instrument. We pretested the survey by sending it to 100 of the 1,610 full-time faculty members. The response rate for the pretest was 27 percent, 21 percent for the final version of the survey—low response rates, but not particularly low for web-based surveys. I do not reproduce the survey instrument here, but you can find it at the following website: http://jonathanrcole.com/survey.

40. The full results of the survey can be found in Bilgrami and Cole, *Who's Afraid of Academic Freedom?*, 343–394. It also can be found online (see note 39).

41. Bilgrami and Cole, *Who's Afraid of Academic Freedom?*

42. We are putting aside here that Columbia University is a private school and therefore is not bound by the current court's views on the scope of protection under the First Amendment.

43. In fact, the research on which this case was built did discover the gene that causes the disease that was being studied. Both the anthropological and the genetics research contributed to this discovery. I will discuss federal regulations in Chapter 11, but note here that the existence of certain forms of federal regulations can actually prevent important research from being done—work that could lead to benefits for millions of people. Principal investigators simply won't spend their time complying with federal regulations when it takes up so much time with uncertain outcomes.

44. Philip Hamburger, professor of law at Columbia, argues that institutional review boards are actually unconstitutional violations of the First Amendment—that in the name of protecting human subjects they do far more harm than good, and that they are comparable to restrictions on speech in seventeenth-century England. Whether or not one agrees with Hamburger, this topic has not been the subject of proper debate within the framework of academic freedom.

Chapter 10: Reconstructing the University-Government Compact

1. While the NSF and the NIH were the principal sources of funding for fundamental and biomedical research, other federal agencies, such as the Department of Defense, also funded research at the major universities or at entities run by those universities.

2. A substantial amount of the auditing of federal grants and contracts to research universities was done by the Office of Naval Research as the cognizant oversight organization.

3. The federal government divides the costs associated with sponsored federal research into two categories: direct costs and indirect costs. Direct costs include, for example, the salaries of the scientists, students, and staff; indirect costs include, for example, the cost of maintaining or building new scientific facilities and the costs of administering those laboratories (for example, the cost of proposal preparation and compliance with federal regulations). It is the latter category that the government began to cap in the 1990s, thus not paying for the full, audited cost of the research taking place under federal government sponsorship—research that led to scores of incredibly important discoveries. For a large set of examples of those discoveries, see Jonathan R. Cole, *The Great American University: Its Rise to Preeminence, Its Indispensable National Role, and Why It Must Be Protected* (New York: PublicAffairs, 2009), part II.

4. There was substantial variability in the indirect cost rate for different research universities. A good deal of the variance could be explained by the location of the research university and the costs associated with doing research in a specific geographic area, such as New York City, Boston, or San Francisco as opposed to more rurally located universities. There were six changes in Circular A-21 (which dealt with the calculation of the cost of research grants) between 1961 and 1976.

5. In 2016, universities represent the second largest contributors to the research enterprise in their own university. That was not the case just a few decades ago. Obviously, this cost sharing had a set of consequences for how the cost structure of the university evolved.

6. The government auditing was carried out by a cognizant federal agency, such as the Office of Naval Research, but the universities were also subjected to audits by the federal Inspector Generals (IGs) office, whose primary function was to identify waste, fraud, and abuse of government funds. These IGs would select universities and often report to Congress totals of large sums of federal funds being misspent. In most cases, upon appeal, these large sums, which caught the eyes of Congress and of the public through media reporting, were reduced to a trivial proportion of the number claimed by the IGs—numbers never reported either to Congress or to the public through the media.

7. Antidiscrimination laws, for example, are valuable laws and regulations that affect everyone in our society.

8. Other than by direction of the president or the board of trustees, there is no incentive for lawyers to take on risks. To the extent that the university either loses a high-profile case or is embarrassed by adverse publicity, this may reflect poorly on the lawyers in the cases. Because university lawyers are salaried employees who often work in various parts of the law and are asked, if possible, to hold down legal costs, there is an impulse to settle cases that should not be settled or to not take up principled cases because the litigation is expensive and the odds of winning the cases may not be great. So one expects most of the very able university lawyers to take a risk-averse position.

9. As of 2015 I have been a participant in an effort mandated by Congress to reduce regulatory burdens on universities. The work of the Committee on Federal Research Regulations and Reporting Requirements: A New Framework for Research Universities in the 21st Century is being carried out by the National Academy of Sciences in conjunction with the National Research Council. I have received a great deal of information and data from participating in this project with the very able members and staff. This chapter was written before I joined the

committee, but I have been able to use in this chapter some of the statistics from other studies reported to the committee. That committee is limited to regulations and legislation related to research; this chapter goes beyond the research enterprise. See National Academies of Sciences, Engineering, and Medicine, *Optimizing the Nation's Investment in Academic Research: A New Regulatory Framework for the 21st Century* (Washington, DC: National Academies Press, 2015). This committee was established in response to a congressional mandate to examine the burdens and costs associated with federal regulations of research conducted at the nation's leading research universities. The committee was co-chaired by Larry Faulkner, former head of the University of Texas, and Harriet Rabb, chief counsel and vice president of the Rockefeller University. For anyone interested in ideas about how to reform the regulatory system that governs academic research, I recommend that they read this report, which differs in a number of ways from the opinions that I've expressed in this and the following chapter of this book. It is also a far more detailed analysis of the federal regulation of academic research and the burdens it places on working scientists.

10. The Federal Demonstration Partnership (FDP) asked more than 23,000 faculty members who were principal investigators or co–principal investigators on federal research grants to answer questions on a web survey that "contained questions on the nature, size, and impact of the administrative task associated with their research projects." The response rate was only 26 percent, about average for these web-based surveys. As was the case with our pilot study of full-time faculty members at Columbia when we were studying academic freedom, it remains unclear and unexplained in the papers published whether the 6,081 faculty respondents were representative of the entire sample or were a highly self-selected group. There is reason to believe, a priori, that those faculty members who felt the greatest burden would be most likely to respond. So while the 42 percent is rapidly becoming a "fact," it would be premature to say that there is a possibility that the number is this high (or it could possibly be higher). See Sarah Rockwell, "The FDP Faculty Burden Survey," http://sites.nationalacademies.org/cs/groups/pgasite/documents/webpage/pga_087667.pdf.

11. This estimate comes from work done by Vanderbilt University. In many ways, this estimate is less robust and perhaps somewhat misleading if our focus is on research-intensive universities. The FDP survey results are perhaps more appropriate here because the Vanderbilt study had a small sample of highly disparate types of schools—some intensive research universities and others with little research activity. Nonetheless, clearly there has been a trend of rapidly increasing administrative costs associated with compliance with federal research and other educational programs at our major research universities.

12. Source: NSF Office of Inspector General (OIG) and Two-Month (summer) Salary (rate calculation). These numbers are publically available, but the public rarely sees them except when the initial claim is identified and reported in the media.

13. There are many examples of scandals or unfortunate outcomes in the process of doing normal research and clinical trials that trigger the flow of events I've described. Of course, the famous Tuskegee syphilis experiments with black men led to the Belmont Report that led to passage of legislation that created protection of human subjects through Institutional Review Boards and the use of the Common Rule; but there have been a significant number of isolated cases at major universities that triggered scandals. For example, there was the gene therapy case at a major research university that involved the death of an eighteen-year-old patient, Jesse Gelsinger (1999), who had volunteered to participate in a gene therapy trial involving a rare

disease; the death of monkeys that were used for experiments and housed at the Primate Research Center (2015) of a renowned university; and the case of the death of a psychiatric patient who was, apparently, pressured into choosing between participating in a clinical trial experiment or spending some undetermined time in a mental hospital—surely a form of coercion. Then there are famous scandals like the Olivieri case at the University of Toronto, in which a researcher was asked to and did sign a nondisclosure form should anything untoward occur during an experiment with subjects in a foreign nation. When the researcher refused to comply with the original signed agreement (and the university had much to gain financially from its relationship with the largest pharmaceutical firm in Canada), she was fired from her job and an international scandal broke out. There are many similar cases like these, but there are no data to suggest what proportion of all experiments in a field result in unethical behavior on the part of researchers. This is akin to the absence of data on scientific fraud and fabrication of data that periodically surfaces. Are these truly rare events or are they more widespread? Could they be handled in ways other than by passage of regulations or legislation that requires all researchers to jump through many hoops before receiving their research funds? Unfortunately, the universities are often guilty of trying to cover up these incidents of bad behavior rather than boldly dealing with them. This may be more so in non-research areas of university activity, such as cases of sexual assault.

14. An example of sanctions might be the adverse publicity, or university sanctions, that would come from a patient accidentally dying during a clinical trial on an experimental drug. In short, no clinical research that tries to find important new drugs or ways of curing disease is risk free. But if scientists are singled out for noncompliance with some federal regulation or other, this can damage their careers significantly. Because many of these scientists have alternative projects that are risk free, they may choose to take the easier route.

15. Of course, most of the discussion of immigration reform centers on those who come for work from south of the U.S. border. Current law is in need of reform here, and it would be worthwhile for members of Congress to put aside ideology and fiction for some good demographic and sociological facts. But here, I'm concerned principally with features of the immigration act that influence our universities, rather than the full complement of needs for reform that exist in the area of immigration.

16. Source: Institute of International Education (IIE), *Open Doors Report on International Educational Exchange*, November 17, 2014. More international students study in the United States than any other country, and this number is increasing. The IIE produces these data annually and works in partnership with the U.S. Department of State's Bureau of Educational and Cultural Affairs.

17. Except for universities with large endowments, foreign undergraduate students are rarely offered financial aid, or minimal financial aid. They tend to pay full freight, akin to the tuition paid by out-of-state students at some of our most prestigious state universities.

18. We ought to rethink what we mean by "needy." Those students who come from really socioeconomically disadvantaged backgrounds are clearly needy and should receive federal, state, and institutional support. But there are also those families who would be defined as middle-middle, or even upper-middle, class—those who may have family incomes as high as $200,000 a year—who cannot afford tuition at top colleges because their incomes appear to be too high to be eligible for this financial support. What is not taken into account sufficiently is the cost of the education without substantial financial aid (which exists for most colleges and

universities—even at the top), especially when we consider that the families are using after-tax dollars and may have more than one child in college at the same time. If denied financial aid, children from such families are less apt to be able to attend the college of their choice that has admitted them than is the youngster from a family with far less nominal income who has been accepted to the same college or university.

19. *United States v. Brown University*, 5 F.3d 658 (3d Cir. 1993).

20. Lyndon B. Johnson signed the Age Discrimination in Employment Act into law in 1967, although age was a protected category in the 1964 Civil Rights Act. The later bill pertained to workers over the age of forty and protected them against discrimination in hiring, promotions, wages, or termination from employment and layoffs. Since 1986, the act has prohibited mandatory retirement in most sectors of the economy, with a phased elimination of mandatory retirement for tenured professors taking full effect in 1993.

21. The same issue exists in the federal judiciary, of course, and perhaps other institutions as well.

22. Many of our more distinguished universities have some variation of this type of program; but they vary enormously in what they offer faculty members, and they vary as well in salaries and perquisites available to older faculty members.

23. If the faculty member continues to work for the same institution at the point of reaching seventy and one-half years of age, he or she does not have to start drawing down the retirement funds saved while working at that university or college.

24. At federal funding agencies, like the NIH, only about 10 to 15 percent of submitted proposals are funded after peer review evaluations. Nonetheless, researchers have to complete a full application, which includes things like receiving IRB approval, before they have any idea of whether their proposal is likely to be funded. "Just in time" is a way of reducing this burden by requiring that researchers provide only that information initially required for peer review. Then, if their grant is likely to be funded, and they are among the 10 to 15 percent who are winners, they submit "just in time" all of the other federal requirements for grants before the grant begins. Because most proposals are not funded, this would take a heavy weight off the applicants who needlessly have to jump through many hoops before even submitting an application for a grant.

25. Source: http://sites.nationalacademies.org/cs/groups/pgasite/documents/webpage/pga_087667.pdf, 4.

26. To read the University of Michigan affirmative action decisions, see *Grutter v. Bollinger*, 539 U.S. 306 (2003) and *Gratz v. Bollinger*, 539 U.S. 244 (2003). For the *Bakke* case, see *Regents of the University of California v. Bakke*, 438 U.S. 265 (1978).

27. In fact, diversity effects have not been demonstrated empirically, even in the materials presented to the Supreme Court in the Michigan cases, despite the rhetoric used by the psychologists presenting the data on diversity. Statistical tricks are used to foster the belief that diversity results in more informed citizens, etc., but the weak measures used actually explain almost no variance in student attitudes and behavior, and there is enormous selection bias built into the Michigan study.

28. The facts of this study are far more detailed and nuanced than those that reached the press and triggered the process of regulation. Over time, the "facts" became simplified, reified, and a symbol of racism and a lack of interest in the consent of human subjects when they participate in experiments or clinical trials. As W. I. Thomas said, "If people believe something is real, it is real in its consequences."

29. Source: http://en.wikipedia.org/wiki/Belmont_Report. The report was published in the *Federal Register* in April 1979. The Common Rule, which outlined rules of ethics when dealing with human subjects in the United States, came into effect in 1981.

30. The law created the National Commission for the Protection of Human Subjects of Biomedical and Behavioral Research. The commission was to consider the appropriate boundaries between biomedical and behavioral sciences research and whether they called for handling of cases differently; an assessment of the risk versus the benefits in determining the research that involved human subjects; appropriate guidelines for the selection of human subjects; and the nature and definition of informed consent. Source: http://en.wikipedia.org/wiki/Belmont _Report. The government provides a set of standards in what is known as the Common Rule, but the government also encourages (through outsourcing the oversight of these research efforts) local IRBs to strengthen the rules surrounding research protocols.

31. In New York State, IRBs were required for all research conducted at a university located in New York after the state passed a law that made universities liable (a tort) for the mistreatment of human subjects. To my knowledge, New York is the only state that has passed such a law as of 2015.

32. Arendt was, of course, a German political theorist. She discussed this concept in her widely read book *Eichmann in Jerusalem: A Report on the Banality of Evil* (New York: Penguin Books, 1963), which had appeared first as a series of articles in the *New Yorker* magazine in 1961, which focused on the trial of Adolf Eichmann. The concept implied that rather than being extraordinary, most people, placed in the "proper" context, would commit evil acts that would offend their own moral sensibilities. This idea was the subject of the social-psychological experiments at Yale.

33. For a full description of the study and its results, see Stanley Milgram, *Obedience to Authority: An Experimental View* (1974; reprint, New York: HarperPerennial, 2009).

34. This research was summarized briefly and used as one vignette in the survey on academic freedom and free inquiry of Columbia faculty members. For a discussion of the faculty reactions to the case, see Chapter 9.

35. For the best treatment of this argument see Philip Hamburger, "IRB Licensing," in *Who's Afraid of Academic Freedom?*, ed. Akeel Bilgrami and Jonathan R. Cole (New York: Columbia University Press, 2015), 153–189.

36. Ibid., 156.

37. For a particularly interesting discussion of the ways that IRBs conflict with basic values of the university—those contained in the Kalven Committee Report and other statements of the mission of the University of Chicago, see Richard A. Shweder, "To Follow the Argument Where It Leads: An Antiquarian View of the Aim of Academic Freedom at the University of Chicago," in Bilgrami and Cole, *Who's Afraid of Academic Freedom?*, 190–238.

38. Quoted in Philip Hamburger, "HHS's Contribution to Black Death Rates," www .libertylawsite.org/2015/01/08/hhss-contribution-to-black-death-rates/.

39. Ibid.

40. This example is also used by Hamburger in the paper cited above. Hamburger is one of the few legal scholars working on this problem; and he often must feel as if he is a lone ranger, since few others have pursued this line of inquiry.

41. There is ongoing debate among scientists and bioethicists about "how far to go" to prevent unethical behavior. For recent examples, see Steven Pinker, "The Moral Imperative of Bioethics," *Boston Globe*, August 1, 2015, and the response to Pinker by Julien Savulescu, "Pinker

Bioethics: What Should We Learn?," http://blog.practicalethics.ox.ac.uk/2015/08/pinker-bio
ethics-what-should-we-learn/.

42. In fact, there may be universities located in areas where the district attorney is, in fact,
loath to bring before a grand jury an accusation of rape by a student who, for example, might
have been dating one of the local sports heroes, whose Saturday exploits on the football field
drew in thousands of fans and voters. But the failure of the criminal justice system to do the
right thing in these instances should not lead us to conclude that universities ought to be the
site to adjudicate these kinds of alleged felony crimes.

43. In my experience as provost at Columbia, a very high percentage of cases of accusations
of sexual assault came from individuals who were either dating or had hookups and had been
drinking themselves into a stupor. It is very difficult, of course, to handle these cases and to get
at the facts, and universities are not the best institutions to try to do this. Universities should,
however, do all that they can to educate students about potentially risky situations and how to
avoid them. They also should create mechanisms that allow students who believe they have
been sexually assaulted to come forward immediately and be helped in dealing with the local
district attorney's office in a compassionate way.

44. The legal requirements for universities taking action in sexual assault cases come from
both the federal and state governments. Title IX of the Civil Rights Act of 1972, 20 U.S.C. §§ 1681
et seq. (1972), which originally was read to require gender equity in intercollegiate activities,
has been expanded to include issues of sexual assault. In 2011 the Department of Education
and the Office of Civil Rights sent a "Dear Colleague" letter to universities and colleges in the
United States that was considered a "significant guidance" letter. It outlined steps universities
must take to create a safe environment and to deal with sexual assault cases under the potential of losing all federal grant support. This directive came in conjunction with the so-called
Clery Act (for Disclosure of Campus Security Policy and Campus Crime Statistics Act, 20 U.S.C.
§ 1092 (f) (1990). The Act is named after a nineteen-year-old Lehigh University student who
had been raped and murdered in 1986. For a good discussion of the breadth of this issue and
how universities can deal with the various forms of assault, see a statement by the American
Association of University Professors' Committee on Women in the Academic Profession and
its Subcommittee on Sexual Assault on Campus, "Campus Sexual Assault: Suggested Policies
and Procedures," 2012, http://www.aaup.org/report/campus-sexual-assault-suggested-policies
-and-procedures. See also, among many news and opinion pieces on the subject, Zoë Heller,
"Rape on the Campus," *New York Review of Books,* February 5, 2015.

45. Maria Testa and Jennifer A. Livingston, "Alcohol Consumption and Women's Vulnerability to Sexual Victimization: Can Reducing Women's Drinking Prevent Rape?," www.ncbi
.nlm.nih.gov/pmc/articles/PMC2784921/.

46. The draft regulations issued in 2013 that interpret the Violence Against Women Act
would essentially amend the campus-crime law known as the Clery Act.

47. Robin Wilson, "Why Colleges Are on the Hook for Sexual Assault," *Chronicle of Higher
Education,* June 6, 2014.

48. Monica Vendituoli, "Colleges Face New Requirements in Proposed Rules on Campus
Sexual Assault," *Chronicle of Higher Education,* June 20, 2014.

49. Richard Pérez-Peña, "Harvard to Bring on Specialists to Examine Sexual Assault
Claims," *New York Times,* July 2, 2014.

50. Cass R. Sunstein, *Simpler: The Future of Government* (New York: Simon & Schuster, 2015).

51. Ibid., 11–12.

Chapter 11: Structural Change

1. If we take 1876 as our point of departure, rather than 1636, when Harvard College was founded, we realize that we are a very young system—especially when we compare ourselves with some of the older European universities. And now I'm suggesting that our great American research universities are entering a period of potentially productive adolescence, which requires that we rethink the idea of the research university and how we structure our efforts at higher learning and research discoveries. Adolescence is often a difficult period; and if we do not rethink features of our great universities, this could be a fraught time for them as well.

2. I want to thank Hanna Holborn Gray, former president of the University of Chicago, who put me to thinking about this issue after a talk at the University of Chicago where she asked why there can't be more differentiation among great universities. And although I believe there are certain fields in which every great university must have a significant presence and without which it will be difficult for them to carry out pathbreaking research, there is no reason why there can't be more universities that are not full-service but are among the very best in certain areas of knowledge creation and its dissemination.

3. Charles Huckabee, "Arizona State and edX Will Offer an Online Freshman Year, Open to All," *Chronicle of Higher Education*, April 23, 2015.

4. Jonathan R. Cole and Stephen Cole, "The Ortega Hypothesis," *Science* 178, no. 4059 (October 27, 1972): 368–375. In that paper we concluded that since a small proportion of scientists contribute disproportionately to the development of knowledge, it might be possible to reduce the total number of scientists. We note, however, that this is difficult to do, and perhaps inappropriate, for two reasons: Redundancy is needed in the system because it is extremely difficult to predict early on who will make pathfinding discoveries and because if it becomes too difficult to be successful in an occupation, individuals contemplating entering that profession are apt to opt out and enter different lines of work.

5. The presses named here are reasonably well endowed, but many outstanding university presses, particularly known for publishing superb art history or architecture books, or books dealing with East Asian history and society or other subjects, for example, are barely making ends meet.

6. Clark Kerr, *The Uses of the University*, 5th ed. (Cambridge, MA: Harvard University Press, 2001), 28.

7. For an illuminating discussion of the relationship between academic freedom and the governance of public universities, see Matthew Goldstein and Frederick Schaffer, "Academic Freedom: Some Considerations," in *Who's Afraid of Academic Freedom?*, ed. Akeel Bilgrami and Jonathan R. Cole (New York: Columbia University Press, 2015), 247–274. This essay is based on former chancellor of the City University of New York (CUNY) Matthew Goldstein's difficult but successful efforts to produce structural changes in the organization and curriculum of CUNY—changes that allowed for more mobility between the community colleges and the senior colleges in the system but that were met with significant faculty resistance. It took more than forty years to implement what was part of New York State Education Law: that CUNY was one university that must establish pathways to enable students in one part of the system, generally community colleges, to move to a higher level of the system without losing academic credits in the process, requiring curricular alignments among the different units in the system.

8. Matthew Goldstein and Frederick Shaffer, "Academic Freedom: Some Considerations," in Bilgrami and Cole, *Who's Afraid of Academic Freedom?*, 260.

9. William G. Bowen and Eugene M. Tobin, *Locus of Authority: The Evolution of Faculty Roles in the Governance of Higher Education* (Princeton, NJ: Princeton University Press, 2015).

10. Boston University, which has undergone enormous change since Robert Brown became its president, and as a result was asked to join the prestigious Association of American Universities (founded in 1900 and today having a membership representing sixty of the most research-intensive universities in the United States and two in Canada), has tried hard to pursue best practices for its board members. I had known Brown when he was provost at MIT. When he became president of Boston University, Brown asked me and another academic to join the board in order to help new board members, as well as some carryover members, learn more about the nature of universities. That took a good deal of intellectual courage by Brown and the board because we were not individuals with the background of most Boston University board members. In fact, the board members with business and professional school backgrounds turned out to be receptive to this idea. Brown realized that it was important to have academic voices other than his own to speak about universities' structures and practices.

11. William G. Bowen, *Lessons Learned: Reflections of a University President* (Princeton, NJ: Princeton University Press, 2011), 12–13.

12. Many European universities and those in other parts of the world elect their president. The university faculty elects its leader. Although it is necessary to have faculty support to govern, this method of choosing the university's leader tends to turn selection into a political process—a bad idea. It also gives the rector or president less independence from the faculty than is optimal.

13. At the time of the report, 87 percent of CUNY community college freshmen needed remediation, compared with 40 percent nationwide, and 72 percent of senior college first-year students in the system failed placement exams before entering college, compared with roughly 20 percent nationwide. So open admission, which was touted as a great effort to improve access to the CUNY system, was failing, and the dropout rate had become enormously high. Those were a few of the conditions that the system faced when Schmidt and Goldstein took over. Goldstein was such an ideal academic leader for the system and Schmidt had such respect among the largely politically appointed board that it became possible to make major changes in the system, including the rejection of the open-admissions idea, without abandoning the idea of access. Students who previously could enter any of the CUNY colleges would have to begin in the community colleges (which were coordinated with the K–12 high schools in New York City) before moving on to the senior colleges. In short, the initial stratification and placement of students was based on their achievements in high school.

14. Of course, some of the components in the CUNY system had great histories as colleges that fostered social mobility for the children of immigrants and for other talented youngsters who did not have the means to attend Columbia or other great private colleges. City College and Hunter College (when it was solely for women) were among the great colleges in the United States for many decades in the twentieth century—until the collapse of the system under the weight of open admissions, which had good intentions behind it but became a form of remedial education that impeded the education of the truly gifted. If we examine the history of these two places, we have to be impressed by their graduates. Some of the great women scientists of the twentieth century and great teachers in the New York City public school system graduated from Hunter; and an astounding array of talent held degrees from City College (and Brooklyn College) during the 1930s, 1940s, and 1950s. In fact, a great historical treatment of these educational institutions remains to be written.

15. Trustees ought to have opportunities to visit labs and to talk with faculty and students on their own—not as a means of end-running the academic leadership, but as a way of gathering unfiltered information. Of course, this must be done in a way that does not undermine the academic leadership of the institution.

16. I've used these two great research universities as examples because both are known for their historical adherence to a model that is referred to as "every tub on its own bottom." Because these are both very influential universities, change toward greater centralization would influence other universities with similar budgetary structures to experiment with structural changes.

17. Here I'm referring to the late nineteenth- and early twentieth-century sociologist Max Weber, who developed the concept of "the ideal type." Weber's ideal types were hypothetical categories that were not necessarily realized in practice but were to be viewed as idea constructs based on various characteristics of a given phenomena that help to order our thinking about social behavior.

18. Recently, historians have used Big Data to better understand the 1918 Spanish influenza pandemic. It was part of the digital humanities programs at several American research universities. Brett Bobley, who directs the digital humanities office of the National Endowment for the Humanities, said that the Spanish flu project "really demonstrated how historical research in the humanities could address a very pertinent contemporary challenge in our society— namely, how public-health policies influence the spread of pandemic diseases." See Jennifer Howard, "Big-Data Project on 1918 Flue Reflects Key Role of Humanists," *Chronicle of Higher Education*, "Research" section, February 27, 2015.

19. Source: shc.stanford.edu/digital-humanities.

20. Source: citris-uc.org/mission-statement/.

21. Sources: http://bids.berkeley.edu/ and http://vcresearch.berkeley.edu/datascience.

22. These new initiatives, which combine disciplines and use the intellectual resources of other universities as well as Berkeley, is testimony to the enlightened leadership of its former chancellor, Robert J. Birgeneau, and its current chancellor, Nicholas Dirks.

23. Prior presidents of ASU, such as Crow's immediate predecessor, Lattie F. Coor, were exceptionally fine and talented individuals, but they were not inclined to make dramatic changes to propel the university into the category of research-intensive universities with a clear ideological commitment to access and excellence.

24. Michael Crow worked with me at Columbia when I was provost and dean of faculties at the university between 1989 and 2003. He spent ten years working in the provost's office, and we established a close working and personal relationship. I know his work in detail and his many unusual abilities and talents, at least as I assess the many academic leaders that I've worked with. But the reader should know that this close set of ties existed and our association continues to this day.

25. The "New American University" has, using President Crow's terminology, eight "design" aspirations: (1) leveraging its location in Phoenix and in the Southwest; (2) changing society by creating discoveries that have very practical applications; (3) transforming the academic enterprise from the bottom up, trying new combinations at both the undergraduate and graduate levels as well as in the professional schools; (4) producing "use-inspired research"; (5) focusing on the individual and his or her needs and interests; (6) creating an intellectual fusion among exceptionally able people from across the university who work on a set of problems together; (7) producing social embeddedness by blurring the lines between the larger society

and the university—embedding the university in the large community rather than walling it off; and (8) forming global and national partnerships. The mantra of the New American University is to produce greatness without exclusion. There is an open acknowledgement of the greatness of the older established Eastern, highly selective universities as well as some prestigious seats of learning in both the Midwest and West. But ASU is not trying to compete directly with this older model, but to create a different one. Each of these objectives can be found elaborated upon on the ASU website.

26. If we were to look at the number of new buildings that are up and running after just ten years, we might think that we were looking at a growing campus in China.

27. While at Columbia, Crow also had innovative ideas. Many in the faculty welcomed them; others with a more traditional point of view resisted them, as did some of the deans and vice presidents. But no one doubted that he was talented, and most faculty and administrators considered him a positive force for change at the university and admired him greatly.

28. The details of the agreement between ASU and Starbucks are not fully known as of this writing, and we have no idea how many Starbucks employees will take advantage of this opportunity or succeed at it. But if we want to improve the chances of individuals who are well-treated by their corporate employers but nonetheless hold low-wage jobs to enter the middle class, then programs of this type that involve collaborations between universities and industry provide incentives for students who otherwise could not attend college because of their economic circumstances. See also Julie Jargon and Douglas Belkin, "Starbucks to Subsidize Workers' College Degrees: Coffee Giant Offers Tuition Rebates to Baristas through Program with Arizona State University," *Wall Street Journal,* June 16, 2014.

29. Steve Kolowich, "Coursera Chief: Reach of Teaching Will Define Great Universities," *Chronicle of Higher Education,* June 19, 2014.

30. Source: https://ucsd.edu/explore/about/index.html. This quote was taken from the website for UC San Diego. It changes from time to time so the exact wording of this mission statement may not be precisely the same quote that you find if you go to the website. A slight variation, for example, is: "The University of California, San Diego is a student-centered, research-focused, service-oriented public institution that provides opportunity for all. Recognized as one of the top 15 research universities worldwide, a culture of collaboration sparks discoveries that advance society and drive economic impact."

31. I would exclude from support the for-profit set of community and undergraduate colleges. Too many of them, to date, represent a misguided way for large corporations to obtain government funding for the financial aid of their students (e.g., Pell Grants), when they know that those students are very likely to drop out and to default on their loans.

32. Also known at the Land Grant Act, the Morrill Act was signed by Abraham Lincoln into law on July 2, 1862. The act gave each state 30,000 acres of public land for each senator and representative, which was based on the census of 1860. Of course, since the Morrill Act was passed during the American Civil War, the grant of public lands did not apply to the southern states that had seceded.

33. Of course, not all state universities' births were a result of the Morrill Act. Nonetheless, when those non–Morrill Act state universities were formed, there was a commitment of substantial funding to the universities to cover a good deal of the cost of an undergraduate or graduate education. The sharp reduction in state allocation to their universities that we've seen over the last quarter-century includes states that were not beneficiaries of the Morrill Act of 1862.

34. While the federal government could pass laws to curtail federal financing of universities in states that have given up supporting the universities, it is far more problematic as to whether the federal government has the power to determine the public or private status of state-controlled universities.

35. My favorite example of the consequences of Proxmire's award was when the NSF directed its chemistry section to be careful about the titles listed on the grants, because that apparently was all Proxmire's staff (not highly conversant in science) looked at. The NSF didn't want to see any titles that contained the term "radical ions" because Proximire had flagged this term. Fortunately, the NSF did not insist that the titles contain the term "conservative ions."

36. Stanley B. Prusiner, *Madness and Discovery: The Discovery of Prions—A New Biological Principle of Disease* (New Haven, CT: Yale University Press, 2014), 255.

37. This point on full recovery of indirect costs is a major feature of a recent report from the National Academy of Sciences entitled *Research Universities and the Future of America: Ten Breakthrough Actions Vital to Our Nation's Prosperity and Security* (Washington, DC: National Academies Press, 2012). See the summary of the recommendation, pp. 4–24.

38. If the foundations are willing to pay any indirect costs at all, they are generally in the range of 10 to 15 percent of the direct costs in the grants. Fields like public health have suffered from such policies because a relatively high proportion of their grants come from foundations that refuse to cover anywhere near the full cost of the research undertaken. The foundations expect that universities will cost share on these grants, but that amounts to a subsidy that must come from other budgets (representing opportunity costs). This puts extreme pressure on those school budgets when they ask for space and facilities that will require cross-subsidization by other parts of the university.

39. Council on Foreign Relations, *U.S. Education Reform and National Security*, Task Force report (New York: Council on Foreign Relations Press, March 2012). An online source of an overview of the report can be found at http://www.cfr.org/united-states/us-education-reform-national-security/p27618. The committee was co-chaired by Joel I. Klein and Condoleezza Rice.

40. There is an important distinction between scientific and technological literacy and knowledge. One does not need to know in detail the content of a specific science to judge its value, but one has to know how to ask the right questions and to understand what differentiates fact from fiction.

41. Source: Interview with retiring congressman Rush Holt, *Science* 343, no. 6174 (February 28, 2014): 954–955.

42. Source: www.hhmi.org/programs/biomedical-research/investigator-program.

43. The Federal Reserve System, better known as the Fed, was established in 1913. Its initial activity was to deal with financial panics, such as runs on banks. Its scope of authority has expanded, and until recently it has focused primarily on setting monetary policy. In the financial crisis of 2008 it began to take a much more proactive position beyond setting interest rates in order to control unemployment and create a stimulus for the economy. Obviously it has often been a body in the middle of controversies over its policy choices. For our purposes it does represent a powerful, quasi-independent body, which has a powerful say over the movement of the American economy. We need to create such a body for academic disciplines and new, revolutionary, scientific, and technological multidisciplinary efforts.

44. As of 2015, the most highly endowed private operating foundations in the United States include the Bill and Melinda Gates Foundation ($42.3 billion), the Howard Hughes Medical Institute (HHMI) ($16.9 billion), the William and Flora Hewlett Foundation ($8.7 billion), the

Andrew W. Mellon Foundation ($6.18 billion), and the John D. and Catherine T. MacArthur Foundation ($6.0 billion). In Britain, the Wellcome Trust, which has goals similar now to that of the HHMI, has an endowment of $25.9 billion. Of some interest is that not one of the ten most highly endowed American foundations was formed after the year 2000, despite the huge accumulation of wealth by many Americans since the latter part of the twentieth and the first decade of the twenty-first centuries. The closest is the Gordon and Betty Moore Foundation, which was formed in the year 2000 and has an endowment as of 2015 of $6.0 billion, equal to that of the MacArthur Foundation.

45. Since the growth areas in science change rapidly, one would want the endowments to specify a general area of work rather than to become too restrictive, so that the funds could be used in perpetuity for great work of the day. Overly restrictive endowments can lead to legal battles when science or technology, or behavioral science and humanistic work, moves beyond what seemed important at the time of the gift.

46. To my knowledge, there is not a single National Public Radio program that is devoted exclusively to issues related to education at all levels. I will be initiating such an effort in 2016.

47. As I've suggested earlier, the federal government should not be reducing the cost of financing higher education only to see the colleges and universities increasing their tuition levels beyond what is minimally necessary. There has to be built into the program disincentives for colleges and universities acting perversely in light of lowered interest rates on federal student loans.

48. The idea of lowering interest on federal college loans is certainly not my idea. It has been proposed by Senator Elizabeth Warren (D-MA), but as of 2015 it has not gotten much support in Congress.

49. Trudie Lang, "Embed Research in Outbreak Response," *Nature* 524 (2015): 29–31. Professor Lang works in England, but the same forms of delays and excessive regulation are present in the United States, and we remain extremely poorly prepared to deal with pandemics that could kill far many more people than foreign terrorism is apt to destroy. This institute would also act as a defense against possible forms of bioterrorism in the future.

Afterword

1. *Citizens United v. Federal Election Commission*, 558 U.S. 310 (2010).

2. Keith E. Stanovich, "The Matthew Effects in Reading: Some Consequences of Individual Differences in the Acquisition of Literacy," *Reading Quarterly* 21, no. 4 (Fall 1986): 360–407.

3. Of course, Finland is a completely different type of country from the United States, being far smaller and more homogeneous, but within several decades it transformed its K–12 system from also-rans in the international standings to the top position in the world. It did this through a combination of factors, including completely reinventing the reward system open to teachers— giving them the respect and compensation that placed them alongside the higher-paid, more prestigious professions. This new system began to draw the top talent in the nation to teaching. We need to do the same in the United States. Importantly, the rise to the top was not done with test scores in mind—they were the consequence of actions that the government took to ensure that teaching young people was again a truly honored profession.

4. Joseph E. Stiglitz, *The Price of Inequality: How Today's Divided Society Endangers Our Future* (New York: W. W. Norton, 2012), 7.

5. Ibid., 4.

6. Ibid., 289.

7. A Nobel Prize–winning economist told me in conversation that he would estimate that far fewer than 10 percent of the American population could accurately define what a marginal tax rate is. Consequently, the vast majority think that a tax on the wealthy that is graduated and rises at different income levels is actually a tax on them—when most would experience little, if any, increase in taxes.

8. Ibid.,114. See also, for a later and more in-depth analysis of the last one hundred years of income and wealth inequality in multiple countries, including the United States, Thomas Piketty, *Capital in the Twenty-First Century* (Cambridge, MA: Belknap Press of Harvard University Press, 2014). See also the work on wealth and income inequality by the British economist Anthony B. Atkinson, *Inequality: What Can Be Done?* (Cambridge, MA: Harvard University Press, 2015). Atkinson offers many potential actions to deal with the inequality problem. He, like Piketty and Stiglitz, depends a great deal on changing the marginal tax rates in order to achieve greater equality. Many of these potential solutions are particularly appropriate for Britain. It's unclear whether some of his proposals, such as a Sovereign Wealth Fund (pp. 174–178) or his idea of a "capital endowment (minimum inheritance) of some amount paid to everyone at adulthood" (p. 303), would be applicable for the American setting.

9. Jeffrey D. Sachs, *The Price of Civilization: Reawakening American Virtue and Prosperity* (New York: Random House, 2011) 22, 25. See also Thomas Piketty and Emmanuel Saez, "Income Inequality in the United State, 1913–1998," NBER Working Paper no. 8467 (September 2001).

Index

Note: Page numbers followed by *f* indicate figures.

Structural changes, proposed for university-
government relationships, 273
business and industry cooperation, 314–316
educational broadcasting network,
311–312, 388n46
federal government's unpredictable
funding and, 305–307
federal institute for disease prevention
and vaccine production, 313–314,
388n49
National Research Foundation, 307–311
state support reduction as threat to
federal support, 303–305, 386n32,
386n33, 387n34
Students
active participation needed from, 59–60
curriculum's challenges to, 50–52, 344n14
proposal to allow movement at own pace,
60
undergraduate curriculum evaluation,
43–44
undergraduate curriculum goals and,
45–46
Summers, Lawrence H., 344n12
Sunrise Semester program, 149
Sunstein, Cass, 271
Supiano, Beckie, 355n19
Sweden, 129
Sympathetic imagination, humanities and, 74

Takacs, Christopher G., 160
Taxes
contributions to proposed foundation
and, 310
faculty retirement laws and, 250
financial aid and, 122, 124–125, 128,
355n19, 380n18
marginal rates, 139, 168–169, 320–321,
389n7, 389n8
on government profits from student loans,
proposed, 313, 388n47, 388n48
on offshore earnings, proposed, 312
public reactions to raising of, 89, 320, 353n8
in reform budget plans, 288–289, 363n33
state aid cuts and, 139
value of education to taxpayers and, 130

Taylor, Mark, 117–118
Teaching, 98
college space redesign, proposed,
202–205
as mission of universities, 2, 332n2
rebalancing research and, 290–291
See also Faculty
Teaching hospitals, 104–105
Technion–Israel Institute of Technology and
Industry, 311, 315
Technology. *See* Science and technology
Tenure
billets reversion to provost's office and, 290
at law schools, 105, 106, 110
retirement laws and, 249
Terman, Fred, 10–11
Testa, Maria, 266–267
Testing movement. *See* Standardized
intelligence testing
*Test of Leadership: Charting the Future of U.S.
Higher Education, A* (Spellings), 130
Texas A&M University, 357n31
Thielens, Wagner, Jr., 229
Thomas, Douglas, 342–343n46
Thomas, W. I., 381n28
Thrun, Sebastian, 152–153
TIAA-CREF, 250
Title IX, of Civil Rights Act of 1964, 26,
331–332n5, 380n20
Title IX, of Civil Rights Act of 1972, 268,
382n44
Tohti, Ilham, 374–375n27
"Translational researcher," medicine and
value of, 103
"Trigger warnings," 51–52, 344n14
Trilling, Lionel, 74
Truman, Harry, 9, 307, 335n13
Trust
erosion between universities and
government, regulation and, 213–214,
241–245, 317–318, 377n3, 377n4, 377n5,
377n6, 377n8, 378n9, 378n10, 378n11,
379n13, 379n14
as fundamental value of university, 12,
216, 217–218, 371–372n6, 372n9
Trustees. *See* Boards of trustees and regents

JONATHAN R. COLE, currently the John Mitchell Mason Professor of the University at Columbia University, is widely known throughout the United States and abroad for his fourteen years (1989–2003) as Columbia's provost and dean of faculties. He is a member of the American Academy of Arts and Sciences and the American Philosophical Society. He lives in New York.

PublicAffairs is a publishing house founded in 1997. It is a tribute to the standards, values, and flair of three persons who have served as mentors to countless reporters, writers, editors, and book people of all kinds, including me.

I. F. STONE, proprietor of *I. F. Stone's Weekly*, combined a commitment to the First Amendment with entrepreneurial zeal and reporting skill and became one of the great independent journalists in American history. At the age of eighty, Izzy published *The Trial of Socrates*, which was a national bestseller. He wrote the book after he taught himself ancient Greek.

BENJAMIN C. BRADLEE was for nearly thirty years the charismatic editorial leader of *The Washington Post*. It was Ben who gave the *Post* the range and courage to pursue such historic issues as Watergate. He supported his reporters with a tenacity that made them fearless and it is no accident that so many became authors of influential, best-selling books.

ROBERT L. BERNSTEIN, the chief executive of Random House for more than a quarter century, guided one of the nation's premier publishing houses. Bob was personally responsible for many books of political dissent and argument that challenged tyranny around the globe. He is also the founder and longtime chair of Human Rights Watch, one of the most respected human rights organizations in the world.

·   ·   ·

For fifty years, the banner of PublicAffairs Press was carried by its owner Morris B. Schnapper, who published Gandhi, Nasser, Toynbee, Truman, and about 1,500 other authors. In 1983, Schnapper was described by *The Washington Post* as "a redoubtable gadfly." His legacy will endure in the books to come.

Peter Osnos, *Founder and Editor-at-Large*